Praise for Sheila Weller's *RAGING HEART*

"**DEVASTATING.** . . . *RAGING HEART* is the emotional case against O.J. . . . Exhaustive. . . . The book abounds in hard news."

—Jeff Simon, *Buffalo News*

"**GRIPPING.** . . . *RAGING HEART* paints a tale . . . [of an] 'obsessive relationship spiraling out of control on both ends.'"

—Kitty Bean Yancey, *USA Today*

"**COMPELLING.** . . . Sheila Weller gained great access . . . for those who want to learn all sides of the sordid story."

—Maureen O'Brien, *Publishers Weekly*

"**IMPRESSIVE.** . . . *RAGING HEART* is the closest thing to an 'objective' journalistic account so far."

—Alan Dumas, *Rocky Mountain News* (Denver)

***RAGING HEART* IS "FASCINATING."**

—Jeanne Beach Eigner, *San Diego Union-Tribune*

Also by Sheila Weller

Hansel & Gretel in Beverly Hills
Marrying the Hangman: A True Story of Privilege, Marriage and Murder
Amy Fisher: My Story

RAGING heart

The Intimate Story of
the Tragic Marriage of
O.J. and Nicole Brown Simpson

SHEILA WELLER

POCKET BOOKS
New York London Toronto Sydney Tokyo Singapore

POCKET BOOKS, a division of Simon & Schuster Inc.
1230 Avenue of the Americas, New York, NY 10020

ISBN: 0-671-52146-2

First Pocket Books paperback printing October 1995

10 9 8 7 6 5 4 3 2 1

POCKET and colophon are registered trademarks of Simon & Schuster Inc.

Printed in the U.S.A.

To the memory of Helen Hover Weller

Contents

Author's Note

UNDERNEATH THE PUBLIC O.J. SIMPSON SAGA—THE ONE WE have all been watching on television and reading about, in media high and low—there is private story, a different story: the real story of the principals and the community they lived in.

This is the story this book tells.

It has not been told before.

This book was based on exclusive interviews with Denise Brown, Juditha Brown, and other members of the Brown family; on extensive, largely exclusive interviews with Nicole and O.J. Simpson's closest friends and confidantes; and on interviews with numerous relevant acquaintances and authorities. Approximately eighty people were interviewed in all, from one to six times each. In addition to the interviews and follow-up interviews, every day from early July until the completion of my writing at the end of December, I spoke at length to at least one member of a core group of six people—three men and three women: people very close to Nicole and/or O.J. Simpson—who I came to think of as my "brain trust" for the telling of this story—and who I also came to think of as my friends. From their insight, their familiarity—and from their pain—I achieved a visceral sense of my subjects, their world, and their marriage. From them I absorbed the emotion of the story.

In my decision to report this seemingly overtold tale purely from the point of view of its intimates—from the inside out, instead of from the outside in—I have included (with the one exception noted below) only those scenes and accounts that my sources participated in or were told about directly, usually by either O.J. or Nicole. When someone is reported to have said or done something or to have looked a certain way (been angry, been laughing, had tears in his eyes), the information and description were given to me by an eyewitness. Where the attribution was more indirect, I have noted this fact in the text.

Unless otherwise verified, dates are reported as described by those interviewed. Although all the incidents described did occur, certain names and a few identifying details have been changed.

The only part of the book in which secondary sources (previously published interviews) have been used is the section on O.J. Simpson's childhood in chapter 2 (and to a far lesser extent, passages on his football career in chapter 3), in which I drew from the excellent interview Lawrence Linderman did with Simpson in *Playboy* magazine in 1976. Despite my several conversations with Joe Bell and Howard Rogers, two of Simpson's best friends from childhood, both men declined to talk about their life with him in Portrero Hill, San Francisco. My questions to other friends of Simpson's about his childhood were met with a cryptic, "We have been told [by his defense team] that we cannot talk about that."

Did something happen in his childhood that the defense does not want journalists and the public to know about?

One friend of Simpson's paused, then answered, "Yes."

When confronted with the intriguing possibility that there is a "Rosebud"-logo'd childhood sled that is already up in flames, a curious writer works all the harder to turn over every other object left in the subject's attic. That's what I have done. The "Rosebud" on the sled is this whole book.

And in this book, I have set out to explore and to try to explain how domestic violence and murder can spring out of a context of enormous adulation, bonhomie, luxury, and love. To me, this story, with its tight ensemble of identifiable and quite fetching characters with perpetually intersecting lives, could easily be lifted whole out of West Los Angeles and dropped tomorrow into any wealthy, young-at-heart, close-as-a-small-town American suburb. Not much looked wrong with that pretty picture—until it all exploded in violent tragedy on June 12.

I'd like to think we all can learn from that violent tragedy. I know the people whom I've talked to—who became, without thinking that they ever would be, characters in this lumbering, full-dress, outsized saga—would like to find a quiet lesson, a clear picture to reflect upon.

In exchange for their hard-delivered confidences, shared in grief and trauma, I owe them my best attempt at assembling that picture.

Here it is.

—Sheila Weller,
New York City, December 28, 1994

He loved her and she loved him
. . . .
Her looks nailed down his hands his wrists his elbows
He gripped her hard so that life
Should not drag her from that moment
He wanted all future to cease

—Ted Hughes,
"Lovesong"

RAGING
heart

1

"Dreams"

AT 12:10 A.M. ON TUESDAY, JUNE 14—EXACTLY TWENTY-FOUR hours after the bodies of Nicole Brown Simpson and Ronald Goldman were found in the courtyard of Nicole's condominium at 875 South Bundy Drive—O.J. Simpson walked upstairs into his master bedroom suite at 360 North Rockingham Avenue.

He was not alone. He was accompanied by a man he had known for many years. This man, whom we will call Leo, was experienced in criminal procedure and had some knowledge of the techniques of determining guilt from innocence. What Leo learned by talking to Simpson in his bedroom that night—an exchange whose mere existence has never been revealed before, not even to the prosecution—would leave him deeply troubled.

That bedroom conversation was part of a week in which O.J. Simpson said other things about—and *to*—his dead wife. These words and actions have never been reported anywhere. They might be construed as cries of the heart.

Or they might be construed as something else, something considerably more significant.

* * *

An hour earlier, O.J. Simpson was downstairs, sitting on a couch between two of his best friends. Swirling around him, through the rooms of the house, all decorated by Nicole, with bleached floors, white couches, plants, and Tiffany lamps, were some of the people who loved him: his sisters, Shirley and Carmelita; their children and grandchildren; and his frail mother, Eunice Simpson. Simpson's sisters were worried about both their mother's health and their brother's circumstances, most immediately his exhaustion. Between his landing in Chicago at 4:15 A.M. and his being summoned by police at 5:45 A.M. and told to fly back to Los Angeles, he had gotten little sleep.

On that plane ride home, Simpson had placed several calls from his cellular phone. One was to Nicole's parents' house in Laguna at 7:15 A.M. Nicole's sister Denise had answered the phone. "You *murdered* her! You sonuvabitch!" she had shouted.

"Me?! *Me?!*" he had exclaimed.

"You fucking murdered her! You always said you would!" she continued.

After his flight had landed, Simpson had been driven by limousine to his house, been handcuffed, dehandcuffed, and taken to police headquarters, where he had allowed himself to be questioned for over three hours without his attorney, Howard Weitzman, present. Then he and Weitzman had a conversation. Or rather, O.J. Simpson talked, as he often did.

At 6 P.M., Bob Kardashian had driven Simpson back to Rockingham. A few of Simpson's intimates had assembled, in states of disbelief and shock, and for this group Simpson's housekeeper Josephine (Gigi) Guarin laid out platters of her home-cooked food. All of them had been in this house, with its pool table and trophy room and sports den with four TVs, on the happiest occasions: the Christmas Eves and Thanksgivings, the Fourth of July post-softball-game barbecues where people played basketball on the tennis court and everybody got thrown in the pool with their clothes on. The

Super Bowl and Fight Night parties. (O.J. always won the bets.) The nights playing Scrabble and Monopoly. (O.J. always cheated.) The poker nights. (O.J. was the peacemaker when fights threatened to erupt.) Nicole's evenings of Password and her improvised Newlyweds Game. Her famous Couples Nights featured an egg toss, a scavenger hunt, and trophies. For an entire community of close friends, these nights and days had been the highlights of the first half of their adult lives. The Simpsons' life had been troubled in the last two years—they had divorced without ever letting go of each other—but for so many years their front door had always been open.

They organized events, they took care of people. Nicole always gathered in strays for the holidays. The whole crowd vacationed together in Hawaii and New York and Mexico and Colorado. Their children trick-or-treated together on Halloween. (O.J. and his buddies went along in costume, too.) There had been so *many* good times in this house overflowing with kids and friends and food and flowers and O.J.'s and Nicole's extended families. "Their life was storybook," one of O.J.'s best friends, tennis-pro-turned-entertainment-agent Joe Kolkowitz, would later say.

"They made a dream life. They had the *world;* they should have been laughing at the world," Linda Schulman, Nicole's best friend for many of those years, would agree, sick at heart and incredulous, as so many were. Linda added in a whisper: *"How* could *this* have happened?"

All those in the house tonight seemed to silently be asking that question, but more in sadness than in innocence. All those close to the Simpsons knew about the couple's fights. And about their love, and their dependence. One seemed inextricably tied to the other.

Jason Simpson, O.J.'s once-troubled twenty-four-year-old son by first wife, Marguerite Whitley, walked around, greeting his father's friends, trying to remain upbeat for him. But his sister, Arnelle, twenty-five, was visibly distressed and had gone, early, to her bedroom in the guest house. Arnelle had been the first member of either the Simpson or Brown family to learn of the killings. Police had awakened her at 5 A.M. With her father's best friend, Al (A.C.) Cowlings, she had rushed to the police station to retrieve her half-siblings, Sydney, eight, and Justin, five.

Others in the house harbored secrets. Simpson's rent-free lodger, Brian "Kato" Kaelin, thirty-five, the sometime-actor with the permanently bemused expression and the hiply disheveled dark-rooted blond hair, had been with Simpson at almost every point in the evening except for the hour—9:45 to 10:45 P.M.—during which the murders were committed. In exactly one week, Kaelin would be the first witness called before the secret grand jury where he would refuse to answer every single question, relenting only after being threatened with jail time.

This evening, the usually funny, loose, and charming Kato, a gifted mimic and prodigious flirt, was, someone who spoke with him noticed, "a nervous wreck." Was Kato hiding something?

Rockingham neighbor Ron Fischman, a short, plump physician who was the husband of Nicole's current best friend, Cora, walked from room to room, exuding a kind of solicitous authority, apparently suppressing the memory of words he had heard from Simpson the previous afternoon. At the conclusion of the dance recital at which both men's daughters, best friends Leslie Fischman and Sydney Simpson, were performing, O.J. had spoken to Ron about Nicole. In these exact words (as Ron relayed the conversation to a third party), O.J. had said, "I'm not done with her. I'm going to get her, *but good.*" Despite whatever might be inferred from these words, Ron would become a supportive figure in the house during the week. The next day he would bring in restaurant food for everyone. Cora Fischman stayed at home, distraught. Of all of Nicole's close friends, Cora and her daughter Leslie, who adored Nicole, would have the hardest time putting their lives back together. But once Cora did so, she would, to the astonishment of Nicole's other friends of the last two years, come out in apparent defense of O.J.

As for O.J. Simpson himself, he had spent much of the time since coming home from the police station seated on one of two facing couches in his den, wearing the same white golf shirt and black pants he had put on in his Chicago hotel room that morning. Mostly, he was flanked by two men who, after Al Cowlings and football star Marcus Allen, were closest to him. One was restaurateur Joe Stellini, a thin, intense, wiry man whose Bronx street-kid gruffness had survived thirty years' polish as an actor, maître d', and host in Los Angeles; the other was former lawyer and music-industry businessman Robert Kardashian, a short, calm, thick-haired self-made millionaire and son of a prosperous southern Californian Armenian family. Though completely unknown to the world tonight, Kardashian's name would become a household word four days later, as he stood before an army of television cameras and read Simpson's "suicide" note.

Both Stellini and Kardashian went back twenty-five years with O.J. They were "Stiff" and Bobby (O.J., of course, was "Juice"), and much of Simpson's life in L.A., including his courtship of Nicole, was intricately tied to one or both of them. In fact, almost every one of Nicole and O.J. Simpson's friends had entered their lives, directly or indirectly, through either Joe or Bobby. Along with three other men—garment businessman Allen Schwartz ("Schwartzy"), medical-technologies-company owner Thomas McCollum ("Mr. Straight"), and Joe Kolkowitz ("Chokowitz")—these were O.J.'s white brothers. This was his inner circle. (Sports commentator Ahmad Rashad and professional football players Reggie McKenzie and Lynn Swann were, besides A.C. and Marcus, the only black friends who had been as close to O.J., but in recent years Simpson's friendships with Swann and Rashad had faded.)

These men loved O.J. and they had loved Nicole. They

were crushed by her brutal death but almost religious in their touted belief in his innocence.

For now, at least. And for most of them.

The whole time Simpson sat between Stellini and Kardashian, he was waiting for one phone call—from his current girlfriend, Paula Barbieri, who had played second fiddle to Nicole for two years. Simpson's desperate fear of losing control of the women in his life had emerged as a dominant part of his personality, and now that Nicole was dead he had quickly trained his obsession on Paula.

A compulsive telephoner and compulsive talker (his mother-in-law, Juditha Brown, was known to set down the telephone receiver while O.J. was talking, then return ten minutes later to find he hadn't even paused enough to notice the inattention), he had been looking for Paula for over twenty-four hours. He had called her home and her pager from his car phone minutes before the murders and had just discovered earlier that she had been in a Las Vegas hotel with singer Michael Bolton.* Paula had with her the antique diamond-and-sapphire bracelet O.J. had recently given her. That bracelet had been his gift to Nicole on her thirty-fifth birthday on May 19. When Nicole returned it to him three days later because she had finally decided to end their relationship, he had given the bracelet to Paula. Now *Paula* was betraying him! And despite the incalculable trouble he faced—this double-murder charge looming—he was, once again, relentlessly focused on a woman.

"If Paula calls," someone said loudly to the person manning the telephones, "put her right through to O.J."

With Kardashian seated on one side and Stellini on the other, and a friend of Stellini's named Neil Sloan across from him, Simpson wielded the television clicker. Other nights, the four TV sets in this room (a large set and three smaller ones surrounding it) showed various sporting

---

*Bolton has publicly denied any involvement with Barbieri, stating that Barbieri was simply there to appear in the music video he was shooting.

events. Tonight, the viewing choice was different: There were Nicole's and Goldman's sheeted bodies being carried through the courtyard's thick foliage; there was O.J. in handcuffs, talking to Detective Phil Vannatter; and there was O.J. strolling, solemn, head down, into police headquarters. Every report implied that he was the only suspect.

"Can you *believe* this? Can you *believe* what they're saying about me?" he called out. ("Can you believe . . . ?" and "I can't believe . . ." were frequent preludes to Simpson's indignation.)

The re-reporting of his 1989 New Year's Day beating of Nicole made him particularly angry. "They're making a bigger deal out of this than it was!" he complained. He hadn't beaten Nicole; it was a *mutual* fight that had gotten out of hand and they had both been drunk: This had always been his public position. Many of his friends agreed. They saw O.J. and Nicole as equally provoking parties. They saw O.J. as a man who had been madly in love with his wife since the first day he met her in 1977. A man who did not know what to *do* with that love, perhaps, but who *had* it. And they saw Nicole as a wife who had jerked O.J. around over the last two years. A wife-beater was *not* what O.J. was!, most of his male friends would tell you. A womanizer, a compulsive talker, a heart-on-his-sleeve guy, but not a "wife-beater."

"Look how they're talking! Can you be*lieve* this!" he said now, shaking his head at the TV sets.

His secretary, Cathy Randa, stood and shook her head with him. Cathy, a loyal, warm woman who most of Simpson's friends were very fond of, and who had been Bob Kardashian's secretary before becoming O.J.'s twenty years ago, was as angry as her boss was. "As soon as they find out who really committed those murders," she was heard to say, "they'll stop doing this!" Cathy was the divorced mother of a teenage son. She and Nicole had hardly been the best of friends. The fact that Cathy sent presents, under O.J.'s instructions, to his girlfriends on their birthdays did not exactly endear her to his wife, and she had recently won her job back after a leave of absence, a leave in part lobbied for by Nicole. Her employer's crisis seemed to galvanize Cathy. With his arrest, she would become the rallier of his supporters, and the scheduler of jail visits. Reportedly, she had already helped him purchase a disguise (mustache and beard), part of which may have been found in the white Ford Bronco after the freeway run on Friday.

Tonight, however, she was calling the Browns' house in Laguna, putting O.J. in touch with his best friend, Al Cowlings, who was helping Nicole's parents, Lou and Judi. A.C. was grief-stricken. He had been extremely close to Nicole—close and protective. ("If O.J. started yelling at Nicole in front of A.C.," says Nicole's older sister Denise Brown, "A.C. would say, 'Shut up!' and stop him.") A.C. had *loved* Nicole like a sister. In fact, intermittently for much of the eighties, Nicole *had* been a virtual sister-in-law to A.C.: A.C. had dated Denise. It was a bond that rendered the two families closer than most married couples are with their in-laws. A.C., who had never married and had gone through a serious addiction to freebase cocaine in the early eighties (the habit had cost him his romance with Dionne Warwick), was more a permanent adjunct to O.J.'s life than an independent person; and Denise, after a successful career as a New York model and a brief marriage, had come home and, faced with personal difficulties and a young son, moved back in with her parents.

Still, O.J. and Nicole's more "independent" life together held deep, dark strands of dependence. They had explosive fights. He was chronically obsessive about her. His style of telephoning friend after friend after friend after friend to lament their breakups and seek advice was startlingly emotional (unmasculine, some thought) and very, very O.J. It took years for Nicole to decide to break away from his domination, and yet when she finally did, she came running back to him at zero hour.

Earlier in the day on June 13, A.C. had driven Sydney and Justin to their grandparents' home, withholding the news that their mother was dead. A.C. spent a lot of that day crying. He was more vulnerable than O.J. was, and he had a hard time defining and looking after his own interests.

Some thought Cowlings to be an inveterate freeloader who had long ridden on his successful friend's coattails. Others saw A.C. as a man who reined O.J. in, protected him, and lived half his life for him, sometimes sacrificing himself in the process. A.C., people said, had no ego. He procured and delivered $24,000 worth of free turkeys to families in South Central L.A. every Christmas. He got ghetto kids jobs with West L.A. businessmen. There was scarcely a Simpson child's birthday party video that didn't feature the large, smiling A.C. in a party hat, bouncing a child on his shoulders, often while their father was out of town on business. His white buddies' parents *loved* A.C. "Why can't *you* be that much of a gentleman?" the father of one of A.C.'s beach club gin buddies asked his son, upon meeting the former football player. Says Allen Schwartz: "A.C. would give you his last hundred dollars, even if he didn't have a place to sleep. If you asked him to drive your daughter cross-country to college, he would do it."

Still, A.C. had a violent streak that threaded all the way back to San Francisco. It has been reported that he was suspended from high school five times, mostly for brawling. Once, eight years ago, because he didn't like a softball play, he picked up a friend on the opposite team and threw him against a fence. More recently, a restaurateur friend of O.J.'s was forced by what he said was A.C.'s irresponsibility and complete lack of bartending skills to fire him from a job. A.C. had looked the man in the eye and said, "If you ever come back around [implying: to O.J.'s house], I'm gonna kill you."

After most of the others left, Simpson turned to an old friend, a man who was in town tonight from his home in another city. He asked this man to accompany him to his bedroom. It is likely that Simpson chose this man, Leo, for a reason. Leo was a principal in a business within which those who worked below him often collaborated with police officers. Leo had a good working knowledge of criminal forensics.

Just after midnight, Simpson's worried sisters approached their clearly exhausted brother. "You get some sleep, now," Shirley had said. "Yes, go on upstairs," Carmelita seconded.

Simpson walked over to Leo and said, "Come on upstairs with me."

"Sure, man," Leo said casually. But Simpson's request did not make Leo happy. Driving over to Rockingham this evening, Leo said to himself, "I hope he doesn't have a wound on his hand. And I hope he doesn't want to get me in a corner and ask me questions." When Leo saw the Band-Aid on the middle finger of his friend's hand, the first tiny alarm bell went off in the back of his mind. But when Leo asked, "Where'd you get that cut?" and O.J. said, "In Chicago," Leo took the answer at face value. Like all the other men in this house tonight, Leo loved the Juice. The Juice could not have done this.

The two men walked into the large light-beige-and-off-white bedroom, the creamy carpet of the stairs continuing into the room. The suite, redesigned by Nicole, had a country-style couch and table, a bookcase-headboarded bed with a beige bedspread. It gave on to beige-tiled his-and-hers bathrooms and a terrace that allowed O.J. Simpson to sit up in bed and see the tops of the backyard trees surrounding his swimming pool.

O.J. Simpson asked Leo to open the white cabinet across from the bed and turn on the television. Leo did so, then sat down on a small couch.

Leo watched his friend take off his shoes, socks, and black slacks. He folded the slacks over a chair, keeping on his white golf shirt. He was wearing brown briefs.

Simpson complained about how the police had messed up his house during their search. They had really ransacked it, he said angrily. O.J. Simpson was a man to whom neatness and cleanliness meant everything. The contents of his closet were color-coded, each garment on an identical hanger an equal space from the next one. He had been known to ask guests in his home who were breast-feeding their infants to please move from the living room sofa. If someone put a drink down on his pool table, he snatched it up and rubbed the spot with a rag, fluffing the felt back up. He never opened his Christmas presents until he brought out a wastebasket within which to stash the wrappings, and then he ran around picking up everyone else's discarded wrappings and throwing them in the wastebasket. (Nicole had been the *opposite.* She was thrilled to get out of her demanding husband's fussy orbit. Though she loved all-white rooms, she never worried about getting them dirty. Guests could park their kids and dogs on her furniture, could spill red wine on her pale couches.)

As Simpson turned the bedspread down, he told Leo what the police had informed him they had against him.

"They said they found a glove . . . ," Simpson said.

"What kind of a glove?" Leo asked.

"A glove with blood on it. A bloody glove." Simpson's baritone had the advantage of enabling him to infuse any word with derision. "I don't know what that means . . ."

"It doesn't mean anything, since you didn't *do* it," Leo said, hoping this was true.

Simpson kept talking. "They said they found a *cap.* And they said they found blood in my car. And in my house."

"Juice," Leo made himself say, "this is all unbelievable. . . ." That much was true. But, glove? Cap? Car? House? That was a good deal of evidence—*if* it was legitimate. Leo navigated the few seconds' awkward silence. Was he now expected to plausibly say that the cops fabricated the bloodstains?

The silence was broken by the urgency in Simpson's voice. "How long does it take for DNA to come back?" he wanted to know.

The question made Leo uncomfortable. "A couple of months," Leo said. He avoided O.J.'s face. He did not want to see any anxiety in his brown eyes.

"They asked me if I would take a lie detector test," O.J. Simpson said as he turned off the light.

Leo's heart pounded. Polygraphs were something he knew about; he had sat in on a dozen of them. And he knew that it is the opinion of many that people often approach a test with a pre-set alibi for failing. "I didn't kill the guy, but I sure thought about it," the person might say, setting up a reason for a false positive. Or: "I gotta be honest; there were times I wanted to strangle the bastard. But I never laid a hand on him." Or: "I've had *fantasies* of taking a rock and smashing his skull, but I'd *never do* it." Fantasies, urges, temptations. People moved the action to their subconscious, building up a case that their *imagined* deeds, not their *real* ones, were the reason for failing the polygraph.

Simpson got into bed. "I don't want to take it," he said.

Leo did not ask why. He just wanted his friend O.J. Simpson to *stop* talking—*immediately.*

But Simpson kept on. "'Cause," he said, with what Leo recalls as "a kind of chuckle," "I *have* had some dreams about killing her."*

* * *

---

*For purposes of this book, three authorities on polygraphing were read the statement that Leo reports O.J. Simpson made that night—"I don't know if I want to take it [the polygraph test] 'cause I have had some dreams about killing her"—without being told who made it. They were then asked if they could infer anything about the potential polygraph-taker on the basis of that statement.

Investigator Don Delaney of the New York State Police, who has administered approximately 400 polygraph tests over eight years, said, "If I heard that, my ears would perk up. I would tend to believe the person committed the crime—both because of the desire not to be tested and the fact they were giving the dreams as alibis."

Sergeant Tony Sanchez, who is in charge of the Los Angeles Police Department's polygraph section, and who has administered or supervised approximately 1,250 polygraph tests over four years, said, "If somebody says they thought about or dreamed about

The phone at Simpson's bedside rang. Leo picked it up and set it down, then reached down by the bed to unplug the phone jack. His shuffling woke Simpson, who opened his eyes and smacked his mouth as if thirsty. He regarded Leo drowsily.

In that moment, O.J. Simpson looked at Leo with, as Leo would later recall, "those big brown eyes, *just* like a little boy, a scared little boy in trouble he knew he would never get out of." A lifetime of bravado drained from his face. His vulnerability, his misery, left Leo breathless. "Oh, Leo," he asked, rocking his head mournfully, *"what am I gonna do?!"*

"Get some sleep. Get some sleep, Juice," was all Leo could answer. He sat at his friend's bedside for twenty minutes, until Simpson's breathing was even.

Leo spent that whole twenty minutes trying to come to terms with what he knew was the meaning of his friend's statement. When he left the house and got into his car, he

---

killing someone, they're saying, 'There's no way I'm going to pass.' They're setting up a way out in advance, for when they fail the test."

And one of the nation's top authorities in the field, Dick Arthur, director of the National Training Center of Polygraph Science, who has administered or supervised approximately 26,000 polygraph tests over forty-three years, said that unless the person in question did not know what a polygraph test was all about or unless the test was not explained properly, he would believe "That person was lying about his innocence. [That person] did the homicide."

It should be noted that the results of polygraph tests and the opinion of polygraph examiners are not determinative in any way of someone's guilt or innocence of a crime. Further, due in part to questions about the reliability of polygraph exams and the credibility of testimony about them, information regarding polygraph testing is generally not admissible in criminal trials. In California, the results of a polygraph examination, the opinion of a polygraph examiner, or any reference to an offer to take, failure to take, or taking of a polygraph examination are not admissible into evidence unless all parties stipulate to the admission of such results.

had to sit for a while before he turned on the ignition. His entire body was shaking.

This was the last night O.J. Simpson spent in his home. Only a handful of people know this. To this day, it is taken as fact that O.J. Simpson remained in his Rockingham home until Thursday, June 16. In truth, however, he said goodbye to Rockingham Avenue shortly after he woke up on Tuesday, June 14. He had gotten up, put on sweat pants and another golf shirt. He appeared tranquilized—"distraught and completely out of it," remembers one person who saw him. By 9 A.M., the press corps was already camped outside the gates. Bob Kardashian, who was present, thought O.J. should get out of his house immediately.

Simpson packed clothes and toilet articles in a black duffel bag. It is a virtual certainty that at that time he also put something else in that duffel: a gun, one of several he kept in the house (including an Uzi), this one purchased for him with the help of a police officer friend. In three days, that gun would turn up, along with $8,000 in cash, in the white Ford Bronco after O.J.'s and A.C.'s freeway pursuit.

Kardashian's plan that Tuesday morning was simple. It relied on the fact that Simpson's tennis court adjoined that of neighbors Eric and Valerie von Watt. You could walk from one court to the other, and guests of the Simpsons and von Watts had often played on their hosts' neighbors' tennis court. So, as the press minivans massed in front of his house, O.J. would simply walk out to his backyard, through his tennis court, then through the von Watts' court and property and out to the corner of Ashford. There, a mere thirty yards from the throngs of cameramen and reporters, O.J. Simpson, viewed by no one but perhaps one or two quietly startled gardeners, would stand with his duffel bag like any fellow awaiting a ride from a friend.

The plan continued. Kardashian would get into his car and swing around the corner. (He would manage to slip out of the house and into the car only when another of Simpson's friends stepped out of the house before him, providing a body for the press to momentarily descend upon, leaving Kardashian unnoticed.)

Bob Kardashian's car would skid to a brief halt in front of the von Watts' house and wait for O.J. to get in with his duffel. Then they would be off, en route to Kardashian's. It was down this very street that O.J. and Nicole Simpson took a walk one day in April of 1993. It was an encounter that one of them desperately sought and the other had firmly resisted. They had been separated for fourteen months and divorced for six. As they walked, there were protestations of love from the initiator of the encounter, wariness and defensiveness from the other. One of them proposed a reconciliation and the other was stunned by the proposal, then angry. This person had finally accepted the breakup and had started a new life. Why undo the healing *just* when the wound had closed?

Hours later, however, the resistant partner became so gripped by the idea of putting the marriage back together that sleep was impossible. A call was placed, from one to the other, in the middle of the night. It was decided. They would try to reconcile.

This was a point of no return, but neither one knew it.

The initiator had been Nicole and the won-over resister had been O.J. Looking back on things now, had it not been for that walk, it is very likely that Nicole Brown Simpson and Ronald Goldman would be alive today.

It was shortly after Simpson's surreptitious retreat from Rockingham that prominent friends—Dionne Warwick, Jermaine Jackson, former Buffalo Bill and Oakland Raider Bob Chandler—arrived at his home. The press cleared a path for them as they entered and, after each left, shouted questions: "How's O.J.?" "How are his spirits?" Not one of the reporters seemed to have guessed, despite the vague answers given, that the guests had not seen O.J. Simpson at all. He had already fled.

Except to surrender to police, three days later, he would never come home again.

* * *

In the jumble of memories that the Simpsons' friends would soon examine for clues to the events of the night of June 12, one inconsequential afternoon attains an odd significance.

It was late 1984, a few months before the Simpsons' wedding in February 1985. They had had a fight and Nicole had gone to her parents' home.

A friend dropped by and found Simpson sitting at the counter in his country kitchen, watching TV, clicker in hand, channel-surfing. He looked annoyed and distressed. Nicole had gone and he felt, as he always did when she left, abandoned, bereft—and obsessed about it.

Suddenly, clicking on MTV, he got excited. He pressed the volume key to force up the sound on a skinny young English rocker, describing lost love in a trembling voice that ascended in the refrain—about his missing her—to furious denial.

"I love that song! I *love* that song!" Simpson shouted. In his growling basso he sang along with John Waite's alto-soprano. It was not unusual for Simpson to sing along with a record; he did it all the time, happily oblivious to what friends unanimously called his "terrible" singing voice. But this time he went further. "This is me and Nicole's song!" he announced. "This is my song for Nicole!" Then, like an earnest kid on a Top-40 request line, "I *dedicate* this song to Nicole!"

In the song, a man makes the best of his woman's decision to leave him. He catches his breath when he thinks of her. When he hears her name mentioned within their circle of friends, he smiles. Maintaining this wistful acceptance, however, becomes difficult, then impossible. He's *got* to reach her. It is unbearable to let her go, even though every appropriate measure and convention says he must. You're *supposed* to let your woman go if she leaves you, the plaintive, struggling-to-be-reasonable man knows. But *he cannot.*

The gathering force of his obsession is hidden: "You don't know how desperate I've become," he whispers, "and it looks like I'm losing this fight." There's a storm "raging" in his "heart tonight," he warns—twice. A *raging heart:* The juxtaposition of vulnerability with fury, tenderness with mayhem is trite and unremarkable when it's heard in a pop song.

But it is something else in real life.

The song described O.J. Simpson's last two years with Nicole, almost ten years ahead of time.

"This is my song for Nicole!" O.J. Simpson had shouted that afternoon, in the kitchen at Rockingham.

Nine and a half years later in his bedroom he keened, *"What am I gonna do?"*

And the next morning Bob Kardashian was driving a man who had had dreams about killing away from his dream of a life.

The evening after O.J. Simpson slipped off to Bob Kardashian's house, a viewing of Nicole Brown Simpson's body was held at the O'Connor Mortuary in Laguna Beach. The modern adobe mortuary was right off the 405, just down the Alicia Parkway from Monarch Bay, the gated community of plant-hugged, glass-walled homes poised between rolling hills and flawless white-sand beaches. Nicole had lived in Monarch Bay as a teenager; her parents and sisters still live there today. It was home.

The viewing was attended by only about twenty-five people. Susie Kehoe and Linda Schulman, Nicole's girlfriends from the days of her marriage to O.J., were stunned as well as rocked by grief. Not only had Nicole been brutally murdered, but the memory of the happiness of their mutual past was shattered by the crime, and by the talk of O.J.'s involvement, talk resisted by both women (fervently so by the fiercely O.J.-loyal Susie).

The unvoiced question could not be ignored: *Had* those days really been so wonderful? In that world of six or eight couples including the Simpsons, had things really been what they had seemed?

To be sure, the two women viewed those recent Good Old

Days of the seventies and eighties through the opposite vantage points of their very different marriages. Linda had a marriage to garment executive Ricky Schulman so loving and so equal it seemed different from all the other marriages in the group. Linda and Ricky were the happy, normal couple you wanted to tell your troubles to. Tiny Italian Linda, with her Long Island accent and her plain-spoken ways, was the neighbor who had the most common sense and basic self-respect of anyone you knew. Susie, on the other hand, was the nice Jewish girl who wound up married to Billy Kehoe, the wildest, most colorful, and most outrageous member of the group. A high-living Rodeo Drive Irish charmer, liar, fighter, scam artist, bon vivant, and severe alcoholic, Billy died of cirrhosis of the liver after serving time in prison for defrauding scores of people in a major pyramid scheme (in which O.J. had briefly participated). The Schulmans' marriage had been Nicole's platonic ideal; Nicole listened to and confided in Linda. The Kehoes, on the other hand, often cast the Simpsons in the role of hands-on professional counselors. O.J. was Billy's more sober and solvent running buddy. He had applied the brakes on Billy, the Wild Man of Beverly Hills, much as A.C. (when he wasn't freebasing or running off somewhere with O.J.'s car) applied the brakes on *him*. O.J. offered to pay for Billy's alcoholic rehabilitation, and when Billy's drinking became uncontrollable, Nicole persuaded Susie to leave him. O.J. helped out the Kehoe kids when Billy was imprisoned in 1989 and he paid for Billy's funeral four years after that.

Neither Susie nor Linda had seen much of Nicole after her divorce from O.J. in 1992. Their lives had diverged. For Susie—whose sufferings had been overwhelming and who had moved to a desert community, remarried, and embraced Catholicism—God would help the police find the *real* killers of Nicole and Ronald Goldman and let the wrongly accused O.J. grieve in dignity. For Linda, things were more complicated. She had been Nicole's best friend for seven years; "Nick," the five-foot-eight, unperturbable, big-boned, barefoot California girl, and Linda, the five-foot, ninety-pound, fast-talking New Yorker, had been inseparable, bound by their common desire to make wonderful homes for their husbands and children, and by their total lack of affectation and pretense.

Linda had once advised a tearful Nicole *not* to marry O.J., "great guy" though she thought he was. Nicole had always been very private, very proud, and very protective of O.J.'s image, and Linda had respected that. But *things had happened—serious* things—between O.J. and Nicole, and Linda Schulman had some idea of what they were and some idea of just how badly they had hurt. Now, waiting for the mortuary doors to open and drenched in unbearable sadness, vague guilt, and disbelief, Linda cursed herself for having lost touch with her dear friend during the obviously confusing two years that had turned out to be the last two years of her life.

The friends Nicole had drawn close to since her divorce knew a different woman from the one that Susie and Linda had known. They saw a woman who had struggled to free herself from a charismatic but mostly impossible man, a man who had controlled and defined her entire post-high-school life. They saw a woman who embraced her new freedom—sometimes naively, hungrily, and injudiciously after having being largely dominated for fifteen years—but one who could not let go of her ex-husband any more than he could let go of her.

This close group consisted of four very distinctive women. There was Cynthia "Cici" Shahian, a stylish, thin, vivacious office administrator and Bob Kardashian's first cousin. The only one of the group who had never been married, had no children, lived in an apartment instead of a house, and who had always worked for a living, Cici was inherently warm and practical, the anchor of the group. She came from a family that, like her cousin Bob's, was as reliable as an old clock: long-married, frugal, business-wise parents who never, ever fought; who socialized principally with other frugal, business-wise, long-married Armenian couples; who sat down with their daughter for a balanced and sensible dinner (meat, vegetable, Armenian pilaf) at 5:30 P.M. on the dot every night of her childhood and adolescence. With her wry perceptions, her authoritative love of fashion (she knew which one of the girls *must* switch her look from Valentino to Alaïa; she knew when the big silver crosses over the Chanel were right and when they were excessive), and with her ability to concentrate on her friends' problems, Cici was a favorite sister figure to all the others in the group and a favorite aunt to their ten children.

Cora Fischman's unvarnished style was the opposite of Cici's polished buoyance. Cora was a Philippines native (and since her marriage to Ron Fischman, a convert to Judaism) who, despite her upscale house and car and clothes, had an unmistakable Asian working-class air about her. She was not a smiler, and she spoke in blunt, grave words in a deep register in the accent of her birthplace. Her doctor husband had met her in New York when she was a relatively recent immigrant, working in a medical office, and her life had changed overnight. Cora was emotional and absent-minded. Almost as tiny as Linda Schulman, Cora replaced the equally un-Hollywood Linda as Nicole's best friend. She and Nicole jogged nine miles a day together; sometimes Cici joined them. For over a year, O.J. had called Cora persistently to lament about Nicole after their divorce.

Becoming best friends with Nicole just as Nicole was becoming a single woman had turned Cora Fischman from one kind of Brentwood woman to another. She came to want to experience freedom as much as Nicole did. Out went the stock-tied ladies' luncheon suits, suitable to the parent of three who cooked kosher to please her mother-in-law; on went the tight designer jeans and tiny tops, the henna-streaked hair better suited to the foxy Starbucks fixture she had become. Then Cora had an affair with a young black grocery stock boy and nothing had been quite the same ever since with her doctor husband, in *their* home on Rockingham Avenue. (In November 1994, Cora broke with the rest of Nicole's friends, who had become briefly fractious with one another, and began writing her own book, which is said to be sympathetic to O.J.)

The third member of this group spanned both Nicole's old married life and her new single one. She was the lone, consistent female witness to the White-Guys-Plus-O.J.-and-A.C. world that had begun in the seventies. She was Kris Jenner, a tall, wholesomely pretty brunette with an air of pert primness unusual in the fast-track environment she had entered, and mastered, twenty years earlier when she became the girlfriend, then the wife, of Bob Kardashian. "Kris was always the Donna Reed of our crowd," says mutual friend Robin Greer. "'Appropriate,' churchgoing, always pregnant, and never did drugs."

But after she had four children in eight years with Kardashian, Kris rebelled. She had an openly admitted affair with a much younger man. For this transgression, Kris was instantly ostracized by the small clique of socialite girlfriends she had joined—a group very different from the funky Bobby-and-O.J. crowd.

Kris' young boyfriend quickly broke her heart by being unfaithful. O.J., despite his close friendship with her husband, stepped into Kris' life and briefly took on the role of her advice-dispensing big brother. But relief was short-lived. Her divorce from Bob was ugly; she was cast as the adulteress and was humiliated in the process.

The ordeal gave Kris added perspective—she could now see life from both sides of the respectability divide. And the unhappiness and soul-searching that preceded her break from Bob would soon give her something in common with Nicole. Still, Kris had managed to rescue herself: She married former Olympic decathlon medalist Bruce Jenner, became his agent and manager and, as president of Jenner Communications, was a principal in his exercise-products business; she had also launched a motivational-speakers bureau. Meanwhile Nicole, more confused than any of her friends really knew, had bobbed in the dangerous ocean of single life, divorced yet not dissociated from the very obsessive father of her children.

Kris and Bruce and their combined families lived in a large home atop the highest-stratosphere Beverly Hills canyon. Her supposed ambition was to have her own television show. She was well on her way to succeeding.

Nicole's murder had devastated Kris. Every morning for the next two months, Bruce would have to remind her to get out of bed and to put on her jeans.

The most exotic and controversial of Nicole's new circle of friends was Faye Resnick. Where the other women, while they may have enjoyed a good party, were grounded, health-conscious women with open pasts, Faye (whom Kris introduced into the group) was like a character out of a Judith Krantz novel: a self-invented, at once vital and self-destructive high liver of mysterious ethnicity. (Faye's mother was of Spanish and Italian descent but many people thought Faye was black.) She had supposedly been married to a vacuum cleaner salesman and a drug dealer by the time she found her third husband, a rich Beverly Hills businessman named Paul Resnick, whose weakness for pretty young women had led him to marry five times. (He fathered seven daughters from these unions.)

Faye was an on-and-off-again cocaine abuser whose cross-addiction to tranquilizers had landed her in rehabilitation clinics. Once she had overdosed in a Wilshire Boulevard luxury apartment, where she was out cold for the better part of two days. Her then-seven-year-old daughter Francesca (whose real father may have been one of Resnick's previous husbands although Paul Resnick assumed paternity) was at her side, helpless and alarmed. Despite these habits, however, Faye was determined to establish herself as a proper West Side socialite—and she did so. Wearing Chanel suits, she pushed herself to the front lines at school fundraising and school-board election committees. Once there, however, her substance emerged. "I can't say a bad thing about Faye," says a woman prominent in the Beverly Hills volunteer community. "She was the rare volunteer who was able to rise above the leadership fights and *do* what needed to be done. She worked her tail off. She may have sat on desktops and tossed her hair, but she was one smart, strong lady. I admired her."

Still, the character that emerged in her PTA work did not necessarily shine elsewhere. Toward the end of Nicole's life, Faye was having hard times financially—and Nicole was said to have been generous. And whether or not she intentionally capitalized on Nicole's vulnerability, many believe that Faye led Nicole into a world that had the power to further provoke the already obsessed O.J. In addition, Faye became O.J.'s confidante, not an enormously rare distinction. Like Cora, Faye accepted his many, long, Nicole-obsessed phone calls.

Faye claims to have heard something that Cora, apparently, did not: She heard O.J. threaten to kill Nicole.

Denise also heard O.J.—repeatedly—make this same threat. "I heard O.J. say to Nicole, many times over the years, 'If I ever find you with another guy, I'll kill you,'" Denise says. "I heard it with my own ears."

Nicole's newer friends had been shattered by her murder, and Ronald Goldman's, not least because they could not help feeling that if their counsel to her had been wiser and more prescient, the two would still be alive. "We are all guilty," one said. For, picking up on Nicole's own clearly expressed longings, they had encouraged her to go back and try again with O.J. fourteen months before. Then on May 22, when she announced that she had broken off with him—for good, this time—they applauded that decision as well. They could see the difference in her; there was about her now a finally grounded sense of freedom, an understanding that O.J. would never change: not his womanizing, not his obsession with her, not his stalking and not his violence. If these new friends experienced a different Nicole, they also experienced a different O.J. than did the old group. This was an O.J. torn apart by the fact that Nicole was living her life as a single woman; an O.J. who alternately swooped down on her and spied on her and dominated her, and yet who earnestly, sometimes touchingly, sought to understand her need for freedom; an O.J. who *tried* to let go of her, and who had once succeeded . . . at which time she came back to him.

On May 22, however, Nicole seemed at last to have moved on from the relationship that had begun in her adolescence and that had dominated and defined her entire adult life. "She was different. She had let him go. He *had* to have seen it. You couldn't help but see it. *We* did," Cici Shahian says. The switch in Nicole's attitude represented a sea change because, Cici says, echoing the sentiments of many other of the couple's friends: "She was as locked into him as he was to her. There was nothing they didn't know about each other. Whether they were together or apart, they each knew there would never be a relationship like the one they had with each other. They just couldn't *finish* this thing between them. They were totally in love."

Nicole's body, along with Goldman's, had been discovered when her children's Akita, Kato (named for Kato Kaelin), led neighbors Sukru Boztepe and Bettina Rasmussen, who were out walking a rescued dog, to the entrance of the courtyard of her condominium at 875 South Bundy Drive. She was lying barefoot in the black halter sundress she had worn to Sydney's dance recital. O.J. considered that dress provocative but Detective Tom Lange, who had been called to the scene, had termed it a "shapeless black shift." She was on her left side in a half-fetal position, her legs bent, one ankle wedged beneath the lowest rung of the open gate, her body lying in what the detective called "an extreme amount of blood."

She had been slashed left to right, up and down, at the neck. Then—though the fact, at this writing, has still been withheld from the public—she was slashed again, right to left, at her breasts and left to right at her waist. The first wound was by far the worst. It severed both carotid arteries and nicked both jugular veins, four of the major paths of blood in the body. It was called a "large, gaping wound" by the detective and the coroner, and it was so substantial that the smaller adjacent stabs intersected and melded with it, making it a megawound: a canyon. "The entire neck [was] opened up," the coroner said succinctly. One viewer of the autopsy pictures said, "It was as if her throat were sliced open and stuffed with a mass of black strawberries."

Detective Lange told the grand jury he believed that the killer came at Nicole from above. And came at her, Lange and his colleague Detective Philip Vannatter would conclude, after he had already stabbed Ronald Goldman, who had just walked in the building's outer gate holding the white envelope containing Nicole's mother's glasses. Goldman had been stabbed nineteen times: in the neck, head, chest, stomach, and thigh. Four of the wounds—to his ribs and his abdomen—were enough to kill him. He had been found slumped against a tree on his right side. He had tried to fend off his killer. He had died with his eyes wide open.

The detectives believe the killer was crouched in the bushes *inside* the outer gate. This detail is important because the outer gate is opened only with a key from the outside or, from the inside, by a manual two-step procedure: the turn of a knob and the flip of a lock. If Nicole were expecting a visitor, she would have had to make sure that the outer gate were open. Otherwise it would be locked. (Nicole's notorious sloppiness about personal security—she kept doors and windows open and didn't like curtains—had tightened considerably during the last weeks of her life. She had discovered, with some alarm, that a door key was missing from her key chain. She also had purchased multiple copies of the book *Obsessive Love,* by Dr. Susan Forward—a primer on men who become stalkers, among other things—and had placed them in several rooms of her house so she could pick up the book in a panic without having to stop and remember which room she had left it in.) If the killer was an intimate—someone who had used the gate and knew the policy for locking it at night when no visitors were expected—the fact that it was unlocked would immediately signal that Nicole expected company.

O.J. Simpson knew this house well. Although most of their reconciliation time was spent at Rockingham, he had spent many nights with Nicole at Bundy Drive. According to what Nicole told her friend and realtor Jeane McKenna, they were together in her bed on January 17, 1994, when the earthquake hit. (He had been more frightened by the quake than she, Nicole had added.) A friend who once left the condo with O.J. saw him, in one quick gesture, flip the lock and turn the knob on the outer gate, "and I thought, 'Man, he knows how to get in and out of this place fast.'"

O.J. Simpson would only have had to look at the gate from the outside on June 12 at 10 P.M. to know it was unlocked.

Whoever the killer was, it appears that at the sight of Goldman, he attacked. Then when Goldman, who had already rung Nicole's buzzer, did not show up at her door, Nicole walked outside to see what had happened. There she met her attacker.

Nicole's fingers were closed, but when they were opened they revealed "defensive wounds." Like Goldman, she had tried to fend off her killer.

Although she died from the first wound, it was the second, lower wound upon which Nicole's friends focused. Says one, "When we heard her breasts were slashed, we knew who killed her. We knew who would want her breasts ruined so that no other man would enjoy them—had wanted that so badly he had to slash her again, even though the first slashing had obviously been enough. The worst thing for us is: She *saw* him. She *had* to have known it was him, no matter what he was wearing. She saw him and she struggled. She knew that he was killing her. And she knew that she was dying."

* * *

At 10:48 P.M. on the evening of the murders—one hour and three minutes after Ronald Goldman set out from the Mezzaluna restaurant (on San Vicente Boulevard) for Nicole's condominium and the same length of time since O.J. Simpson was last seen (by Kato Kaelin), and thirty-three minutes after a neighbor of Nicole's heard a dog's "plaintive wail" coming from the direction of the condominium, a woman named Jill Shively was driving hurriedly in the eastbound lane on San Vicente Boulevard to try to make it to the supermarket before their salad bar closed at 11. According to Shively's grand jury testimony, just as she drove into the intersection at Bundy—she had the green light—she was startled to see a white Ford Bronco, with no lights on, shooting north on Bundy into the intersection, running the red light. Shively clutched her steering wheel and swerved sharply to the right to avoid a collision.

The Bronco screeched to a halt at the grassy median that divides San Vicente's eastbound and westbound lanes. Slamming to a halt right in front of it—the two cars formed a T-square—was a gray Nissan, driving west on the green light. The Nissan blocked the Bronco.

The Bronco's driver turned to stare at Jill Shively, giving her, she said in grand jury testimony,* "a real quick look, like he was mad or angry and like what was I doing to him?" Then he yelled at the Nissan driver, "Get out of the way! Get out of the way! Move the car!" like a "maniac, gone crazy or something," Shively remembers.

---

*After hearing Shively's testimony, the Simpson grand jury was told by prosecutor Marcia Clark to disregard it because Shively had sold her story to a tabloid TV show for $5,000 and then, Clark claimed, was untruthful to Clark about the sale. Shively says a D.A.'s office representative approved her talking to the media. In a highly unusual move, the grand jury was disbanded in July, on the grounds that the frenetic media coverage, including police leaks about evidence, had made it impossible for Simpson to get an impartial grand jury. A preliminary hearing was held instead, during which Shively was not called as a witness.

The Nissan driver seemed frightened. He moved forward to try to accommodate the Bronco, but the Bronco moved forward at the same time. The Nissan then moved *backward,* just when the Bronco started *behind* the Nissan. The Nissan and Bronco both moved forward—together—again, blocking each other a third time.

Finally, the Bronco driver gunned his engine, backed up, and sped north on Bundy, past the Union 76 station, toward Sunset.

Before he took off, Jill Shively got a look at his face. "I recognized him immediately," she said. "It was O.J. Simpson."

Nicole's close friends stood waiting outside the closed mortuary doors while Nicole's family privately viewed the body.

Nicole had always been so *alive:* kissing her kids, jogging, skiing, playing tennis, flashing the peace sign; popping out of her white Ferrari convertible, into which she had packed dog and kids; leaning on the low stucco wall of Starbucks on Gorham and San Vicente in her lycra jogging tights and bra; striding around her children's birthday parties in an ironed, rolled-sleeved white T-shirt and faded cutoff jeans, video camera on shoulder, calling, in her crisp voice: "Hey, Justin! Hey, Sydney! Wow, look at the Ninja Turtle! Smile for the camera!" It was so hard to imagine her face and body mutilated; so hard to think of her dead.

Nicole was, in equal parts, hip, windswept, upscale surfer girl and pious, hardy German fräulein. She was the one Brown sister who had mastered their Oma's [grandmother's] way with spaetzle-and-goulash and breadbaking, who once authoritatively stopped her high-school best friend's salad-making to show her the *correct* way to get the sand out of lettuce. She was an avid gardener and a talented decorator who, in that no-nonsense way she had, hauled potted trees and furniture in the back of her car rather than have them delivered; who did her own furniture finishing and exuberantly decorated her friends' homes. When she was doing Linda Schulman's house, she would bound in every morning without ringing the bell, barefoot, opened Coke can aloft, calling "Lin . . . ! Lin . . . !", then go in the backyard, pick an orange off Linda's tree, rip it open, and eat it. She walked around barefoot *everywhere;* O.J. always said, "Nicole! Put on your shoes!" And everyone noticed that she had the *heaviest* walk—"like," her sister Denise recalls, "a marching sergeant."

Nicole seemed incapable of pettiness. She gave her babysitters $100 bills to take the kids to dinner and a movie and she did not ask for change; when dining with girlfriends, she would grab the check, never stopping to figure out who paid last time. She was equally inept at bullshit: If she didn't like your new haircut, she would tell you. If O.J. got too talkative or obnoxious, she immediately called him an "asshole." Nicole *could* provoke O.J. She gave as well as she got. She did not suffer in silence. "She knew how to push O.J.'s buttons." Five people, independently, uttered that identical sentence.

Intimates of the couple are even more undivided in describing Nicole as a devoted mother who lived for her children.

She was very loyal to the people to whom she made commitments. As a sixteen-year-old at an Allman Brothers concert, she had turned down the Brothers' invitation to go backstage because she did not want to abandon the girlfriend she had come with. That habit of loyalty—and of liking people for who, not what, they were—continued into Nicole's adulthood. She didn't have a snobbish bone in her body. Her post-O.J. beaux were a shoe buyer, a young law clerk, and a bar manager. The *last* thing she wanted was another rich, older man. She hated Hollywood galas—she couldn't be dragged to Donald Trump's wedding to Marla Maples. (O.J. took these things seriously; he ended up going to that wedding with his mistress Tawny Kitaen.)

She couldn't stand shopping for clothes and was so

spontaneous and indifferent that, "unlike me," Linda Schulman says, "she could wear the same clothes all week." She didn't know designers' names but she was knowledgeable and fussy about music; there wasn't a black group she didn't know. She played the Isley Brothers' "Twist and Shout" at Justin's fourth birthday (along with the Beach Boys). She bopped around her Laguna summer house, the last summer of her life, a shift over her bikini, singing along to "Would I Lie to You, Baby?" and "A House Is Not a Home."

She never passed the San Vicente Market without giving a couple of dollars to the rhyming beggar Wendell Brown (about whom Arrested Development wrote the hit song "Mr. Wendal"). And she once donated money and solicited donations for a woman (whom she had only briefly met) whose children had been kidnapped and taken abroad by her ex-husband. "Oh, to lose your kids like that!" she had said, jogging with Cora and Cici—never imagining that the loss of her own children would come so fast, and be so much worse. Finally, she was a serious romantic who always lit white candles, who had spent her teen years conjuring up images of true love over slow, moody rock songs, who watched her parents go through forty years of life together and who strongly believed, even more proved for herself, that there is *only one love* in one's life.

"It's not her! It's not her! No, this is *not* my Nicole!" Nicole's mother, Juditha Brown, was crying to the mortuary owner Joe O'Connor, as the viewing room doors were about to be opened. The reconstruction of Nicole's face was dismaying; her mouth seemed distorted. Judi was in tears.

A serious beauty with dark hair, deep-set eyes, a charming light German accent and a palpable vulnerability, Judi implored Nicole's friends, "Is it okay with everyone if we close the casket?" The guests sympathetically assented. Judi then rushed back inside to consult with O'Connor about the possibility of fixing Nicole's mouth. The guests waited.

Viewing Nicole had been overwhelmingly emotional for the family and hardest, perhaps, on Nicole's older sister—and best friend—Denise, thirty-seven. A former Ford model who had been Nicole's idol, who came home to live with her parents and date Nicole's husband's best friend, Denise had a crisp, brisk, uncontemplative style that often hid her feelings, but her protective love for Nicole ran deep. As a two-year-old, she had been so proprietary toward her baby sister that, Judi recalls, "anyone who *breathed* on Nicole, Denise would push away, saying, 'Not so close; not so close.'" As six- and four-year-old German emigrées who, despite their American father, spoke not one word of English, Denise and Nicole had clung to each other for weeks in their brand-new southern California school.

Now, standing in the characterless viewing room, Denise Brown was saying goodbye to the sister who had almost been her twin, and she was quietly preparing for what she now knew was her destiny: absorbing her sister into herself; raising her sister's children. "Please dye your hair blond," Sydney later begged her, "so you'll look just like Mommy."

Just as sad were Dominique ("Mini"), twenty-nine, a Smith Barney computer systems processor, a rounder-faced version of her two older sisters, and Tanya, twenty-four, the softest-edged Brown sister, the only one who spoke no German, and the only one with Lou Brown's open face, generous features, and fair hair, rather than Judi's more intense beauty. Weeping, too, was Judi's nephew, Rolf Baur. A fair-skinned, emotional man whose pure blue-collar-southern-California manner and accent yielded no hint of the Germany of his first sixteen years, Rolf had been close to Nicole ever since he moved into the Brown home when she was nine. All the Brown daughters referred to him as their "brother." Rolf had worked as the Simpsons' gardener; he married O.J. and Nicole's Mexican housekeeper Maria. Rolf and Maria were Nicole's favorite relatives. In 1983, the Simpsons and Baurs traveled to Munich—two German-Americans with their black and Hispanic spouses, disparate in status yet cross-linked by blood, employment, and marriage—visiting the recent world center of racial purity, defying their Aryan ancestry.

Whatever else you could say about this family, their choices were solely, unaffectedly, their own—and their lives defied stereotype.

Lou Brown was stoic and pained. A Kansas- and Texas-bred Baptist (his daughters had been raised in their mother's Catholic faith), he was used to being the anchor in a house full of women. In addition to having these four daughters, he had had two daughters and a son from a previous marriage. He was no stranger to the untimely death of a grown child. One of his older girls had recently died after a harrowing fight against amyotrophic lateral sclerosis. But nothing—not even his training as a World War II fighter pilot—had prepared him, or any of the Browns, for the brutality of Nicole's murder.

When Joe O'Connor told the Browns there was nothing he could do about Nicole's mouth, Judi became highly emotional, walking in and out of the room, looking like a deer caught in headlights. Mini Brown voted for a closed casket. "I wouldn't want anyone to see me like that," she said. Then David LeBon spoke. A successful advertising photographer with blond, round, postsurfer looks, David had been so close to Nicole since both were teenagers that he and his wife, D'Anne, were considered by the Browns to be part of the family. It was he who had taken Nicole to Los Angeles right after high school. They had roomed together in a studio apartment. David had helped her decide what clothes to wear on her first date with O.J., and, like a protective older brother, he had been waiting up for her when she got home that night.

From Nicole's appearance at the end of that date, David LeBon had suspected that O.J. Simpson had violent tendencies. Alarmed, he had tried to caution her, but Nicole was so young—eighteen years and one month old. And it was clear: She was already falling in love.

"I know I need to see Nicky one last time," David told the

Browns now. "I have to resolve the fact that she's really gone."

"All right, we'll leave the casket open," Judi said softly.

There was just one more thing to do. Before every party, just after she had finished cooking the dinner and laying out the individualized favors, Nicole would run upstairs and shower; then, running back downstairs, she would take out her tiny plastic vial of lip gloss and dab it on her lips. Never color. Never lipstick. "Always," Linda Schulman recalls, "that stupid clear lip gloss."

"Please take that off her," Denise Brown told the mortician, indicating the pasty dark red lipstick he had applied to Nicole's mouth. All the Brown sisters huddled around as the mortician did as he was told. "It was as if," D'Anne LeBon recalls, "they were guiding his hand." After this was accomplished, Denise reached into her purse for something she had had there for two days.

With a little sigh whose understated sorrow covered a lifetime of closeness, Denise handed Nicole's clear lip gloss to the mortician.

Then she signaled for the viewing room doors to be opened.

Nicole's friends filed into the small room, its few chairs, couch, and Victorian loveseat against the walls. On a table next to the casket, photographs of Nicole showed her as everyone knew her: confident, happy, gorgeous. Eyes shifted from the pictures to the blond wood casket.

One at a time, friends approached the casket. Many placed single roses inside. Nicole had always filled her homes with flowers.

The family had selected a long-sleeved, high-necked, loose-flowing black dress for Nicole. The choice was dictated not just by the wounds it had to hide but by the buttresses required to hold her head upon her body. The mortician had pulled the collar up to almost cover her chin. Her face looked enlarged, puffed by the embalming, but the wax and makeup were effective. She still looked beautiful.

Her hair was down, loose to her shoulders, as it always had been.

The large Simpson party arrived—Eunice, Shirley, Carmelita, their children and grandchildren; Arnelle; Jason; Jason's girlfriend, Jennifer Green. They waited in the hallway.

O.J. strode in alone, through the double doors. People moved quickly, deferentially aside, to let him pass. He walked right to the casket and leaned over, gripping the casket's sides with his strong hands.

He began to shake his head and keen.

His exact words were: "I'm *sorry.* I'm *sorry.* I'm *sorry.* I'm *sorry.*"

A few people standing close by shuffled around distractedly, pretending, as they listened, that they did not hear those words.

He lowered his knees onto the kneeling rail. "Oh, Nick! Nick! Nick!" he wailed, his hand cupped to his mouth and his nose. "Oh, my God! Oh, I loved her!"

Then O.J. Simpson broke down and sobbed.

Judi Brown took a photograph of Nicole from the table, where it was propped near the foot of the casket, clutched it, and walked the few steps to where O.J. knelt. "This is not our Nicole; this is just a shell," she said, indicating her lifeless daughter to her son-in-law. "Our Nicole is in heaven," Judi went on, staring earnestly into O.J.'s eyes. *"This"*—Judi gazed at the photograph—"is our Nicole." She placed the photograph on Nicole's chest. "Remember her *this* way," she said, hugging O.J. But O.J. was still crying despondently.

The scene was a strange contrast to that Monday morning, when Detective Tom Lange had called at 6:20 with the news of the murders. Then Judi had screamed and Denise had run and grabbed the phone. "Oh, God! He did it! He *did* it!" Denise had shouted.

"Who did it?" Lange had asked her.

"O.J. did!" Denise had said.

Now Judi found herself leaning over the man whom one of her daughters had accused of killing another; found herself stroking O.J.'s back, reflexively the sympathetic mother-in-law.

They had always been close. O.J. raved to his friends about his beautiful German mother-in-law, closer in age to him than he was to Nicole's sisters. And his friends knew there would be hell to pay from the Juice if they ever took a business trip or vacation and *didn't* use Judi's travel agency to book the ticket.

There was a terrible dissonance—an unbelievableness—to all of this. Three months later, Judi Brown would show a guest scrapbooks full of pictures of the Browns and the Simpsons. "Look at these! Did we *not* have fun?!" she exclaimed. The pictures showed a dazzling, multicultural extended family smiling on ski trails, in hotel rooms, on beaches, under Christmas trees. "And to end *this* way . . . ?" Judi whispered.

O.J. was still sobbing. Now Lou Brown came over and softly asked, "You okay, Juice? You okay . . . ?"

When O.J. and Nicole became lovers, Nicole and Judi hid that fact from Lou for one whole year. Then fifty-three years old, he was an Army man from the South and lower Midwest. The word "nigger" had more than once passed his lips.

But despite their concern, Lou never hit the ceiling, and almost as soon as he and O.J. met, the two men had become friends. In fact, they grew to love each other—the tepid-voiced, white, grain-belt Baptist and his urban-housing-projects-born-and-bred famous black son-in-law.

"Easy, Juice, easy," Lou now said consolingly.

Calmed, Simpson walked to a chair. He sat and lowered his head. "His mouth was hanging open and he was staring into space, his arms between his legs," recalls one woman. "Even though I had been mentally sending him daggers a moment before, I felt *such pity* for him now. 'I love you.

Everything will be okay,' I said. People were hugging him, patting him on the back, saying the same thing."

Simpson was handed a glass of water; then he brought his older children into the room, his arm around Arnelle. Jason and his girlfriend, Jennifer, followed. But Jason became hysterical the minute he got inside. "I can't look at her! I can't look at her!" he cried out, jerking his head right and left. A few people in the room tensed at the young man's evident pain. They knew about his emotionality, his vulnerability, and his teenaged cries for help. "He's like his father that way," one family friend whispered to her mate.

Jason ran out the door and into the limousine. Judi ran after him, O.J. following suit.

Together O.J., Jason, and Judi huddled in the front of the limousine, Judi between son and father. Both adults comforted Jason, who was sobbing angrily while they appeared to be trying to encourage his return to the viewing room.

According to an eyewitness who saw and heard the entire following scene, Jason crawled over Judi and O.J., out of the car. Then Judi crawled out over O.J. As she backed out, she suddenly turned and—uncharacteristically—gripped her son-in-law's shoulders. Judi had often taken O.J.'s side when Nicole complained about O.J.—for example, about the lack of time he spent parenting. And when O.J. sought to win Nicole back after their divorce, Judi had told him that he was foolish to have confessed his infidelities to Nicole. *Why,* she asked him, go back and dredge up the past? But this mother-in-law-as-supportive-buddy persona was gone now, replaced by Judi's determination to get one central, pressing question answered—nothing more, nothing less.

"O.J.," Judi said, looking right into his eyes, "I *have* to *know:* Did you have anything at all to do with my daughter's death?"

O.J. Simpson's precise words were: *"Oh! Oh! Oh!* Judi, I *loved* her. I loved her *too* much!"

Too much? Judi stared at him for a few seconds. *"So* much," "very much," "more than life itself." These would have been more comforting. But *"too"* much? "Too" much for *what?*

Judi took her hands off his shoulders and walked back inside, for one final look at her daughter.

O.J. was helped out of the car. He re-entered the viewing room, too. He walked back to the casket. He reached inside, moved aside the flowers, and put his hand on Nicole's hand. He began pulling Nicole's dress up at the waist—as if, one witness surmised, to see if it was a two-piece dress, in which case her slashed stomach would be visible underneath. Then he pulled the dress *down* from the *chin.* My God, two friends independently wondered, is he trying to look at her *wounds?*

The Browns were going back to their house to relieve A.C., who was babysitting Sydney and Justin. Before she left, Judi whispered to close friends, "Wait here till A.C. comes. I don't want to leave O.J. alone with Nicole's body."

O.J. continued to touch Nicole's cold, embalmed body for about five to seven minutes, one viewer estimates. He stroked her face, her hair.

Meanwhile, sixty miles north, a resolute assistant district attorney named Marcia Clark was quietly preparing for what she and her boss, Los Angeles District Attorney Gil Garcetti, expected to be Simpson's imminent arrest. Three years before, Clark had obtained a conviction of Robert Bardo, the stalker and killer of actress Rebecca Schaeffer. The case was one of the few big wins that office had been able to wrest from the courts in the last several years. Shortly after that victory, Clark won the conviction of two Russian immigrants who were on trial for killing another Russian and hacking off his fingers. The day before, Garcetti had assigned *The People v. O.J. Simpson* to Clark, even though no arrest had been made as yet. Simpson was not unprepared. That afternoon he had met with Robert Shapiro and had hired the tanned and personable, if slick, criminal attorney who had made his name as a plea-bargainer for athletes indicted on felony charges—Vince

Coleman and Darryl Strawberry—and for Marlon Brando's son Christian on charges of killing his sister's boyfriend.

Simpson had needed, not wanted, a new attorney.

His previous attorney, Howard Weitzman, had resigned from the case—abruptly. He announced: "I have decided because of my personal relationship with O.J. Simpson and my many other professional commitments [to, among others, Michael Jackson, who was being investigated on child-molestation charges], I can no longer give O.J. Simpson the attention he both deserves and needs. I will continue to advise and consult with O.J. and provide whatever support I can."

As the prosecutorial artillery massed, unseen, against him, O.J. Simpson lingered over the body of the only woman whom he had loved who had dared, twice, to leave him. He moved the cuffs of her dress up. A Brown family friend approached and tactfully reminded O.J. that the mortician had advised against touching. "I'm looking for something," O.J. said. It is thought that he hoped Nicole would be wearing a beautiful ring he had given her several years before. He had promised to buy it if she stopped biting her nails. She didn't stop the nail biting, but he bought the ring for her anyway. To a large and very sad extent, that's the kind of husband he had been.

The ring, however, was not on Nicole's finger. He looked chagrined.

He turned from the casket and sat down on the Victorian love seat next to his mother, who was seated in a chair. Nicole's casket was about seven feet away, facing him. Flanked by the two most central women in his life, O.J. Simpson sat impassively in the bright, light room—surrounded by the darkness that had become his life.

Family and closest friends repaired to the Browns' open, rambling, sliding-glass-doored house, the site of the family's yearly Easter party. O.J. and Nicole's two kids, Rolf and

Maria's three, and Mini's and Denise's sons (like Denise, Mini was a single mother who lived at home) always scooted around the driveway, looking for the eggs and candy Nicole brought. "Hey, those baskets aren't filled up yet! Keep looking!" Nicole had cheered them on one year in her white, short-skirted Easter suit and high heels. The videotape of that day shows O.J., in off-white golf shirt and khakis, racing a just-starting-to-walk Justin (who had a cast on his arm from a recent spill) down the driveway, anxiously trying to block him from a fall. "Be careful! You'll crack your head!" he nervously calls to his little son. The Brown sisters wave and flash bright smiles into the video lens. "Happy Easter, all!" says Denise. And, "Oh, Nicole, there's so much *stuff!*" "Keep going! There you go, you found one!" Nicole says, as the toddling, self-conscious children inched around, bending to pluck egg after egg out of the hedges. Linda Schulman would later say, "I never saw Nicole so happy as when she was with her family—the whole, extended family—at Easter. She was so happy with her life."

Tonight, two months after the last happy Easter, O.J. Simpson huddled with Justin and Sydney in a bedroom. In another room A.C., who had just returned from viewing Nicole, was crying. Earlier, A.C. had been telling Rolf that he was *sure* O.J. had been framed "because he's gotten so famous." Such typically loyal-to-O.J. talk was gone right now, however. Having just seen Nicole dead, A.C. was left to weep for the woman he had so long protected and defended from his best friend's lesser self. Still, when Rolf and others asked A.C. where O.J. was now staying, A.C. would not say. How complex and ambivalent, yet how undying, his loyalty to O.J. was.

Also present but quickly wearing out his welcome was Kato Kaelin. A friend of the Browns was dispatched to politely inform Nicole's and O.J.'s nonpaying houseguest that while it had been very nice of him to come, the family now requested privacy.

As another of the couple's friends was leaving, he hugged

Simpson and said, "Hang in there." O.J. closed, then opened, his eyes slowly. He looked morose. "This is only the beginning . . . ," he said solemnly.

In time, O.J. kissed his children, then slipped out of the bedroom and was driven back to Bob Kardashian's. The next evening, after the funeral, he would make the same trip from the Browns', this time wearing A.C.'s shirt, and A.C., his, so the press would not descend. That trip would be his farewell to Monarch Bay. He had spent so many Easters and weekends there. He and Nicole owned several condominiums in this complex; here they had spent their summers. Each morning at six he was on the country club golf course across the street, teeing off with Tom McCollum and Joe Kolkowitz.

As the car pulled past the complex's guard house, with the moon high in the sky and the huge, black Pacific stretching past the golf course, another piece of O.J. Simpson's life was over.

And, whether or not he knew it, he had just left his children with what would indefinitely be their new family, in what would indefinitely be their new home.

Nicole's funeral was held the next day, Thursday, June 16, at 11 A.M., at St. Martin of Tours Church in Brentwood, the same church in which Sydney Simpson had, a month ago almost to the day, received her first communion. O.J. had not made it to that event, a lapse that had greatly upset Nicole.

O.J. Simpson was here today, however. Tranquilized, wearing dark glasses, he held his children's hands and walked them through the phalanx of cameras. Press minivans massed at the curb. Helicopters hovered. Police leaks about a ski mask (the mask leak eventually proved false) and a bloody glove coursed through the TV and radio wires.

Simpson and his children took seats in a front pew, with the Brown family. "My mommy's in there!" Justin said as

Nicole's flower-draped casket was wheeled in. "That's funny. What's she doing in there?" Justin did not seem to understand his mother's death. He twitched around and laughed, as confused children at funerals do. Sydney was more solemn. Her father spent most of the service comfortingly stroking her long, golden brown hair.

Reverend Monsignor Lawrence O'Leary ascended the pulpit and addressed the departed's "grieving husband." According to some guests, the monsignor seemed to have geared his entire sermon toward Simpson. We must keep ourselves clear and clean in the eyes of God, the priest declared. We must treat others with respect and kindness. We can't have any dark spots on our consciences.

We must ask God to forgive our wrongdoings.

Forgiveness and getting on with the joy of life seemed to be the theme of the funeral. Alfred Lord Tennyson's poem "Crossing the Bar" was engraved on the program. The cover of the program was an orange- and blue-hued photograph of an ocean's ebbing tide at sunset, a scene of solace and great familiarity to Nicole. The poem counseled loved ones to not be saddened at the death. "And may there be no moaning of the bar, when I put out to sea," the poem read. ". . . . And may there be no sadness of farewell, when I embark."

Denise and Tanya Brown stepped to the pulpit and spoke about their sister's hope and spirit. Kris Jenner started crying uncontrollably. When the Brown sisters exclaimed, "We love you, Nicole! We miss you!," everyone in the church began to cry.

At the burial an hour later at Ascension Cemetery, near the Brown home, Nicole's casket was borne to a freshly dug space next to the spot where her maternal grandparents (her "Oma" and "Opa," as she called them) had been laid to rest years before. This was to have been Judi Brown's resting place. Several years before, the son of close friends of the Browns had been killed in a car crash. At a graveside just like this one, O.J. had then sadly recalled his baby daughter Aaren's death by drowning in 1979. "You know, there's nothing as bad as losing a child," he had said. "It's unnatural. *You're* supposed to die first." Now Judi's face was suffused with grief as she watched her daughter's casket lowered into her own plot.

O.J., however, had apparently steeled himself. For at least part of the interment, he was the O.J. Simpson of Monday night—the one who had sat in his den, angrily concerned about the destruction of his image, rather than last night's emotionally overcome husband, unable to take his hands off his dead wife. When a woman next to him let out a moan at the lowering of Nicole's casket, he turned to her and dryly remarked, "Shit happens." The woman was stunned.

A female friend of Nicole's recalls that he was making a virtual pass at her. "Poor Nicole!" this woman thought. "She can't even have peace from his womanizing while they're putting her into the ground! He was checking me out—coming *on* to me—right then and there. At her *burial!*"

O.J. then made his separate peace with Nicole's current best friends. "You gave her the best years of her life," he told Cora Fischman, according to another guest present, to whom Cora disclosed the conversation. This same guest was told that O.J. told Faye Resnick, "I loved her." Resnick would soon disappear with a tabloid editor to write her steamy book. After it was published, Sydney Simpson would tell her grandma Judi, "I guess Mommy's best friend wasn't such a good friend after all."

Finally, O.J. said to the practical, unmarried Cici Shahian, "Please help Arnelle take care of Sydney and Justin." Did he know that incarceration was forthcoming?

But the most significant remark made during the whole funeral was one that Simpson's just-resigned attorney Howard Weitzman made, after the church service, to a close friend of the Browns. Simpson had requested that Sydney and Justin be brought to see him for a few hours.

"Whatever you do," Weitzman said now, "do *not* let the kids go back up to O.J.'s."

Weitzman said the words gravely but matter-of-factly, "As if," said the person he was addressing, "he had something important to tell me that he knew that I knew he could not say."

The next day, Friday, June 17, after being informed by Bob Shapiro that his arrest was imminent and that a surrender to police had been worked out, O.J. Simpson got into Al Cowlings' white Ford Bronco with his gun, about $8,000 in cash, and a photograph of Nicole and the children that Judi had given to him at the funeral.

While A.C. drove, O.J. huddled in the back of the Bronco and did what he always did in times of stress—he picked up the telephone. While news and police helicopters crowded the air above, and all four major networks interrupted their scheduled programing, as if for the outbreak of a war or a presidential assassination, and drivers ran out of their vehicles to hang signs over freeway overpasses and cheer on the Juice, as if he were running for a touchdown, O.J. Simpson, Fugitive, telephoned no fewer than twenty-two people, telling one, "I'm in trouble, man. I need all the friends I can get." Simpson's and Cowling's location on the freeways was determined by tracing the calls from the car phone. O.J.'s telephone addiction, through which he had always looked for but never found relief from his obsessive love, had succeeded in getting him captured.

At sundown, inside the gates of 360 North Rockingham Avenue, O.J. Simpson finally set down the gun and stepped out of the white Bronco, and over one-third of the American public was spared the horror of watching a beloved hero blow his brains out—a suicide that most viewers were nonetheless unwilling *not* to witness.

O.J. Simpson then went back into his house of dreams and surrendered to the charge of killing two human beings.

On Sunday, July 3, a number of Simpson's friends visited him at Men's Central Jail. They walked through the front door, then passed through a metal detector into a holding area where a deputy behind a window had them fill out slips of paper.

Joe Stellini was one visitor; Cathy Randa and her son Gary were two others.

Two at a time, guests filed into the stark visiting area. The long counter separating inmate from guests was dissected vertically into cubicles and fronted by a long glass pane. A lawyer associate of Kardashian's—a young woman with the unsettling name Nicole—stood chaperone. Eventually she would become Simpson's official "babysitter." Simpson, in his jail jumpsuit and slippers, walked through the door from the hall that led from his seven-by-nine-foot cell.

He stepped up to the glass partition to greet his friends. The glass came only to his nose, but all were instructed that no one touch the prisoner and that the prisoner touch no one. Under the watchful eye of the chaperone and the guard, each guest obeyed.

"I can't believe I'm here; isn't this something?" Simpson mumbled angrily. Disbelief at unfair cards dealt him had been his leitmotif from the beginning of this saga: his what-are-you-doing-to-me? look—the one motorist Jill Shively said she saw at the corner of Bundy and San Vicente; his angry disbelief at the press coverage, as he watched television the night after the murders; the same words—"I can't believe what is being said"—in his "suicide" note. "Sometimes I've felt like a battered husband or boyfriend," he had written. He had used that same description—"battered husband"—five and a half years earlier in a heart-to-heart talk with a friend, days after his 1989 beating of Nicole. The friend was trying to tell Simpson that he was a batterer, that he *had* to change. No! Simpson protested. *He* wasn't the batterer! In *both* marriages, *he* had been the victim.

Why did he feel so wronged?

Where did that keen sense of victimhood, especially at the hands of women, come from?

Simpson "touched" hands through the glass with each of his guests. Cathy Randa brought encouragement and humor. "We've got to find out who framed you!" she said. Simpson seemed weakly gratified that the loyal woman, to whom he had written in his "suicide" note, "I love you. . . . Without you, I never would have made it through this far," was coming through in this hour of need.

Cathy said, "I heard a joke." She paused. "It's about you."

"Tell me." He seemed amused.

She worked up her best mock-football-commentator voice. "He's at the fifty . . . the forty . . . the thirty . . . the ten . . . the five . . . the four-oh-five."

Simpson managed a desultory smile. Over the next few weeks, none of the O.J. jokes would get much better than this tepid reference to the San Diego Freeway, the meaning of which he and A.C. had forever changed.

Another visitor that Monday was Marcus Allen. He brought along his new wife, Kathryn, a thin, sweet, pretty blonde. They had gotten married at Simpson's house in the summer of 1993 after a relationship as plagued by Marcus' womanizing as O.J.'s with Nicole's had been. In his "suicide" note, O.J. had written, "You've got a great lady in Catherine [sic]. Don't mess it up"—much as an older, unreformable womanizer might have written to O.J. about Nicole.

Marcus was a brilliant running back, just as O.J. had been in his prime. Like O.J. had been, he was a lean, handsome man in a beefy, unhandsome man's game. Marcus, however, was, as one businessman friend of O.J. puts it, "a wholesome kid from a stable lower-middle-class San Diego home." O.J.'s childhood had been lived in the projects, the ghetto.

Both on his new team of one season, the Kansas City Chiefs, and on the L.A. Raiders, where he spent the bulk of his career, Marcus' number was O.J.'s old number: 32. Marcus was O.J.'s protégé; O.J. was the mentor, the *hero.*

The night Marcus won the Heisman Trophy as the outstanding college football player of 1981, he had celebrated with O.J. at Morton's restaurant and, as the third dinner celebrant, Hertz commercials director Fred Levinson, recalls, "Marcus was in awe of O.J. all night long."

Now it was Marcus' turn to enter the visitor's cubicle. He walked in, sat down, and he and O.J. were observed praying. It was not the first time the two men would pray together. Along with Bob Kardashian's brother Tom, they had been in a men's prayer group led by Reverend Donn Moomaw—a former UCLA All-American lineman—of the Bel Air Presbyterian Church. The focus of that small prayer group had been fidelity—in retrospect, a very appropriate subject for concerted reform, not only because of Simpson's and Allen's reputations, but also perhaps because of Reverend Moomaw's eventual fall from grace: In 1993, he resigned his prestigious pulpit (Ronald and Nancy Reagan were among his flock and he officiated at Reagan's first Inauguration), saying that he had "stepped over the line of acceptable behavior with some members of the congregation."

Whatever Marcus Allen and O.J. Simpson said to each other in their private visit at the jail, the subject of infidelity and betrayal that had linked the two men in prayer before had attained a far graver significance: Marcus had had an affair with Nicole after her divorce from O.J. "It was very serious; it was very passionate; they were crazy about each other," says one of Nicole's best friends. She and another best friend of Nicole's would smile as "we'd leave her off jogging and see him driving up and down her street, waiting until it was safe to park and go in."*

---

*Ed Hookstratten, Marcus Allen's attorney and agent of fourteen years, says that allegations of a romantic relationship between Nicole and Allen are "totally ridiculous. He was very friendly with O.J. and Nicole and that was the size of it." Hookstratten further stated that to "drag" a person of Allen's stature in the sports world into the "O.J. and Nicole story," as he put it, was deplorable. This denial notwithstanding, two close friends of Nicole have unequivo-

That affair had been bad enough. To make things worse, Nicole had *resumed* her affair with the now-married Marcus just before she gave O.J. back the sapphire-and-diamond bracelet and broke up with him on May 22. Nicole's best friends knew how dangerous Nicole's behavior was. Marcus Allen wasn't some pretty but unaccomplished white boy like Nicole's other post-divorce boyfriends had been. He was a younger, *better* O.J. Could there be a more pointed insult?

During the last weeks of her life, Nicole reassured her friends that she saw Marcus only when she knew O.J. was out of town. Still, they were deeply worried, especially because Marcus and Nicole were so sloppy about discretion. "Once I was driving down Bundy and I saw Marcus' *car* in Nicole's driveway! I *flipped!* Her other boyfriends had been so afraid of O.J. they parked around the block. There was Marcus' car, which O.J. would recognize much faster than I did, clear as day."

The best friend continues: "Toward the end, we only used three words whenever she talked about Marcus. Those words were, *'Nicole! Be careful.'* I truly believed that if O.J. had found out she had started seeing Marcus again, he would have killed them both."

Right after his Sunday, July 3, visit with Simpson, as he walked out of the Men's Central Jail visiting area, Marcus Allen was observed to have had tears in his eyes.

Slightly less than two weeks earlier, on Monday, June 20, several of O.J. Simpson's friends had a meeting to discuss support strategy for him and, as one put it, "to find the real killer." Kardashian, Stellini, Schwartz, and Kolkowitz were among them. A few days later, a conference call was placed to those who could not make it to Los Angeles; these men included Michael Militello, the Buffalo restaurant owner

---

cally stated, to the author of this book, that Nicole said she had an affair with Allen both after her divorce from Simpson in 1992 and for a brief period of time before her murder in 1994.

who had been Simpson's friend since his days on the Buffalo Bills. All these men, and others, would remain staunchly supportive of their friend, visiting him frequently in jail. Some would even ask others to "keep an open mind about O.J."

And yet, during the month of November 1994, a rumor raged through certain very-close-to-the-case quarters in Los Angeles—and among O.J.'s friends. The rumor was that Howard Weitzman quit the case because of something—a confession?—that O.J. told him on June 13.

In a conversation with an acquaintance in December, Howard Weitzman said, "I decided not to take the case when I found out he left at eleven o'clock at night for Chicago." He also said, "It's okay if Shapiro does this thing, but I told Johnnie [Cochran] over and over again, 'Do not take this case.' He still took it." When asked by this acquaintance (who was sympathetic with the prosecution) if he thought O.J. would be convicted, Weitzman replied, "They have so much evidence, you don't have to worry."

The Simpsons' marriage is a domestic tragedy like no other and like all others. They were two people who could not let each other go, who found in each other an irreplaceable—an *unabandonable*—home. They worked very hard on a marriage that had largely conquered differences of age, race, public recognition, temperament, and background. But that marriage could never vanquish other problems: those of infidelity, obsession, provocation, violence—and the blinding hero worship that obscures deeper truths.

The Simpsons did not live in abstract, ruinous "Hollywood," but in a highly identifiable, surprisingly traditional community where people played softball and Scrabble and Password together every week and celebrated Christmas and Thanksgiving and the Fourth of July in family gatherings year after year after year. The group consisted of regular, up-from-the-working-class, self-made, sports-mad guys—and a group of women who juggled their desire to make homes and have children with these men with their need for freedom, independence, and adventure, women who rebelled from the "Boys' Club" of their "Couple's Night" life with a "Girls' Club" of their own.

It is a very typical American scenario.

The Simpsons took the notion of family very seriously and, in this day of fractured households and families Lite, they were heartfelt and talented domestic practitioners of the old-fashioned kind. They longed to preserve the family they had created; they made their friends feel like a part of that family; and they very successfully blended that family *and* their friends with the families they had been born into and created before. You cannot look at the life that, on its surface and several layers under, looked so ideal and not be struck by the tragedy that it inexplicably—and yet inevitably—led to.

Nicole and O.J. Simpson were two extremely romantic people—dangerously romantic, you might say—and their inability to live apart is what created their fate. One of them died in an effort to make real her own words, "I want to come home." The other's severe "lovesickness," so disarming and affecting for the vulnerability it displayed to the hero's awestruck friends, was never dealt with as the pathologic obsession that it almost certainly was.

A sports superstar's life is arranged so that what can plainly be seen in others as sickness and cruelty is in him excused as the idiosyncracy of a hero with vast appetites. When that man has generosity and charm galore, the process of seeing other truths about him is harder still—even for the kindest and most intelligent of friends. Every day of his football career—and after it was over—O.J. Simpson was told, in words and especially in actions by his fans and by his male friends, that he could do anything he wanted and never have to pay for it. That he could walk on water.

* * *

Three weeks before the murders, one of Simpson's closest male friends said to another, "One of these days, one of them is going to kill the other." The remark was accompanied by something more rueful than laughter but less than literal conviction. Such comments are not meant to be taken seriously because most of us do not live in a world where murder happens to those we know, and, even less often, by the hand of those we know.

Yet sometimes it does happen.

In cases of spousal murder (which the judicial system has yet to decide whether this is), it often turns out that friends of the victim and the culprit have made this very remark to one another, weeks or months or years before the murder.

The victim, however, almost always knows what her fate will be. She senses it in her body; she reads the invisible writing that no one else can see. Whether or not Nicole was such a victim, she certainly fit the profile. For years, Nicole Brown Simpson said the very words that other wives of wealthy, well-connected—and obsessive—men have said before their murders: "He is going to kill me, and then he will get away with it." Denise Brown says, "Nicole said this *many* times to me: 'O.J. will kill me and he'll get away with it—he'll "O.J." his way out of it.'"

About five weeks before she was murdered, Nicole left a list of O.J.'s abuses of her in the Bundy Drive condominium. It is now in the possession of the prosecution. Four weeks before she was murdered, she made out her will. Her outcries about her husband—which were so hard to hear during her life because of her constant reconciliations with him, her confusion and bravado, and her own minimization of them—are plain and eloquent in the substance and the timing of these documents that survive her.

But this story is not about a man and a woman in a vacuum; rather, it is about the development of a troubled relationship within a circle of good, loving, but ultimately helpless friends.

Any reader who has lived in a community of close-knit friends and families and seen how the year-by-year shift in the other members' lives and marriages affects and is affected by its most charismatic but star-crossed couple—that compelling but aggravating pair that embodies the best and the worst qualities of the group—will come away from these pages knowing in their bones that the Simpsons' soaring, flawed love story is not as isolated as it looks.

2

Californians

SUNSET BOULEVARD BEGINS AT THE PACIFIC OCEAN AND, AS IT curves along its undulating eight-mile course into Brentwood, its thousands of eucalyptus trees—lemon, blue gum, silver dollar, and ironwood—define the route. Drooping, shaggy, and fringed, their trunks parched and peeling, they teeter over the winding boulevard like shawled, exhausted widows.

However native to the land they seem, the eucalypti's presence here is accidental. They were shipped from Australia in the 1880s to be made into railroad ties, but their bark proved too delicate so they were planted instead. They survived their destiny as perishable workhorses to become the most dominant, glamorous, and soulful part of the landscape—to literally *change* the land.

Rockingham Avenue is just about the last point on Sunset before the eucalypti taper off, giving way to more ordinary trees. So if you're going east, it is here that the poignant gives way to the banal. But if you're driving west, then Rockingham Avenue is where the trees' soft hint of sorrow starts.

O.J. Simpson lived at 360 North Rockingham Avenue, two blocks north of Sunset, for seventeen years. Like the trees, he started as an outsider, destined for a purely physical, fast-burnout life. Yet, once ensconsced, he immediately seemed as native as the trees were to the hills.

O.J. Simpson is a Californian. This is never unimportant. The California state history book started not with Pilgrims nor with tenements full of dark-garbed people from an Old World, but with a sandaled, staff-bearing man in a mud-brown Old Testament cape—Father Junipero Serra—walking through the empty land, creating chalk-white missions amid the donkeys and the stones. It was a biblically bare, blank-slate landscape, a grandly naked canvas on which to paint a life.

In Portrero Hill, the San Francisco housing project where O.J. grew up, you could always feel the damp fog, a reminder of the closeness of the bay. The bay led to the same ocean that the drive west from Rockingham to Sunset leads to. It was that ocean, the Pacific, that always signaled the goalpost of possibility.

And Brentwood Park, his "goalpost" neighborhood, was, as late as the 1920s, almost as undeveloped as Mission California had been. It was then that oil magnate Alphonso Bell financed and cajoled the extension of Sunset Boulevard through his acreage and on to the ocean. Bell owned 30,000 acres that included Brentwood Park, of which Rockingham Avenue is a premier street, as well as the Riviera section of Pacific Palisades, on whose Riviera Country Club course O.J. Simpson played golf at 6 A.M. every day, including the morning of the murders. With the swath cut through this land by the broad new boulevard extension—which gently zigzagged left and right to accommodate the grooves cut by Mandeville, Sullivan, Rustic, Rivas, Temescal, Las Pulgas, and Santa Ynez Canyons—the tracts laid out by the Santa Monica Land and Water Company over the old avocado and citrus groves and cattle farms were rapidly sold and developed.

The beautiful homes of northern Brentwood—Spanish Colonial Revival or Mediterranean, mostly; some later ones, like Simpson's, modified Tudor—were constructed on this acreage. This is the best of old, studio-era Los Angeles. Photographs from those days show residents squinting in the sun against bougainvillea-braced Spanish stucco walls backed by orange trees and newly planted Washingtonia palms.

There is an air of borrowed drama in these old photographs of Brentwood, supplied by the chance meeting of evocative topography and glamorous vocation. The residents themselves were usually nowhere as exotic as either their work in the film industry or the land that they lived on. When a genuinely romantic character—a foreign spirit, a restive soul—did turn up among them, the prosperous yet more ordinary residents often became infatuated.

It made sense that O.J. Simpson moved here. His public life was a classically American uphill thrust past limits, right to the shore of possibility. The rickets-afflicted ghetto boy destined for a hoodlum's life becomes America's most gifted football star, then a beloved and "colorless" celebrity.

Nicole Brown Simpson was the cool, blond beauty, a child of the beach, that western edge. She was blithe where he was heated, understated and ironic where he was hyperbolic and heart-on-sleeve. The life they lived among their friends on shady Rockingham had a destined charm. "Being invited to the Simpsons' was like being invited to Camelot, and O.J. was King Arthur," says actress and realtor Robin Greer, who, with her husband at the time, party-rental company heir Mark Slotkin, was part of the Simpsons' circle.

Greer's half-tongue-in-cheek metaphor suggests a sought-after closed world, and this is apt. The canyons, the hills, the shaded streets were naturally conducive to a kind of huddled, seductive group intimacy, and the history of the land—wild and marginal for so long—brims with examples of bonhomie among its pioneering residents' self-ordained elite. The big family barbecues the Simpsons gave every Fourth of July were like the legendary barbecues given several blocks away and one hundred years earlier, by the Marquez ranching family for their neighbors, the Carillos, Lugos, and Reyes. The guys' nights that O.J. hosted for his buddies—the practical jokes they played on each other and the twenty-four hours of pie-throwing that preceded his birthday—had precedent in the antics of the Uplifters Club founded in the 1920s by Will Rogers, Hal Roach, Harold Lloyd, and L. Frank Baum so they could get drunk and crazy a few times a year in their clubhouse, just down the street from Rockingham. The weekly softball games that O.J.'s All-Stars—including Ahmad Rashad, Reggie McKenzie, Kareem Abdul Jabbar, and Bobby Chandler—played in Mandeville Canyon against Jack Hansen's Daisy team were heirs of the polo games played a few blocks west by Will Rogers, Spencer Tracy, Walt Disney, and Darryl Zanuck. Eventually that polo field was razed and on its leveled grounds was built Paul Revere Junior High School. It was in the auditorium of this school, at 5 P.M. on June 12, 1994, that Sydney Simpson danced—the day of her mother's murder.

North of those polo fields-turned-junior-high, north of the Will Rogers estate, which is now preserved as part of the state park bearing his name, way up Rustic Canyon in the middle of a tangle of forest, a huge and mysterious compound was constructed between 1932 and 1934. It was called Murphy's Ranch. It was a 40,000-square-foot collection of buildings designed by the one distinguished local architect who had the time to take the job because he needed work and—for reasons probably particular to what, not who, he was—could not get assignments. His name was Paul Williams.

The day after Pearl Harbor was bombed, the FBI raided Murphy's Ranch and discovered that it was a site of the Nazi Party, an advance command post for Adolf Hitler. The Brentwood residents were stunned. Had the thousands of eucalyptus trees, all this time, really shrouded *that* much evil?

Paul Williams was known as a laudable entrepreneur, a romantic and a focused man. He was a barrier breaker, a token success. Paul Williams was African-American.

A black man designing the U.S. headquarters for the

führer's "master race"? The irony and mystery were a rich mix. This was a local scandal involving a dashing, successful, ambitious black man who turned out to have done a shocking thing that no one could understand. Did he get stuck in a world he wanted to win, and largely *did* win, but did not create?

The Brentwood residents were stunned and chastened, and then they got over it. It was, after all, too much of an anomaly. It carried no lesson. Nothing like this had ever happened here before and—of this they all were certain—nothing like this would ever happen here again.

I.
Crippled Boy

For forty-five years, Eunice Simpson has reportedly felt guilty about O.J.'s rickets.

The disease, caused by a nutritional deficit, a lack of vitamin D in the bones, is preventable. O.J. Simpson was two years old when he was diagnosed with it and, as he once told an interviewer, it "made my legs skinny and left me bowlegged and pigeon-toed. I needed braces to correct both of those things, but my mom couldn't afford them, so I wore a pair of shoes connected by an iron bar. I'd get into that contraption a few hours every day and until I was almost five, I'd be shuffling around the house."

Over the years, Eunice, a friend of hers reports, has nursed the nagging feeling that somehow *she* had brought on her son's disease by not properly nourishing him *in utero.* Eunice initially did not welcome the pregnancy that resulted in O.J.'s birth, and she fears she may have sabotaged it.

Eunice became pregnant with her third child unexpectedly and so quickly after she had had her second child, Truman, that she was uncomfortable telling her co-workers at San Francisco's Laguna Honda Convalescent Home, where she worked as an orderly. "She tried to keep that pregnancy a secret," her friend says. "Her co-workers looked at her and said, 'Are you pregnant *again?* Didn't you just *have* a baby?' You know how women are: She didn't want to have to say she was. She was a little embarrassed to be 'that way' again so soon. She didn't want to be showing. Eunice's friend indicates she may have tailored her eating accordingly. "Eunice always felt that O.J. didn't get enough nutrients from her, and that that's why he got sick. She still feels that way."

O.J. appears to have been a little boy unhappy and fearful in many ways. He was "sensitive"—his word—about his crippled, skinny bowlegs. He was equally "sensitive"—again his word—about his oversized head, which his playmates in the project thought resembled a watermelon and thus earned him the taunting nickname "Waterhead." He was angry that he had to walk around in the primitive iron contraption he was consigned to because his mother could not afford the more conventional and efficient braces. And he hated his strange first name, Orenthal, so much that he refused to use it. His initials—O.J., for Orenthal James—became his permanent name.

Just as his mother had put him into those onerous nightly braces, one of his mother's three sisters, Jonnie, had given him the hated name Orenthal. The received wisdom is that she *thought* she had heard that Orenthal was the name of a French actor, but Eunice Simpson has told a close friend that Orenthal was the name of a well-respected local church organist.

In childhood, O.J. was surrounded by his mother and his mother's sisters. His aunt Jonnie Durton lived in Las Vegas but visited frequently. While another aunt resided in Chicago, the aunt closest to O.J., the woman who was a kind of second mother to him, lived in San Francisco. Her name was Ruth Tucker. "Ruth was O.J.'s favorite aunt," says a minister who knew the entire family. "Ruth and Eunice were very close. Ruth was with O.J. all the time." In fact, Ruth lived with Eunice and her children and helped raise O.J. for part of his childhood. "Ruth counseled him," the minister continues. "O.J. relied on her. Ruth was always giving him candy and things, and yet she was stricter with him than Eunice was. If he didn't behave, boy, he got it from Aunt Ruth."

What do the terms "stricter" and "he got it" mean, exactly? the friend of Eunice's is asked.

The friend replies, "Ruth, and Eunice, probably spanked him on his butt, and she may have hit him with a switch."

Whether or not Ruth Tucker struck him in this way, two childhood friends declare that Eunice did. Childhood friend Joe Bell told *The Los Angeles Times* a week after the murders, "If Mrs. Simpson saw me doing something wrong, she'd slap me quick. And if my mother saw O.J. doing something wrong, she'd slap him." A quick slap, of course, is not unusual discipline. But a boyhood friend of O.J.'s named Willie Dickens goes further. He told *Newsweek* magazine: "He used to get whupped with anything [his mother] could find: a belt, a bottle . . ."

Thus, Simpson's early childhood was dominated by the understanding that women he felt attached to and dependent on could hurt him, could control him, and could abandon him (by going off to work for eight hours every night). Women were the center of his boyhood universe, yet they exerted an awesome power with often cruel and frightening consequences. He seems to have rebelled against that power, or, at any rate, to have been angry at *something.* Interviewed on a tabloid television show after the murders, Jonnie Durton said that she called her sister Eunice after hearing about O.J.'s New Year's Day beating of Nicole and that Eunice told Jonnie that when O.J. was a child she couldn't do anything with him when he went into a rage.

Whether to prevent or mollify those rages, Eunice coddled O.J. just as much as she punished him. He seems to have learned the somewhat mutually contradictory message that women exist to spoil as well as strike you. *His* wishes mattered most to Eunice, even at enormous sacrifice to her own needs. Once, in the middle of a hard-earned vacation, a visit to her sister in Las Vegas, Eunice noticed O.J. moping. The vacation—the first his mother had been able to afford and take in years—conflicted with the season opener of his Little League game. Eunice was relaxing, plunking quarters in a slot machine, just about to get lucky, but her younger son wanted to go back to San Francisco. Eunice Simpson acquiesced to his wishes and drove the ten hours from Las Vegas to San Francisco so O.J. could play in his season opener.

Despite his daunting macho personality, O.J. Simpson would grow into a man saddled with health neuroses and phobias. He is a hypochondriac, his friends report, so nervous about the proper use of medicine that, says one, "if a bottle of Sudafed had a stamp on it that said 'Do Not Use After February 1,' and it is February *second,* O.J. will send an assistant out to the drugstore to buy a new bottle rather than take one drop." He is afraid of water; no matter how many times Nicole tried to teach him over the years, he has never learned to swim. "He flaps around in the pool, at waist level, scared and awkward and ridiculous looking. I was *shocked* that my hero was so afraid of water," says another close friend. He was an anxious parent, quick to fly into a rage at what may or may not have been his wife's lack of concern for the safety of his young children, rather as if his own vulnerability were never far below the surface. Such anxiety and rages were a motif in his marriage to Nicole.

When O.J. was five, his father, James Simpson, for whom he received his middle name and who was a custodian and later a cook, left the family apartment. In the Portrero Hill Housing Project, it was not unusual for a man to abandon his wife and children. But most men left their wives for other women. Jimmy Lee Simpson left Eunice for a man. He lived in the community as a homosexual, and he came to be referred to as "Mama Simpson" and "Sweet Jimmy" because of his effeminate manner.

Eunice Durton probably did not know that handsome Jimmy Simpson was a homosexual when she met him in the late 1930s. Both were poor teenagers in the tiny rural town of Rhodessa, Texas. It was a bigoted time and place. They migrated to San Francisco as many blacks did at that time, to find work at the Hunter's Point Naval Yard or with the railroad. They settled into menial jobs; Eunice had five babies—one, a daughter named Patricia Ann, died. Then the secret that had become increasingly apparent was declared. Jimmy left Eunice. He had fallen in love with a man in the neighborhood.

Having a homosexual father was a devastating burden for a young black male in the ghetto in the 1950s and early 1960s. It guaranteed constant ridicule. Friends of Eunice report that O.J. was teased relentlessly about his father's sexuality. To make matters worse, despite the atmosphere of homophobia, Jimmy Simpson did not slink away. He remained part of the Portrero community, participating with Eunice and the kids at holidays and family events.

A woman prominent in San Francisco's black community met Jimmy Simpson at a discreet Christmas party in 1978. As the assembled gentlemen in the living room were greeting one another with hugs and kisses on the lips, less than a mile away, O.J. was scoring touchdowns for the San Francisco 49ers. The men at the party were all black, mostly middle and lower-middle class—utility company unit supervisors and bank tellers. Except for a few in dashikis, they all wore suits—no army boots, white T-shirts, and black jeans. Even though the just-peaked disco craze had brought homosexual culture to most big cities, and Armistead Maupin was writing his *Tales of the City* about this most "out" city in the country, the group at the party was conservative, uniracial, cautious. These black men in their late thirties to early sixties gathered not at bars or bath houses but exclusively in private homes; they were men who understood the risks and limits of proclaiming themselves within the community that was their only home.

Jimmy Simpson was effeminate "but not wildly so," says the prominent community member. "He was certainly no drag queen. He was affectionate with his companion, a polite, thin, good-looking, dark-skinned black man about his age. This man, I was told, had been with Jimmy for years. They did not kiss in front of me but they acted insinuatingly.

"Jimmy talked so proudly about O.J. He said his apartment was full of memorabilia from his son's career—it was almost a kind of shrine. But others at the party said that, although O.J. did recently buy him a car, he never visited his father." Whether or not O.J. actually visited his father at his father's apartment, the implication that O.J. rejected his father is an inaccurate one. He did keep up with his father during these years. Jimmy Simpson was present at at least two barbecues at Rockingham (Tom McCollum met him there on both occasions), and at least once O.J. had him there for Christmas. "O.J. got along great with his dad," says his friend Joe Kolkowitz. Still, however well he got along with the man, the fact of Jimmy Simpson's gayness never lost its power to disturb O.J. "We never discussed" his father's sexual orientation, says McCollum. "It was brought up very unpleasantly one time at the house by one of his friends and the conversation was definitely over."

Jimmy Simpson appears to have been a charming, idiosyncratic man. He lived in a nicely furnished bachelor apartment in which photographs of O.J. lined the wall by the stairs. (This is a decorating penchant Nicole would later share: She hung her family photographs on the counterpart wall at Rockingham, but they were frequently torn down when O.J. threw tantrums.) Jimmy collected decorative crystal and he was a natty dresser with a weakness for nice shoes. He like to drink, gossip, travel, cook, play whist, and sing and listen to spiritual and jazz vocalists (Carmen McRae was a particular favorite). And he was an actively religious man; despite the fact that the Baptist church frowned on homosexuality, he served as an usher in the Tabernacle Church and was ordained as a deacon there in 1982.

Soon after becoming a deacon, however, Jimmy Simpson walked closer to the wild side in his personal life. Because he was an excellent cook, he was often hired to cook for the parties of affluent gay white men. He moved into the bath house crowd.

By 1985, Jimmy Simpson had full-blown AIDS. He and another gay black man, a friend named Sonny, frequently visited each other as their illnesses worsened. Ironically, Sonny was the uncle of one of O.J.'s former-running-back friends. To judge by Sonny's life, the crowd that he and Jimmy ran with was violent. Somebody had it so in for Sonny that he came to Sonny's house with construction worker's tools, banged out the bricks from the side of the house, burst in through the hole he had made in the wall, and shot Sonny.

Jimmy Simpson visited Sonny in the hospital, where he was recovering from the gunshot while also fending off the blindness induced by his AIDS-enabled cytomegalovirus. Jimmy himself had AIDS-related cancer.

Within months of that hospital visit, both Jimmy and his friend Sonny died. O.J. was a pallbearer at his father's funeral on June 9, 1986, exactly one month to the day before his thirty-ninth birthday.

O.J.'s childhood friend Joe Bell spoke at Jimmy's funeral, which was held at Providence Baptist Church in the Bayview section of San Francisco. The minister sang one of Jimmy's favorite hymns, touchingly titled "He Looked Beyond My Faults."

A few days after O.J. beat her on New Year's Day 1989, Nicole said to a confidant, "O.J.'s father was gay, did you know that? *That's* why he did this. I think he gets aggressive and violent like this because his father was gay."

Indeed, the argument that triggered the bad mood O.J. was in just before New Year's had *everything* to do with O.J.'s strong negative reaction to AIDS-infected gay men. Even if that were not so, Nicole's theory may be more than speculation, according to Dr. Richard Majors, America's emerging authority on the psychology of black males and the co-founder of the National Council of African-American Men.

Whether or not his difficulty with his father's sexual orientation contributed to O.J.'s violence, Jimmy Simpson's being gay, Dr. Majors says, "meant that O.J. was abandoned by his father *three* times: once by his father's leaving the house; ultimately by his father's death; and, in between, by the fact of his father's homosexuality. This means that O.J.'s mother was *three times* all O.J. had left. Who did he insist on seeing before he would surrender to police?* *His mother.* She was paramount. In black families, there's a high degree of father absence and, as a result, a high degree of closeness to the mother. You see more role flexibility with black males—by the time they're teenagers they can cook and sew and change diapers. The father's not there; these boys have to *be* their fathers. They have to take care of mom. And it all falls on the mother to hold their world together."

Without a father, this son-to-mother dependence can be insupportably threatening. If there is no man for him to turn into, then who *does* he become? A *woman?* The boy may sever that bond through radical, stylized verbal liberation. Amplifying on the work of an earlier clinician, Dr. Majors contends that the ghetto "dozens" game, whereby boys one-up one another in making obscene rhymes about one another's mothers, is an attempt to break the intense, identity-confusing bond with their female parents.

Or they may *not* break away at all. If his adult attitude is any kind of marker, it is inconceivable that O.J. Simpson played the dozens, ever spoke disrespectfully (much less obscenely) about his mother. "O.J. is like a European

---

*While police were negotiating with Simpson and Cowlings for Simpson's surrender as the two were driving the southern California freeways, Simpson made seeing his mother a condition. However, Eunice Simpson had been hospitalized in San Francisco, a result of stress over her son's circumstances. It was arranged that he would talk to her by phone once he got back to Rockingham.

gentleman around his mother," says Tom McCollum. "Always being gallant, pulling out her chair. That part of him is something those who know him do not miss." Every year, on her birthday, Eunice Simpson receives one dozen long-stemmed red roses from her son. But while that gallantry is charming and affecting, there is another side to it. "He's a real mother's boy," another friend notes. "You could see it the day he was captured: He wanted to crawl back into the womb."

"O.J. Simpson," Dr. Majors theorizes, "may have become obsessive toward his mother—and then transferred that obsession to the other women he loved."

Eunice Simpson was, indeed, the favorite mother among O.J.'s friends. O.J.'s friends from the projects—Joe Bell, Howard Rogers, Al Cowlings—loved to hang out at his apartment. Eunice was a second mother to Cowlings, a large, shy, mischievous boy who stuttered. A.C.'s daily hours in O.J.'s apartment, eating Eunice's fried chicken and watching her television, marked the beginning of a lifelong pattern through which Cowlings found sustenance in O.J.'s hearth and home.

"You just don't know what it is to be eight years old and all your friends think you have the best mother in the neighborhood," O.J. said emotionally, of and to Eunice, at his induction into the Football Hall of Fame in 1985.

Eunice was a pillar of the community and her values, spirituality, and resourcefulness were inspiring. Despite her week of all-night work, she was at the Portrero Hill Housing Project's recreation hall almost every Saturday night from 1949 on, helping a local minister set out the folding chairs, move the organ, and generally transform the impersonal concrete and linoleum room into a homey makeshift church and Sunday school. In fact, she chose her exhausting work hours expressly so that she could have Sundays off to go to church. On Sunday mornings, she got up and bathed and dressed Carmelita, Truman, O.J., and Shirley, and then walked them over to the transformed recreation center for the 9-to-11 A.M. session. The minister gave all the children

K-Ration candy. O.J., he recalls, "was a cute little fellow" who always took a heaping portion; candy, not religion, is the reason he came. Then they sat down and dutifully recited their Bible verses. It is not known what passage, if any, made an impression on O.J., but many years later, after his arrest for murder, he would sit in his jail cell reading and rereading the Book of Job. Its protagonist's "Why me, Lord?" matched his own well-developed sense of victimization.

After the minister read Bible passages, he customarily led the group in prayer, then delivered his sermon, which generally had an inspirational you-can-make-it-against-the-odds theme. The parishioners were hardworking blue-collar people who had menial jobs in still-largely-segregated San Francisco. The spirit of the place was contagious. Over the years, the congregation grew from sixty to four hundred. O.J. and his siblings listened to the minister's scriptural readings, then clapped along as he played the organ while the choir sang gospel songs made popular through the recordings of Mahalia Jackson, Reverend James Cleveland, the Dixie Hummingbirds, and the Pilgrim Travellers.

O.J. had already been baptized at the nearby Evergreen Baptist Church, the church that Eunice still belongs to to this day and which O.J. has endowed, over the years, with baskets of candy and flowers and cash donations.

Portrero Hill was never left totally behind. Years later, when O.J. was living on Rockingham with Nicole, he frequently flew friends to San Francisco, sometimes just for weekends of staying at the Fairmont and dining at Chez Michelle restaurant. These trips sometimes included a quick drive through the streets of Portrero Hill. "Look at this!" he once said to Ricky and Linda Schulman, indicating the projects out the car window. "His attitude," Linda recalls, was, " 'I'm proud that I got out.' I remember a kid pointing to our car and telling his father, 'Look, Daddy, there's O.J. Simpson!' The father said, 'So fucking what.' "

When Simpson was interviewed by Lawrence Linderman

for *Playboy* magazine in 1976, Simpson put a positive—indeed, a romantic—spin on his childhood home, where, by his own estimation, seventy percent of the residents were on welfare. "The Portrero Hill district of San Francisco . . . to me was the greatest place in the world. Me, my brother, and my two sisters always had a terrific time. Blacks talk about other blacks being your brothers and sisters, and that applies even more in the projects, where everybody's momma is your momma and three or four nights a week you'll be eating over at somebody else's house. It's like living in a federally funded commune. . . . It's bullshit to think [the fathers] sat on their asses waiting for government checks, because the fathers were always out looking for jobs, but there wasn't any work for them. I wasn't aware of that, of course. To me, Portrero Hill was America the Beautiful, and I think most of the people who lived there felt the same way. At World Series time everybody would crowd around a radio to listen to the games, and when the national anthem was played, the whole room would stand up. *Everybody*—mothers, fathers, kids—would be on their feet."

According to his telling, O.J.'s childhood had a Tom Sawyer quality. "Mostly, I remember the adventures we had. There was a polliwog pond, railroad tracks, a lumber yard, and lots of factories nearby, and in the summer, when there wasn't anything to do, somebody would say, 'Hey, let's go hit the pie factory!'

"So we'd go down there, sneak around the fence and set up what looked like a little bucket brigade, and we'd steal maybe fifty pies. My favorite was blackberry. Man, that was *good.* Or we'd hit the Hostess Bakery or the milk factory."

O.J. kept himself "in lunch money" through a series of resourceful scams. "During football season, we'd go down to the Forty-niners game and sneak in, and then afterward, when the game was over the management would give you a nickel for every seat cushion you turned in. Me and my friends would grab all the cushions we could, and sometimes we'd also grab all the cushions *other* little dudes had picked up. It was a *dogfight.*"

But the way to really make money was to hustle tickets, and for this, "you needed a little dough, up front, to work with. If my momma would lend me a few bucks, I was over like a fat rat. But most of the time I'd have to get the money together by myself. So on Fridays I'd go fishing down at the pier and then sell my catch in the projects. On Saturdays, I'd hustle bottles for the deposit money and by game time on Sunday I'd have $3.50 for a reserved-seat ticket. That wasn't to get in, because we'd *sneak* in; that was money to work with." He would go around, currying sympathy and begging extra tickets from spectators whose friends didn't show; then he would scalp *those* tickets. "By game time, I'd pick up about $40, and this was a little dude whose momma gave him a quarter a day for lunch." Years later, O.J. Simpson would cultivate as friends a number of extremely wealthy entrepreneurs and executives: Charles Olson, CEO of Hertz; Louis Marx, Jr., who is in oil and toys with his Noel Group, Inc.; Tom McCollum, who made his fortune in immunodiagnostics (he developed and patented, among other medical products and devices, the forerunner of the HIV blood-testing kit); and others. He would also become very close with Eddie DeBartolo, Jr., who eventually purchased the 49ers, in whose stadium O.J. had, as a teenager, hustled those seat cushions and scalped those tickets. It was a team on which he himself would later play, at the very end of his career.

According to a mutual friend of Simpson's and DeBartolo's, "'Eddie D.'"—as O.J. and his friends called the Forbes 500 millionaire son of a billionaire owner of shopping malls and racetracks—"idolized O.J. And still does." That a second-generation multimillionaire team owner would end up idolizing the son of a custodian and an orderly, who as a boy was thrilled to have made forty dollars scalping in the stands of the team owner's stadium is a prototypic American story. Our society's sports worship creates its own royalty for American men, demolishing every other rule of status, birthright, entitlement. There is really no other hierarchy quite like it, enabling once-poor men to socially vault so far so fast—and rich men to be so unabashedly starstruck.

Simpson's friendships with Olson, Marx, McCollum, and DeBartolo, contends one of these four men, were actually more equal and substantial than those "gut-level friendships" he enjoyed with Stellini, Kolkowitz, Schwartz, et al. With the latter, "there was a lot of sycophancy from them to Juice," this man says. "But on the level of friendship I was on with him—what I call the middle level of Juice's hierarchy of friendships (the top level was his fantasy level: he wanted to be friends with the Sinatras and Kissingers)—there was mutual respect. O.J. wanted to learn from us, and we were able to mentor him." Part of that mentoring, this friend says, was listening to him talk about his dream of running for a seat on the California state senate.

"Juice eventually decided that a run was not in the cards. There were too many skeletons in his closet. And he couldn't get past a certain level, in social and business connections. The eminences he was in awe of may have played golf with him and had their picture taken with him" (indeed, a whole enclosed hall of his house displays these pictures, including shots of Simpson with Presidents Reagan, Bush, and Ford*) "but he could never sustain the friendships. He couldn't control himself about things that are not socially acceptable. He brought his dirty laundry to the table. He could sit there in a social setting with somebody he just met and talk about his family problems."

O.J.'s entrepreneurial streak was briefly sidelined into street fighting when he became a teenager. You almost couldn't *not* join a gang if you lived in Portrero, he has said. Life there was too dangerous without a group's protection. After being president of a nonfighting gang, the Gladiators, at thirteen ("me and all my little cronies got these great

*Three weeks before the murders, Simpson played golf with President Clinton, a fact about which the White House has kept silent.

burgundy satin jackets"), he moved on to the inevitable next step: a fighting gang, the Persian Warriors. The Warriors had a ladies' auxiliary, the Persian Parettes ("and, man, they gave *me* an education!" he has said of his initiation to sex in his early teens). "We did a pretty good amount of fighting, and the big showdowns would usually take place on holidays, when everybody would get on down to Market Street. You'd hear cats saying, 'You gonna be at the Golden Gate theater tomorrow night? The Roman Gents are gonna fight the Sheiks!'"

When O.J. was sixteen, he and Al and Joe—by now this threesome was known in the neighborhood as "the Three Musketeers"—joined a gang called the Superiors. They threw rocks at buses, stole cars for joy rides, and sometimes were hauled into the station house by the police. O.J. would set up fights, then split on A.C., leaving his friend to take the licks for him. And there was nothing, Joe Bell has said, that O.J. could not talk his way out of. His bequeathing of his hassles to A.C. occurred so often it became a piece of family folklore.*

The Superiors eventually became entrepreneurial. "We started stepping out of all this rowdy shit and giving dances instead. . . . We made us some *bucks*. One year we rented a hall in the Sheraton Palace Hotel and gave a Halloween

---

*Indeed, in the early afternoon of Friday, June 17, 1994, just after Bob Kardashian read O.J.'s "suicide" note, Simpson's worried family—Shirley, Carmelita, Arnelle, Jason, and Jason's girlfriend Jennifer—sat in the Rockingham den waiting for news about him. Once they got word that he was not dead, they collapsed in relief, even though they had no idea where he was or who was with him. The relief turned to reminiscence. They started telling stories about how O.J. repeatedly roped A.C. into *his* fights and *his* jams. In the middle of the family's laughing recollections, all four networks interrupted their regularly televised broadcasts and—as if joining the family's conversation with the topper of them all—beamed live footage of A.C. driving the Ford Bronco down the 405, with fugitive O.J. in the backseat. O.J.'s sisters and children burst out laughing.

party that hundreds of kids came to. We cleared $3300 for the night—which to us was almost unbelievable." By now, it was clear that O.J. had a way with the ladies. He and Joe, Alan, and Howard Rogers spent a lot of time listening to the Temptations—they jockeyed to outdo David Ruffin's raspy solo on "Beauty's Only Skin Deep" and they loved listening to Diana Ross purring out "Baby Love," closing their eyes to imagine they were hearing the song up close and personal. When they went to parties, they put the songs to work. They would go down to the recreation center, where those hits were alternated on the record player with the more plaintive sounds of Curtis Mayfield singing, "Some day I'll find me a woman, who will love and treat me real nice . . . ," Levi Stubbs moaning, "Can't help my*self,* I love you and nobody else . . ." and Major Lance imploring everyone, "You get yours and I get mine in the Monkey Time." O.J. and his friends would try to grab some action. O.J. would pull his long, white, brimmed, Iceberg Slim-style hat down over one eye, take a long, slow look at the room and figure—not inaccurately—that he could have pretty much anyone he wanted.

"If I saw a girl who looked good, I'd go right up to her and start rapping, even if she was with a guy. I didn't care *what* the dude said, 'cause I'd tell him, 'Hey, I'm talkin' to her, not *you,* man. If she don't *want* me to talk to her, she'll *tell* me she don't want me to talk to her.' It rarely got into punches," Simpson had bragged, "because most of the dudes didn't want to fight me."

One night, a member of the city's toughest gang, the Roman Gents—"this loud little sucker—an older O.J.—comes up to me and says, 'What did you say about my sister?' I'd heard of Winky—just about everyone had—but I didn't know that was who this was, so I just said, 'Hey, man, I don't know your sister. I don't even know *you."* As the legendary Winky walked away, "still talking crap to me, I yelled back, 'Fuck you, too, man!' " O.J. was game. Fights were a staple of his weekends. As he put it, "I only beat up dudes who deserved it. . . . At least once a week, usually on

Friday or Saturday night. If there wasn't no fight, it wasn't no weekend."

Winky was game, too. Despite a group of Roman Gents attempting to restrain him, Winky wanted to fight. "He shouts, 'Motherfucker, I'm gonna kick your ass!' And then—bingo!—the music stops and I hear everybody whispering, 'Winky's getting ready to fight.' *Winky!* Damn, I didn't want to fight *him*. So as he walks up to me I say, 'Hey, man, I really didn't say *anything* about your sister.' But before I can say anything else, Winky's on me and swinging. Well, I beat his ass—I just cleaned up on the cat—and as I'm giving it to him I see this girl, Paula, who I just loved, so I started getting loud. And as I'm punching I'm also shouting, 'Muthafuckah! You gonna fuck with me?'"

It is noteworthy that O.J. started shouting and swearing to *impress* a girl. Given the time and place, that kind of macho behavior was a turn-on. Thirty years later, on the night of October 25, 1993, O.J. Simpson would burst into Nicole's Gretna Green house and shout menacingly at his ex-wife through her closed hall door. Using the same street epithets he used on Winky, he would rant on about an intimacy between Nicole and Mezzaluna restaurant principal Keith Zlomsowitch that he had witnessed months before by staring into Nicole's window. The rhythm of O.J.'s rant was half-stylized; it was almost as much stagey, for-effect "testifying" as it was spontaneous anger. The whole ordeal was recorded by a police hot-line operator. Nicole's voice—it would be the only time the American public *heard* her voice—literally quivered with fear. Simpson's behavior during this now-famous 911 call is something that the white and feminist communities view as a prime example of nascent domestic violence, but many black males see it as a case of a man shooting his mouth off at a woman whose behavior with another man has brought disrespect upon him. In this latter interpretation and rationalization, the fact that the man and the woman are divorced is essentially irrelevant.

"Masking strategies," and the need for them, is the thesis

of Dr. Richard Majors' important 1993 book, *Cool Pose: The Dilemmas of Black Manhood in America,* co-written with Janet Mancini Billson. "Striving for masculinity," Majors contends, "presents dilemmas for the black male because it is so often grounded in masking strategies that rest on denial and suppression of deep feeling." Psychologically surviving in essentially racist America, Majors believes, involves wearing numbing and destructive psychic masks: adopting a "cool pose" of speech, walk, and demeanor in order to navigate through daily land mines, to "bring balance, stability, confidence, and a sense of masculinity"; to "render the black male visible and to empower him; [and to ease] the worry and pain of blocked opportunities. Being cool is an ego booster for black males comparable to the kind white males more easily find through attending good schools, landing prestigious jobs, and bringing home decent wages. . . . For many blacks, life is a relentless performance for the mainstream audience and for each other. Creating the right image—the most impressive persona—is part of acting in a theater that is seldom dark."

It may not be a coincidence that the early and incorrect news leak that a "ski mask"* was found at the crime scene was so instantly inflammatory, much more so than mention of the "bloody glove" or any other single piece of real or imagined evidence. A masked black man is a threatening image to white America because it is a thin metaphor for what is both a social necessity and a psychologic reality for black males in the U.S.

Simpson himself has been candid about his masking.

*Although the "ski mask" falsehood has been laid at the doorstep of the Los Angeles Police Department, the genesis of this inaccurate rumor may lie in the proceedings of the ultimately disbanded O.J. Simpson Grand Jury. The knit cap found by the detectives was, at one point early in the secret testimony, referred to as a "*ski* cap." Some knit caps designed for very cold weather include face protection. Hence, from one telling to another, "ski *cap"* became "ski *mask"*—and an innocent accessory became a loaded symbol.

"The ghetto," he wrote in his autobiography, *The O.J. Simpson Story,* "makes you want to hide your real identity —from cops, from teachers, and even from yourself. It forces you to build up false images."

O.J. Simpson had a "hot" or a "warm" rather than a "cool" pose; keeping his mouth *shut* was the problem, but the effect—successful integration into the mainstream—was the same. In fact, Simpson succeeded beyond anyone's wildest dreams: As he became lionized as an athlete and as a spokesperson and celebrity, he didn't have to drop his ghetto style for a black bourgeoisie or a white one; he was able to keep it, polishing it into a personableness that somehow managed to *seem* as middle-American and "colorless" as Johnny Carson's or Clint Eastwood's.

But the masks and the poses were there, born in the bravado of his fights with the Roman Gents and his posturings with the Winkys at the dances. Back in Portrero Hill, he had found a way, despite his childhood infirmity and despite his homosexual father, to win in almost every social encounter. Having a conveniently soft-hearted and uncalculating best friend—Al Cowlings—fortified O.J.'s performance in that "seldom dark theater," as Richard Majors puts it, in which he played out his life. A.C. was a buddy—and an asset.

O.J. Simpson would take all those tools, including A.C., into every single successive stage of his future, and those tools would be as essential to his ultimate success as his athletic brilliance.

But what happens when the tools start to fail? Bursting through Nicole's door on Bundy Drive, O.J. Simpson reverted. He was back at the youth dance with the pimp hat and the attitude. But it all seemed out of place. Besides, it wasn't working. He may have successfully terrified Nicole—and his posturing may indeed have rewon her (she was back with him a week later)—but the marriage, on *his* terms, was torn asunder: She couldn't unsleep with the men she had slept with since their divorce. He must have known that, though its embers were not all extinguished, the marriage was over. At frustrated moments like that, of which there were many in those last two years, there was very little protective material left to mask the deepest, most vulnerable layer of his childhood self.

Simpson would later tell his adult friends, "My whole childhood was in the playground." Sports grounded him. They were everything. Baseball was his first love; he dreamed of being a major league catcher.

It was while he was standing at the edge of a vacant lot in which a gang of kids were shooting that O.J. Simpson realized he was a runner and a real athlete. "I had to get through that lot," he would later tell his friend Joe Kolkowitz during one of their all-night post-tennis-game backgammon sessions in O.J.'s game room in the basement of Rockingham. "I stood there and figured I was gonna run this way, then that way, then the other way—to get my ass through those bullets. I saw the *course.* I saw myself doing it *before* it happened. That was it, man: visualization." After that moment, O.J. Simpson knew he was an athlete.

But it was Eunice Simpson who steered him past the bullets of his own worst self and *made* him an athlete.

Eunice felt a special responsibility to her third child. He had always been the sickest, the prettiest, the loudest, and the wildest. Shirley and Carmelita would eventually marry and have children; Truman eventually served in Vietnam, then came back and held a series of unskilled jobs. In the early eighties, he was a doorman at the luxurious Clift Hotel. (Eunice's friend says that O.J. may have chosen the Fairmont in order to avoid the awkwardness of staying at a hotel where his own brother "had to be at O.J.'s beck and bow.") Eventually, Truman moved to Pittsburgh.

Eunice Simpson focused on her third baby, O.J. As she had once stuck his spindly little legs in the steel brace to strengthen his body, she now ushered him from school to school to try to strengthen his shaky character. Emphatic that he not go on to Mission High, a hotbed of gang life, she talked the baseball coach at the parochial St. Ignatius into giving O.J. a scholarship. The man did so, but withdrew it after O.J. went out partying and missed a crucial baseball practice. Undaunted, Eunice got O.J. into Galileo High, a whole bus ride across town. Al Cowlings and Joe Bell followed. O.J. left baseball for track, and broke school running records. But he was needed elsewhere. The Galileo population was mostly Asian and their football record was desultory. O.J. and his buddies were standouts because of their heights, frames, and toughness. They were quickly drafted.

O.J. took his running into football.

Meanwhile, across town from where O.J. was scoring touchdowns and hustling girls away from the Roman Gents at Superiors' parties, a whole new culture was emerging somewhat similar to what the Beatles and Rolling Stones were bursting out with across the ocean, but definitely Bay Area. The rich white kids from art and finishing schools were starting bands with intentionally absurdist names like Jefferson Airplane, Quicksilver Messenger Service, and Sopwith Camel. Cool, pretty, upper-middle-class girls whose parents had been in the tight, inbred San Francisco aristocracy for generations—girls like Grace Wing Slick and Signe Anderson—became the bands' lead singers. Two decrepit theaters, the Fillmore and the Avalon, showcased the bands, whose appearances were advertised on posters with swirling, liquid graphics so dense and baroque one could barely read them. Young people flooded O.J.'s hometown as if it were Mecca. The white kids sitting shoeless on the stoops of the Haight and hanging out of parked vans wore their hair, beards, beads, and shawls long; spoke slow and rarely; smiled constantly, dreamily, and mysteriously.

O.J. was baffled by all of it. Here were "all these weirdos . . . coming in from all over the country. The only thing they talked about was 'margarine' or 'marinara.' I finally found out it was called 'marijuana.' Up until then, me and my friends thought dope was something you only put in your arm, so we decided to make it over to Haight-Ashbury and see what was happening. We'd go down Page and Stanyan streets and walk into parties and see bald-headed Japanese cats praying and all *kinds* of characters smoking that shit and to us it was just *weird.*"

Later, one of the Superiors brought a couple of joints to school. "When they passed it around, I just *pretended* to take a hit. I was a diehard athlete and I didn't want to get *deranged,* right? I finally tried it one day and didn't get high—but I ran all the way home from school, breathing real hard to get it out of my system. I believed every horror story I'd heard about grass and while I was running I remember thinking, 'God*dam,* why did I do *that?* I'm gonna get *addicted!*'" (Eventually, Joe Bell would come to school with two thin joints, which he was going to sell to a teacher for a dollar apiece. Bell invited A.C. and O.J. to join him; they declined only because of football practice. The teacher turned out to have been set up by a narcotics agent and Joe Bell served two years in prison.)

Seventeen years later, on an evening in 1980, O.J. Simpson would be in the wine cellar of one of the Bay Area's finest restaurants—a stone's throw from the projects he grew up in, hanging out with some people, leaning with rolled-up dollar bills over several lines of cocaine. This restaurant was a favorite of now-upscale former hippies, the same rich white kids who had started out in the Fillmore bands and at those parties O.J. and the Superiors found so weird and foreign. And O.J. Simpson was no longer the nervous ghetto boy, afraid he would get deranged, but an easygoing player among these people whose own provincial lives his own now-worldly life had handily surpassed.

Simpson's famous meeting with Willie Mays when he was fifteen—Eunice had had a neighbor pull strings to get the baseball star to give O.J. a tour of his home, just after O.J. got home after a week in a juvenile detention facility (the result, according to Simpson, of a fight he was involved in)—has always been considered a turning point, the moment he focused all his energies on being a football star instead of a hoodlum. Simpson himself has fostered this impression in various interviews and it certainly makes good copy. But Dr. Majors speculates, "It wasn't the meeting with Willie Mays that was so central to his life; it was the ongoing relationship with his mother—with a woman. *That* was where the energy came from."

By his third year in high school, O.J. had met a girl who would take over his mother's role in steering him straight. Her name was Marguerite Lorraine Whitley and she was as quiet and conservative as he was big-mouthed and wild. Characteristically, he met her by taking her away from A.C. As the reverse-Miles-Standish story goes: A.C., self-conscious about his stuttering, asked O.J. to tell his girlfriend Marguerite something for him. O.J. did—and took her over. A.C. was initially so upset, the story continues, that he tried to overturn a car they were in. Then he got over it. Perhaps he was beginning to resign himself to his fate: O.J. was the charismatic one and he was the support unit.

As for Marguerite, she seemed to calm O.J. down, to rein him in, and give him direction, as Eunice always had. She would soon tell a reporter that when she met him he was a "terrible person with no goals." She was won over by him, nonetheless.

There *was* a male mentor in Simpson's life who helped him get out of the ghetto, who became one of his best friends, and who has always been there for him. His name is Wayne Hughes and he is the billionaire owner of Los Angeles' Public Storage warehouses.

In 1967 Hughes was a major alumnus from the University of Southern California (USC), and remains so today. USC (often referred to as SC) was a school O.J. had dreamed of attending ever since he heard the vivid description of the school football team's mascot Trojan horse being rolled out onto the field during a radio broadcast of the 1963 Rose Bowl game; O.J. was thrilled and impressed by the dramatic pomp. SC was an elite school—not academically, but socially. Despite its location on the crime-ridden edge of downtown Los Angeles, it had catered for decades to the children of the city's generally aloof old-line families. It was, after all, a private (not a state) university and, unlike UCLA, it was not located on what the old-line families considered the nouveau-riche entertainment-industry-saturated West Side.

O.J. Simpson was impervious to the details of SC's snob value but he was taken with its aura. The Trojan horse ceremony on television—with the real horse galloping and the bugles blowing—had made him sit up straight. SC was compelling to him. He *had* to go there. He got a dramatic invitation after he scored three touchdowns in a San Francisco/Long Beach game and was responsible for bringing his team back from twenty points behind to a 40–20 victory. Right after Simpson was named the game's Most Valuable Player, USC coach Jim Stangland strode up to him and asked, "How would you like to be a Trojan?"

"The man had just said the magic word," Simpson recalled to *Playboy* reporter Lawrence Linderman. "Inside my head, bugles were blowing and that white horse was galloping!"

The elite school did not immediately make good on Stangland's burst of enthusiasm. Marv Goux, SC's defensive line coach, encouraged Simpson to finish junior college and bring up his grades and continue playing football. It took two years of his breaking junior college rushing records at San Francisco City College to overcome USC's skepticism about his woeful grade point average, but finally he was accepted.

Wayne Hughes quickly traveled north to meet O.J.

A fair-haired, heavyset man of about six feet, Hughes was a very wealthy man. He was also confident—quietly confident in a way that O.J. Simpson had never before experienced. He was a brilliant businessman and a very kind man. Wayne Hughes wanted to help O.J. and A.C. The two boys came as a package; it was clear. Hughes knew the new SC recruits had a lot of rough edges. "Wayne knew O.J. and A.C. were *wild,*" says a friend of both Hughes and Cowlings. "He as much as said, 'I will be your father figure. I'm going to help you guys get jobs, put you on the right path. Come with me.' "

Over the coming years, Wayne Hughes' advice would serve O.J. well. "You'll never get anywhere if you keep hanging around with guys like that," he had once told O.J. about his friendship with Billy Kehoe, reports a mutual friend of the two men. O.J. always listened. And though the friendship between Simpson and Hughes would eventually equalize as the years went by into more of a peer relationship, Simpson never lost his respectful admiration of him.

In July of 1994, just weeks after the murders, Wayne Hughes, upset by the ugly depiction of Nicole in the tabloids, spoke to O.J. in jail. He knew that Simpson's defense team was encouraging the negative and mostly inaccurate portrayals of her. The false image of a callow and promiscuous Nicole would destroy sympathy for the victim, perhaps even create the basis for a legal defense of justification—she was such an emasculating, provoking wife, she *drove* him to kill her!—in case he changed his plea to guilty.

The trashing of Nicole had distressed Hughes. He had felt close to Nicole for years. She had ridden his horses at his Malibu ranch, just as she had ridden her own horse as a girl. Wayne Hughes had even paid for Nicole's casket.

Nicole had been killed once by a knife; now she was being killed a second time, by the tabloid press. And her family was made to suffer with every falsehood, every rumor.

But the most innocent victims of the trashing of Nicole, Wayne Hughes knew, were her children. They had lost the mother who adored them, who had been a devoted parent. They would have to live out their childhoods with a black hole where an endless fount of love had been. On top of that, every jaunt to the drugstore and supermarket for months to come would mean confrontation at the checkout stand with headlines about their mother's "secret life" of partying in Mexican resorts.

Wayne Hughes knew about children's pain. Late in life he had married a woman he loved who had had their first child, a son, when she was comparatively old to have a baby. The little boy had been diagnosed with leukemia in early childhood—at just about the age, in fact, that O.J. Simpson had been diagnosed with rickets. But rickets could be cured. Leukemia was different. And Hughes' fortune was now irrelevant to him in the face of the constant heartache of his parenthood.

"You're the only person who can stop these stories," Hughes reportedly told O.J. that July day. Hughes was confident that his protégé-turned-friend would hear him. He had helped move this boy out of the ghetto and into football glory. Simpson had so respected him, had always leaned on him to learn the ways of business, of polished living. "Do the decent thing and get those ugly stories about Nicole stopped," Wayne Hughes is said to have pleaded.

O.J. Simpson's response to Wayne Hughes signaled that the relationship—the mentorship, the gratitude—was over in an instant. He opened his mouth and it was as if he were back on the dance floor at the recreation center, facing down a Roman Gent. He stunned Wayne Hughes by saying, "Mind your own damn business."

Back in 1967, however, life was ahead of, not behind, O.J. Simpson. With the help of Hughes, he was heading for a college for rich white L.A. boys and girls who had grown up in the gated homes of Hancock Park and Pasadena, kids whose parents were members of no-Jews-allowed country clubs and who had known blacks only as maids, chauffeurs, and Bullocks Wilshire elevator operators.

He had been a Gladiator, a Persian Warrior, a Superior. Now he would be the coolest thing of all: a Trojan.

Shortly after receiving a full scholarship, O.J. married Marguerite in a Catholic church ceremony (reflecting her faith) on June 23, 1967. They moved to Los Angeles and took a small apartment near campus. Marguerite got a job as a clerk in the science library. She watched over O.J. With Marguerite around, O.J., by his own admission, stayed home and did his homework instead of running out and partying. O.J. became the eminence at Julie's, the SC sports bar/restaurant at Exposition and Figueroa. Marguerite bought their groceries at the 32nd St. Market. Next to that market was a hamburger stand that, after O.J. won his Heisman, had a super-life-sized portrait of him painted on its wall.

Simpson became the greatest football star the university had ever known. In his first season, 1967–68, SC, with a 10–1 record, was the top team in the country. The Trojans won the Rose Bowl; the dream he had had while watching the game on his small TV in the projects had become a reality beyond his imagining. He rushed for 120 yards and scored both of his team's Rose Bowl touchdowns. He led the nation with 1,415 yards rushing and 1,700 all-purpose yards, scored 11 touchdowns, and came in second in the voting for the Heisman Trophy.

The next season, 1968–69, he led the nation with 1,709 yards rushing and scored 22 touchdowns. He entered the Rose Bowl as a brand-new father (Arnelle had been born on December 4, 1968) and although his team lost the Bowl game, he played brilliantly. He rushed for 171 yards in the game and made an 80-yard touchdown run. He won the Heisman and was a member of the school's world-record-setting 440 relay team—running the hundred-yard dash in 9.3 seconds.

Strikingly, however, despite his status as SC's Trojan knight in shining armor, the university's preppy elite patronized their new hero in words that would be shocking today. The profile of Simpson in the daily *Trojan* included this sentence: "His environment shows through in his grammatical inconsistencies in his deep, rumbling speech, but he absorbs and understands as well as any man."

The profile's startlingly casual racism opens a window on the SC world. Old-line Angelenos in the mid-to-late sixties were an oddly entrenched lot. They had spent so many years disdaining and buffering themselves from the Jews (who had

had the audacity to invent an entire medium and build a major U.S. industry around it rather than merely, as their co-religionists on the East Coast had done, taking over a déclassé industry: garments, or working their way into a lofty one: finance), that they never noticed the blacks, whose status as essentially the servant class seemed assured. The university was mere blocks away from the Watts Riots of 1966, but that riot had seemed, to the university's guardians and most other affluent Angelenos, to have "come out of nowhere." Other than vague understandings that some eccentric man had built a Gaudiesque tower there out of thousands of shards of Coca-Cola bottles, rich white people in L.A. not only did not know *where* Watts was, they did not know it existed. It was never a name like "Harlem."

Today, "South Central" (as the neighborhood is now known) has become, thanks to native filmmaker John Singleton, a synonym for the beleaguered black neighborhoods of L.A., but in the early to mid-sixties, such neighborhoods *had no* names to the geographically segregated white community; they were *that* invisible.

White people did not know that the riot's rallying call—"Burn, baby, burn!"—came from the theme chant of a popular black disc jockey, the Magnificent Montague. They did not know that communications-central for the black radio-listening population of Los Angeles was a little record store off Central Avenue called Dolphin's of Hollywood. They knew little of the neighborhood's Fremont High, which would eventually provide a lion's share of talent to major league baseball teams: Willie Crawford and Reggie Smith to the Los Angeles Dodgers, Doc Ellis to the Pittsburgh Pirates, Bob Watson to the Houston Astros, Bobby Tolan to the St. Louis Cardinals, and Eric Davis to the Cincinnati Reds and then to the Dodgers. (Darryl Strawberry, New York-Met-turned-L.A.-Dodger, went to Crenshaw High, four miles away from Fremont.)

Despite the mainstream success of Berry Gordy's Motown Records, most black music was still "ghettoized."

Only a few years before she would break out as the Queen of Soul, Aretha Franklin was playing dingy clubs in segregated L.A. neighborhoods with no fanfare; and a few years before their Vegas nightclub careers and number-one pop records, Lou Rawls and Billy Preston were, respectively, singing gospel and playing gospel organ at Central Avenue black churches.

Black men who walked down the streets of Beverly Hills after dark were routinely stopped by cruising police cars. Not too many years before, Johnny Mathis had moved into a home on Elm Drive and Sunset only because his white manager, Helen Noga, had signed the purchase papers for him. Lena Horne could buy because her husband, Lennie Hayton, was a Caucasian. (This did not keep people from throwing trash on her lawn.) Home sellers in Beverly Hills wanted to *meet* Sam Cooke but they did not want to lease their homes to him. Crowds flanked the Beverly Hilton Hotel to gawk as the "controversial" newlyweds Sammy Davis, Jr., and Mai Britt alighted from their limousine for their wedding reception. The city was only a few years away from these moments.

Even though the insular little world of USC stayed stuck in this era, the late sixties had vaulted ahead. Stokely Carmichael had coined the term "Black Power." H. Rap Brown had proved even more militant than Carmichael, proposing, among other things, that Madison Square Garden be blown up to protest the Olympic Committee's decision to allow South Africa to participate in the nineteenth Olympiad. The New York Athletic Club, which had no black members, had planned a track meet as a preliminary event and many organizations withdrew from the event in protest. With a telling choice of maternal emphasis, O.J. himself said he would not participate in that track meet even "if my mother was holding [it]." Still, he did not agree with his friend, basketball player Lew Alcindor (soon to rename himself Kareem Abdul Jabbar) that the Olympics should be boycotted.

As a star college athlete in the first flush of getting out of the ghetto, Simpson's relationship to his blackness in those heady political days was similar to white working-class students' distance from and disdain of their upper-middle-class classmates' radicalism. As he told *Playboy:* "A lot of middle- and upper-middle-class black students were having a tough time discovering who in the hell they were. All of a sudden USC had a black student union and then—bingo!—the black student union was talking about who was *black enough.* I'd tell those cats, 'Hey, I don't have to go through any changes to prove that I'm black *enough;* I am *black,* I grew *up* black, I knew it the day I was born, I knew it when I went to school—I knew it *all* the time. You're just finding it out, but that's *your* problem, not mine. . . . Don't judge my trip by yours.' "

In 1969, O.J. Simpson was the number-one football draft pick in the country, signing with the Buffalo Bills for a reported $350,000 for a four-year contract. A.C. was signed to the Bills as well—where one went, so went the other.

While at SC, Simpson was well known to two brothers who had functioned for the football team as glorified water boys. They were Robert and Tom Kardashian. Their father, Arthur, had made a fortune in the meat business, and he and his wife, Helen, were among the most highly regarded members of Los Angeles' Armenian-American community. Helen's and Arthur's parents, like many parents in that community, had fled their native land during the Armenian massacre prior to World War I. The drama of that exodus, as well as the group's strong values, gave the Kardashian boys a sense of family so solid it was protective. "You almost lived your life for your parents," their cousin and Nicole Simpson's close friend Cici Shahian says. "Your family instilled pride in you. I can't tell you how many people have come up to us and said, 'I always wanted your family.' "

The elder Kardashians appear to have had a natural respect for cultural diversity before the word was coined.

They resided in an area of Los Angeles, Windsor Hills, that was adjacent to the upper-middle-class black community of Baldwin Hills, and Tom and Robert attended Dorsey High, whose student population was largely black. Four years of admiringly watching the Dorsey Dons handily vanquish their rivals on the football fields and basketball courts around Los Angeles may have led Tom and Bob to volunteer for their water boy positions for the Trojans.

Just as O.J. and Marguerite—and A.C.—were leaving for Buffalo, Tom Kardashian was taking over the family's meat business and Robert, the social one with the easy charm, was entering the University of San Diego Law School. While O.J. was at Buffalo, each Kardashian boy would become very wealthy in his own right—Tom with the meat business; Bob, through a music industry publication called *Radio and Records*. They would move to Beverly Hills and become two of the town's most eligible bachelors, Bob dating Priscilla Presley, among other women.

An older man like Wayne Hughes could be a mentor for a boy from the projects, an uncle to a nephew, but to have the kind of life that O.J. Simpson wanted to have for himself in Los Angeles, he had to learn it at eye level. That life meant tennis and skiing and backgammon. It meant knowing how to think of yourself as a businessman. It meant having an internal picture of healthy family life. It meant knowing all of these things as if you had always known them, as if the expectation of getting them had been absorbed into your skin from the very air of your childhood household.

All of these things would come later for O.J. Simpson, and his USC classmate Bob Kardashian, whom O.J. would not officially meet until they were introduced on a Beverly Hills tennis court in 1970, would supply a good many of them.

Although he was leaving Los Angeles, on the winged feet of his galloping Trojan horse, a $350,000 Bills contract in hand, the move was only temporary for O.J. Simpson. He would come right back and make his life in southern California. It was home now.

II.
NICKY

Judi Brown wept when she arrived in Long Beach, California, in 1963.

She was almost unbearably homesick for the whole first six months as she walked around sprawling, beachside suburbia, speaking no English, while her six-year-old Denise and four-year-old Nicole got strep throat, measles, and earaches.

She was a Frankfurt girl—she had been Juditha ("Yoodeeta") Baur before marriage to an American had given her a name more suited to a middle-American cheerleader than to the smoky, elegant, deeply European young woman that she was. She was used to cities—old, cobblestoned cities with windowboxes, milk wagons, and church towers where everybody knew everybody else's grandmother, where you *saw* people when you walked out the door. How, she wondered, would she ever get used to the gerrybuilt suburb, "Park Estates," in this characterless, history-bereft, aerospace-and-naval-industries neo-city?

In 1954 Judi had been a twenty-three-year-old secretary for the fiscal director of the U.S. military newspaper *Stars and Stripes*. She remembers, "All I ever heard about, from other women in the office, was Lou Brown. He was the paper's circulation manager. Lou Brown. Lou Brown. Lou Brown. He was so popular with the women. I said to myself, 'Who *is* this guy? Let's see if I can catch his eye.'"

As Lou himself remembers, this was not hard for Judi to do. He was driving out of the office parking lot, indifferently watching the stream of German workers walk the two hundred yards from the administration building to the bus stop. "And there was Judi. I stared so long I bumped into the car in front of me. I was driving a company car—and I bashed it."

At the time, Lou Brown was married and had three young

children, but that relationship had lost its luster and was now eclipsed by his infatuation with the beautiful young German secretary. He and Juditha moved in together. They lived together for several years, and, because of Lou's pending divorce, one if not both baby daughters, Denise and Nicole (born in late 1957 and on May 19, 1959, respectively), may have been born before a marriage that would be legal in the United States could be performed. Once Lou and his first wife were divorced, he and Judi were married in Switzerland.

Daughters who are close to their mothers often unconsciously pick up patterns from them, so it is not surprising that Judi's first daughter, Denise, as well as her third daughter, Mini, would become mothers without benefit of marriage, as their own mother may technically have been. But most striking were the patterns Judi seemed to pass on to her second daughter, Nicole—or Nicky, as she came to be called. Like her mother, Nicky would grow up to be a young beauty who immediately and dramatically turned the head of a man who was married, a man who had three young children,* and whose reputation as the focus of women's attention was substantial. Nor would it be surprising that Nicole, like her mother, would live with this man while he inched his way toward an inevitable, though not immediate, divorce from his first wife. (Denise, too, followed the pattern to some extent. The father of her son, Sean, is a man who, she eventually discovered, was raising a family elsewhere.)

And there would be an even more significant similarity: Parental pressure to keep the marriage intact.

For Judi, the initial adjustment to southern California had seemed all but impossible. Once little Denise and Nicole mastered English—in just three weeks they went from knowing only "yes" and "no" to being comfortably

*Actually, Nicole and O.J. fell in love before his then-wife, Marguerite Whitley, gave birth to their third child, a daughter, Aaren, on August 27, 1977.

bilingual—they started gently informing their mother of her other cultural gaffes, most notably their school lunches. While all the other kids had big, messy American sandwiches—peanut butter and jelly, tuna fish with lettuce, ham and cheese dripping with mayonnaise—the two little Brown girls had German sandwiches: a slice of sausage between two pieces of barely buttered European hard bread. They sat by themselves at the lunch table, then came home, ashamed, and said, "Mama, nobody else has sandwiches like these. They're so dry and tiny!"

Concerned that his wife was so homesick, Lou Brown came home one day and announced, "Okay! We're going back to Germany!" Judi was thrilled. But when they arrived in Frankfurt, "suddenly Lou was always out of the house—busy, busy—and so were my mother and brother. I had never *seen* my mother busier!" Judi's romanticized vision of Coming Home was dashed. Her family seemed to have no time for her. She was left all alone with her daughters, just as she had been in Long Beach. Finally she told Lou, "We might as well go back to America." Only later did Judi realize that her mother, Denise and Nicole's "Oma," had *wanted* her daughter's marriage to the American man to work—so much so that she subtly forced her homesick daughter out of the family nest and into the arms, and the country, of the man she had married.

As Oma had taken Lou's, and not Judi's, side and had supported the marriage on her son-in-law's terms, so would Judi Brown, years later, frequently support O.J.'s position when the couple argued or separated. And the Browns would lobby for their daughter's reconciliation with her husband as surely as Oma had implicitly lobbied for Judi's return, with Lou, to America.

Even before they left Germany, Denise and Nicole had developed into a pair of headstrong, adventurous tomboys who teased and challenged and outdid each other. Denise remembers, "Nick would always come running after me and say, 'Wait, Denise, I'll go with ya!' and then she'd take off, running ahead. One day in Frankfurt we were running down the street with our little wire milk trays to bring back six bottles of milk from the store on the corner. We were walking together. Then all of a sudden Nick started teasing me and running ahead and I said, 'Nicole! *Warte! Warte!* ["Wait! Wait!"]' But she ran ahead and I tripped and fell on the cobblestone street and the milk bottles fell out of the wire tray and broke all over my hand and sliced my finger—and Nicole went running home and got our aunt, who bicycled over and came back to find my finger just *hanging* there. To this day, I still have a scar from it."

Returning to Long Beach, the Browns moved into a new middle-class housing development, Vista del Golfo, and a year after that, to the Royal Palm estates in Garden Grove, a more prosperous housing development, a move made possible by Lou's new ownership of several car washes. The large, comfortable house had a resort-style, jagged-edged, rock-lined swimming pool and high-dive board. The girls had shared a stuffed-animal-filled bedroom in the Vista del Golfo house. In the new Royal Palm house, their twin-canopied beds were placed in separate bedrooms, linked by a cozy low-ceiled sitting-room. Their parents, of course, thought they would be thrilled with the separate rooms, but Denise and Nicole—only a year and ten months apart in age and linked by their memories of Germany and their own private language—missed each other. Most nights, the girls sat "in our little cubbyhole," as Denise recalls their name for it, hugging their knees to their chests, their toes sticking out of the bottoms of their nightgowns "talking, talking, talking—and reminiscing about Germany until all hours." After much yawning, they had to force each other to go to their respective bedrooms. Before they went to sleep, they said their prayers in German: *"Lieber gott mach mich fromm das ich cu dir in den himmel komm."* ("Dear God, make me holy, so I can come to you in Heaven.")

"Did we have German characteristics?" Denise mulls it

over. "If it's German to be stubborn and hard-headed, then, yes!" Nicky, especially, their mother says, was Germanic: impeccably neat ("the messiness came later, as a rebellion against O.J.'s pressuring her to *be* neat") and self-disciplined. "She hated diapers and toilet-trained herself at one year. She insisted on keeping all her food completely separate on her plate at mealtime. Even if she was starving, she would not take a bite if the peas even slightly touched the mashed potatoes or the mashed potatoes even slightly touched the meat." And she was determined and hardworking enough to skip fourth grade. The teachers at both Gilbert Elementary School and Skylark, the special school that she later went to, often peppered their reports and parent conferences with the words "Nicole knows exactly what she wants" and "She has a mind of her own. You can't force her to do anything she doesn't want to."

Many years later, Tom McCollum, who became a trusted confidant to the couple, would say, "Nicole's and O.J.'s problem was that they were so alike. They were two 'sames.' Both strong-willed. Both confrontational. A same should be with an opposite."

Denise wasn't as fussy as her younger sister; she was more hang-loose, less patient with domestic rituals. Nicole, a romantic even at ten, loved long baths; "I get nervous sitting in a bathtub!" says Denise. Nicole stood in the kitchen carefully picking up tips on cooking pot roast and spaetzle and goulash; Denise could not be bothered. Denise wanted to be a rock singer—though it was Nicole, not Denise, who listened to the pop stations and knew all the songs.

They took dancing lessons together—ballet, acrobatic, tap, Tahitian—and through their dancing school put on performances for retirement homes. Denise was the brunette with the square jaw, upturned eyes, and the striking, chiseled features that were accentuated by the harlequin glasses that her poor vision required. Nicky had slightly softer features and more baby fat, and she was blond. They were both beautiful little girls, but as often happens, the older sister led. Denise would be anointed the Beauty, the one everyone said should be a model. Nicole became Denise's slightly pudgy, awestruck younger sister.

Several friends of Nicole say, "Nicole idolized Denise."

Today, Judi Brown says that it puzzles her when her two older daughters are referred to as "typical California girls." "I think of them as typical *European* girls. I always have. Especially Nicole. To me, everything about them was European: their manners, their flair, the way they carried themselves. Their way of decorating their Christmas trees—simply, with the lighted candles sticking up."

Judi's parents—the girls' "Oma" (grandma) and "Opa" (grandpa)—came over from Germany and lived in the Garden Grove house. "The minute the girls walked into the house after school, they'd call out, 'Mama? Oma? Opa?' When we all answered, they knew everything was okay." Each evening, the extended family sat down to dinner together. Denise believes that her sister's insistence on trying again and again to preserve family life with O.J. is rooted in those solid, comforting evening meals—and the sense of what a family was and is and should be.

After Oma and Opa died, Nicole made it a habit of getting down on her knees to pray for them every night throughout her adolescence. She even continued this practice in her new life in Los Angeles.

But piety and placid domesticity hardly defined the Brown girls in their entirety. "The two of us were real little hell-raisers," Denise says. "We were always getting in trouble." When they were fourteen and twelve, respectively, they used to go ice skating every week at a rink four miles from their home. One week, however, they had misbehaved and Judi grounded them from skating. "I'm *not* going to drive you to the rink!" she declared.

"Okay, Mama, we're going bike riding instead," Denise said, elbowing her younger sister in the ribs.

"Yeah, Mama, we're not going to the rink!" Nicole called out as she and her sister shot out the back door to the garage, where their bikes were. "Just to the plaza."

The girls got on their three-speeds and pedaled wildly to

the rink, where they skated two sessions, then got back on their bikes to hurry home before their mother would realize how long they had been gone.

"We were biking so fast, Nicole hit a pothole and went head over bicycle. She crashed up her whole elbow, got tar from the street all over her arm, and her bike was totally mangled." The girls found a sympathetic trucker to haul their bikes on his flatbed and give them a lift home. "We're like, 'Oh, my God! They're gonna find out we went to the ice rink! They're gonna kill us! They're gonna *kill* us!' But we just walked in the house and said calmly, 'Oh, Nicole just fell in the plaza and this man gave us a ride home.' "

The girls stood solemnly while their parents took in the story, looking from one unsmiling face to the other. They decided to believe them. In their cubbyhole that night, Denise and Nicole collapsed in relief and laughter.

"We were naughty girls," Denise says. "Whenever I'd get caught for something—smoking, going out with boys—Nicole would go, 'How *can* Denise do that? Ahhh! *I* would *never* do *that!*' And then she'd turn right around and do something ten times worse than *I* did!" It may not have been O.J. and A.C. joyriding on Nob Hill or rolling dice in the Galileo High bathroom, but it was the little-white-Orange-County-girl's equivalent.

As they approached adolescence, the girls, who by now had a little sister, Mini, fell in love with horses. Lou bought them each a horse—Denise named hers Tiki, Nicole's was Diablo—and after school and on weekends they would go down to the stables and ride, Western saddle, down the Santa Ana riverbed, right up to the Newport Beach jetties. One day Diablo bucked Nicole straight off his back; she fell onto the ground, her head smashed into the pebbled dirt. Blood spurted. Denise, her heart pounding, rode down the dry riverbed to the nearest gas station phone booth.

When Judi Brown got a call from the hospital emergency room later that night, she said, "I had a *premonition* that something happened. In fact, I was even going to pick you girls up early."

(The next time Judi had a premonition that something bad would befall her daughter was when she kissed her goodbye at Mezzaluna restaurant.)

After she recovered, Nicole got right back on Diablo. "Nicole was fearless," Denise says. "She was *never* afraid. Of anything."

Within a year, however, Lou Brown sold both horses. The Brown girls' attention turned from the equine toward the romantic. Nicole's first teenage crush was on bubble-gum singing star Bobby Sherman; then she focused on firemen. (Years later, Denise says, "When Nicole was living on Gretna Green, there was a fire station right up the block on Sunset, and one day she walked the kids there to show them the fire trucks. She called me later and said, in this excited voice: 'Denise, you'll never believe it! One of the firemen here is Bobby Sherman's sister's husband!" She had been married to and divorced from a celebrity and was the mother of two children, but underneath it all a part of her remained the starry-eyed twelve-year-old.)

By the time the girls were at Rancho Alamitos High, Nicole had outgrown bubble-gum music and she and her sister were a matching pair of one-person English-rock fan clubs. The walls of Denise's room were adorned with pictures of David Bowie, and Nicole's, of the Who, especially the group's lead singer, Roger Daltry. The tall, narrow-faced, light-haired, big-toothed English singer was Nicole's dream lover. "Oh, was she a Who fan! She loved Roger Daltry more than life itself! Once we went to a Who concert and he tossed his tambourine—and Nicky caught it! She was in heaven!" She used to lie on her bed in her room, talk dreamily to girlfriends about one day going to England and driving around and finding him on some foggy London street corner. Their eyes would lock and then she and the author of the rock opera *Tommy* would fall in love on the spot and go off and live together.

Nicole's romanticism was becoming a dominant part of her character. When a boy she had a crush on named Larry

Case gave her his letter jacket to wear at a football game because she was cold, she went home that night and *slept* in it.

"Aren't you . . . un*com*fortable?" Denise asked, staring at her sister swaddled in the thick leather under the blankets.

"Yeah, but it's okay," Nicole said.

But as romantic as she was, she was also tough and forthright. Later, the combination of these traits would make for her great vulnerability: the romantic in her preventing her from walking away from even supremely unhealthy love; the tough German in her making her impervious to the precautions necessary in dealing with a volatile partner. But at fourteen years of age, that toughness was useful: It kept hooligans from ruining her party.

She and Denise, then sixteen and just back from a trip to Germany, held a summer swimming party that ended up being attended by the entire teenaged population of Garden Grove, as well as the group of surfers and their girlfriends whom the sisters used to hang out with at the 17th Street beach in Huntington Beach. (One of these beach pals, who also came to the party, was someone Denise remembers as a "nice, sweet, plain, normal girl named Michelle Pfeiffer.") "There was a line around the block," remembers Rolf Baur, who had now joined the family. "People were jumping naked into the swimming pool." Denise says, "They were coming out of the bushes; they were wading in our fishpond, as if it were another swimming pool. They were all *over* the place. It was just incredible!"

Even through the loud din of the partygoers' voices and the blaring stereo sound of Barry White and Fleetwood Mac, the roar of gunned-up motorcycles was ominously audible. Into the party marched a cadre of stocky, tattooed, long-haired, booted Hell's Angels. They walked over to the edge of the pool with wide, slow, proprietary strides.

"Our mother freaked!" Denise recalls. "I was in the swimming pool—I felt vulnerable! Who goes over and walks up to them? Nicole. She says, 'Hey, guys, party's over.

See ya.' There was just something so cool and confident in how she said that. Like, You don't for a minute think you're going to get away with staying here, do you? They turned around and marched out, and that was the end of that. I'm no coward but, boy, she was tougher than I was."

Just before Denise's senior and Nicole's sophomore year, the girls succeeded in talking their parents into moving from inland Garden Grove to coastal Laguna. Lou Brown moved the family to a bright, modern, rambling house in greater Laguna's Monarch Bay community. The house, with its fifty-two glass doors and windows, right across the street from the ocean, is a testament to open, indoor-outdoor California living. The move meant leaving Rancho Alamitos for a new high school, Dana Hills. Denise would be voted Homecoming Princess shortly after she got there; the next year, Nicole would also receive this honor.

Nicole's good grades at her previous schools earned her a place in Dana Hills' experimental "Crossroads" program for gifted students. The progressive system gave students a peer-like, contractual relationship with their teachers and made daily classroom attendance voluntary. Among the members of the group was a tall, strikingly pretty Chinese-American girl named Eve Chen. Eve would later become a theatrical director and would marry a considerably older man. The authority and maturity that would find a natural outlet in both of these future life choices were already apparent during Eve's adolescence. She was more dignified and sophisticated than the typical beachtown girl; some people wrote Eve off as "stuck up" without even knowing her.

Nicole had had a similar reception at Dana Hills High. She was so pretty and yet so cool and private that the kids pegged her as icy. The two girls—both tall, both reserved on the outside but wild and complex underneath, one black-haired, one blond—looked at each other and saw a kind of mirror. At the end of the first week of the program, each student was asked to write an essay about one other student and then to read it out loud. Eve wrote: "Now that I've gotten to know Nicole, I realize you have to look beyond her coolness and her prettiness. There's such a caring person, such a deep soul, underneath."

Nicole had written an almost identical sentiment about Eve.

One day, they took advantage of the flexibility of their school schedules to take a half day off "and 'do' lunch, like grown-up women," recalls Eve. "We got dressed up and went to a little French restaurant in Laguna and we thought it would be really grown-up to order escargots, which neither of us had ever had before."

When the plate of escargots was set before them, Eve and Nicky tried to act confident and sophisticated as they picked up the tongs to remove the meat from the shell. Eve remembers, "When Nicky plucked the first escargot it went whoosh!—flying from between the tongs, through the air, between this elderly couple seated by the fireplace. Nicky and I laughed so hard, we couldn't finish our lunch. When I saw Julia Roberts do the same thing in the movie *Pretty Woman,* I gagged from laughing so hard."

Nicky and Eve started the day by getting on the phone with each other. It would be a habit Nicole would take with her throughout her life in her friendships, first with Linda Schulman, then with Cora Fischman. "First thing in the morning, Nicky would call me or I would call her, literally the moment we woke up," Eve recalls. "We were full of teenage girl talk. 'What do you wanna do today?' 'I dunno.' 'I'll hop in the shower and then I'll call you back.'

"We were happy kids—growing up in Laguna was like growing up in heaven—and our moms were strong and stable. I used to walk into the Brown house—the door was always open, day and night—and there was the smell of bread baking, and there were the parents and the girls and the grandparents, all together. I thought, 'Now, *this* is what a family is supposed to be like.' "

In the same way that Eunice Simpson was a favorite mother to O.J.'s boyhood buddies, Judi was the mother all the Brown girls' friends could confide in. "I don't know where I would be without Judi," Eve says. "I could confide in her about boys and things like I couldn't do—like you never can do—with your own mother. And Lou was always the one who took care of everything, just like O.J. did. Judi never had to deal with the finances. Lou was a very strong father and a gentle man. He never got upset with us, no matter how wild we got. Once in a while he would say, 'Girls, simmer down, now'—that was all. There were *no* bad moments."

Still, a neighbor hangs this heavy footnote on that glowing portrait: "I don't know how many times I've heard, from Judi, over the years, 'You don't know how hard it is to live with that man! He tells me what to do.' She'd say it in exasperation, certainly not in pain. But she'd say it. In his own quiet, calm way, Lou Brown was very controlling. He was this innocuous-looking, mild-mannered man surrounded by all those extravagantly beautiful women—his wife and his daughters—but *he* was in charge. You did not want to displease him."

Neither Eve nor Nicky had a steady boyfriend, according to Eve. "It was a time when you looked at a guy and said, 'Oh, he's so cute,' but you really group-dated with friends. We had this one friend, Jim Mitchell, who we hung out with. He was a gangly surfer kid who was one class ahead of us and so tall he could always keep guys from hitting on us and we would never lose sight of him at rock concerts. We went to every Elton John concert we could drag our little butts to." Nicole went to Led Zeppelin concerts with Denise.

But Rod Stewart and especially Roger Daltry were her true loves. "Nicky's attitude about how she would meet Roger Daltry—'I'll just go to England and drive around and meet him'—that innocent, fairytale idea of life, *that* was Nicole," says Eve.

"Yet she was serious—not flippant—about love. To her, even then, romance was not a trivial thing. It was something she was going to throw herself into, all the way. We would be in her room, listening to this one really sad song—'I Don't

Want to Talk About It' from a Rod Stewart album—so many times in a row that once Judi came in and said, 'Girls, that record is going to break in half *right there.* Even *I* can sing that song now!' Nick would just pine and pine away about love. She'd ask, 'When is that person going to come into my life?' She was waiting for someone wonderful."

One day in the summer of 1974, Denise and Nicole were walking along Monarch Bay in their midriff tops and bell-bottom pants when two slightly older young men drove by in a Porsche. One was a casually good-looking, blond-haired young man, David LeBon, whose parents were neighbors of the Browns at Monarch. Driving the Porsche was David's friend Mike Purcilly. They were in their early twenties and were students at Brooks Photography Institute in Santa Barbara. To the Brown girls, they represented male versions of themselves: confident, good-looking, local middle-class boys who had waded out into the world the girls wanted for themselves. Denise by now was well on her way to becoming a professional model. (A young man who had pestered her at an Emerson, Lake and Palmer concert months before had snapped her picture and had gotten it to local modeling agent Nina Blanchard, who had called Eileen Ford, the top modeling agent in New York.) Nicole wanted to be a photographer.

Both guys had Porsches, actually: Mike, a brown one; David, a white one. What better way to impress the girls than go Porsche racing, with stunt turns, in a big open area of Laguna Niguel. So later that afternoon, Denise got in Mike's car and Nicole in David's and, as David recalls, "I took this one turn super fast and Mike went through it and I spun out and did a three-hundred-sixty-degree turn."

"Mike and I, we made it," Denise recalls. "And we looked back and we see Dave and Nicole coming. And it was like they did two—*three!*—three-sixties. And we were like 'Oh, *shit!*' "

Denise froze in fear, then collapsed in relief when Dave's

car didn't turn over and, instead, her sister emerged laughing.

As summer turned to fall and 1974 to 1975, David and Nicole became best buddies. "I loved her," he says, "like a little sister." Excited to know a real photographer—David had apprenticed in Dallas after going to school at Brooks—Nicole showed him prints she had made of Mini and her new little sister, Tanya. He gave her pointers on lighting, developing, and enlarging. He did test shots of her modeling, and of her, Mini, and Tanya leaning on his Porsche. Whenever he was down visiting his parents, they hung out, sometimes with Eve and Jim Mitchell. They shared a love of Bob Marley and the Wailers, continuously playing "No Woman, No Cry" and "I Shot the Sheriff" and singing along with perfect off-beat reggae accents.

David LeBon had a nickname, "Pinky," given because he only turned red—never tan—in the sun, and Nicole never called him anything but that. He was a car freak, his love of the fine points of automotive design eventually made him one of the country's foremost advertising photographers of automobiles. After he graduated from Brooks, he moved to Los Angeles, got a funky little apartment downtown, and worked as an assistant to a major advertising photographer. He would call Nicole and tell her about the shoots he was going on, for Lockheed Aircraft and Hilton Hotels and Honda motorcycles. He also told her about his softball team, the Protectors, made up of a bunch of advertising guys. They played every week at fields and parks all over Los Angeles.

L.A. sounded great to Nicole. Maybe, after high school, if Pinky was still there, she would join him.

Meanwhile, she was about to have an adventure. It was the summer of 1976 and Nicole was flying off to Greece to visit Denise, who was there on a modeling shoot. Denise's new life as one of Eileen Ford's young star models captivated Nicky and Eve. When not traveling to exotic locations, Denise lived in Ford's townhouse in Manhattan, which was a virtual dormitory for beautiful young models, and even though she was one of the younger models (the profession had yet to recruit thirteen- and fourteen-year-old girls for high-fashion work as it routinely does now), she was one of the few in the house who spoke English, so Ford had made her, of all things, a kind of chaperone.

Denise's life was thrilling. One week she was parading down the runways in Milan. The next week she was posing in the Francesco Scavullo studio in Manhattan for *Cosmopolitan*—she was featured in a layout in the magazine almost every month. At night, she went dancing at Studio 54, surrounded by the likes of Calvin Klein and Warren Beatty and Liza Minnelli. Nicole wouldn't exactly mind a life like that, she sometimes thought, though not in a place as far away from her family as New York.

Nicky had been excited about flying to Greece to rendezvous with Denise. Her camera was loaded, her passport ready. She kissed her parents and Eve goodbye and boarded the plane, prepared for the Acropolis and adventure. But not long after the sisters had had a few days together, Denise got called off on another shoot in another European city, and Nicole had some time alone in Greece.

She found she had not quite picked up her older sister's new independence.

"She wrote all these sad, sweet letters," Eve recalls, "that said, 'Greece is really interesting but it's so different, so noisy, and I can't read the signs. I feel really sad and alone sometimes. *Please* talk your mom into letting you come and visit.' Then I got a phone call from her. She was crying. She said, 'I'm so scared! I don't know where anything is! Oh, I wish you were here! If you were here, I know we would figure everything out. Please come over!' "

Eve Chen hung up from that phone call, touched and a little worried. As tough and headstrong as Nicky was—as able to kick Hell's Angels off her property, to recover from bicycle spills and horseback accidents and three-sixties in Porsches, to fake out her parents over forbidden trips to the ice rink—she was not beyond being terrified. The comforts of life at home with its mix of Old World household and typical Laguna Beach lifestyle had kept her innocent. For all her outward cool, she was a naive, sheltered girl. Softer than she looked.

Nicole Brown was, at heart, a dependent, vulnerable person.

3

The Inner Circle

From 1969 through 1971, when Nicole Brown was still saying her German prayers by the side of her canopied bed in Vista del Golfo and developing her crush on Bobby Sherman, O.J. Simpson was restless and angry in Buffalo. Still, the first seven years of the seventies would be important years—years during which he solidified around himself a group of friends who would be a crucial part of his life from there on in—a gang of disparate but tightly connected people within whose midst eighteen-year-old Nicole would meet and fall in love with O.J.

O.J.'s dissatisfaction with Buffalo had him running back to California every chance he got. The weather he encountered in his new home port, right across Lake Erie from Canada, was far colder than anything he had experienced in San Francisco. In contrast to San Francisco and especially Los Angeles, the large upstate New York city—white, blue-collar, its steelworks being dismantled and its rusty industrial base turning obsolete—was depressing. After playing in the dramatic Los Angeles Coliseum, which was visible a half-mile away, Simpson found Buffalo's rundown War Memorial Stadium very disappointing. The locker room for the team's practices was located in a public ice rink and the team shared those facilities with teenagers suiting up for hockey games. Team meetings were held in the ice rink's hallway, with a sheet hanging over a wire so that the hockey team wouldn't intrude.

But all these complaints were minor. What really made the season dismal for Simpson was that Bills head coach John Rauch failed to appreciate his star rookie's gifts and insisted on using him as a wide receiver instead of as a running back. By his second season, Simpson was having regular run-ins with Rauch, who stubbornly refused to change his position. The negativity between the two was about "as hot as it could get," Simpson reported. Only Simpson's knee injury in the eighth game of his second year (which allowed him to go back to Los Angeles) and his affection for Bills' public relations man Bill Horrigan, who consoled him and encouraged him to "ride things out" even though he himself was dying of leukemia, kept Simpson from asking to be traded. On top of all this, the team's white and black players were Balkanized into separate, sometimes angry camps. Simpson hated this.

Meanwhile, however, he had signed a lucrative contract with ABC Sports in 1969, his rookie year. Shortly after the birth of their second child, Jason, on April 21, 1970, he and Marguerite moved into a Tudor home on Deer Run Road in Woodstream Farms, which is Buffalo's version of Brentwood.

Marguerite was not happy. A woman who is consistently called "conservative," "reserved," and "quiet" by all who know her, she was married to the most attention-getting, extroverted, and flirtatious rookie star in all of football. "She was having problems with O.J. because he was wild and she was a homebody, a Bible-carrying churchgoer," says another star athlete's wife who was her friend for many years. "Marguerite and I had a lot in common. We were both our husbands' high-school sweethearts and we watched our husbands go from having nothing to being able to have anything they wanted. Being an athlete's wife is rough.

Every city you go to, women are pulling on your husband. Black women with famous husbands—it wasn't easy for us. Marguerite and I sort of read each other's minds. There were hurts we didn't even have to talk about."

In the late sixties and early seventies, Mulligan's Café and Nightclub was Buffalo's trendy night spot. Whatever young entertainers on tour passed through the city—Mick Jagger, Stevie Wonder, Van Morrison—stopped at Mulligan's. So did astronaut Alan Shepard, Bob Hope, Frank Sinatra, as well as two very different kinds of local hero: football-star-turned-conservative congressman Jack Kemp, and singer Rick James, who would soon become a major funk star with his song "Super Freak" (as well as a prodigious freebase cocaine addict).

Rick James was a friend of Mulligan's owner, a young man named Michael Militello. Mike and his brother Bobby, a saxophone player who toured with Dave Brubeck and eventually signed with Motown Records, were as hip as you could get and still stay in Buffalo. During the 1970-71 Bills season, Mike became friends with Al Cowlings. By late 1971, A.C. was bringing O.J. into Mulligan's. They would be there when the action in the place shifted from the front of the restaurant, which Militello had patterned after the popular Manhattan Upper East Side restaurants Maxwell's Plum and the Sign of the Dove, to the dance floor in the back, which Militello hoped would be a Bills fans' equivalent of Studio 54.

"Man, you and O.J. gotta meet," A.C. would say to Mike. Mike, however, wanted to give Juice his space. You didn't hassle celebrity customers; you deferred to them by granting them privacy. But A.C. knew O.J. would like Mike. All three men were the same age, twenty-five. Back in 1968, A.C. and O.J. had beaten one draft—the Army's—with another—SC's. But Mike Militello *had* been drafted. He had gone to Vietnam. In August of 1968, while O.J. and A.C. were in Bills training camp, Mike was ambushed by the Vietcong when he was separated from his Army patrol unit near the

Cambodian border. He was shot three times, in both legs, and was wounded when a hand grenade exploded. As blood gushed out, Mike fired his automatic weapon furiously. He knew he was dying. Trapped and alone, he rolled into a ditch and he passed out. He was almost dead by the time a helicopter rescued him. When he opened his eyes in an Army hospital five days later, he was told that both of his legs might have to be amputated.

Fortunately this did not happen, and the first day he *could* walk, in December 1968, he was released from the hospital. In full, medal-bedecked uniform, he boarded a transport on crutches and was flown to the States. On the second leg of that flight, a gun-brandishing hijacker took over the flight and ordered the pilot to fly to Cuba. Mike was the first Vietnam war hero ever to be so hijacked.

O.J., who had a natural respect for any man who served in the war he had gotten out of, was as in awe of Mike's experiences as Mike was of his. (Moreover, Mike's stories were as good as O.J.'s—and *that* almost *never* happened.) As with most of Simpson's subsequent friendships, a man had to have pulled himself up from something in order for O.J. to want to spend time with him.

For the next few years, Mike, A.C., O.J., and Rick James hung out together. Cocaine was snorted—Militello admitted this to the local press shortly after O.J.'s arrest. Tom Higgins, who is currently Sheriff of Erie County and was with the Buffalo Police Force's narcotics squad during those years, says, "There were rumors in police circles in the mid-seventies that O.J. did cocaine, but cocaine was so pervasive then—I can tell you, they said that same thing about half the teams." After his press statement during the summer of 1994, Militello, who currently owns a restaurant named the Bijou Grill and who is very active in civic affairs, told Higgins that he and O.J. had never sold, distributed, or purchased cocaine. Higgins believed him. "O.J. was well liked here, and of course Mike's very well known in Buffalo. He's deeply involved in the community," the sheriff says, letting bygones be bygones.

Back then, however, Higgins and his peers in the Buffalo narcotics squad were a bit more suspicious of Militello. "In late April 1975, we were doing a raid on another building, not too far from Michael's residence," Higgins recalls, "and nothing materialized there so one of the detectives came to us with information that led us to get a search warrant for Mike's apartment. We executed the warrant—myself, as the senior officer of the narcotics squad, and members of the New York State Police."

Militello wasn't at home, nor was the friend of Militello's, a man named Casey Sucharski, who was his houseguest at the time. However, a search of Sucharski's coat pocket turned up cocaine and a search of the apartment turned up two guns. Sucharski was arrested a few days later and charged with possession of a controlled substance in the seventh degree and two counts of weapons possession in the fourth. He was released on $250 bail. After he pled guilty on the minor drug charge, he was never seen by the authorities in the Buffalo area again.*

The professional impasse broke for O.J. during the 1972–73 season. John Rauch, O.J.'s bête noire, was replaced by Bills former head coach Lou Saban. Saban knew what to do with Simpson: He restored him to his natural position as running back rather than wasting him as a wide receiver. Simpson signed a new, multiyear contract and led the NFL in rushing, as he would also do the following year. It was also during the 1972-73 season that O.J., Mike recalls,

---

*In a coincidence that briefly unnerved Sheriff Higgins, days after the murders of Nicole Brown Simpson and Ronald Goldman, the long-vanished Casey Sucharski was murdered in Florida. And in a second coincidence, one month after Simpson's own arrest, Militello's old Buffalo friend, singer Rick James, was sentenced to five years in prison after being convicted in connection with assaults on two women. (After O.J. and Nicole's divorce, James, at that time an L.A. resident, had once asked a friend of O.J.'s to arrange a date for him with Nicole. She was not interested.)

personally broke the impasse between the white and black players. "Hey! This is baloney! Let's all go out to dinner!" Militello says O.J. said in the locker room. By season's end he had flowered into what Dan Jenkins of *Sports Illustrated* called "the light, the spirit, the guru of all running backs." He broke his hero Jim Brown's record for yards rushing in a single season. He was named Most Valuable Player and AFC Player of the Year. He was placed on the Pro Bowl team, and his number—32—was requested by the Pro Football Hall of Fame. By season's end, demonstrating a generosity that his friends would identify as characteristic, he gave his coaches and his blockers $20,000 worth of gold bracelets (the five-man offensive team, composed of Reggie McKenzie, who was now a good friend, Joe DeLamielleure, Mike Montler, Dave Foley, and Donnie Green, would be nicknamed "The Electric Company"), each inscribed with "2,003" for the record-breaking number of yards rushed, and signed "Juice."

In 1973, however, something else happened: Marguerite initiated the first of what would be many separations. She even consulted a lawyer to talk about the possibility of divorce.

Many tensions had eased in O.J.'s professional life, yet his wife had become unhappier.

Interestingly, what Simpson most preferred about the change of coaches had to do with his pride, not his playing. Even more important than Saban's returning him to his running-back position, Simpson has said, was that "he treated us like men." Rauch had humiliated the players, he said, by coming into their rooms after curfew and actually checking to see if they were in bed; by giving them written tests three hours before games; by instituting dress codes that stipulated, among other things, that players were not allowed to wear long or full hair or bell-bottom pants. Saban's abolition of those practices made O.J. later "look back and wonder how I ever put up with that crap."

Rauch's humiliating treatment of the players was not

racially based—the Bills roster at the time was less than forty percent black—but Simpson's racial pride *was* surfacing. In 1974, he shot the first of his series of commercials for Hertz. New York commercials director Fred Levinson was hired by the Ted Bates agency to direct them. Levinson, who would become a good friend (and, when he was in Los Angeles, a Rockingham regular), remembers that O.J. was very confident but that his lack of on-camera experience showed up in the way he talked.

"A lot of accents are accepted in commercials today," Levinson says, "but twenty years ago, this wasn't the case. O.J.'s speech wasn't quite what the agency wanted. A line would be written, 'Hertz will get you in the driver's seat' and he'd say, '*git* you in the driver's seat.' He got very obstinate when they wanted him to change the enunciation. Finally, he said to the writer, 'If you wanted a honky, why didn't you hire a honky?!' "

This same year, 1974, a young Seattle player named Bobby Moore joined the Bills. He was buddies with fellow Seattlean and O.J.'s star blocker, Reggie McKenzie. O.J., A.C., Reggie, and Bobby became a unit. Moore would soon change his name to Ahmad Rashad, and his friendship with O.J. would continue until the mid-eighties. (Nicole once described the cooling of Rashad's friendship with O.J.: Rashad was at Rockingham playing tennis when Simpson received a phone call from an executive at NBC Sports, for whom both men worked as commentators, Rashad in a notably higher position. In that phone call, O.J. was told that, in an upcoming broadcast, *he* would be doing the main commentating that Rashad usually did, while Rashad would merely be doing field interviews. When O.J. went back out to the tennis court, he chose not to tell his friend about the call. Later, when Rashad found out that Simpson had gotten the news while he was at the house, he was hurt that O.J. had been, as Nicole had paraphrased it, "sneaky.")

Simpson may not have ever considered changing his name, as Rashad and Kareem Abdul Jabbar had done; such was not his style. He was a complete assimilationist. Yet, as his remark to the Hertz copywriter shows, he was by no means the self-loathing black man that magazines seemed eager to portray right after the killings.* Nothing riles his white friends more than charges that Simpson is an Oreo. They may be both naive and unintentionally self-serving in this respect, but they are enthusiastic. "He's an American!" says Tom McCollum. "He lived in a completely mixed world. If you look at a picture of his softball team in 1982, you'll see it was as black as it was white!"

"O.J. Simpson is the most unprejudiced man I have ever met," says Joe Kolkowitz. And from Allen Schwartz: "I used to have a lot of respect for *Newsweek* magazine, but not after that terrible racial article. O.J. accepts *everybody*. He doesn't look at color." Joe Stellini: "He has black friends, white friends, Jewish friends, all kinds of friends. He was always O.J., no matter who you were." However, a black friend, who chooses not to be identified, says, "It is interesting that, aside from A.C., Ahmad, and Marcus, all of his best friends are white. I don't know what you want to make of that."

He is proud of being black, his friends say. "In private, in our little group, he liked to call himself 'the Prince of

---

**Newsweek*, *New York*, and, to a lesser degree, *Esquire* magazine all portrayed Simpson as a man whose problems sprang from, or whose character weakness was evidenced by, his corrupting embrace of white values. This strangely separatist line (taken by mostly white journalists and white editors) may have been an attempt to couch criticism of him in political correctness—to blame his alleged violence on his wrongful rejection of his blackness. Still: Michael Jordan also loves to play golf; Quincy Jones has long lived with white wives and girlfriends, and his children from these relationships, in posher-than-Brentwood Bel Air; Lionel Richie weathered a report of domestic violence scandal (his wife burst in on him and another woman and attacked him). Yet nobody calls *these men* "Oreos." Perhaps being arrested for the murder of two Caucasians is what makes a famous black man "self-loathing" to the mainstream press.

Darkness' and talk about how blacks were the superior race," says Tom McCollum. "And he would call me a 'bigot' because I'm a free-market Republican. (Since I was a Freedom Rider in my youth, I'd answer, 'Hey, you wouldn't have gotten to play ball in the sixties if it wasn't for guys like me getting the crap beat out of us in Mississippi and Alabama.' Besides, O.J. was a Reagan and Bush supporter himself.")

Recalls Kolkowitz: "The proudest I've ever seen him was a few years ago, when he told me that Arnelle had quit SC to enroll in Howard University as a black-studies major." Arnelle graduated from Howard, has been a member of the choir of a local black church, often wears her hair in long cornrows, and dated Shaquille O'Neal. At the same time, however, one of her oldest and closest friends is Jonah Wilson, the son of Beach Boy Carl Wilson, who epitomized the same white, Orange County culture that Nicole grew up in.

As "colorless" as he is touted to be, raw racism has pierced through the thick, shiny coat of public adulation that supposedly protects O.J. Simpson. He once lost a very-much-hoped-for position on the board of directors of the major company of one of his white friends because another, more powerful board member objected to having a black man appointed, and O.J.'s friend could not dissuade him. "When I told O.J. the reason he'd been voted against —racism—he was not surprised; he accepted it as something that happens," the friend says. "He was also very hurt and very disappointed."

And he once had occasion to tell a fellow who worked for him and had displayed a propensity for what might be called white working-class bar talk, "Don't you ever use the word 'nigger' around me."

Joe Kolkowitz says gravely, "I have been with O.J. when somebody called someone a nigger and it hurt him. I can tell you he was affected by that. He was very offended and hurt."

* * *

Through all his years in Buffalo, Simpson never really left L.A. He and Marguerite purchased their primary home—a large, modern house on Elvill Drive, just off Mulholland at the juncture of Bel Air and the San Fernando Valley's Encino—in the late sixties. Both of them greatly favored their adopted southern California hometown over Buffalo and would spend as much time in Los Angeles as they could manage.

Besides, O.J. had professional reasons for wanting to be in L.A.: He wanted his next career, once he retired from football, to be acting. Unfortunately, his movie and television performances, though benefiting from his likable persona, would turn out to be limited by a talent generally described as mediocre. As with the other post-sports careers he eventually fancied (business and politics), he dreamed big. The breakthrough role he really wanted—that of Coalhouse Walker in the Milos Forman adaptation of E.L. Doctorow's *Ragtime* (which went to Harold Rollins, Jr.)—would likely have been lost to him by virtue of his woodenness even if the initial hurdle (the production's timing conflict with his football schedule) could have been vaulted.

The movies in which he did appear in the mid-seventies were boilerplate action-adventures, with the exception of *The Klansman* (working with Richard Burton and Lee Marvin was "like being paid to take acting lessons"). One was *The Towering Inferno,* the multi-star catastrophe epic featuring Steve McQueen, Paul Newman, and a host of other actors in large and small cameo roles. The other was *Killer Force,* an action-adventure piece about diamond mining in South Africa.

What was significant about this otherwise unmemorable movie was the depth of feeling he apparently acquired for his co-star, Maud Adams, during its filming.

"I'm in love," he told one very close friend, in a tone of voice, the friend says, that seemed to mean, "This time it's different." According to two close friends, Maud Adams would be in his life at least until he met Nicole in 1977.

Adams had been born Maud Wikstrom in Lulea, Sweden, the daughter of a comptroller father and government-tax-inspector mother. As many beautiful models later claim to have felt, she considered herself "odd" and "tall and skinny and all the boys came up to my navel." Her oddness, she once told Chris Chase of *The New York Times,* left her dreaming of leaving Sweden, which was apparently too conventional, to become "an interpreter at the UN or a stewardess." She arrived in New York in the sixties and became a favorite with fashion photographers. She was one of a gallery of major models in the late sixties and early seventies—among them, Cristina Ferrare, Cheryl Tiegs, Verushka, and Lauren Hutton—who would be called "supermodels" today. She had married graphic artist and fashion photographer Roy Adams in 1966. The marriage was not unhappy ("He knew how to entertain; how to be witty—he took care of that for me"), but it ended in 1973.

A year later she met O.J. on the *Killer Force* set and, three friends of Simpson's say, romance bloomed. He was still married to Marguerite, but this had not stopped him before. Nor did his feelings for Adams stop him from dating still others. "He was feeling his oats," Fred Levinson recalls. "Being a major name kind of exaggerated his prowess off the field. Wanting all the pretty girls: this was a natural outgrowth of someone who came from the ghetto and could suddenly get anything he wanted." (Later, when he was living with Nicole and his apparent dalliances with other women still did not abate, Levinson says, "I think O.J. was having an identity crisis. He was afraid of losing it. He had to prove he was in demand.")

Eventually, O.J.'s taste in the opposite sex started to run to the young. In late 1974, when eighteen-year-old Kris Houton was new to L.A. and just recently involved with Bob Kardashian (whom she would later marry), Bob's best buddy O.J. walked over to her at Bob's house in Beverly Hills' Deep Canyon and asked her if she would make a phone call for him. O.J. had met his fellow SC alumnus a couple of years earlier. Now, O.J. was practically living with Bob and Tom during one of the frequent "off" spells in his troubled, on-and-off marriage to Marguerite.

"Dial this number for me," O.J. told Kris, "and ask can you speak to Jennifer."

Kris did as O.J. requested. Once she got the breathlessly high-voiced Jennifer on the phone, she realized why O.J. had wanted *her* to make the call: This Jennifer still lived with her parents. She sounded so young, she might even still be in high school. O.J. had wanted another high, sweet, female voice—not a low, mature, male voice—to be asking for Jennifer in case the girl's parents answered. Which they *had.*

"I never asked too many questions in those days," Kris Houton Kardashian Jenner says today. "I was so young, I just watched. But I did think it was strange that O.J. was always over at the house with Robert and Tommy, and always calling these girls. I mean, wasn't he *married*? I remember thinking, 'Boy, if *I* ever get married to someone who travels, I'm never going to let him travel without me. Look what happens!' "

Kris had met Robert Kardashian at the Del Mar racetrack, near her native San Diego, a few months earlier. At thirty, he was twelve years older than she—and he had no trouble telling her he was successful. He seemed not unpleasantly full of himself. But she, a brand-new flight attendant with American Airlines, was determined not to give him an easy time. "He came up to me and said, 'You look like somebody I used to go out with.' I thought it was a line. I wouldn't give him my name. But he found out my name from the person I was with and he just assumed, correctly, that I lived in the area. When he found that I had an unlisted phone number, he called a friend of his who had an in at the phone company and got my number. Robert was *very* resourceful."

The first time Kris went to Robert's house, she says, "I rushed into the guest room and closed the door and called my mother and whispered, 'You're *not* going to *believe* this place! This is incredible!' I mean, I was raised comfortably middle class, but we never lived like Robert and Tom did, with a tennis court, a swimming pool, and Mercedeses and Rollses in all different colors!" Kris was a fresh-faced teenaged girl—dark, short hair framing her softly pretty features—in awe of her brand-new older boyfriend. Bob Kardashian, says someone who knows him well, "always kept his eye on having his life 'look right.' Well, Kris looked right, like the kind of girl he should marry." Besides, he was intensely family-oriented, and she, unlike the career-oriented young women and the starlets he had dated, wanted to have a lot of children, right away. (She delivered the first of their four babies nine months after their wedding, when she was not yet twenty-three.)

O.J. was over at the Kardashian boys' house all the time. "Robert, Tommy, and O.J. were the Three Musketeers," Kris says. (O.J., A.C., and Joe Bell had been the Three Musketeers in Portrero Hill.) "O.J. admired and looked up to Robert," Kris recalls. "O.J. enjoyed the fine things in life. He wanted to be successful. He saw how Robert and Tom lived, in that beautiful home, and he wanted it.

"Robert and O.J. got into several business ventures together." A clothing store at USC, named JAG, was one of them. "He really respected Robert's opinion in his personal life. When O.J. needed somebody, Robert was there. O.J. would always stop by Robert's law office. Robert acted as his attorney." And when Bob Kardashian left his law practice to become an executive at the Music Corporation of America, he passed almost every piece of his deconstructed business life and law practice over to O.J. O.J. got Bob's secretary, Cathy Randa; his office, on not-yet-trendy San Vicente Boulevard at Barrington in Brentwood; and, most important, through Bob, O.J. met Leroy ("Skip") Taft, who would become his business manager and day-to-day financial mentor. "Skip Taft's importance in O.J.'s life cannot be overstated," says Tom McCollum. "He was O.J.'s financial guru, legal mentor, personal stabilizer, and guidance counselor." Taft kept O.J. on a strict budget.

O.J.'s eventual purchase of the Rockingham house was not made without consulting Kardashian. "I remember O.J. saying, 'I'm going to buy a new house. Why don't you come. I want to get your opinion,'" Kris recalls. Kardashian's approval of the house clinched O.J.'s decision.

What was left, perhaps, was for O.J. to get his own Kris: a wholesome, impressionable eighteen-year-old beauty, just like Kardashian's.

Kris noticed how unhappy O.J.'s marriage to Marguerite seemed to be. "Whenever O.J. was around the Deep Canyon house, he and Marguerite were either separated or having a fight. So when it came down to me meeting Marguerite, those were solemn times, very serious meetings. She never had a smile on her face." Kris was particularly struck at her wedding rehearsal dinner that "Marguerite seemed so unhappy."

The athlete's wife mentioned earlier says that she never saw Marguerite angry. "I never met a woman in our situation who kept her complaints hidden as well as she did. Marguerite didn't complain."

But Marguerite Simpson did confide her unhappiness in the marriage to a woman who was an actor's ex-wife. "Marguerite was the sweetest person I ever met in my life," this woman says. "We had lunch a lot. We stayed friends for years. She told me the marriage was very painful for her. She was madly in love with him. She said she just couldn't take his fame; she couldn't take all the women. She felt totally shoved in the background—like a nonentity in this grand, enormous life he was having for himself. She said something I never forgot. 'I feel very abused in this relationship.' 'Abused.' That was the word. But I never knew if she meant physical or only mental."

Cyndy Garvey, who was then married to Los Angeles Dodger Steve Garvey, believes it was the former. She says,

"Back then, among the people in sports circles, it was generally believed that O.J. was beating Marguerite. I can't tell you *how* we knew—we just *all* knew it, just as everyone knew that certain Dodgers were doing cocaine during games. Marguerite was known to wear sunglasses all the time, inside as well as outside. I remember being at some sports event in Hawaii and seeing Marguerite with those sunglasses on. The person next to me said, 'Well, he hit her again.' "*

Yet whatever violence there may have been was hidden. O.J. wowed everyone. Of the man who would eventually become "a friend I could always gossip with, giggle with, and confide in," Kris Jenner recalls thinking when she first got to know him, "Here was a guy with incredible charisma. He had a great personality. He could charm the pants—I mean, the socks—off anyone. When you're in a room with O.J., you're taken in. You're in awe. There's nobody who can have more fun at a party than O.J. Simpson. And what fun we had."

Indeed, through an interlocking series of fast friendships sparked throughout the late sixties and mid-seventies among sports, restaurant, and clothing people, an ensemble had formed. Its existence confirmed the vision of filmmakers Alan Rudolph (in *Welcome to L.A.* and *Choose Me*), Lawrence Kasdan (in *Grand Canyon*), and Robert Altman (in *Short Cuts*): that L.A. is a huge, anxious city populated by only twelve or sixteen people, linked to one another by appetite, adventure, eros—and a Dickensian abundance of coincidence.

---

*In the investigation of its murder case against Simpson, the Los Angeles District Attorney's Office discovered that on at least two separate occasions Marguerite Simpson called the police about feared or actual physical attacks by her husband. As of this writing, the police officers who responded to those calls are scheduled to testify for the prosecution at Simpson's murder trial, and Marguerite Simpson has been subpoenaed by the prosecution.

This group of people would comprise the population of O.J. and Nicole Simpson's Peyton Place, their Main Street, from the first day they met until the end of their marriage. They would populate the entire second half of what would turn out to be Nicole Brown Simpson's brief life. If you drew a thick line down the center of Beverly Hills—from the tops of Coldwater and Benedict canyons, down Beverly, Rodeo, and Bedford drives, and ending at Pico, off Bedford—you would have the grid on which to place the dots for tennis-courted houses, restaurants, menswear shops, and public parks with softball fields on which this group of people interacted.

You could start with any one member and circle your way around to all the rest. But when Nicole stumbled upon that world and met O.J. in it, she did so through its elder statesman, a suave, handsome man named Jack Hansen.

You didn't grow up female in West Los Angeles in the late fifties and early sixties and not yearn to wear Jack Hansen's clothes. Both the design and contents of his store, Jax—across the street from the Beverly Wilshire Hotel and a block east of the Beverly Hills Brown Derby—were ahead of their time for the era of flip hairdos, shirtwaist dresses, Courrèges-and-white-Jackie-Kennedy-gloves pertness. Jax was a dramatic building with long, thin, awninged windows showing dark, headless mannequins in clean-lined, tight, avant-garde dresses. The clothes seemed designed for actresses with a whiff of the beatnik, say, Tuesday Weld or Jean Seberg. They were clothes for sitting at a Left Bank café or hearing Chet Baker at a club at the beach after a Synanon meeting. They projected a hipness at a time when no other retail women's clothes did.

Jack Hansen's true love, however, wasn't fashion design but sports. He was quite the athlete. He had played pro baseball for Los Angeles when the city's team was in the Pacific Coast League, before the Dodgers were transported from Ebbets Field in New York to Chavez Ravine. He was also an excellent tennis player and the court of his home on the 600 block of Beverly Drive* was considered so ideal (the surface played very quickly, it had a beautiful sound, it had perfect north–south placement) that the best young tennis players, including John McEnroe, flocked to it and perfected some of their winning strokes there. Jack Hansen was always trying to get O.J. Simpson to play on his court and when he did, the two men became friends. Eventually, they would become opposing captains of two softball teams—O.J.'s All-Stars and Hansen's Daisy Team—whose games in nearby Coldwater Canyon and Roxbury Parks lasted until Hansen's recent death and then turned into an annual Fourth of July event, always topped off by an exuberant party and barbecue at O.J.'s Rockingham house.

Jack Hansen's diverse group of friends included writers like A.E. Hotchner and Gay Talese (who wrote his book on American sexual mores, *Thy Neighbor's Wife,* in Hansen's guest house) as well as men who, like himself, were former athletes who had become enormously successful mining what were then the wide-open economic possibilities of West Los Angeles. (Much of Hansen's own mining of those possibilities came from his then-wife, a beauty products entrepreneur whose "Sally Hansen's Hard As Nails," a fingernail strengthener for women, made them both extremely wealthy.)

One such friend was former Stanford football star Jon Douglas, whose realty business would become one of the two largest in West Los Angeles during the era of exploding home prices in the late seventies and early eighties. Another was tennis player Thomas McCollum, who had grown up in Minnesota, moved to San Jose with his family in his adolescence, and quit UCLA medical school in his last year to join a medical firm, Kallested, which became the world's largest in the esoteric field of immunodiagnostic blood

*Hansen's house would later be purchased and razed by Jose and Kitty Menendez, the ill-fated parents of Lyle and Erik. As future chapters will reveal, the next Menendez home (the eventual crime scene) will also figure in this story.

testing. This company developed the ground-breaking endoplate and quantiplate and was a pioneer in developing HIV beginning test kits. When this company and a second (specializing in computer personnel for the medical industry), of which McCollum was director, were bought out in the public stock markets in the early eighties, he essentially retired. (He returned to the fray a few years later to develop and patent the first pulmonary catheter to detect pneumonias in AIDS patients and a coronary balloon angioplasty catheter for the cardiovascular field.) McCollum was a gracious, enthusiastic, yet slightly formal man, more genteel, learned, and traditional than the rest of the crowd that O.J. assembled around him. But he relished raw jock talk and pranks, and had a tropism for difficult women (which O.J. eventually helped him get over). He lived in an historic estate in Coldwater Canyon and a villa in Marbella.

McCollum and Hansen became tennis partners.

Hansen's Jax's distinction had long since faded by the early seventies, by which time many dozens of breakthrough designers and clothing trends had come and gone. Though the store was still open, Hansen had moved his energies one block east: He bought Romanoff's, the landmark fifties restaurant owned by Count Mike Romanoff, and turned it into a brick-patio'd private club, the Daisy. Backgammon and disco dancing were featured at night. Celebrities and nightlife types flocked there. Spoiled kids cruised one another and did drugs in the bathrooms.

"The Daisy was the first really exclusive club in Beverly Hills," remembers Rocco Cedrone, who owns a men's clothing store down the block and used to be the manager of the prototype Rodeo Drive boutique, Giorgio. "I remember the first time I walked in—I saw Sinatra, Gregory Peck, a very young Joan Collins, Claudia Cardinale. It was intimate, it was dark. You rubbed up against people who had money, but it didn't matter if *you* didn't have any. Things were different then. Not so materialistic."

O.J. Simpson was a regular at the Daisy. It was there that he had met Hansen. Cedrone, however, had known Simpson even longer than Hansen had, from the time when the football star first walked into Giorgio to buy a new wardrobe for his Hertz shoots. Cedrone, working-class Boston Italian turned Beverly Hills men's fashion arbiter, coached O.J. on his haberdashery. O.J. was a quick study. He developed a dead-eye taste for conservative clothes—nothing flashy, ever—and he took to Rocco, whose gruff North End voice popped out of his otherwise suave new persona as surely as Portrero Hill popped out of O.J. From that point on, O.J., A.C., and others would make pit stops at Rocco's new store on Brighton off Bedford, and sit under the grand chandelier imbibing Cokes, shooting the breeze, making phone calls. Like many other men who became O.J.'s friend, Cedrone speaks of how "humble" and "regular" and "approachable" he was, how unceasingly he chatted with fans and signed autographs. "Don't ever change," Rocco often said to O.J. "You're handling your fame perfectly."

Beverly Hills clothiers were a macho lot. Most would rather have spent their days coaching sandlot than ordering yardage. They had a natural affinity for athletes. Marvin Chanin, who owned his own self-named menswear store (now a thriving mini-chain), got to know A.C.; it was through A.C. and Chanin that Alan Austin, whose women's clothing store was then on the same street, got to know O.J. For the last eight years, Austin has been one of Simpson's thrice-weekly golf partners at the Riviera Country Club.

Several days a week, O.J. and A.C. and their friend Billy Kehoe cruised down Rodeo and Camden, dropping in on their garment pals Hansen, Cedrone, Austin, and Chanin. At night, all these men stopped by the Daisy. In warm weather, Hansen held court outside on the Daisy's brick patio, his red telephone receiver pressed to his ear. Hansen named sandwiches for his esteemed regulars—the Rod Steiger Sandwich, the Jack Lemmon Sandwich, the O.J. Simpson Sandwich; Tom McCollum was one of the rare non-household names who got a sandwich named for him.

Through Hansen, O.J. met Tom McCollum.

McCollum knew Sean Connery, which impressed O.J.

McCollum recalls: "He was still a little black kid from the street and he'd made it, and he loved that. And I loved him for it. He was in awe of all those people—the Sinatras and all of them. We used to talk about it and he'd say, 'God, I can't believe it, man. They like the Juice!' He had that amazing ability to communicate with everyone, from the President of the United States to a crack dealer in Watts.

"He was always so full of himself—confident and arrogant, but in a nice way. You couldn't help but love the guy—and overlook all those little foibles that in other people you'd find so repulsive, you wouldn't talk to them. Like, later, when we became golf partners, he cheated at golf—all the time! If you didn't catch him, he'd take your money. If you *did* catch him, he had that childish ability to turn around and give you that grin that said, 'Aw, come on, man, it's just the Juice. . . .' He'd feel horrible. He'd get repentant, just like a little kid. Then he'd take you to dinner."

This sequence—misbehavior, charm, repentance when faced with rejection, finally material compensation—was effective. It was a sequence that O.J. Simpson employed not just on his male friends, but on his women.

McCollum says, "You just couldn't ever stay mad at the guy."

What went for friendship would prove to go double for romance.

O.J. never totally warmed to Tom McCollum until he learned one key thing about him: Tom's upper-class airs were acquired. McCollum had grown up as squarely on the wrong side of the tracks in the wealthy town of Wayzata, Minnesota (home to the Pillsbury and General Mills families), as O.J. had in San Francisco. O.J. Simpson's father had been a cook; Tom McCollum's father had been a butcher. The ice had really broken between the two men when O.J. understood that his new friend was every bit as self-made as he was.

McCollum had the sort of voluble kindness and penchant

for verbal analysis that made O.J. want to pour his heart out to him. McCollum was a perfect straight man for a hustling prankster like O.J. Their friendship would come to be peppered with April Fools' jokes from Simpson to McCollum that bordered on but never quite approached meanness. McCollum's solid-citizen quality was a godsend ("Whenever anyone in that crowd got in trouble, it was, 'Get the Skip Tafts! Get the Tom McCollums!—the *straight* guys' "), and his easy camaraderie with the venerable expatriate set intrigued O.J. (Irwin Shaw, Deborah Kerr, and Peter Viertel were his friends and he introduced O.J. to the son of the king of Saudi Arabia.) Over the years, O.J. sought Tom out for social advice and strategy—and Tom was happy to try to help him.

"I don't know how many times I'd be at Juice's house and we'd get a whole strategy planned about what he was going to do and who he was going to take to some celebrity thing he was invited to," Tom says. "Nicole liked to party, but she was definitely selective, and she really hated that he had the attention all the time—that was her jealousy thing—so she'd say, 'Go with somebody else.' And he'd sit down and map out who.

"He'd go through a list of ten guys, rating them for the occasion. He'd ask me, 'Or should I take Arnelle tonight?' Or he'd say, 'McCollum, I don't want you tonight'—right to my face! He had his own version of who was appropriate for each particular occasion.

"If it was a rock-and-roll-type situation—someplace Nicole *definitely* did not want to go—he might take a record producer friend. If it was a more conservative or intellectual event, it might be me or Skip Taft. I remember one time Juice and I went to some event at the Shubert Theater. Whatever and whoever it was, there was a lot of strategy to it. O.J. was absolutely a social climber. He was socially driven. He did *really believe* he could be a state senator. He did *really believe* he could be on the board of Hertz. He would go into these almost dream-like trances where he believed he had a future in politics, where ego and naive power and delusions of grandeur took over. We had conversations about these aspirations of his for ten years. He was addicted to people and he was addicted to his celebrity status. But O.J. was ultimately stiffed where it counted. He wasn't going to make it—not as a potential candidate, not as a social eminence. And when he realized that, there was always a hint of sadness he carried around with him."

Mike Militello flew out to L.A. one summer with O.J. and stayed at Jack Hansen's. The next morning, the Vietnam War hero pulled his car out of Hansen's driveway and practically ran over Jack's next-door neighbor, Paul Newman, who was bicycling to the store he had opened. (He hadn't yet gotten to the salad dressing.) Newman's blue eyes knocked Militello out. Hanging out with O.J., getting to know O.J.'s lady friend Maud Adams and other top models, houseguesting next door to Paul Newman—not bad for a provincial boy from a working-class steel town. Such was Mike Militello's life now that O.J. Simpson was his friend.

Mike and O.J. had instituted a tradition: Mike would fly out every July for O.J.'s birthday—July 9—and give his pal twenty-four hours of pranks and pie-throwing (the rules were midnight to midnight, anything goes). In the course of these marathon frat-house-style celebrations, and in the midst of O.J.'s trying to work out his problems with Marguerite, "Jack Hansen became my very best friend," says Militello. The Buffalo restaurateur sat at his Beverly Hills counterpart's table on the red-brick Daisy patio, eating and greeting the other regulars as Jack said hello to his famous friends and manned the ubiquitous red telephone. O.J. would join in on the cool glad-handing. Visitors to Hansen's table were thrilled to meet the Juice. "O.J.," Militello says, "can make the whole world feel close to him."

In the circle of friends he was entering and weaving together and becoming the center of, O.J. Simpson orchestrated a chorus of quiet awe and gratitude. Being O.J.'s friend *anointed* a man, laid an invisible mantle on his shoulders. That unspoken sense of consecration seems to have enabled a lot of men to look at O.J. and see him selectively, as we do anyone we openly admire and secretly idolize. And it produced the immense loyalty these men had for O.J. after the murders.

The man who became as close a friend of O.J.'s as Bob Kardashian was Joe Stellini, then the maître d' at the Luau restaurant, which was located on Rodeo Drive, just up the street from the Daisy. Like Trader Vic's at the Beverly Hilton, the Luau was of the totem-poles school of Polynesian restaurant architecture. The Luau was where wealthy realtors and plastic surgeons took starlets to dinner so both members of this "Item" or this "New Two You" could get their names in Mike Connelly's column in the *Hollywood Reporter* and in George Christy's in the *Daily Variety*.

Steve Crane owned the Luau. His daughter, Cheryl, had been O.J. Simpson's direct predecessor in providing the neighborhood with a celebrity knife-murder scandal when, as a juvenile, she stabbed a minor hoodlum named Johnny Stompanato to death in the bedroom of her mother, Lana Turner, in 1958.

Joe Stellini was Crane's maître d' at the Luau from the mid-sixties through the mid-seventies. Stellini was an intense, somewhat thin-skinned, macho but personable young man—a working-class Bronx boy who had gone into the service, then did some acting in New York, and had come to Los Angeles to try to make it in films (the dream, of course, was Brando or Pacino casting). That hadn't happened. The restaurant world, however, had proved to be Stellini's forte. He was the kind of maître d' most owners wanted in the relatively innocent sixties: Stellini was a guy's guy—part seating master, part genial host, part bouncer. He was comfortable around the famous and the powerful.

That ease enabled him to strike up an immediate friendship with Simpson one day in 1970, when O.J. had been sent home early from Buffalo after being injured. "Nobody introduced me to O.J. He was just waiting for a table and I was standing there with Rocco Cedrone and I walked over and introduced myself and we started talking about football," Joe says of the man whom he has counted a best friend for twenty-four years. "Me being enraptured with sports, and O.J. being the kind of person he is, we became fast friends."

It was Stellini who, shortly after their first meeting in 1970, introduced O.J. to Bob Kardashian on mutual friend and businessman Harry Rothschild's tennis court. As the Luau host, the Bills star, and the prosperous young music businessman whacked tennis balls back and forth in the sun, talking sports and women, none of them could foresee a dusk, twenty-four years hence—when Kardashian and Stellini would be flanking Simpson on the couch in his den, offering him moral support on the last truly free evening of his life before he became, in a frantic succession of four surreal days, a murder suspect, a fugitive, and a defendant.

O.J. Simpson had the ability to make his friends feel like the most important people in the world, like they had won some jackpot. Joe Stellini was touched and surprised when O.J. devoted the night before he had to fly back to Bills football camp "to coming over to my house to look at me and my wife's newborn son. Here the guy was—had a million things to do that night. But he calls and says, 'Stiff'—he gave me that nickname 'cause I'm regimented and he's lackadaisical—'I want to see the baby. I'm comin' right over with a six-pack.' That was O.J."

Similarly, O.J. had once surprised Hertz commercial director Fred Levinson's son by running up and greeting the boy as he arrived at Newark Airport on a holiday vacation from Duke University. Fred and O.J. had been shooting in another part of the airport, so why not say hi to the kid?, O.J. thought. Levinson's son was stunned, as were all the other travelers on his flight. Here was everybody's hero—O.J.!—rushing up to meet a college sophomore with a bookbag, flying standby!

Another time, many years later, Joe Stellini had a couple of his boyhood friends from the Bronx visiting. "These were

Italian guys from the old neighborhood. I asked if they could come over and see his Heisman" (with its misspelled inscription: *Atletic* instead of *Athletic*)—"and he said, 'Sure.' We drove to Rockingham, we went inside, there was O.J. saying, 'Hi, guys, make yourself at home.' He let them invade his home. He not only showed him his trophies, he took them for a walk through Brentwood. O.J. *did* things like that.

"Still," Stellini continues, "it was very hard being a friend of his. He always got all the attention. Once I was walking down a street in Beverly Hills with O.J. and A.C. and I ran into this guy I knew—and he was gushing all over O.J. and A.C. He didn't even say hello to me! Okay, I'm with these two, big, well-known black guys, but *I'm* not exactly nondescript! I had my restaurant! I'm standing here, being ignored —I'm sick about it! I said to the guy, 'What are you, a schmuck?! Acknowledge me!' This would happen *all* the time. You have to have a very strong constitution to be friends with O.J. I never envied Nicole, what she had to go through, dealing with it all the time."

When O.J. returned to L.A. from Buffalo in 1973, right after breaking Jim Brown's rushing record, "O.J. and I went to somebody's house to film a TV spot," Joe remembers, "and then we went into Beverly Hills to have lunch. I'm telling you, people followed us like O.J. was the Pied Piper. Truck drivers were honking their horns when they saw him! And O.J. loved it—he *loved* being the center of attention. Sure, you got pushed aside if you were his friend. But it wasn't *his* fault."

It's the lore among O.J.'s friends that A.C. once said, "There are guys who would give O.J. a blow job on the freeway just to get to say they know him."

Stellini, who admired the élan and success of Jack Hansen, had dreamed of opening his own restaurant. He knew so many athletes, garment guys, and movie stars from his years at the Luau that he was sure a place of his own could make it. He had tried to launch one restaurant, Faces, but the place he had in mind was more genuine—nothing Hollywoody, nothing gimmicky—just good food (Italian, of course) and good company. Simpson offered to support his friend's dream and invest in it when the time came.

As unlikely as it was that either of them ever realized it, Simpson and Stellini had in common their temperaments and their strong attachments to their mothers. Both were emotional, quick-to-boil men whose mothers had influenced their lives well into adulthood. Joe was as connected to and deferential toward the woman who had steered him through the pitfalls of his rough childhood neighborhood as O.J. was to the woman who had done the very same for him. Joe's mother flew to California frequently and always stayed with Joe, where she dispensed Italian common sense to her son's new friends and decried his adopted town's excessive divorces. In fact, Mrs. Stellini had been visiting her son one night in 1966 (years before Joe met O.J.) when another meeting key to the formation of the group that ultimately surrounded Simpson took place.

On that night in 1966, Joe's friend Susie Cantor Kopel was over at his house. Susie was a sweet, pretty, not enormously motivated nineteen-year-old who had grown up without a father and had quit Dorsey High School (the same school Bob and Tom Kardashian had gone to) to attend beauty school. A year earlier, she had met and married Jack Kopel, a thirty-year-old man who had been Joe Stellini's roommate.

Kopel's friend Joe made Susie's life glamorous. "Joe was handsome and had that great job at the Luau. It was a high-status restaurant and you saw movie stars there and Joe always got tips for seating people at the 'good tables.'" Just like Kris Houton Kardashian—and, later, Nicole—Susie was a teenaged girl who did not go to college, who was entranced by West L.A. fast-track life, and who was in love with a man-about-town twelve years her senior. Actually, in Susie's case, it would be *two* men, one right after another. No sooner had she married Kopel than she met yet *another* of Stellini's friends at his house ("his mother was there, like she always was," Susie recalls). The sight of this man made her want to jettison her marriage to Kopel.

The man's name was Billy Kehoe, and he had a wife and family back in Cleveland, Ohio, but Susie didn't care. "Billy was gorgeous and fun and charismatic," she says. He was big—six-foot-two, about 230 pounds—bushy-haired, handsome, and very well dressed, and stories and mischief and bravado just poured out of him.

Billy Kehoe turned to Joe Stellini's mother and said, "You see that girl there? I'm gonna marry her someday!"

"No! No! No!" Mrs. Stellini had said, according to Susie. "She's already married! And so are you!"

Billy had hugged and nudged Mrs. Stellini, like *he* knew better. "I'm gonna marry her," he said again.

Within months, Susie got an annulment from Kopel (this was 1966) and moved to Cleveland with Billy. "I didn't know that he was an alcoholic," Susie says. "I was so young. Billy's drinking looked normal." By their marriage's end, three children later, Susie would be reduced to hunting the house for hidden empty vodka bottles and sniffing opened soda cans for their secret contents.

One night in 1976 (ten years after they had first met at Joe Stellini's house) Susie and Billy—newly returned to L.A. from Cleveland, married with two young sons—were at Joe Stellini's house on another evening. Billy was "in construction—in the home improvement business," Susie says and believed. But many members of this group say that what he was really doing was defrauding people in Watts with a crooked aluminum siding business and doing business, and pleasure, with Mafiosi. It was hard to really know exactly *what* Billy did, or had done, in his life. Rumors abounded that he had been a hitman and a leg-breaker. Strange buddies of Billy's would turn up at the group's softball games. One man was on crutches with two bandaged knees; his kneecaps, Billy said, had been snapped with a giant nutcracker-type device because he had talked too much. A few years later that same man was indicted on several felonies in a decidedly Mob-related roundup.

Billy was a high roller's high roller. He cut a dashing figure in his Baroni suits and expensive jewelry zipping around Beverly Hills in his silver Rolls Corniche convertible, buying sartorial clothes at Cedrone's and Austin's stores, sending steaks back at the Polo Lounge three and four times before he pronounced them satisfactory. He and Susie bought two glassed-in penthouses on Palm Drive and Burton Way, just to be close to the action. The grid of Beverly Hills boutique streets—Rodeo, Camden, Bedford, from Little Santa Monica to Wilshire—became his turf and he worked it like a suzerain. Guys loved Billy Kehoe. Today at the mention of his name, big smiles sprout and heads snap back—"Billy *Keh*oe!"—in full-dress reminiscence. "Billy Kehoe stories would fill two books," Joe Stellini says, "and seventy-five percent of them would be lies."

That night in 1976 at Stellini's house, the Kehoes were introduced to an attractive black couple. "The woman was conservative; the man very outgoing and regular." He was going to be a major investor in Joe's planned restaurant; she was his wife. Susie didn't know football, so she had no idea why Billy "was so excited. *So* excited! I *never* saw him so excited as the night he met O.J."

After that evening, Billy and O.J. became solid, almost daily, running buddies. They hit the shops, the restaurants, the clubs. Billy filled O.J. with his demi-truthful stories. Billy could make a scam out of the most commonplace events—to *not* rip someone off was a challenge for him—and O.J. was as convenient a patsy as anyone. Billy once made a great show of having a flagpole installed in the front yard at Rockingham as a birthday present to O.J. Then, after the drilling, the installing, the unfurling, he stuck O.J. with the bill for it. Another time, after O.J. lost his luggage on a trip they had all taken together with Eddie DeBartolo, Billy claimed the lost luggage was *his* and *he,* not O.J., got reimbursed by the airline.

But Billy also had a heart of gold, despite the attendant thuggery. He was always whisking Jason and Arnelle off to Disneyland. And when the prominent surgeon father of one of his son's Little League teammates said that the boy couldn't get excused from sleepaway camp to play in the team's All-Star game, Billy took it upon himself to drive the two hours to the camp, push his way into the boy's tent, and hijack the kid while camp counselors ran after both of them in alarm. "The surgeon could never have done that," he said, arriving with the kidnapped boy at game time.

He sometimes carried a gun and he often used his fists. Once, for example, two Iranian men pulled into the space in front of the Daisy where he always parked his Corniche. Billy was not pleased. He got out of his car, pulled both of the men through their car windows one after another, banged their heads together, and proceeded to make a long, ranting, expletive-rich anti-Ayatollah speech. A crowd gathered, most jeering, "Shut up, you asshole!"—to *Billy.* The two Iranians finally struggled free of him, got in their car, and fled. Billy was entirely unchastened.

Billy was twice the strutter, brawler, and hustler that any of the Superiors or the Roman Gents O.J. had known in Portrero Hill had been. Everyone told O.J. that Billy was dangerous but, says one friend, "Juice just loved the guy, he *loved* him." In time, Billy and Susie would become the Fred and Ethel to Nicole and O.J.'s Lucy and Ricky.

One night, Billy, O.J., McCollum, and a few others flew to New York for a party. "Hey, Juice, Juice—this is a Mafia function, a Mafia function," McCollum remembers that Kehoe kept insisting. "And, Juice, you *gotta* come: They need a token nigger."

McCollum recalls: "Billy gets us to this huge, beautiful restaurant under a bridge, in Little Italy. You had to enter as if it was a speakeasy. There were celebrities and politicians around. It was great! We were excited, like kids. Now we all head for the bathroom and Billy's taking out a vial of coke. 'You want a hit? You want a hit?' I decline, of course—I'm Mister Straight—but the rest of them go in. Billy and Juice and the rest disappear into a toilet stall and then when they come out, they're talking like crazy, Kehoe especially.

"And we're all sitting there—by now, Kehoe's got us convinced we're practically all Sonny Corleones. Me, Juice, all of us—we're buying it! (To this day, I don't think Juice or any of us know if it was a Mafia function or not.)

"They have these Tiffany lamps hanging over the tables. And sitting across from us is the guy who later arrives kneecapped at our softball game and eventually gets indicted. So the guy starts talking to Juice and Juice says, 'Hold it right there.' Then, as a joke, Juice grabs the Tiffany lamp and talks into it, as if there's a microphone hidden inside. 'If you're listening,' he says to some imaginary FBI agent, 'McCollum and I are perfectly straight, man.' The guy across the table was furious! We barely got out of there. I always loved Juice for that childish humor he had."

A final member of the pre-1977 group was a once-scraggly sojourner who arrived on Tom McCollum's far-off doorstep in 1969. "I had separated from my wife and had taken a house with a tennis court, up a fjord in a completely isolated part of western Canada, twenty-eight miles north of Vancouver," McCollum remembers. "One day I was all decked out in my tennis gear and this little kid—the weirdest-looking little hippie you ever saw—came up to me. He had on a lumberjack shirt and black hightops and he had hair all over, slicked down by a green do-rag, like the ones black guys wear under their football helmets. He was twirling an old wooden racquet with a press on it. He said, 'Hey, man, I've never seen you play, but I'll play you for anything you wanna bet.'

"I was intrigued. He couldn't have been more than fifteen. I said, 'Okay. Whaddya got?' He said, 'A hundred dollars.'

He didn't look like he even knew what a hundred dollars looked like.

"Well, we played—and I lost to him. He was an unbelievable player, this little teenaged tennis hustler. He had run away from home. He was broke. I had this fabulous place with no electricity, no road access. I had to cut maybe fifty cords of wood a day to keep the place going. He looked around and saw that. He said, 'Hire me. I can do that, easy. On the way up here, in Oregon, I was a choke-craner in a lumber yard.' I said, 'Okay, you're hired. Go to the top of the tree. Here's a chain saw.' Only when he was up in the tree and the chain saw bucked back and almost cut his head off did I realize he was lying."

In short order it emerged that McCollum's unbidden guest was from the San Fernando Valley, a three-minute drive across the canyon from Tom's house in Coldwater. The kid was a tennis-obsessed high-school drop-out runaway, the son of a mathematician and an English teacher. McCollum couldn't get rid of him. He let him stay with him in Canada, then took him back to California. He referred to him as "my stepson" and made him finish high school. The kid was such an amazing tennis player, he once beat John McEnroe, aced a job as the tennis pro at the Hillcrest Country Club, and became the freelance tennis guru of West L.A. Even though the kid coached studio executives Sherry Lansing, Irving Azoff, and Alan Hirschfield, and even though his Hillcrest locker was next to Frank Sinatra's and he regularly listened to the stories of club members George Burns, Groucho Marx, and Burt Lancaster, when he met O.J. Simpson (through McCollum) he was so awestruck that he opened his mouth to say hello but couldn't squeeze a word out. He choked. Literally.

And that's why O.J. gave his soon-to-become good buddy Joe Kolkowitz the nickname "Chokowitz."

O.J. took an immediate liking to Kolkowitz (who today is a lean, trim-haired, precise-speaking talent agent, with no trace of the wild hippie tennis hustler left in him) and he became a daily buddy and longtime confidant. The two men became so close, in fact, that Kolkowitz would eventually be the only white usher at O.J.'s wedding to Nicole in 1985.*

Perhaps it was their shared hustler instinct that was the root of the affinity between Simpson and Kolkowitz. Or maybe it was the fact, as Joe himself believes, "that I could keep up with O.J. We'd play tennis all day—he talked incessantly during the lessons; he didn't listen; he wouldn't hear anything; he just wanted to hit balls and compete—always his tongue hanging out, talking. Then go back to Rockingham and play backgammon downstairs in his pool-table room till five in the morning." Then again, as another friend suggests, the relatively unprepossessing Kolkowitz was "safe as a close friend, once Nicole was in the picture. O.J. didn't have to worry that she'd be attracted to him."

For despite Nicole's fidelity to the very end of their marriage, O.J., this friend says, is an enormously insecure man who was compulsively jealous. Another friend seconds this perception and adds that Lynn Swann and Tom Cruise were two men who incited Simpson's irrational jealousy. Once Swann was at Rockingham among a group of others. Music was playing, people dancing. "When Nicole danced with Swannie," this friend recalls, "O.J. stood looking in the window at them: *staring.*" At least Nicole *knew* Swann. Cruise, on the other hand, was just someone she thought attractive; they never met although he was a guest at a party Tom McCollum once gave, which O.J. attended alone—"to try to get some ass," a party guest remembers. But as different as Swann and Cruise were physically, Simpson's groundless jealousy did turn out to have a prescient logic: The football player and the movie star represented precisely the two types of men—black athlete and young, dark-haired, preppy white man—that Nicole *did* get involved with once her marriage to O.J. was over.

* * *

*The other ushers were A.C., Lynn Swann, Marcus Allen, and Reggie McKenzie. Jason was best man for his father.

In 1976, the restaurant of Joe Stellini's that O.J. had agreed to back was ready for business. The neighborhood—Pico and Cardiff, off Bedford—was too far south to be fashionable, which, in a way, was the point. The new place, which he named simply, "Stellini's," had its own insider cachet. It held only fifteen tables. The bar, however, was commodious. Joe brought the chef from the Luau, who did crowd-pleasing ribs, and Joe's wife, Donna, contributed what became known to the regulars as "Donna's Salad." The group had a second home, along with the Daisy, and Joe Stellini was sharing the mantle of host with the man he had for so long admired, Jack Hansen. O.J. came in with a party of ten on opening night, and from the first year of its opening until a few years before its closing in 1993, his table was the main seat of action at the restaurant's large, boisterous, private New Year's Eve party.

Stellini's had a mixed-bag clientele: everyone from all the city's sports figures to the occasional movie star (Stellini's friend Burt Reynolds, McCollum's acquaintance Sean Connery) to a few feisty little old ladies. Whenever Billy Kehoe sauntered in, a chorus went up, "'ey, the *Key* is here!"

"Billy was loud, intimidating, imperious," says one woman who was part of the group. "He was always, 'Get this! Get that!' A lot of people were scared of him. But O.J. was always the top guy. We all went to the Daisy on Wednesday night—you'd run into Tina Turner, Tommy Smothers, or Jerry Buss—and Stellini's on Thursday—you'd see Lynn Swann, Bobby Chandler, Don Klosterman. O.J. was always at Stellini's on Thursday night, sitting with Billy and their friend, Pierre Dineen, who has since died, like Billy. The three of them had their own table, but they'd be all over the place, especially Billy. Oh, those days were fun."

Stellini's was such a comfortable place for these men that, as Allen Schwartz, who joined the group a few years later, says, "Sometimes we didn't even go *into* Stellini's, we just met there and left our cars there. It was, 'You wanna go to the game? I'll meet ya at Stellini's. Let's go in, grab a salad, see if Joe wants to come . . .' " If O.J. was there, and the kitchen was backed up and the diners were getting impatient, "he'd work the room," Joe recalls, "going from table to table, shaking hands, calming everybody down for fifteen, twenty minutes while the chef caught up. People were charmed enough to forget they were hungry."

The group traveled together, often courtesy of O.J. A goofy jock camaraderie ruled. Life was a frat house, with first-class airfare and four-star hotel rooms.

One year, Stellini, A.C., O.J., and the Kehoes went down to Miami, where O.J. was doing commentating for the Super Bowl. Stellini and his wife had separated by now, and Joe had moved in with A.C., just as O.J. had moved in with Tom Kardashian (now that Kris had moved in with Bob) during his separations from Marguerite.

"I'd been having a ball in L.A.," Joe recalls. "I just bought a new yellow Ferrari. But in Miami, I was miserable. I didn't have a date. I was rooming with Billy and Susie Kehoe and their kids. One morning I woke up and said, 'I've had it! I'm leaving!' Billy says, 'You can't leave!' I say, 'Oh, yeah?' Billy runs and tells O.J. And before I know it, A.C. and O.J. drag me out of a restaurant and out into the parking lot and pull my pants off."

O.J.'s circle of friends would serve two purposes for O.J., says a black friend who has observed him with them for years. They would get him past the transition to his post-athlete life in a diverting and nonthreatening manner, and they would allow him to feel accepted in the white world.

"He wanted to be accepted," this man says. "And they hailed him as the Juice. The Black Superjock. That was a safe, flattering way to go for him. Because when it came to doing something beyond parading his image, when it came to acting and doing commentary, he wasn't very good, and he knew it. He was a terrible actor (people told him so, and *certainly* Nicole did), and when it came to commentating, he had to hire a coach to work with him so his shoulders wouldn't move when he talked. He really tried, but he just couldn't make it. He wasn't going to be a Frank Gifford, John Madden, an Ahmad—and he knew it. He was really insecure about that, and he had trouble with very intelligent people who were really good at what he wanted to be good at, people like Howard Cosell and Bob Costas. Once someone said, 'How do you like Bob Costas?' And he said, 'He's very cocky.' I knew he was intimidated."

In the spring of 1977, realtor Elaine Young heard that O.J. and Marguerite Simpson had been looking for a new home and could not find anything they liked. Marguerite was expecting their third child. The pregnancy, which O.J. would later tell Nicole was something Marguerite had "tricked" him with, was an attempt to save their marriage. As was the house purchase.

In the growing house market, selling L.A. real estate was becoming a stylized, high-stakes game of war, informed by stealth, panache, and cult-of-personality. Realtors were strategists and players, much like film agents. The most successful—Mike Silverman, Fred Sands, Jack Hansen's friend Jon Douglas—were considered city-builders. Elaine Young—with her big blond hair, huge sunglasses, ebullient "I know *everybody!*" attitude, and six ex-husbands—was out there, hustling with the best of them. She called Jack Gilardi, O.J.'s manager (and Annette Funicello's then-husband) and said, "Jack! Darling! *Quick!* You *have* to get me O.J. Simpson's phone number! You *have* to! Darling, I've got *the* house for him!"

In the language of the city that gave the world vanity license plates, the sentence "I've got the house for him!" did not simply mean that Young had a house Simpson would love, although her remark did include that sentiment. Rather, it meant that a bedrock resident was finally persuaded to sell the not-for-sale house he and his family lived in because Elaine Young had finally found him that *one* right celebrity who could render the owner starstruck enough to accept the sacrifice, the *one* buyer whose name as a fill-in-the-blank in the sentence "I just sold my house to ———" would make temporary homelessness worth it.

Elaine Young had discovered the manipulability of West L.A. luxury home traders through personal experience. When she was married to actor Gig Young at the height of his fame in *They Shoot Horses, Don't They?*, prospective purchasers of a house the couple was selling would ask, "Look, I'll give you $50,000 extra if you'll include the bed, so I can say I'm sleeping in the bed Gig Young slept in." If celebrity lust worked on buyers, she reasoned, why couldn't it work just as well on sellers?

Elaine had heard through the realtors' grapevine that O.J. Simpson and his wife, Marguerite, had been looking at houses for a long time with just about every broker in town and could not find anything that was right. The house had to have north light, because Marguerite's hobby was painting. It had to have a pool, a tennis court, be private, and be gated.

Elaine had been trying for several years to pry this one lovely Tudor in Brentwood Park away from its intractable owner. She had leased the house to Carly Simon. Simon wanted to buy it. The owner said no. She then leased it to Tony Orlando. Orlando wanted to buy it. The owner said no. Acting with the brio of a rogue prospector, Young played a hunch and called the owner one day in late winter 1977. "I know you haven't been willing to sell the house before," she said, "but what if I got you O.J. Simpson?"

"O.J. Simpson?!" the owner shouted into the phone. "Oh my God! I'm the biggest football fan in the *world!* He can *have* it! When can he come *over*?"

Young frantically called Jack Gilardi to *get* the client she had told the owner she had in her pocket.

Gilardi came through. He gave Simpson's number to Young.

Simpson saw the house and fell in love with it. The owner was predictably besotted as he shook hands with O.J. Robert Kardashian approved it as a good buy for his friend. In style and neighborhood and grounds, it was infinitely classier than the Elvill house, which was stark and cold and undistinguished—a "starter."

When Young returned to the house alone to seal the deal, however, the football fan/owner looked like a little boy whose mother had just pulled him in from the street by his ear. Young presented him with Simpson's check for the asking price: $650,000. (Today, the house is valued at between $3 million and $5 million.) The owner turned evasive. "My wife doesn't want to sell," he blurted out.

Elaine Young heaved a large, hopefully guilt-inducing sigh and said, "But you *promised!*" The minute she said it, she thought, "Jesus Christ! Listen to me! 'You *promised?!*' A promise is for third-graders. It doesn't mean anything in this business!"

But the man had a strong streak of piety. He looked at the check in his hand, signed by one of the greatest running backs in NFL history. "Okay," he said, sighing louder than she had.

He and Young shook hands. He would—somehow, *somehow*—deal with the wrath of his wife later.

The new house was warm, used-brick and country and charming. Soon, it would be modernized, room by room—unattractively, in Elaine Young's judgment. ("I love O.J., but every year he lived there, the house lost more of its original character.") A life-sized black bronze statue of O.J., wearing his number 32, running with his football, was erected in the backyard, near the brick-edged swimming pool. Hewing to the relaxed standards of safety in those years, the previous owners had put aesthetics over caution. They had not installed a metal gate around the swimming pool.

Marguerite was six months pregnant when the move from 3005 Elvill to 360 Rockingham began in late May 1977. Things were not good. A woman whose luxury-jewelry-store-owner ex-husband socialized with O.J. got a call from her young daughter, who was with her father at Rockingham one afternoon shortly after O.J. and Marguerite moved in.

"My daughter was crying," the woman recalls. "She said, 'Mommy, come pick me up. They're doing bad things.' I asked, 'What?' She said, 'He yells at his wife and he shoved her and Daddy was weird'." This woman, who contends that her ex-husband snorted cocaine with O.J. regularly, drove to the house, where a housekeeper brought the child out to her car.

A few days before this event, Nicole Brown graduated from Dana Point High School in Laguna.

Nicole was ready to move to Los Angeles on May 20, 1977, the day after her eighteenth birthday. " 'Well, is she moving? Is she moving?' " Denise remembers Judi Brown walking around the house asking anxiously. "The next day she was saying, 'Bye, Mom, bye, Dad.' She was out the door with Pinky [David LeBon]."

Lou and Judi had given their second daughter permission to move into David LeBon's one-bedroom apartment on First and Virgil in downtown L.A. Nicole slept in the bed; Pinky, in a sleeping bag on the floor. David hated telephones so the apartment didn't have one, which didn't thrill Nicole. But living in L.A. was great. One of the first days she was there, Pinky brought her to one of the softball games he played with his team, the Protectors. "The players—all advertising guys—thought she was the most beautiful girl they had ever seen," David recalls. Several wanted to date her.

One day about a week into her stay Nicole came back to their little apartment, excited. Pinky was making popcorn and listening to his Credence Clearwater Revival record—he was a freak not just for cars but for popcorn and fairly recent golden oldies.

"I got a job at this neat store," Nicole told her buddy. It was called Jax and it was in Beverly Hills. From the way she was talking about the store and the area, David could tell she really liked it.

Jack Hansen himself had hired her. She was just the kind of tall, cool, slightly ironic beauty—still innocent, but waiting to be made sharply knowing—that he had designed for years ago, when his vision of the L.A. woman was so prescient. Nicole stayed at Jax for two weeks; then Hansen decided she would be better utilized at his other business. She was too pretty to be merely a salesgirl in a store principally patronized by women.

How would she like to be a waitress? he asked her.

Sure, she said. Yes. She'd like it. But she had never been a waitress before; she didn't have any experience.

Hansen decided to break her in in the afternoon. He was planning on opening for lunch—a new move and one which made sense, given the newly booming tourist business along Rodeo Drive.

The whole group watched O.J. fall in love with the beautiful young blond waitress on the red-brick patio of the Daisy during the end of the last week of June and the beginning of the first week of July 1977.

"Jack, who's that girl?" he had asked Jack Hansen on Tuesday. Jack was sitting at his table talking on his red telephone.

Hansen introduced them. O.J. started flirting. Nicole flirted back.

That night, O.J. called Mike Militello, who was staying at Hansen's. "I want you to meet this fabulous girl," Mike recalls O.J. saying. "We have to go to lunch at the Daisy tomorrow."

Mike met O.J. for lunch at the Daisy the next day. And the next. Bob Kardashian joined them. "Nicole was beautiful, smart, and funny—and totally unimpressed with who O.J. was," Mike says. "He was intrigued by her. He was in awe of her. He was probably in over his head," Mike says. "He came back day after day and just sat and talked to her. It was a simple attraction—it had no heavy past. It was like, 'Hey girl, you're affecting me on a day-to-day basis that I only realize when I go home and think about it.' This is the only time I saw him so infatuated—in love."

"Who is he, again? I don't really watch football . . ." Nicole asked Mike, of this man who seemed so smitten, so pursuing.

Mike briefly ran through his record.

On Thursday, Tom McCollum joined O.J. and Jack for lunch and met the girl his friend was so smitten by. He noticed, as she laid the plates of food on the table, that her fingernails were bitten to the quick. He immediately saw something in her that others would be slower to discover: her insecurity.

After lunch on Thursday, O.J. walked down Rodeo and turned the corner to Alan Austin's store. "He said, 'Alan, I met the most beautiful girl,'" Austin recalls. "I knew by his voice that it was not frivolous, that this was going to be permanent."

The next day, Friday, at a little before noon, Tom McCollum was driving down to the Daisy for lunch in his "Roller" (Rolls-Royce) after his tennis game with Hansen. Hansen was already there.

O.J. had just arrived—to see the waitress. Again.

Militello, who was now starting to plan O.J.'s big birthday blow-out the next week, would be by later.

Billy Kehoe was home, sleeping off a hangover. Susie was in the next room, taking care of their young sons, Sean and Christopher.

Joe Kolkowitz was giving a lesson at Hillcrest.

Kris Houton was out by her pool. Bob Kardashian was in his office working.

Alan Austin was in his store, around the corner on Brighton Way. Rocco Cedrone was in his store as well.

Joe Stellini was walking down Rodeo with a bunch of his friends, on his way to go see both Rocco and Alan. Joe was looking for a shirt to wear to a party he was giving at his restaurant that evening.

"Hey, Stiff, come on over," Stellini remembers O.J. calling out across the street to him, from the Daisy patio.

Stellini strode across the street and joined him.

"And here comes Nicole," Stellini remembers. "It was instant infatuation. O.J. was very attracted to her. It was clear."

They all started kidding around. Then O.J. asked her if she wanted to go out that night, to Joe's party at the restaurant.

He had been asking her out for the last two days but she'd always put him off, even though she liked him.

Today was different. It was time for their flirtation to kick into second gear. It was time for her to take a chance.

This time she said "Yes" to him.

4

Love Affair

"I'M GOING OUT WITH HIM TONIGHT!" NICOLE ANNOUNCED TO David LeBon when she got back to their little apartment at the end of the day. Dave knew the "him" she referred to. He had lived through the week-long flirtation she had had with O.J. Simpson. Like Mike Militello, he had had to tell her, "He's a famous football player!" It was amazing to guys that she didn't know who this man pursuing her *was.*

Now she asked David, "What should I wear?" She seemed nervous and excited.

"Wear a pair of nice jeans," David advised. "You always look great in those. And a nice top."

After trying on a couple of different jeans and tops, Nicole settled on a pair of tight stretch jeans and a button-down silk shirt, gave Pinky a kiss on the cheek, and went out to wait for O.J. in the lobby.

Like an anxious big brother, he waited up for her.

When she turned the key in the lock at two in the morning, David turned on the light.

"What *happened?!*" he asked, because she was standing with her hands awkwardly holding her jeans together at the waist. The jeans were unclosable. The metal button had been pulled off and the zipper was yanked off its ribbon mooring, leaving a gaping slit down the front of her jeans. Nicole looked embarrassed.

"He ripped my pants," she said.

"I can't believe it," David said. He shook his head, upset for her, and looked around the room frantically as if to pick up a weapon to go out and protect her.

"No, no," Nicole said, calming him down. "Dave," she said softly, "I *like* him." When she called him "Dave" and not "Pinky," he knew she was really serious.

Nicole proceeded to tell David about the evening. O.J. had arrived to pick her up in his vintage black Rolls Silver Cloud—its license plate read "JUICE"—and had taken her to Stellini's, which she described as a "great" restaurant with wonderful food. (Joe Stellini remembers that when he observed them together that night, "They had a definite chemistry.") Then they had taken a drive and parked in a secluded spot, and O.J. had ripped the button and zipper on Nicole's jeans so that they could make love as fast as he wanted to.

O.J. had to be back in Buffalo for Bills football camp in twenty-two days, so the next almost three weeks of their courtship were conducted at an accelerated pace. Because he could not abide the fact that Nicole was living with a man, even a Platonic friend, in an apartment with only one bed, he set up Nicole—three days after that first date—in a small apartment in Westwood, conveniently near Rockingham. The apartment was sparsely furnished; its virtue was its proximity to O.J.'s home. He could be with Nicole until four or five in the morning and then be home in minutes.

There, a very pregnant Marguerite was still getting boxes of furniture unpacked from their recent move from Elvill Drive.

It is not known just when O.J. told Nicole that he was married and that his wife was expecting their third child in mere weeks. But when he did tell her, he put it this way:

Their marriage had been over for many years. He had tried to reconcile one last time. She had gotten pregnant without his knowing—their arrangement was that she would use birth control, so she had "tricked" him—and their separation was imminent, this time for good. Nicole's reaction, according to Denise, was that while she did not want O.J. to stay married, *she* did not want to be the cause of her new lover leaving his wife.

On July 9, O.J. celebrated his thirtieth birthday with his brand-new girlfriend. "It was a great night, a key occasion," says Mike Militello, but he otherwise refuses to divulge the "special" content of the evening.

Nicole was crazy about her new boyfriend, and she was smart enough to know that with someone as flirtatious, as desirable, and as married as O.J. was, you had to play games. "She told me," Denise says, "that she wanted him *so* bad she pretended she was out with other guys, just to make him jealous. She said, 'I would sit there in that little apartment at night and hear the phone ring and I wouldn't answer it, even though I was *dying* to pick it up and hear his voice. Then I'd hear him on the answering machine.'" Denise imitates Nicole imitating O.J.'s low, deep voice: "'Yeah, yeah, it's me . . .' She laughed when she imitated him. She would say, 'I knew if I gave in to him he wouldn't really want me.'

"She knew right away that this was the man she really wanted. That this was the man she was going to be with."

Nicole quit her job at the Daisy. She was O.J.'s woman now. That meant, as it would mean from here on in, that she always had to be available to him. Gone was her talk of applying to the Brooks Photography Institute, which David LeBon thought she could get into and do well in. Gone was her presence at David's softball games. She was the young, kept woman of a charismatic, possessive, by all accounts besotted man. And a man who could afford to keep a woman: He was still enjoying the fruits of his unmitigated success as a professional athlete (his less-than-grand career as an actor was still just gravy). He was starting the third year on his $2.5-million contract with the Bills, the high figure wrested after his contention that he had been treated poorly by the management and by his demand to be traded to a West Coast team, ostensibly to preserve his relationship with Marguerite. In the broadcasting department, he had switched from ABC to NBC, signing a handsome five-year contract—all of this augmented by his thriving deals with other corporations, Hertz foremost among them. (The dip in his fortunes as a commentator would not come until later.)

The hastily acquired Westwood apartment was relinquished for a much nicer one on Bedford and Charleville, the latter avenue parcelling off a lovely, urbane section of Beverly Hills, just south of Wilshire. With domestic instincts honed by growing up with Oma and Judi, Nicole nested. "That apartment was all Nicky," Eve Chen remembers. "It was all warmth and sunshine. It was natural, simple, warm-looking—white sofas, white candles, flowers, big pillows. You walked in and you just knew this girl was a romantic."

Eve had gotten a call from Nicky a week after she met O.J. "She said, 'Eve, I've met somebody and you'll know who he is.' She said she was absolutely crazy in love. 'He's so wonderful!' she said. 'I know you're going to like him.' "

A meeting between Eve and O.J. could not be arranged before O.J. had to leave for Bills camp, but a meeting between Nicole and A.C. did take place. A.C. became the third party in their love affair, O.J.'s errand-doer and Better Self, Nicole's cushion. The three traveled together to the Caribbean. There, Nicole tore down the white sand toward the surf like a gazelle, but her speed-demon beau dragged his feet. So did his buddy. Once the two athletes approached water's edge, it became clear why they had resisted. Neither man could swim! Nicole watched the big, macho football players wade awkwardly in, up to their waists, their torsos twisting jerkily, their hands stretched out to brace themselves.

Nicole howled with laughter.

"Hey, Nicole, don't you know? Black people can't float!" O.J. called out to his girlfriend. "Why you think you never see any black people on swim teams? We sink!"

Nicole was so young and naive she believed him.

Kris Kardashian, twenty-two, newly married to Bob, and pregnant with their first child, was excited to meet Nicole. "I don't remember the actual day we met," Kris says now of the woman whose life ran parallel to hers for so many years. "I just remember thinking how beautiful she was, and how young, and how blond."

O.J., the man whom she had gotten to know as the honorary third Kardashian brother, was now, Kris saw, transformed. "Nicole brought O.J. a lot of happiness—you could see it. She was a free spirit and she had such a great way about her. She was nice to everyone and she was always happy and up and liked to have a good time. She just . . . *exuberated.* When you're around somebody who's up all the time, I think it really does change your whole life and your whole attitude. I think this was something O.J. wasn't used to being around."

Was O.J. dazzled by this blond California girl? Kris is asked.

"I think he was," she says. "She lit up his life. They were golden together."

As for Mike Militello, he had never seen his friend so smitten. In mid-July, he accompanied O.J. and Nicole on a trip to the La Costa spa, near San Diego. They planned to stop at Disneyland, then travel the short distance to Laguna. Nicole called her mother from La Costa.

Judi Brown recalls, "She said, 'Mama, can I come by? I'm with two friends of mine.' I said, 'Of course you can.' She said, 'Mama, one of them is black.' I said, 'I don't care.' Which is true. I didn't know how to be prejudiced. People are people to me."

At the end of the day, after they had stopped at Disneyland, Nicole arrived with O.J. and Mike. Judi says, "I opened a bottle of wine in honor of the visit, like we do in Europe, and I put out some cheese and bread. Later, O.J. teased me and said, 'I thought you'd bring out more food! I kept waiting and waiting for something more to eat. I was *hungry!'* " (Judi redeemed herself, in O.J.'s eyes, as a hostess to trenchermen by whipping up a thick batch of pancakes the next morning.)

When O.J. was out of earshot for a moment, Nicole shrugged her shoulders "and said casually," Judi recalls, " 'Yeah, I kinda like him, but we'll see how it goes.' But I know my daughter, and I could tell she *really* liked him."

Judi, it was clear, did not know anything about the man who was sitting in her living room. Finally, in front of her new beau, Nicole leaned over and whispered, "Mommy, don't you know who O.J. *is?"*

"Should I?" Judi was flustered.

"He's a famous football player!" Nicole said, a fact she herself had learned only two weeks earlier from David LeBon and Mike Militello.

"Oh. I apologize," Judi said to O.J.

Months later, O.J. told Judi, "That's what I liked about you: You didn't think I was anybody and you didn't care." What he meant, Judi says, is that a black man didn't have to be a "special" black man to be considered a proper boyfriend for her daughter.

This liberal attitude, however, was one Nicole knew not to expect from her father, a man who had made casually bigoted references in conversations and had once dismayingly told his daughter Denise that when he was growing up in Texas, he had known a black boy—and had become prejudiced *because* of him! It was only because Lou Brown was out of town on business that O.J. and Mike spent the night at the Brown house that evening.

"Lou didn't have anything against blacks," Judi says. "He just felt that whites and blacks should each stay on their own side. So I figured, why don't we let this [romance] run a little bit and see what happens before we upset anybody."

In the coming months, O.J. was at the Brown house more than one time when a telephone call led one of the sisters to say, "Daddy's coming!," whereupon O.J. would bolt out the door.

Just as she was about most things, Nicole was blunt and forthright in presenting the situation to O.J. Judi recalls: "She said, 'I don't know if you should be here. I'm not sure my dad is going to accept you.' He said, 'Why?' She said, 'Well, you *are* black, aren't you?' And he said, 'Well, *yeah.*' O.J. always joked about black and white, and Nicole always kidded him about his thinking he *was* white. They could joke with each other."

But O.J. also explained quite seriously that resistance to interracial romance was definitely two-sided. Judi recalls: "He said, 'Well, my mother isn't exactly excited about it either,' meaning his relationship with Nicole. 'See, these things go both ways,' he explained. 'Don't think the blacks want the whites—they don't. It's a two-way street. So you're not sure Lou will accept me? My mother isn't sure she'll accept Nicole, either.' "

On July 22, O.J. flew to Buffalo for Bills training camp. He returned to Los Angeles a month later for the birth of his third child and second daughter, Aaren, on August 27. He and Nicole spent time together in the Bedford Drive love nest. Then she flew to Buffalo in September and set up housekeeping with him in his home on Deer Run Road. Denise flew in from New York and accompanied her sister to what would be Nicole's first pro football game. Mike Militello sat with them in special seats at War Memorial Stadium.

As he tells it, the day couldn't have been more romantic. "It was a sunny day in Buffalo at the very end of September," Militello remembers. "Nicole looked so innocent sitting there. Here she had met this man at the beginning of July and in less than a month had met, through him, some of the most famous people in Hollywood. She'd heard big-time people tell her about O.J. Simpson, but she still didn't know who her boyfriend was or what he did—what he looked like on the field, what he was capable of.

"As he came running out, he looked up and winked at her," says Militello. "She was amazed. She couldn't believe he could even see her. Then the game started, and what a game! He ran over two hundred yards and scored two touchdowns. And, don't forget: He was thirty; he'd been talking about retiring for a year. I knew what was happening. The guy was in love. I turned to her and hugged her a little and said, 'Those touchdowns were for *you*. He's doing this for *you,* Nicole.' She said, 'Really . . . ?' Oh, it was *great!* So incredibly pure!"

Yet the purity of the day would soon be sullied.

"After the game," Denise recalls, "O.J. was down at the gate and he wanted to show a teammate his girlfriend. He pointed up to where Nicole was, just as Nicole was kissing Mike Militello on the cheek as a thank-you for a great day.

"Well. That evening we get home and are getting ready to go out, and she and O.J. have a huge blowout. He was screaming—*screaming*—at her: 'How could you *embarrass* me like that?'

"She was in the bathroom, combing her hair after having showered. She took his little O.J. doll and threw it in the bathtub. She was crying when I came in. 'That *asshole!'* she said, through her tears. 'Why does he *do* this to me? Scream at me like this! He's such an idiot! All I did was give Mike a kiss on the cheek. What's the big deal?!'

"I hated to see her crying," Denise continues. "I said, 'Oh, Nicole, what *are* you doing with this guy?' But then we went out to a party and they had a great time, and everything was forgotten. She wrote it off, like the conversation had never even happened."

On September 18, 1978, less than a month after Aaren was born, Marguerite filed for formal separation from O.J. Although she did not cite Nicole in the papers, it seemed clear to her now that her husband was otherwise occupied; brand-new baby or not, their marriage was irrevocably over.

Whenever Nicole and O.J. were in L.A. during this, his final season with the Bills, they got together with Billy and Susie Kehoe. Susie saw in Nicole "someone who was pretty much a kid, just as I had been when I met Billy. She didn't have experience, she didn't have confidence, but she wanted to learn." Like many girlfriends of still-married men with children, Nicole was earnest in wooing her beau to an alternate domesticity: her own. Susie had been raised in a house with classic Jewish cooking, and one night Nicole called her anxiously: "Susie! Come over! When O.J. comes over tonight, I want to have a nice brisket made. How do you make a brisket?" Susie came over and taught her.

O.J. and Nicole had Thanksgiving with the Kehoes, but mostly the foursome socialized outside, not inside, their homes. "Nicole and I would meet for lunch at LaScala Boutique and then we'd go shopping. And we'd run into the guys on Camden or Bedford." The whole little grid of Beverly Hills shopping blocks was the stage set for their days and, to a large extent, their nights. It was a surprisingly urban life, given that Los Angeles is essentially a suburban city, but then O.J. (and A.C.) had grown up in a housing project, and the volubly Irish Billy had been reared in an urban environment—all three of them had street life in their childhoods and heritage and could concoct for themselves a modern version out of minimal ingredients.

In ten or twelve years, the locus of West L.A.'s young urban population would shift to a three-block stretch of San Vicente Boulevard in Brentwood, and *that* urban life—*designed* for the young and the more-or-less single—would be shared by many more people than a small hip group of boulevardiers hitting the commercial streets of Beverly Hills, heretofore the footpaths of shopping matrons. An urban life—a life lived not in cars and backyards but on streets in plain view, with frequent, chafing, random contact among past, present, or prospective intimates—requires discretion. The externals must be muted so that in chance encounters emotion can be controlled. Eastern city dwellers know this. They dress for the street to neutralize, not to provoke, aggression and attention. But when the made-for-privacy southern California style—tiny, tight, sexy clothes and tight, tiny, sexy cars—is added to a more urban, "European" lifestyle with streets of outdoor-patio coffeehouses, indoor-outdoor cafés, stand-and-read outdoor international newspaper stands where people live, work, play, exercise, mate, and gossip, *all* in the same, snug, walkable area, then private emotional warfare acquires a more visible, public component, and all kinds of things can happen.

In 1978 Susie and Nicole could run into their men on the corner of Camden and Brighton and everything would be fine. But years later—with an intense marriage and unresolvable conflict behind them—O.J.'s and Nicole's chance meetings on the corner of San Vicente and Gorham would be a different—and riskier—matter.

Everywhere they went, O.J. was the star. O.J. was mobbed. Susie watched Nicole struggling to get used to it. "We'd walk into a place and go, 'Whoooaa.' Here was this whole sea of people. Sometimes fans would grab the hamburger out of O.J.'s hand to get him to sign an autograph. Once we were all in Florida and we couldn't even eat, so many people were coming after him. We just jumped in the limousine. At first she liked the attention. Then she realized it was a constant—it would never go away. She got impatient. She always wanted more time with him, without everyone else wanting a piece of him."

Susie thinks Nicole liked the attention brought on by an interracial relationship. "She was very proud that he was black. And she'd open a magazine and say, 'Hey, look at this gorgeous guy.'" When she flashed the page at Susie, Susie was "surprised somehow—even though Nicole was with O.J.—that the man in the picture was usually black."

* * *

O.J. was traded to the San Francisco 49ers at the end of his 1977–78 season with the Bills. Fittingly, he would end his football career where his love of the sport had begun: in the very stadium he used to sneak into, earning a nickel for every seat cushion he turned in.

Nicole and O.J. spent the spring dividing their time between Los Angeles (the Bedford apartment and, when O.J. needed space, a house he leased on Deep Canyon), and the large, loft-style San Francisco condominium he had purchased.

It was from the condo that an excited Nicole called her high-school best friend, Eve Chen, now a student at Long Beach State, one afternoon in the early spring of 1978. "Can you fly up this weekend and meet him? Oh, please, oh, please?"

Eve said she could and asked if there was anything Nicole wanted her to bring. "Yes," Nicole said. "Famous Amos cookies!" They were suddenly all the rage in L.A., but you couldn't get them up north yet.

When Eve arrived, bag of chocolate chip cookies in hand, she looked and looked but couldn't find Nicole. This wasn't like Nicky. Eve got worried. But when she walked outside, there was Nick, honking anxiously from behind the steering wheel of a car. She was wearing a terrycloth bathrobe. "I goofed on the time," she hurriedly explained. "I was jogging and then when I was in the shower I realized, 'My God, Eve's plane's coming in!' So"—Nicole threw her hands up from the sides of the steering wheel—"I just jumped out of the shower."

Leave it to Nick, Eve thought, to drive to the airport in nothing but a bathrobe just to make sure she wasn't late in picking me up.

O.J. was out at the stadium that afternoon and evening, so the girls had the rest of the day to themselves. "Nicky was talking about how wonderful he was," Eve recalls, "but she also kept having to be reassured, somehow. She'd say, 'I *think* you're gonna like him.' 'I *hope* you like him.' 'Now you *have* to tell me what you *really* think of him.' "

Eve slept downstairs and when she awoke the next morning, her host was leaning over the loft railing. "Good morning," he said in his charming, low voice.

"Good morning," Eve said, looking up and smiling. "I've heard a lot about you."

"Good, I hope," O.J. said, smiling back broadly.

"Of course," Eve said. "*All* good."

"Are you guys having a good time?" he asked.

Eve said yes.

Nicole walked out of the bedroom and draped her arm around O.J., a big smile on her face as she watched the duet of exaggerated pleasantries between two of her favorite people. "Are you staring at my boyfriend?" she asked Eve. Her face was alive with a look that seemed to say, Isn't this neat? You guys are *finally* meeting each other!

"Yes, I am," Eve said. "He's a very, very handsome boyfriend."

"*Isn't* he?" Nicole turned and looked right at O.J.

"It was such dear, sweet love," Eve says now. "You could tell they both adored each other."

The three spent the whole day together, "hanging out all over San Francisco"—drinking cappuccino (which was very new) in cafés in Ghiradelli Square and North Beach. Eve drove the car because O.J. and Nicole, like teenagers (which she, actually, still was), wanted to cuddle together in the backseat. Their attraction to each other was more than evident.

"Eve, you drive very well," O.J. piped up from the backseat, apparently getting a kick out of her chauffeur status. "Hey, Nick, I really see what you mean: Eve is someone you can trust." Eve liked this, the kidding, the affection, the studied flattery, his including her in their life as a couple. O.J. would continue to do this with other friends of Nicole's (as well as with Nicole's mother and with at least one nanny). In fact, there was scarcely a friend he didn't try to do it with. It was oddly *high-school*-like—the football player plunking himself down in their midsts was flattering and refreshing to many women used to men with more drably "appropriate" behavior. O.J.'s interjection of himself, and his obsessive Nicole-woes, into these women's lives would become the way he controlled Nicole—lobbying for his cause within her circle of closest advisors, keeping one step ahead of her plans and intentions.

Eve, Nicole, and O.J. drove to look at the new condominium O.J. was thinking of buying, but they did not—this time at least—drive by O.J.'s old neighborhood. They ended the weekend at a friend's house in romantic Carmel-by-the-Sea. "I have this picture in my mind from that day," Eve says. "O.J. is sitting in a lounge chair on the redwood deck, with the beautiful trees around. Nicole is sitting to the side of him. The way he had his arms around her; the way they dealt with each other, there was such sweetness. This is wonderful, I thought. Nicky is such a serious person. This is the first time she's shown so much affection and openness toward a boyfriend."

It was during this stretch of time in San Francisco that O.J. introduced Nicole to his mother. Despite the fact that two people in the community—the minister who ran the housing project Sunday school and O.J.'s second-best boyhood-friend Joe Bell—had very recently attempted to broker a reconciliation between O.J. and Marguerite, by now Eunice Simpson was probably resigned to the fact that the next serious woman in her son's life would be white. According to a friend of Eunice's, she found Nicole sweet, if young. The parent Nicole most charmed was Jimmy Simpson. Jimmy shared recipes with her. If Nicole had mastered German spaetzle from Oma and Jewish brisket from Susie Kehoe, she was now learning how to baste ribs, bake peach cobbler, and simmer collard greens from her macho boyfriend's natty, gay gourmand of a father.

The other father, too—Nicole's—finally had to be confronted. Nicole may not have been facing this fact, but apparently O.J. was.

Nicole had spent the eve of her nineteenth birthday—Sunday, May 19, 1978—with her parents in Laguna. The family was sitting around eating breakfast, "when," Judi recalls, "all of a sudden there's the sound of two cars pulling up to the driveway. Nicole runs out, there's nobody there." Just a black Porsche 914, with a big bow tied to its hood, parked in the driveway. An undisclosed friend had followed O.J., who was driving the Porsche, to the house. O.J. had parked the Porsche in the driveway, then hopped into the other car and sped off, leaving the provocatively extravagant present for all, including Lou, to see.

Lou Brown walked outside. "Where did that car come from?" he asked, more than a little puzzled.

"From someone I've been seeing," Nicole said at last. "Daddy, you probably know him since you know football." She paused. "His name is O.J. Simpson."

Judi says, "I still remember the little reaction Lou had. The expression meant, 'Now let me figure this out. I'm not sure that I like this.' "

"I think my father's reaction," Denise says, "was, 'Well, if it's gonna be a black guy, I'm glad it's someone who's not a bum.' I know he thought that, 'cause that's how he thinks."

Nicole tackled her father's ambivalence and invited him and Judi up to San Francisco for the weekend. O.J. won Lou over that weekend. "I remember my dad saying, 'Yes, he's a very nice man,' right afterward," says Denise. "The learning-to-like-each-other was fast. Nicole was very relieved about that."

Looking back, however, there is a little mystery attached to Nicole's receiving the black Porsche. Right after O.J. beat her on New Year's Day 1989, Nicole told a confidant, by way of beginning to spill out many things she had long hidden, "Do you know what O.J. did to me once, at the beginning? He punched me in the face. Then he felt so bad about it, he went out the next day and bought me a Porsche. I should have left him, but I took it! I was so stupid—driving around in a brand-new Porsche in Beverly Hills with a black eye."

Nobody remembers seeing Nicole with a black eye on her nineteenth birthday. But then, as at least one of her friends would later learn, Nicole became proficient with cover-up makeup.

One day, during O.J.'s season with the 49ers, Nicole arrived unexpectedly at her parents' Laguna house, crying and tired. She had made the eight-hour drive from San Francisco. "I'm never going back there!" she decreed. "He's an asshole!" They had had a fight about his having other girlfriends, Nicole told her mother.

Judi told Nicole to relax. She certainly expected her daughter, exhausted from the fight and the long drive, to spend the night. But Nicole got on the phone with O.J. Then, incredibly, she picked up her purse and her car keys. "I gotta go back," she told Judi. "I'm leaving."

"What?!" Judi said. "You're crazy!"

But Nicole was out the door.

Nicole later told Denise that it was O.J.'s threat on the phone that had made her grab her car keys and run right back to him. "O.J. told her, 'If you don't get back up here, I'm gonna get another girlfriend and fuck the shit out of her.' "

Nicole drove another eight hours, all the way back up to San Francisco that night, without stopping.

Peace had returned to their San Francisco life by August 1979, when Billy and Susie Kehoe came up for a visit. O.J. had a pre-season game and had gone to the stadium to practice.

"The phone rang," Susie recalls. "Nicole answered it and she screamed, 'Oh, my God!' She turned and told us, 'Aaren fell in the pool! She's in a coma!' It was A.C. on the phone. He was calling from the hospital in Santa Monica.

"We got the car keys and all of us—me, Billy, Nicole—got into the car and drove to the stadium. Billy waved O.J. off the field and told him. O.J. looked very, very upset. He went into the locker room and changed quickly. Then we just rushed to the airport and got the first plane back to L.A. He was emotional on the flight—wouldn't *you* be?"

Susie says that the story transmitted to Nicole over the phone was this: Arnelle and Jason were in the front of the house, washing the van. Their baby sister, not quite two, was near them. While their mother was paying the baby-sitter (who was inside and about to leave), Aaren managed to open the side door from the front of the house to the backyard. She rushed right to the pool and fell in.

Billy and Susie sat with O.J. at the hospital; A.C. drove Jason and Arnelle, then nine and eleven, to the Kehoes' apartment and looked after them there. When the decision was made to take Aaren off life support, Billy took over for his distraught friend and arranged for the baby's funeral.

Susie Kehoe says she did not hear O.J. accuse Marguerite of "murder[ing]" Aaren, although it has been widely reported that he ran down the hospital corridor yelling that accusation. "That report is inaccurate," Susie says flatly. "I was there." However, the previously quoted friend of Marguerite's says, "Marguerite told me he *did* come running down the [hospital] hall screaming, 'You murdered my baby!' and that it devastated her. It's bad enough to lose your child, but when your husband blames you for it . . . !"

Aaren's drowning* made the bad relationship between O.J. and Marguerite worse. On March 3, 1980, the two finally signed a separation agreement. Sixteen days later, O.J. was granted an interlocutory divorce. Still, Marguerite would contend for years, through her lawyers, that her grief over Aaren's drowning as well as Skip Taft's intimate

*In a bizarre accident some years later, O.J.'s and Nicole's dog had a baby, whom Nicole and O.J. named Shiba. Shiba, who was blind, fell into the Rockingham swimming pool (it can't technically be called the same pool, because the old one was filled and a new one built in 1989 when the house was completely refurbished) and drowned there, just as Aaren had.

understanding of her business affairs led O.J., through his lawyers, to conceal assets and to take advantage of her in the settlement. That settlement gave her custody of Arnelle and Jason, $600,000 for her half of the Rockingham house (which at that time was valued at $1.7 million), maintenance of $63,300 a year for six years (for a total of $379,800), 50 percent of his deferred compensation from the Bills for the 1976-77 season, $500,000 in spousal support, a Chevy van and a Mercedes, the contents of the Rockingham house, $4,200 temporary support until she vacated Rockingham on June 30, 1980, and $1,500 monthly child support as well as O.J.'s assumption of school, camp, and therapy payments.

Two ex-wives of major L.A.-based athletes (who were also the high-school sweethearts of these men, supporting them through the hard times) believe Marguerite's settlement was insufficient. "Male judges are snowed by sports stars," they say, almost in unison.

O.J. wanted to stay in Rockingham—badly. Though Marguerite lobbied feverishly to get her move-out date of June 30, 1980, extended (the date coincided with the three-year anniversary of his involvement with Nicole), he wasn't having it. Through papers filed by Skip Taft, O.J. was not budging. On that date, O.J. showed up to take possession of the premises and change the locks, only to find Marguerite still in the house with no intention of leaving. According to court papers filed in early July, Marguerite threatened O.J. with physical violence when he showed up at the Rockingham house on June 30.

Fights over houses are common enough in divorce, though generally the husband cedes the house to the wife, especially when there are children. Yet in both of O.J. Simpson's divorces—this one from Marguerite and his 1992 divorce from Nicole—*he* asked for and got the house, despite the fact that in both cases his young children would have to be uprooted. Simpson's steadfastness toward Rockingham is unusual, especially given the high turnover of house ownership among Hollywood celebrities (and among realty-market-minded prosperous Los Angelenos in general). The image of him arriving at Rockingham on June 30 to change the locks and force Marguerite out is arresting. He *loved* the house and was committed to *it*—an inanimate touchstone and port in the storm—in a way that he could never commit to a woman.

Once Nicole and O.J. moved into Rockingham, the house became a center of activity. Thanksgiving moved from the Kehoes' apartment on Palm Drive to the Simpsons' sprawling country kitchen. Nicole would roast a turkey (later, on this holiday and on Christmas, the bird was augmented by two of Linda Schulman's famous lasagnes and a ham by Honey Baked, in which O.J. had a financial interest). The Browns arrived early with covered side dishes—Judi loved to help cook. Nicole got on the phone weeks beforehand and made sure that bachelor friends, permanent or temporary—Joe Kolkowitz, Joe Stellini, Fred Levinson, L.A. Raiders senior administrator Mike Ornstein—knew a place was being set for them at the table.

Christmas Eve was held at O.J. and Nicole's as well, the tradition really kicking into gear after they married and had children. An elegant, traditional Christmas it was—with eggnog, Cristal champagne, a German-style understated tree, rounds of Password being played, and O.J. singing carols in his unanimously-declared-terrible voice,* over Nat King Cole's recorded renditions. Sometimes Christmas Day was spent at Rockingham as well—a fatiguing exercise for Judi because her neat-freak future son-in-law, she recalls, "kept his house *so* clean he was always running around and picking up every paper that was lying around, putting every

*O.J. was apparently no better at dancing than singing. Once Tom McCollum was at Rockingham when Broadway choreographer Tommy Tune was over, giving O.J. tap-dancing lessons by the swimming pool (while Nicole, and Denise and A.C.—together in a hammock—looked on, amused). Tune, McCollum concluded, had found "one black person in America who did not have rhythm."

shoe back in its place, until I finally said, 'O.J.! Can't you relax?!' Oh, he was so *proud* of that house! And it was always *'my'* house—'my,' 'my,' 'my.' He later told me, 'I'm really hanging on to *everything*. I will never be poor in my life again!"

One Christmas, before Jimmy Simpson contracted AIDS, he shared in the Rockingham celebrations. "He made this great Southern cooking—collard greens, okra," Joe Kolkowitz recalls. "It was fabulous."

On these holidays, the Browns got used to seeing A.C. as much as they saw O.J. He came with the territory and, on and off during those years, he and Denise were an item. But even when they were not involved, they were close friends, allies. To this day, despite his driving of the getaway Bronco on June 17 (which Judi calls A.C's "big boo-boo"), the Browns are appreciative of him. "A.C. is a good guy," Denise says, with the solid gravity of one who *knows,* in her bones, what another has done. Judi says, "Whenever Nicole and O.J. had fights and A.C. was there, A.C. took Nicole's side. And if O.J. started rattling and rattling, A.C. was the one who said, 'Okay, O.J. *Shut up! Finish!*' "

Sometimes, in fact, the Browns liked A.C. more than O.J. did. Says a close male friend, "I can't tell you how many times O.J. has written A.C. right out of his life. One time A.C. took Nicole's Mercedes and didn't come back for days, and it was, 'Okay, man, I'm never gonna speak to you *again'* from the Juice. The two of them would have fistfights and everything." But always—*always*—need and shared history drove them back to each other.

What O.J. could only turn into destruction with women, he had mastered, with his male best friend: the art of making peace with a state of mutual dependence.

Early on, Judi Brown and others in the family were witness to glaring examples of O.J.'s violence—toward inanimate objects, at least. Somehow, these incidents were taken in stride. In fact, they were even *laughed* at. How can this be? One reason is that—hard as it is to remember today given the high awareness the public has about domestic violence—the reaction to such violence was *extremely* different in the late seventies. Astonishingly, it was not until *late 1984* that American women's right to receive civil damages for the lack of police protection against husbands trying to kill them was widely recognized.* Another reason is that everyone loved O.J. He was famous, rich, and charming. Clearly, if he threw objects around or out of the house, this *had* to be idiosyncracy, not pathology. Besides, Judi Brown had been raised to accede to a husband—her mother had done so, in gently pushing her out of the family nest in Frankfurt, and she had done so countless times with her quietly, peaceably dominant husband, Lou.

Thus, it did not alarm Judi Brown when, one day shortly after Nicole moved into Rockingham, she, Nicole, and one of Lou's daughters from his previous marriage came home from dinner at the Daisy a little later than O.J. had wanted

---

*And this occurred only when crusading attorney Burton Weinstein of Bridgeport, Connecticut, representing his client Tracey Thurman, who had been left partially paralyzed after a brutal beating by her husband *that police passively witnessed,* sued the local police department. To his peers' surprise, he got a large sum for his permanently injured client. The resulting U.S. District Court decision—*Thurman v. Torrington P.D.*—finally kept police from standing by while women were beaten to the point of unconsciousness. In these enlightened days of mandatory-arrest police policy, that decision appears chilling in the long-held assumptions it calmly takes for granted. It says that "a man is not allowed to physically abuse or endanger a woman merely because he is her husband. Concomitantly, a police officer may not knowingly refrain from interference in such violence, and may not automatically decline to make an arrest simply because the assaulter and the victim are married to each other." The decision was handed down in October 1984, a full decade and a half into the women's movement, and the lateness of that date demonstrates the pervasiveness of the notion that in America "family" arguments are "private," even when they result in serious injury.

his woman to return home. Mother, daughter, and stepdaughter were greeted by a furious O.J. hefting a beautiful heirloom desk of Nicole's out the door on his shoulders. He threw it into the driveway, screaming about how late she was.

"We laughed," Judi recalls, albeit nervously. "Why's he doing *that?"* Judi wondered. She sloughed it off as "stupid," turned to her stepdaughter, and said, "We better go home." They did so, leaving Nicole to deal with her angry boyfriend. The next day, a rather startlingly accepting Judi called and asked Nicole, "What happened to the desk? Are you still living there? Or were you kicked out?"

"Oh, everything's okay," Nicole said.

"So you moved the desk back in?" Judi asked.

Nicole said yes, she had.

While the desk had only one crashing dive onto the Rockingham driveway, Nicole's treasured photographs of her own family, lining the wall by the staircase going from the living room to the bedroom, made many repeat trips to the Rockingham foyer floor, courtesy of a furious O.J. "Every time they had a fight," Judi says, "he cracked those pictures and threw them down." Judi pauses. "Nicole had to keep reframing them and reglassing them."

Even today, Judi laughs as she tells the story that she found even more humorous then. "I asked Nicole, 'Why do you even bother to put them up? Why don't you just keep them down?' But she had a hard head. She said, 'No *way!* Those pictures are going back up!' She put them back up, again and again. And I would say to Nicole, since the pictures are of *my* family, 'You know, I think every time he has a fight with you, he hates me, too.' When I heard they had had a fight I'd say"—she affects a self-consciously matter-of-fact tone—" 'Oh, I heard the pictures flew down the stairs again . . .'

"We never took it so seriously!"

The message coming from Nicole's mother was clear: It's funny, not serious. Accept it, these things happen. Forget about it, till the next time. Go on with your relationship.

Just don't get O.J. too mad. (And is he mad at *me,* at *us,* in the bargain? That isn't good.)

Life in the group went on, O.J.'s charm and his fame bestowing the magic that made simple vacations larger than life. Even when O.J. was the novice, as opposed to the ringleader, he provided the air of specialness—he was the undisputed focus of attention. In January of 1980, for example, O.J. tried skiing for the first time when he, Nicole, and Kris and Bob Kardashian went to Aspen. Says Kris, "O.J. had never skied before because, as a football player, he was always afraid of breaking something. So now that he was retired, he decided that this was going to be his first year on skis. The Hertz van came to take us to the airport at five in the morning because we had a seven A.M. flight. I had just had my first baby nine months before and I was ready to go out and have a ball. We got this instructor we'd been using for years, a guy named Eric, to teach O.J. to ski." He was clomping around on the skis, sticking the pole everywhere, but to his adoring public he was still the king. "When people started to notice that it was *O.J. Simpson* learning to ski, they crowded around him and followed him around the hill like disciples. You'd look up the hill and there was a whole stream of people—like *ants*—skiing down after him. *Everyone* wanted a piece of O.J."

Kris Jenner, from her sad, unique position today as a friend of the murdered Nicole while her ex-husband and the father of her four children is O.J.'s chief friend and champion, becomes wistful about those innocent times. "We were so young then. We just had the *best* time."

A year after the Kardashians' ski instructor turned O.J. into a determined skier, O.J. passed the lessons on to Joe Stellini. "We were all in Vail—me, O.J., Nicole, Ahmad Rashad, a bunch of us," Joe remembers. Nouveau-skier O.J. was kiddingly lording it over the extremely uptight Stellini. As the slender, high-strung restaurateur, whose life as a Bronx street kid, G.I., and maître d' had never prepared him to be the next Alberto Tomba, started inching his way down the bunny trail, "There was O.J., yelling at me, 'Stiff! Stiff!' He's pointing at a guy being carried down the mountain on a stretcher. 'Stiff! Ha-ha-ha! That's gonna be *you,* man.' "

Then there were the yearly Super Bowl trips—to Stanford and to Miami. During one trip, to San Francisco, with Nicole's new best friend, Linda Schulman, and her husband, Ricky, an English-accented, fresh-faced young man came up to the foursome, declared himself to be a big fan of O.J.'s, and introduced himself as Prince Albert of Monaco. "O.J. said, 'Yeah, sure,' " says Linda. "We gave him a hard time. O.J. said, 'Show me your driver's license.' " The fellow diligently opened his wallet and tendered a square of plastic as earnestly as a Mexican day worker at a Texas border checkpoint. "It had a crown on it," Linda says. They read the card and looked at his face. "He *was* Prince Albert!"

And at an event at the Santa Monica Civic Auditorium when Joe Kolkowitz took a group of them to see a fighter he was representing, O.J.'s presence led King World's Michael King to flaunt his magnanimousness by buying beers for everyone. "Not everyone in our *party,"* Kolkowitz explains. "Everyone in the whole Santa Monica Civic Auditorium."

O.J.'s extraordinary charm was allowed to blanket his more serious obnoxiousness and it rendered forgivable things that would never have been countenanced in others. He was "so absolutely incorrigible a flirt," one close friend says, "he'd hit on any woman, no matter whose wife or girlfriend she was." He once came on to Tom McCollum's teenage daughter. (Tom told him to go home.) And his idea of humor occasionally was to walk into the bathroom of his Laguna condo where a male houseguest was showering, "tear open the shower door," says one to whom this happened, "and yell, 'Nicole! Come in here and see what a little white man's dick really looks like!' "

Not that Nicole let O.J. get away with this. She was always the first to roll her eyes and say, "You asshole . . ." ("And whatever O.J. did to her," one friend says, "he never spoke ill of her. Never said a bad thing about her. And she put him down, talked behind his back, constantly.")

Sometimes Nicole was less flippant in her desire to have her beau demystified. Once at Rockingham with another couple, O.J. asked Nicole to go out and buy him some "real Rocky Road ice cream." She refused. Then O.J. asked the man to go and get a pizza. The man stood up and fished his car keys out of his pocket; Nicole, out of O.J.'s earshot, abruptly said, "Don't go. Everybody always gets things for him. Let him learn he can't have everything."

Much of Nicole's cutting O.J. down to size had a large component of jest and goodwill. The two got into goofy adventures with each other, often with their friends along as foils, cronies, and running buddies. When Tom McCollum was along, Nicole and Tom called O.J. "Largehead," a variation of his childhood nickname "Waterhead," and Nicole's usage of it was both bitingly and affectionately condescending, "as in 'There goes Largehead. What an asshole . . .'"

Such was her response once when the three took a flight to New York in the early eighties. "We had this phenomenal trip," McCollum says, "because I was eight hundred and fifty dollars ahead in a gin game. We always took the same first-class seats on the United flight, and if O.J. was losing to me at gin, he could sit there the whole time in those big seats and no one would know it was O.J. Simpson. But if he was *winning,* he was up and down the aisles and everyone was all over him. 'There's O.J. Simpson!' 'Yo! Hi, O.J.!'"

McCollum got double-skunked. He went to the bathroom, safely ahead by $850, "but by the time I came back I not only lost the eight hundred and fifty dollars I was ahead by, but Juice got me for three hundred and fifty dollars more before we hit the landing pattern. And he was running through the airplane saying, 'Everybody saw me play the gin champion! And I *beat* that bitch for three hundred and fifty dollars!' And of course Nicole is saying, 'There goes Largehead. What an asshole . . .'"

Both men were in town for functions—O.J.'s, a celebrity function; Tom's, a medical one. The Simpsons checked into the Sherry Netherland on Fifth Avenue; Tom, into the Plaza, one block downtown from the Sherry. In between their engagements they scheduled some fun, including a trip to visit the home of O.J.'s very wealthy friend Louis Marx, whose son was a great tennis player McCollum wanted to play.

The day at the Marxes' house in Westchester had been capped off by a gift to O.J. and Nicole of a kilo—$5,000 worth—of their favorite appetizer, Beluga caviar. Tom, O.J., and Nicole were inching in a taxi through the slow-moving traffic down Fifth Avenue, the large tin of Beluga in the cab's window nook, when they hatched the idea of solving traffic-jam boredom by hopping out every few blocks, diving into a bar, ordering a bottle of champagne, having a few quick bottoms-ups, and diving back into the cab. As they made their way toward their proposed first pit stop, the bar at the Stanhope Hotel, "We notice the cab driver's license. His name is something like Fijad Furnarshkanarshka. He tells us he's Iranian. We're all laughing."

After tanking up at the Stanhope, the plan was to stop at the bar at the Sherry, then the Plaza. "We're just having a ball, the three of us. We were pleasantly pissed. By the time we get out at the Sherry, we're tanked. We jump out of the cab and it's raining and we have no umbrellas and we run inside and all of a sudden Nicole stops dead at the elevators and says, 'Oh, my God, Thomas! The *caviar!* We left it in the back window!' So here's O.J., Mr. Hertz: running down the hotel carpet, sliding on his butt, out to the street, trying to stop the cab. And Nicole, in her great wisdom, goes, 'Yeah, Thomas. Old asshole Largehead is really bright, isn't he? We leave five thousand dollars of Beluga caviar with an *Iranian* and the driver is going to turn it in to the hack bureau . . .'

"That was Nicole, and that was Juice, for you."

* * *

Nicole took her role as a stepmother-figure in stride. "She didn't think about it; she just plunged in—that's her style," says Judi. "She never worried about it. She always said, 'We'll be fine!' and 'I can handle it.' Given that children don't exactly like discipline in the first place, and when you are only twenty-one years old and you have a twelve-year-old stepdaughter, well, that's hard, but she refused to see it as a problem."

At first, Arnelle was standoffish toward her father's young white, blond, live-in girlfriend, who was, after all, only nine years older than she and who could easily be seen as having stolen her father away from her mother.* Ultimately, however, Nicole won her over. Arnelle recently admitted, in a television interview with NBC's Katie Couric, that Nicole's race was initially an issue for her but that she soon put this behind her. Nicole, Arnelle said, was "the only person I know who could keep up with my father. They were like each other's best friend." Friends of Nicole's noted a closeness and respect between Nicole and Arnelle as Arnelle got older, but they *do* recall that the initial period was bumpy. During the first year, the children harbored understandable resentments. A flight attendant who tended them on their plane ride to summer camp recalls that Arnelle said that she and her brother were being sent away "because my father and his girlfriend have *things* to do," though she added that at least he didn't fight with her as much as he had with their mother.

With Jason, the initial relationship was less troublesome. And the older Jason got, the closer he and Nicole became.

---

*Eventually Marguerite began a new life. According to a confidant, she was briefly engaged to a rabbi. Then, in 1992, she married furniture salesman Anthony Thomas. The two were living in a spacious home Marguerite bought after selling the Encino home she moved into with the children after they left Rockingham. But things were not going well for the couple financially and in early 1994 the bank foreclosed on the house. Marguerite went into virtual hiding after the murders.

"It seemed like we had a common wavelength—we liked the same songs, the same TV shows, we were friends," he told Couric.

During this rough first year, Arnelle was still grieving over the death of her little sister and, to make matters worse, was feeling rejected by her father. A letter from Marguerite's attorney to O.J.'s, sent in January of 1980, posited: "There is a distinct favoritism shown toward Jason. This has had an effect on Arnell [sic] which, combined with the death of her sister Aaren, has created a serious emotional problem of adjustment. Arnell is in need of love and recognition, to the same extent as Jason. O.J. should give her such consideration."

The letter from Marguerite's attorney portrays O.J. as a rather selfish and immature parent who often arrived at Marguerite's house without calling and, once there, spoke to the children while completely ignoring their mother. It also reveals a man with an "apparent determination . . . to 'win over' Jason," by telling him he was going to be living with O.J. and Nicole. "Even if O.J. maintains such feelings and expectations," Marguerite's attorney wrote, "this is not something to be told to his son, who has continued loyalty, love, and feeling for his mother."

Ironically, despite the initial neglect of Arnelle and the inappropriate favoritism toward Jason, the child who would come to feel most neglected by his father would turn out to *be* Jason. And, perhaps not surprisingly, this pattern of preference would repeat itself: After his second divorce, Nicole would claim that O.J. evinced the same sort of favoritism toward his second younger son, Justin, over his second older daughter, Sydney.

Still, whatever else the divorce had deprived them of, Jason and Arnelle had a slew of "uncles," courtesy of their father. A.C. was a second father, plain and simple. Billy Kehoe played both Santa Claus and Pied Piper. Tom McCollum and Joe Kolkowitz would come over at Halloween and, along with O.J. and Nicole, chaperone Jason and Arnelle through the neighborhood. One year, O.J. went as a giant pumpkin, McCollum went as Tom Sawyer, and Kolkowitz dressed as the Pillsbury Doughboy—chef's cap and all—but ended up resembling a Ku Klux Klanner. Eric and Valerie von Watt, who lived next door, got a visit; so did retailer Gary Hartounian and his wife, Amy, who lived down the street. Jermaine and Hazel Berry Jackson received a knock at the door, "Trick or treat!" ringing out in multitudinous octaves, paper bags extended.

The house at Rockingham was a guys' house. One night a week was O.J.'s poker game with Alan Austin, Joe Kolkowitz, and Fred Levinson. Levinson recalls that "Juice was the coolest head there. If anyone was about to lose his temper, O.J. would cool him out and mediate it." Other nights, guys would be over watching sports on TV while Nicole laid out food for them. O.J. loved having a group to watch championship boxing: Ahmad Rashad, Reggie McKenzie, Kolkowitz, McCollum, and the new members of the group, Allen Schwartz and Ricky Schulman. Everyone would toss ten and fifteen dollars into the betting pool and O.J., miraculously, always won. Although he did cheat at Monopoly (says one who often played with him, "He'd hit his marker twice on one square of the board so he'd be able to buy the most expensive properties, Park Place and Boardwalk") and he relentlessly and ingeniously cheated at golf, the wins in the boxing betting pool were legitimate. Still, as the host, he could have relinquished the winnings. Instead, "Thank you very much . . . thank you very much" was all he would say, with an avariciously self-satisfied lilt in his voice as he stuck his hand in the pot and pulled out his hundred and fifty or so dollars. His guests would half-kiddingly complain, "Hey, Juice, man, let somebody *else* win!" "You fucker, you're actually gonna *keep* it?"

"Fuck *you,* man!" he'd answer, smiling.

It was through their mutual love of championship boxing that O.J. had gotten to know the man who would become as close to him as the rest of the group and who would dominate their circle of mutual friends in the eighties: Allen Schwartz. His induction into O.J.'s inner circle is, again, classic, confirming Simpson's pattern of charming his male friends so exquisitely that they dropped all pretense of cool, evincing a near sycophantic delight in their "anointedness."

Schwartz was thirty-two and an on-the-rise garment businessman when he moved from New York to L.A. in 1979, eventually buying a house in Mandeville Canyon, virtually next door to Rockingham. A tall, toothy, good-looking, sports-crazed man, he had, like O.J., recently divorced the woman who had been his high-school girlfriend. Like Militello, like Stellini, like McCollum, like Kehoe—and like O.J.—Allen grew up working class with a vengeance. His father was a dress salesman who had held only two different jobs in forty years; Allen had sensitivities—even a chip on his shoulder—about rich kids. "Self-made guys, regular, solid guys who aren't looking to trade on anybody" were all he trusted, all he hung out with. He used his thick, whiny, slow Brooklyn accent like a weapon against the postures of the upscale world he now moved in. What O.J. had once said of his own unassimilated voice ("If you wanted a honky, why didn't you hire a honky!"), Schwartz would have understood.

Schwartz, whose company, A.B.S.—U.S.A., is today a highly successful wholesaler of women's designer sportswear (selling to stores like Bloomingdale's and Saks, as well as through eleven A.B.S. stores around the country), was new in town and had become buddies with Stellini. He had known O.J. for a month and had casually mentioned that he liked boxing.

"I'm sitting alone in my apartment one night and I get a phone call and it's O.J. He said, 'Hey, Schwartzy, what are you doin'? (All the black guys call me Schwartzy.) I said, 'What do you mean, what am I doin'? Nothin'. Just hangin'.'

"He said, 'Remember you told me you liked the fights?'

"I said, 'Yeah.'

"He said, 'Well, I have two seats at the Forum tonight. How would you like to go?'

"I was *speechless!"* Schwartz exclaims in vivid remembrance. "Now I want to tell you: Here I am, John Q. Public. I just moved to Los Angeles. I didn't know anybody more than a couple of people. I loved the fights. And here's . . . *O.J. Simpson,* who needs me like he needs a headache. But he was gracious enough, whether he wanted to go or not, to remember that this guy mentioned he liked the fights. I'll never forget it. And I saw this a *thousand* different times from O.J.!" Schwartz trots out yet more examples of trips to Florida and Mexico where no one could get out of the restaurant because Juice was mobbed by autograph seekers he couldn't say no to, and goes on about O.J. charming his parents ("Are you Schwartzy's mother?").

Schwartz and Stellini have only recently made up after years of estrangement due to Stellini's jealousy over Schwartz's seemingly usurping his role in O.J.'s life. "I guess I was a little jealous of Allen's friendship with O.J.," Joe says candidly. During all those years that Stellini had to be at his restaurant at night, Schwartz, with his more flexible schedule, got to go on more trips with the Juice than he did, and Stellini, a man whose nose is easily bent out of shape, resented Schwartz for it. But "it was my loss," says Joe. The two men are good buddies again. (Stellini is about to open another restaurant—Carson's—in Beverly Hills, and Schwartz, who bailed A.C. out of jail after the Bronco chase, is an investor.) Together, they recall how they always loved O.J.'s stories. Schwartz: "He would just mesmerize us with football stories. We'd sit around. He'd tell great stories about Dick Butkus . . ."

Stellini: "People like us, who aren't in the huddle, want to know what's going on there. And he would tell us, and explain to us about the vulnerabilities."

Schwartz: "He'd go, 'Man, I was always aware of where Butkus was, because that guy would sock you in the head . . .' "

Robin Greer says, "You have *never* seen such hero worship in your life! O.J. is a *god* to all these men. He can do no wrong. It's disgusting! It was also a little bizarre and scary. For some reason, sports heroes are more important to men than presidents, doctors, philosophers. Why *is* that?"

Robin, a television actress and native West L.A. beauty, became part of the circle through her then-husband Mark Slotkin, an entrepreneur and antiques dealer who, when she met him, was just about the most eligible man in Los Angeles. (His parents owned Abbey Rents, the city's premier party-goods rental company.) She had to weather the fallout of that distinction, hearing about his plethora of dates with *Playboy* centerfolds, whom he ferried in one of his two Ferraris or his permanent on-call limo. By the time she won and married Mark, she had an appropriately wry take on all local young hotshots, and she brought that vinegary judgment to the crowd in the Rockingham living room.

Getting in the door at O.J.'s house, Robin soon understood, was, for men like her husband (who, as of this writing, remains one of O.J.'s staunchest supporters and jail visitors), a bigger thrill than landing any number of nubile young women. "Let's just put it this way," Robin says. "It was a given that if you got in good with Nicole, you won major points with your spouse. In other words, you had a ticket to the inner circle at Rockingham, to King O.J.'s Court. Not that we girls weren't very excited to be in the inner circle—we *were*. We were all having a fabulous time. That house was entertainment central. We felt lucky.

"O.J., especially when he was drinking, had a habit of telling football stories about himself. He'd start in on one and Nicole and I would look at each other and the looks would say, 'Here he goes again.' Then she'd whisper, between clenched teeth, 'This is the tenth time I've heard this story this week.' And yet all the guys—all *our* husbands—would lean forward, mouths open, all ears, like it was the first time they ever heard it."

One whose mouth wasn't usually agape, though he was respectfully interested, was Ricky Schulman. The

Schulmans moved right into the middle of the group, but their marriage took priority over the dazzling new social life afforded them. "Ricky and Linda were my favorite couple—I was over the moon for them," says Robin. "They had a healthier relationship than any of the rest of us. Ricky *listened* to Linda. He respected her. And they knew one another better than the rest of us knew our mates. We'd all go over to O.J. and Nicole's and play the Newlyweds Game. Nicole would set it up, just like on television: The guys would go in one room and the girls would go in another and they'd answer questions about their mates and whoever got the most answers right won. Linda and Ricky won."

When Linda, who had met Ricky while working in New York's garment center, first encountered Nicole in 1981, she was an insecure L.A. newcomer just moving, with Ricky, to a Century Hills condominium that she felt ambivalent about and had *no* idea how to decorate.

"I came home to the condo the day after I met Nicole and there was this big basket of fruit and flowers on my doorstep: 'Welcome to L.A.—O.J. and Nicole.' Then she came over—'Hi, how ya doin'?'—and walked right in and helped me unpack. She made fun of all the stuff my aunts had given me. As we put my glasses on the bar, she lifted them up and pouted a little and said, '*I* am going to help you furnish this house!' The next day she zoomed by in her little Mercedes 450-SL"—this supplanted the Porsche—"and drove me over to the Design Center on Beverly Boulevard."

The capable, briskly pragmatic Nicole took Linda by the hand, whisked her through a maze of intermediaries, and *did* Linda and Ricky's condominium for them.

"She was five years younger than I, but she was like my big sister," Linda says. "I learned so much from Nicole. And I could be myself with her. When I look back on it," Linda says sadly, "I got the best of Nicole."

Nicole took Linda for rides on her moped through Brentwood Park—up Oakshire Drive, the private street right off Rockingham. And when it was time for the

Schulmans to move out of their condominium and buy a home, it was Nicole who talked them past their worry about the enchanting cottage they found near Rockingham and said, with a conviction they themselves lacked, "Ricky! Ricky! We *can* do this!" With what was now her trademark taste—the bleached and sanded wood floor, white couches, and fat pillows, which were about to become the hallmarks of Melrose Boulevard's "California Look"—Nicole brought the cottage to life. "She stayed in it for three days, telling the workers how to put up the wallpaper. She stripped and refinished a wood piece herself." Eventually she did the same thing for Fred Levinson's house.

What Linda later realized was that Nicole was trying to become a decorator so she could use that skill to support herself. And she wanted to be able to support herself because there were times, though she kept them pretty much to herself, when O.J. would do things to her that made her *know* she had to leave him.

The two women would get on the phone and plan their days, much as Nicole had done with Eve Chen. They would go flower and grocery shopping together, do their errands together. "It was fun! It was never, 'What are you wearing?' It was never, 'Let's have lunch.' It was never gossip. We were always *doing* things." Both women loved being ladies of the house, providing for their men.

Rockingham during those years was a jewel of Nicole's making. Linda says what others have said. Taking care of O.J., making the environment beautiful and smooth-running for her fussy man, was her goal, and her pleasure. "There was always music—I remember she liked a James Brown album—and flowers in vases and fruit in bowls. Later, when Nicole and I both had children, if I had my kids at Rockingham, I couldn't get them to leave, the place was so inviting. Nicole had that great play yard built in the front."

Linda and Nicole spent many hours sitting in the park-style benches at the house's entrance, talking and smoking.

Linda was a smoker and Nicole was a sneak-smoker (O.J. hated and forbade it and was forever lecturing people on the evils of nicotine).

Whenever Nicole heard O.J.'s car pull up,* she would hurriedly stick her half-smoked Marlboro into Linda's hand. "So here we are, side by side on the bench: me, 'Oh, hi, O.J.!' Nicole, 'Hi, honey!' Nicole not smoking and me holding *two* lit cigarettes."

Nicole selected and framed the photographs of O.J. with other celebrities that filled an entire enclosed hall, and she painstakingly made a dozen scrapbooks, a chronology of every clipping, award, photograph, and statistic from his careers in football, acting, pitchmaking, and commentating.

Nicole got Linda into running through Brentwood Park, "and when I fell on a sprinkler head and hurt my leg so much I was crying, Nicole *carried* me back to her house," says Linda. When Linda's first baby was stillborn, Nicole comforted her and helped get her through the terrible sadness. That initial stillbirth had made Linda "crazy-uptight that my kids would get hurt. When my son tripped in the driveway trying to take off his sweater and started wailing [it turns out he broke his jaw], I got hysterical, while Nicole, the cool one, ran in and got ice, applied the ice, drove us to the doctor for the stitches, saying the whole time, 'Hey, Linda, he'll be okay . . . he'll be okay.' "

---

*"O.J. *always* parked his car on Ashford," a babysitter who tended the children for years told a friend of Nicole's. During the preliminary hearings in the summer of 1994, when, in the questioning of the limousine driver, the point was made that O.J.'s Bronco was parked on Rockingham that evening, "the babysitter said that she knew from that fact alone—and anyone who knew his parking habits must have known—that something was suspicious," reports the friend. Why, the babysitter had reasoned, would O.J. break a bedrock habit and park on the street he *never* parked on—unless, for example, he didn't want the limo driver, who *was* parked on Ashford (as well as sitting on the Ashford curb), to see him pull up and rush into the house?

Nicole as a toddler with her mother, Judi, in Germany

Baby Dominique (Mini) with Nicole and Denise at the Royal Palm house

Nicole at seventeen, just a few months before she met O.J. Simpson

Copyright— David LeBon

The beautiful Brown sisters at Laguna in the 1980s: Mini, Denise, Nicole, and Tanya

1980—Nicole, O.J., and Bob and Kris Kardashian on the weekend O.J. learned to ski

May, 1981—Nicole and good friend David LeBon at his wedding. Next to O.J. Simpson are Judi and Lou Brown. In the foreground at the left is Mini Brown; at the right, an unidentified wedding guest. Photo by Figge Photography

1982—O.J.'s All Stars. From left to right: Irwin Rennert, (half hidden) Ricky Schulman, Al Cowlings, Allen Schwartz, Lynn Swann, Mark Reede, (in sunglasses) Joe Stellini, Jason Simpson with O.J., (kneeling) Tom McCollum, (children) Chris and Sean Kehoe, (next to O.J.) Billy Kehoe, Reggie McKenzie, (below Reggie) Joe Kolkowitz, Mark Davidson, Ahmad Rashad, Bob Chandler

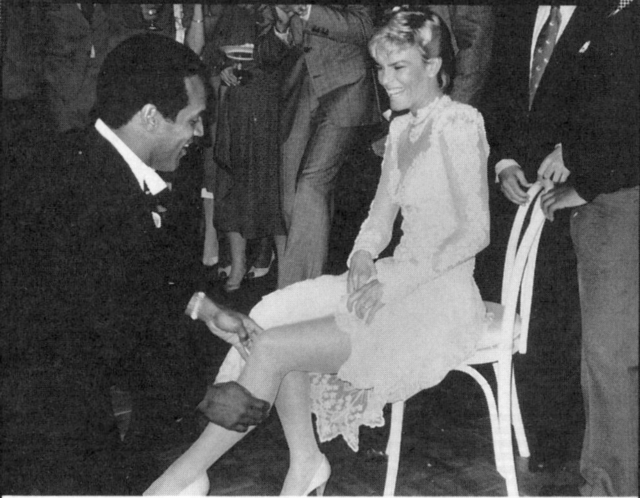

February 2, 1985—O.J. and Nicole at their wedding

Copyright— David LeBon

Denise and A.C. at Nicole and O.J.'s wedding

Copyright— David LeBon

December 28, 1988—Judi with baby Justin, Nicole and O.J. with Sydney in Hawaii—shortly before the infamous 1989 New Year's beating

Christmas, 1989—The Brown and Simpson families in New York. At left, Denise with her son, Sean; Lou Brown; Judi with Sydney; Nicole and O.J. with Justin. In front, Tanya and Mini with her son, Aaron. At far right, Jason Simpson.

O.J. with Sydney at Disneyland

Sydney and Justin on the Simpsons' 1990 Christmas card

Nicole, O.J., and Justin mimic Sydney's habit of finger sucking

"The girls": Faye Resnick, Kris Kardashian Jenner, Cici Shahian, Nicole, and Cora Fischman

Cabo San Lucas, Mexico, 1992—Nicole, Brett Shaves, and Mini

Indeed, Linda Schulman got a lot from Nicole. There was a vulnerability about Linda, whose doe-like, diminutive appearance often resulted in her being taken for half her age. (When Judi Brown first came upon Linda at Rockingham, she thought she was a friend of Arnelle's.) But as their friendship went on and Nicole got a sense of the marriage Linda had with the easygoing, secure Ricky Schulman, she began to lean on and confide in Linda—and sometimes in Ricky as well. Linda was funny and hip and had a toughness to her, but more than that, she had basic self-respect and unyielding values. In her view, a man and a woman who had committed to each other did not sleep with other people, did not scream or throw things at each other, did not humiliate each other.

Later, as they both had their children, the difference between O.J.'s and Ricky's parental involvement was painfully evident to Nicole. "Ricky was always there for his son and daughter, and it *really* bothered Nicole that O.J. wasn't that way. She always said, 'Why can't O.J. be more like Ricky?' " recalls Judi Brown. According to Judi, O.J. used to say, "Nicole, why are you always comparing me to Ricky? Ricky is the way he is but I have more things to do than he does. Ricky works regular hours, he's free at night. *My* day doesn't stop at five—I have appointments in the evening."

Judi took O.J.'s side. "I said to Nicole," she remembers, " 'You know, most daddies are not like Ricky Schulman. He really is an exception. Most men work, make money, come home—they're tired; they don't want the kids anymore.' And I told her, 'Nicole, don't keep saying Ricky's such a better father than O.J. or O.J. will never want to be around Ricky.' "

Two things are evident here: Nicole baited O.J. by comparing him to other men. ("If she saw a guy weight lifting on the beach," one male friend says, "she'd turn to O.J. and say, 'Why don't you look like that anymore?' ") But much more striking is Judi's siding with O.J.; her message to her daughter was to settle and appease rather than to ask for—or even to believe she deserved—any improvement in O.J.'s behavior.

Whatever Nicole's complaints about O.J., they dissolved at the year's quintessential group activity: the annual softball game pitting O.J.'s All-Stars against Jack Hansen's Daisy team. The games, which originated as Saturday and Sunday events in 1981 at Roxbury Park (on Olympic Boulevard, midway between the Daisy and Stellini's), eventually moved to Mandeville Canyon and became an annual event on the Fourth of July.

O.J.'s team boasted Kareem Abdul Jabbar at first base, Lynn Swann as, Joe Kolkowitz recalls, "an incredibly graceful catcher," Kolkowitz in right field, as well as Bobby Chandler, Ahmad, Reggie McKenzie, Jack Gilardi, A.C., and Billy Kehoe. "O.J. was okay as a pitcher," Joe says, "but he was *always* talking."

McCollum pitched for Hansen's team (O.J. called Tom *his* Most Valuable Player), which included Hansen, actor Reed Smith, and producer Joey Vecchio.

After each game, everyone would go over to Rockingham, where all the kids—Jason and Arnelle, Sean and Chris Kehoe, Annette Funicello Gilardi's children, Joe Stellini's son—played PacMan. O.J. and Nicole barbecued chicken, ribs, hot dogs, and hamburgers and everyone played tennis and basketball on the tennis court. One unyielding tradition was that *every* adult guest be thrown in the pool with his or her clothes on. "I remember one year these three black girls—real lookers—came late and did not know about this tradition," Kolkowitz says. "They were dressed to the nines. When they were told, 'Take your car keys out of your pockets and set down your purses,' they went, 'Oooh, no! Please! I just had my hair done!' There was lots of resistance—there always was—but when you have all these big football players picking you up over their shoulders and walking to the deep end . . . Well, sorry, ladies."

As the eighties progressed and O.J. became a golf nut, Allen Schwartz, now married to a sweet, pretty woman named Pamela Sue, took over as chief softball maven. And tennis was played by the whole crowd on either the Simpsons', the Schwartzes' or the Kardashians' court. One afternoon in 1983, Schwartz and Kolkowitz—with O.J. as umpire—faced off against each other in a singles match they called "the Great Jewish Challenge." A banner emblazoned with this title was tied between two trees on either side of Mandeville Canyon; T-shirts were printed; the soundtrack from *Rocky* blared over loudspeakers.

Good times and joking around were what held this group together. At 5:00 one morning in early spring O.J. called Kolkowitz in a panic, waking him up. "A.C.'s been arrested! They found him in an all-night whorehouse. He's down in Watts. He needs five hundred dollars to bail himself out. Nicole won't let me go. I *know* you can get it, man. He's my best friend! Hurry up and get down there, man." O.J. gave Joe the address of an outdoor phone booth to stand next to. A.C. was to call from the police substation.

Kolkowitz drove down to Watts in his 1960 Cadillac. By the time O.J. and Tom McCollum drove by in McCollum's Rolls and yelled, "April Fools, asshole!," Joe had been standing loyally by the designated phone booth for an hour, hit on by dozens of beggars and hoods, secretly terrified, his vintage Caddy several times in danger of being hot-wired.

"You couldn't be thin-skinned around our group," Schwartz says, "or you'd have to be on the couch for the rest of your life."

Other times, humor was provided by fate, mother nature, or human fallibility. At one of the best ever of the yearly birthday parties Nicole threw for O.J., the entertainment at the beachside event included a 300-pound stripper doing the hula and Kolkowitz, Marcus Allen, and two members of the soul group Shalimar, dressed up as the Temptations, singing "Lean on Me" and billing themselves "The Rhythm and Jews Band." However, no one had checked the tide tables. As over a hundred guests in tuxedos and gowns scrambled up the moist sand to safety, a galloping crash of white-capped waves struck down, enveloped and eddied over the tents, the tables, the presents, and the food, pulling half of it into the ocean.

Another time, a jumping-out-of-his-seat-excited Allen Schwartz called O.J. and Kolkowitz to say that Presidential candidate Gary Hart was coming over to his house to play tennis. (A mutual friend had arranged the date between Allen and the person the friend described as "Gary Hart, the politician.") "The Secret Service had to okay it," Schwartz whispered, significantly. O.J. changed a business trip to be there. But as the introductions were made on Schwartzy's court and the balls were lobbed, O.J. took Kolkowitz aside and grumbled, puzzled, "I've *met* Gary Hart. *That* guy's not Gary Hart." O.J. and Kolkowitz looked over at Schwartz, who was blissfully ignorant that the man he had on his court was a *California* state senator coincidentally named Gary Hart, *not* the rock-jawed Coloradan whose bid for the Presidency would shortly be dashed by his dalliance with Donna Rice aboard the *Monkey Business.* An hour of tennis with the man didn't disabuse Schwartz, according to Kolkowitz. "Do you think you have a chance to win?" Schwartz asked his guest, still confusing the minor politician with the Democratic party's top Presidential primary contender. Joe and O.J. razzed Schwartz about it for months afterward.

Allen Schwartz wasn't the only member of the inner circle to be occasionally thick-headed. When, one day at Rockingham, A.C. admonished a visiting policeman friend for not having his watch on ("How the hell are you gonna clock the speeders?"), Ahmad Rashad and Reggie McKenzie doubled over in laughter. "You don't clock speeders with a *watch,* A.C.! You pace them with radar guns," someone had to tell him.

Friends remembering the golden years of this group are quick to recall the happy moments. "Such good times," Linda Schulman says. "Such good times we all had." Linda pauses. "The bad times, they kept to themselves."

"There was always something fun to look forward to; it was always a wonderful life," Kris Kardashian Jenner seconds. But it was all-guy fun, successful-grown-men-in-a-frat-house fun—"a chauvinistic boys' club," as Robin Greer puts it. Kris noticed something then that has been exacerbated since the murders: "The men and the women were always seriously divided on the subject of O.J. He had such a reputation for infidelity. The women cared for Nicole and went, 'Oh, he's such an idiot—he'll screw anything in a dress.' The guys were, 'Oh, he's just a big teddy bear.' The guys were *so* forgiving of him."

And Kris, who was by now busy raising her babies, wondered when Nicole, who had inherited the pack of guys *she* had just kicked out of her house, would tire of playing den mother. "The bachelor pad switched from being my and Robert's house to their house. Kolkowitz, Schwartz, Levinson—they were all at O.J.'s playing tennis." (When O.J.'s court was filled or when he got tired of the ruckus, another friend says, they migrated to Schwartz's.) "And O.J. had his weekly poker game out in the guest house. Nicole fed the players. He used to get ribs from somewhere. She was always organizing the food. She was always supportive of his activities."

Still, Kris says, "Nicole found time to be thoughtful. After each of my kids were born, she was always the first to send a gift or send flowers." Her actions, however, spoke louder than she did. "A lot of people over the years would tell me, 'Gee, Nicole is so private, Nicole is so unapproachable.' I would always say, 'No. Nicole is just shy.' Now I look back and see that Nicole wanted her space and needed to keep her distance because she was going through a lot during those years."

People got disturbing glimpses of what she was going through. Twice, one particular friend received startling phone calls from O.J., who was apparently looking for Nicole. No sooner did the friend pick up the telephone and say hello than she heard O.J. ranting on about Nicole, agitatedly and nonsequitorially—"Did I say this?! Did I say *this?!*"—as if he and the friend had been in the middle of a heated conversation. Or, worse, as if O.J. were having a fight with the absent Nicole. The friend who got that phone call remembers hanging up and thinking, "This is *not* a normal person." The second time she got that kind of call, her appraisal shifted to: "This person is a *monster.*"

On another occasion, a couple was having dinner with O.J. and Nicole at Rockingham. Something was said by Nicole, casually, during dinner that did not strike the couple as provocative, but a half hour later, they heard, as one of them recalls, "horrible screaming and yelling from O.J., out of the blue, in the other room."

One person who knew them both very well says flatly, "He was an animal."

Then there were more troubling things. Maria Baur, who worked as the housekeeper at Rockingham (and was Nicole's "sister-in-law"), thought it odd that Nicole often wore dark glasses inside the house during the day. "And jogged in them, very early in the morning," she says, "when you don't need sunglasses at all and when dark lenses could have made her stumble." Maria thought, at the very least, that Nicole wore the glasses to disguise the fact that she had been crying.

When the Baurs traveled to Germany with O.J. and Nicole during one holiday season, an incident in Munich made Rolf wonder. He recalls, "We were in a very nice glassware store and the saleswoman made a laughing remark about Nicole's leather shorts and all of a sudden O.J. ran out of the store—he was just running, running down the street. Nicole took it in stride. She said, 'He's just having his little fit right now.' "

A woman whose children knew O.J.'s saw O.J., Nicole, Jason, and Arnelle many Sunday nights at Regular John's, a family-style pizza parlor in Brentwood. "He took over the whole restaurant with his jokes and loud voice and huge mannerisms," the woman says. "Nicole was very sweet to his kids but he would get verbally abusive with her. Once he called her 'white trash' for all to hear. She was feeding his kids at the time. She stopped and laughed at his remark."

Twice, Robin Greer was at Rockingham when Nicole

didn't make it downstairs. "Where's Nicole?" Robin asked O.J.

"She's not feeling well; she couldn't come down," was his answer, in that deep basso, as he and all the guys hunkered down on couches watching TV. "He was perfectly charming when he said it," Robin remembers. *"Oh,* he could be charming. There's a lot of duality in that man!"

"Well, then, I'll just go up and say hi," Robin said, heading for the stairs.

O.J. stopped her. "She doesn't want to see anybody," he said.

In a heart-to-heart talk with Nicole right after she separated from O.J., Robin would find out *why* she didn't want to. "I couldn't come down and be seen," Nicole told Robin. "I didn't have enough cover-up makeup."

One day Linda Schulman and Nicole were sitting in front of the house, smoking cigarettes and discussing a recent Christmas present to O.J.—an Uzi.* Linda was shocked and annoyed that anyone would give another person such a present. Couldn't a more appropriate holiday gift than a machine gun be found? Linda had pointedly wondered.

"Aren't you a little . . . scared, Nicole?" Linda wanted to know, according to someone to whom Nicole later told this story. Linda knew that O.J. was amassing a gun collection as a hobby (she did not know he had a knife collection), but still, *she* wouldn't be very comfortable going to sleep at night knowing that the weapon-of-choice of the Medellin drug cartel was in *her* house.

Nicole used Linda's concern over the Uzi as an opportunity to make a disclosure. According to someone to whom

*Two people say they watched O.J. opening the gift-wrapped Uzi and both recall that it was acknowledged to have been from Allen Schwartz. A third person says, "O.J. told me, 'Schwartzy gave me an Uzi for Christmas.'" Allen Schwartz, however, says today, "I absolutely deny ever giving O.J. a gun. Guns are not positive things. O.J. doesn't think guns are positive, either."

Nicole relayed this conversation, she said, "O.J. said he would kill me if I left him. Or if I cheated on him."

"Nicole," Linda asked, "how can you live like this?"

"I don't know," Nicole said, stoically. "But I do." Nicole disclosed more: Once, O.J. was so angry at her he had taken a wine bottle and beaten her with it. "He broke my ribs!" Nicole wailed. "My ribs were all broken!"

Nicole had called the widely used private security company that had been contracted to guard the house, "but when they came, O.J. just talked them out of it. Oh, O.J.! They *all* kiss his ass!" Nicole had said disgustedly.

It is believed that A.C. had driven Nicole to the hospital. Possibly thinking of that childhood day when she fell off her bike and injured herself after she and Denise had pedaled to the verboten ice rink, Nicole had told the emergency workers that her rib injury had occurred when she had fallen off her bicycle. (A lie to her parents had once saved her from punishment; a lie to the doctor and nurse could now save her from humiliation—and O.J. from career-ruining publicity.)

"But how can you stay with him, Nicole?" Linda asked.

"I could never leave him," Nicole said. "There's just something about O.J. that I love."

Linda was dumbstruck.

O.J. apparently favored the wine cellar. It was a very quiet, secluded place for a fight. Notes in Nicole's handwriting, found in her Bundy Drive condominium after her murder (and now in the possession of the Los Angeles District Attorney's Office), detail another incident, separate from the one Nicole told Linda about. On this occasion, after a fight possibly triggered, as so many were, by Nicole's angry lamentations about O.J.'s infidelity, O.J. beat her, pushed her into the large basement wine cellar, and locked her in. He went to watch a sporting event on television, then came back and beat her some more and went back to watching television: The alternating pattern continued while Nicole became more and more distraught and frightened.

Nicole had told her sister Denise the story, but so sketchily and matter-of-factly ("O.J. pushed me in the wine cellar") with a toss of her head and roll of her eyes indicating "case closed"—that Denise never thought that much of it. Both Brown sisters had a quick, don't-look-ahead/don't-look-back way of expressing themselves and framing the world—a refreshing style in these turgidly overanalyzed times but one that nevertheless does not invite nor is conducive to the kind of caution that living with an erratic, if not violent and unbalanced, man requires. Nicole's friends believe—and the history of her struggle with her powerful feelings for O.J. makes clear—that she routinely minimized such incidents, when she talked about them at all, because she never wanted to burn her emotional bridge back to him. As any woman who has ever complained tearfully about her boyfriend to a friend one day and lived to regret it the next knows all too well, you cannot conduct a relationship you're *impelled* to stay in if all of your friends know every bad thing about, and therefore hate, your boyfriend. So Nicole routinely suffered in silence, then woke up the next day, got over it, and got on with her life.

An even stronger reason for Nicole's silence, Linda Schulman believes, was her pride. "She didn't tell people the bad things because she didn't want people saying, 'Poor Nicole . . .' I *know* that is true."

Was cocaine use behind these incidents?

It may have been a contributor, but only that. During the eighties, members of this crowd dabbled in L.A.'s drug of choice and "O.J. did a *lot* of it," one member says emphatically. "If somebody had a bottle of coke, O.J. would take it and start it."

He was seen doing lines through a rolled-up dollar bill during afternoons in his Rockingham office. But the person who witnessed this says, "He made distinctions. He would never do sports on coke, and he mostly did coke just at parties."

"He bought an eightball [an eighth of an ounce] from my boyfriend," says the woman who snorted with him in the Bay Area restaurant wine cellar. "He definitely knew his way around coke; we did a lot of lines."

Still, for better or worse, many people availed themselves of cocaine in those days, and Simpson's dalliance seems to have been recreational and controlled—hardly the raging addiction that put others in rehabilitation clinics, bankruptcy courts, ENT wings in hospitals for nasal-membrane reconstruction, or in morgues.

Furthermore, by the time he developed his passion for golf in 1987, what cocaine nights he might have had were necessarily over: He had a 6 A.M. golf date almost every day of the week.*

"Neither O.J. nor Nicole did that much of it, by the going standard of the day," opines a male friend. "And from what I saw, she did more coke than he did." A female friend is quick to say that Nicole completely stopped the recreational use of cocaine once she had children.

The addiction that *was* worrisome at the time was Billy Kehoe's—to liquor. Although Kehoe's alcohol dependence had not reached its eventual critical point, where an anguished Susie would give her sons twenty dollars for every hidden empty vodka bottle they found crammed in a drawer or closet, his drinking was causing Nicole to say to Susie, "We love you, but it's getting painful for us to be around Billy." And, "Susie, only Billy can make the decision to stop. You can't do it for him." Then, saying what she could not say to herself, Nicole added, "But *you* have to be strong enough to walk away."

"Nicole was supportive, loving, firm," Susie remembers. It is always easier to give advice to somebody else, and women are particularly good at "projecting off" their own

*According to a source directly involved in the investigation, Simpson's blood test showed *no* drug use.

carefully hidden situations by focusing, authoritatively and judgmentally, on another woman's problem with her mate.

One afternoon, an inebriated Billy pulled O.J. into a bank where the tellers would not give him money because his several accounts were overdrawn. "This is my *friend,* O.J. *Simpson!"* he bellowed, for everyone to hear. "Now give me the fuck the money!" It was after this incident that O.J. began thinking hard about Wayne Hughes' warning that he would never achieve what he yearned for—at that point, a state senatorship was still the goal—if he didn't cut loose from Billy.

Still, O.J. did not wish to abandon his friend. In the early eighties, he offered to pay for Billy's alcohol rehabilitation as well as for military school for the Kehoes' older son, Sean, whose parents thought he could benefit from that regimen. Billy and Susie came over to Rockingham one day and O.J. got on the phone with the sergeant at the Connecticut-based school. "I'll write a letter; I'm willing to go to the extent of helping with the tuition," O.J. said. The Kehoes thanked him but decided against the school.

A year or two later, Susie called O.J., more alarmed than ever about Billy's drinking. He was grabbing his flask first thing in the morning, hiding booze in iced tea (Susie could still smell it), staggering around, and passing out at restaurants. O.J. offered to help pay for a stay at the Betty Ford Clinic. Billy refused to go and continued drinking.

For a long time the Kehoes were conveniently, divertingly, the group's "problem couple." Everyone adored Susie—she was so sweet and nurturing—but Billy kept going further off the wall. In the early eighties, he became heavily involved in a large-scale pyramid scheme that was based solely on money rather than on a product. Participants would congregate with hoards of cash. Many were armed. "It got to the point," Tom McCollum, who observed the scheme from a distance, recalls, "where people were carrying around three and four hundred thousand dollars in suitcases, going to pyramid meetings in warehouses in the middle of nowhere. We're talking guns and 'big boys' and people getting hurt and nasty things happening." Billy was an active participant. O.J., to a much lesser extent, also got involved. O.J. asked at least one unwealthy friend, "Give me four thousand dollars—I'll double it for you." ("Nicole," says Eve Chen, "was very upset by O.J.'s and everyone else's participation in the scheme. 'I wouldn't do that; it's not decent,' she said. She had a firm sense of right and wrong.")

Billy's eventual arrest for diversion of funds, and his subsequent incarceration in the state penitentiary at Tehachapee (during which stay his eventually fatal cirrhosis of the liver was diagnosed), resulted in part from his participation in the scheme.

One night in 1982, O.J. and Nicole and Susie and Billy went to a huge party given by L.A. Laker Jerry Buss. The foursome arrived in a limousine and got right in the swing of the lavish affair—all outdoors, with strings of lanterns and a great buffet and Dionne Warwick (A.C.'s sometime-ladyfriend) singing.

Billy, as usual, was downing vodkas, one after another. At one point Susie and Nicole went into the bathroom, then, on the way back to the table, stopped and talked to some people they knew. "I was always a really friendly, huggy-kissy type of person, but my husband would get the wrong idea," Susie says. "He wanted me right there. So when I saw him looking at me, I left Nicole and walked over to where he was standing, by the bushes. He smacked me—so hard—right in my eye—I hit the ground. I got up, stunned! I ran and told the limousine driver to take me home immediately.

"Nicole must have looked for me and said, 'O.J., what happened to Susie?' They had seen that I was pretty loaded myself, so they both left the party right away and came to our apartment. I was sitting there on the couch crying, 'I want a divorce! I'm not gonna *live* like this!'

"The two of them were wonderful. They just took charge. As soon as Billy stumbled home, O.J. took him aside and said, 'What's *wrong* with you?! How could you do something like that? Susie's the best wife! We gotta talk, man. We gotta talk *now*—and get you straightened *out.'* And he took Billy to the other side of our penthouse and talked to him for *four hours.*

"Nicole sat with me. She put a compress on my black eye. (*One* little pop and I had this black eye!) I cried and cried. Gently she said, 'Susie, he's got a problem. He drinks too much. We love you, but . . .' Later she sighed and said, 'Susie, I don't know how you take it.' "

When O.J. and Nicole left before dawn, Susie felt exhausted for herself and Billy, and grateful to her friends. To this day, Susie says she never sensed the irony in their roles as obersided marriage counselors, and that she never saw a dark side to their union.

But then, the interpretation of some events has changed over the years. As Susie puts it, "Some of the things that were funny then have turned, today, into serious stories. I don't know, maybe I have amnesia, but I thought when we all did things—like go to Las Vegas and gamble and have a few drinks and a few laughs (which the four of us did a lot)—*I* thought those times were fun. Now the interpretation is changing."

One such trip to Las Vegas, which predated the Jerry Buss party by a couple of years, culminated in a night of watching Frank Sinatra perform at the Stardust Hotel. Sinatra invited O.J. and his party backstage after his performance. To both Billy and O.J., Sinatra was just about the coolest man on the planet; they wanted to make the right impression. By the time the curtain rang down on "My Way," both couples had had a little more to drink than might have been ideal for a walking-on-eggshells meeting. Susie did not go backstage, but Nicole did.

All Susie remembers is that, the next day, "Nicole was laughing that she had gotten locked out of their room. It wasn't a fight where he hit her, it was more . . . funny."

Nicole would later present a somewhat graver version of this story to Denise and a downright humiliating and horrifying version to Linda Schulman and to Cici Shahian. To both women Nicole said she did not know what it was that she said in Frank Sinatra's presence that had so "embarrassed" O.J., but by the time they got back to their hotel room O.J. was furious.

"Nicole told me they had a big fight," Denise remembers, "and that O.J. locked her out of their room. But she minimized the story, as always. It was, 'Oh my God, I couldn't find the room . . . ,'" just a tossed-off remark. However, Nicole confessed details to these two friends that she had never told Denise: O.J. had "thrown" her out of the room before he locked the door, she told Cici, and she was "half naked" in the hallway for a long time. To Linda she said, "I was in my bra"—Linda never learned if Nicole's lower body was clothed at all—"when he threw me out of the room. It was the most horrible thing in the world."

Nicole told both Denise and Cici that she had wandered the halls on different floors trying to find the room again. Once she found the room, she sat in front of the door until O.J. let her back in.

This incident is one of the instances of perceived abuse that Nicole wrote down in the notes she kept in her Bundy Drive condominium.

5

Marriage

DESPITE THE ABUSE AND THE BAD TIMES, NICOLE WANTED TO marry O.J. and have his babies. Those yearnings were not free of ambivalence—enough ambivalence that she had at least two abortions before the pregnancy that resulted in Sydney's birth in October 1985.* But the yearnings were there. "Nicole was always pushing O.J. to let her have a baby, but he said, 'I already have two kids,'" recalls Tom McCollum.

Everyone around Nicole seemed to be marrying and having babies.

"Let me see your ring," Nicole had said to Nina Shipp, as the two women sat at the bar in the Rockingham den while the guys were watching sports on TV in the other room.

---

*During the summer of 1994, the *National Enquirer* reported that Nicole had had six abortions. This account, a source very close to Nicole concedes, is not untrue. But the *Enquirer* story said that Nicole had the abortions *after* Sydney and Justin were born, and that she had them because she felt that O.J. was clinically insane; relieved that she had had two mentally healthy children, she did not want to press her luck. This is inaccurate. According to a very close friend, she had at least two of the abortions before Sydney's birth.

Nina had just married O.J.'s friend Ron Shipp, after having been his girlfriend since they were seniors—he the football star, she the tall pretty brunette—at a West L.A. high school twelve years before. "Boy, I wish O.J. and I were married, like you and Ron," Nicole said, admiring Nina's gold band. "That's the relationship I want with him."

"Don't worry, you will be," Nina assured Nicole. "You two are such a perfect couple." By that, Nina meant they were both glamorous, energetic, and a little tempestuous. They flew up to San Francisco just to have dinner. They fought and made up on a dime. She and Ron were very different. They were salt-of-the-earth people.

But as different as they were, what Nina and Ron had in common with O.J. and Nicole is that they, too, were an interracial couple. Therefore, Nicole—who to all others both blithely and adamantly denied any concern whatsoever about that aspect of her relationship with O.J.*—turned to Nina with the worries she may have felt she could share with no one else. Sometimes her questions were naive and blunt.

"What's it like getting married to a black person?" she wanted to know now. "Was it hard finding someone to perform the ceremony?"

"No; *that* wasn't an issue," Nina said. "Religion was. I'm Jewish, so we had to find somebody neutral." Ron, however,

---

*"Race was never an issue with her," contends Denise. "She'd look at O.J. and her attitude was, 'So? He's a little darker than me, so what?' It wasn't like, 'Oh, you're a *black man.*'" Cici Shahian, who met Nicole when Nicole already had children, says, "Her attitude was that the children's beauty, and their being O.J. Simpson's children, and O.J.'s wealth and fame—all of this would protect them from any racism. Racism—race consciousness—didn't exist in the world they lived in." David LeBon's wife, D'Anne, says, "Nicole was very idealistic. Her attitude was, 'I don't care whether O.J. is black, yellow, white, or green; so why should anyone else?' About the children she said, 'They're their own people; they won't have to deal with race. If we lived in a place like South Central maybe they'd have to deal with race, but not here in Brentwood.'"

despite being a Christian, had worn a yarmulke for the wedding as a courtesy to his bride.

But then, that kind of empathy was typical of Ron Shipp. Everybody leaned on him. People made him their crisis confidant when their wives walked out on them and they contemplated suicide or when their husbands were killed in helicopter crashes. There were dozens of people in his telephone book who got a call from him on their birthdays. He was the person who picked up friends' cousins at the airport, who never missed a neighbor's father's funeral, who got athletes to speak at boys' clubs. People also turned to Ron when they needed special protection and when they needed someone to plead their case to an unreasonable partner. Ron was a natural mediator. And he was a police officer.

Nina knew Nicole appreciated all these qualities in Ron. She had a feeling that one day she might be loaning her husband to Nicole in an emergency.

The birth of Susie Kehoe's daughter in 1982 heightened Nicole's longing for motherhood. Donna Stellini had given Susie a shower at the Bistro on Canon Drive. The Bistro was an unusually staid venue for this crowd; it was inhabited mostly by the wealthy young Ladies Who Lunched. (This was the crowd that Kris Kardashian had aspired to and had succeeded in becoming a member of. She and several other well-to-do young wives and mothers wore Valentino suits and Judith Lieber handbags to frequent lunches, and collected Baccarat and Lalique glass.)

Billy, O.J., and Joe popped in and said hello as Nicole and Donna helped the very pregnant Susie work tight pink satin ribbons off white boxes. The women swooned as Susie lifted hankie-sized white-eyelet garments out of weightless folds of tissue.

Susie's cake had "HELLO, KELLY!" written on it in icing. (Susie knew she was having a girl, and she and Billy had already chosen a third Irish name for their third child.) O.J., Joe, and Billy took pictures and mugged for the video camera saying, "Hey, Kelly, the gang's all here!" "Hi, Kel! This is your dad and his buddies!"

A few weeks later when Kelly was born, "O.J. and Nicole were the first two people to hold her, after me and Billy," remembers Susie. "They came into my room right after I delivered. I remember O.J. cradling Kelly in his arms and Nicole looking at her and going, 'Oooh!' Right after that it was, 'Kids! Kids! That's what I want!' from Nicole."

Although Nicole did not necessarily believe that marriage guaranteed fidelity, she had faith in that equation in the reverse: O.J.'s decision to marry her, if it ever came, would naturally be motivated by his decision—*finally*—not to sleep with other women. This being so, marriage would not just bring legitimacy ("Nicole was proud and she was traditional; it was a little humiliating for her to just be living with O.J.," Linda Schulman believes); it would also bring relief. Relief from all the cliché indignities she suffered. She went through his coat pockets for names and phone numbers scribbled on napkins; when he was traveling on business, she called his hotel room at 4 A.M., only to hear the operator say, "Sorry, they're not answering; would you care to leave a message?"

O.J. was cavalier about his behavior. Sometimes he had the girls he slept with over to play tennis. Or he invited them to the birthday parties Nicole gave him every year. (*"Three* girls he supposedly had affairs with came to one party," remembers Denise.) In the middle of conversations in which well-known women's names came up in a notably different context, he would pipe up with decided non-sequiturs about his sexual conquests. The exotic beauty turned James Bond girl? "I fucked her," he told a friend. The Charlie's Angel turned TV-movie leading lady? "I fucked her," he told the same friend.

"Sometimes," says a close friend of Nicole's from that period, "O.J. had two or three different girlfriends at a time." Says one of her more recent best friends, "O.J. could get *any* girl in this town." Adds another friend wryly, "And *did."*

When Nicole was at her boiling point, O.J. got others to take the blame for his glaring indiscretions. Once, turning on the television to watch a Lakers game that O.J. was attending, Nicole saw him and a friend sitting with a blonde. O.J. set up the friend to take the blame. Nicole banned the man from the house for two years. (The poor man seems to have been a sitting duck in the Nicole-O.J. crossfire. At O.J.'s raucous bachelor party before his marriage to Nicole, an exotic dancer who was hired for the occasion had, according to one guest, attempted to perform oral sex on this unwilling man while other guests hooted and cheered. When Nicole learned of the incident, she called O.J. and showed her displeasure in no uncertain terms.)

Eventually, Nicole became so obsessed and desperate over O.J.'s infidelity she amassed a list of license plates of his suspected girlfriends' cars. It is not known if she compiled the list by hiring a private detective or by following O.J. when he left the house at night. She presented the list of plate numbers to someone who was in a position to trace them to their owners, saying that these were the license plates of presumably overenthusiastic fans who had stopped their cars in front of the house. When the tracer tracked a plate to one of his friends whose father was a major record-company president, the tracer delicately confronted Nicole and asked her about the *true* purpose of the search. She was embarrassed when she told him. Not wanting to be involved in domestic espionage nor wanting to get on O.J.'s bad side, the man stopped tracing the plates.

There were times when Nicole could not take another day of it. "Sometimes she just cried and cried," Judi Brown says. "She was desperate. She would say, 'Yes I know he's "single," but he expects *me* to be faithful. Why can't I expect him to be?' "

And Nicole *was* faithful. "She used to tell me that when she went to parties with O.J., guys would hit on her," says Eve Chen. "I guess celebrities think they can do anything they want. Nicole was *so* disgusted. She said, 'Don't they know I'm with O.J.? How dare they?!' "

Not that she didn't allow herself secret infatuations. Among Nicole's freelance decorating jobs was the Westwood apartment of O.J.'s protégé Marcus Allen. Nicole made it airy and light. At the 1984 Rose Bowl, which O.J. was commentating, the subject of good-looking football players came up, and Nicole turned to a friend in the stands and said, "That Marcus Allen. I have such a crush on him! If I wasn't with O.J., I'd go after him in a minute."

One day shortly after that Rose Bowl game, Nicole was driving up Brighton Way in Beverly Hills, just past the Daisy. She and O.J. had actually been talking about getting married, so she was even more stunned and hurt than she might otherwise have been when she saw O.J., acting ostentatiously affectionate with another woman, right in front of Alan Austin's store. Nicole later told the Schulmans that he was "hugging and kissing" the woman, and she told Denise that "he had his hand right on her butt." Denise says Nicole "started screaming at O.J. angrily." Then she drove off.

She arrived at the Schulmans' soon after. Denise seems to remember Nicole telling her she went home and packed an overnight bag first, but Linda can't remember one. She says, "Knowing Nicole—Nicole just *did* things, *boom*—she didn't pack." With or without the suitcase, Nicole told Ricky and Linda that she didn't want to go home to Rockingham. Could she stay at their house overnight?

Linda got sheets and blankets and prepared their guest room. She and Ricky spent half the night sitting up with Nicole as she cried and railed against O.J. She hung on them for advice. They took turns giving her variations of this basic speech: "Look, Nicole, you know we love O.J. He's a great guy. He's a terrific friend. But this is *not* a man you can marry. You can't live like this, Nicole. And it's always going to be like this. Some men just *have* to do it all the time, and he's one. A man cheats once, okay. But this is not the second or even the third time this has happened. Forget about it. He will *always* cheat on you, married or single. Nicole, if you marry him, you will be dealing with days like today your whole life."

"You're right, you're right," Nicole said. "I am never going back to him. I am *never* going back!" The Schulmans did not for a minute, of course, believe this proclamation.

The next morning as Linda was making breakfast in the kitchen, the intercom rang. The condominium complex's security guard was calling to say that Mr. Simpson was on his way.

Linda went upstairs and said, "Nicole, O.J.'s here."

"Don't let him in!" Nicole told her.

Linda had seen the shattered photographs of Nicole's family lying on the floor of Rockingham, the result of O.J.'s rages; she knew enough to say, "Nicole, I've *got* to let him in or I think he may break down the door. Just talk to him, Nicole. Be strong."

Linda opened the door and O.J. said hello to her briefly—"He was not rude; he was never rude to us, always nice"—then bolted right upstairs. As badly as he might treat her, O.J. could not bear to feel even temporarily abandoned by Nicole. After her night's absence from Rockingham, he was clearly in a hurry to set things right with any words or deeds that would do the trick.

"She was putting on her makeup in the bathroom when O.J. walked in and proposed," Denise says, on the basis of what Nicole told her right after that day. "He said, 'I'm sorry! Nick, I'm sorry! Marry me! Let's get married! I want to marry you! We can get the ring right now! A diamond as big as you want!'"

The two came downstairs. Nicole told Linda cryptically, "I'll be right back." Linda was confused and a little concerned. Two hours later, Nicole and O.J. walked into Linda's house. Nicole extended her left hand and displayed the beautiful diamond engagement ring they had just bought at a jeweler's on Beverly Drive. Linda's heart sank. She was amazed at how fast O.J. had worked and how complete a turnaround Nicole had made. "It was as if the whole conversation we had with her the night before hadn't even happened."

"Yes, she was excited," Denise says, having heard about the ring right afterward. "But she said, 'Look how it had to happen. . . .' "

"Ricky and I looked at each other after they left," Linda recalls, "and said, 'We are *never* doing *this* again . . .' "

So O.J. and Nicole were officially engaged.

Before the wedding date was set, O.J. insisted on a prenuptial agreement. According to court papers, it took between seven and nine months to negotiate this. In his subsequent divorce declaration, O.J. said that he had asked for the prenuptial because he had entered the marriage with substantial assets and had the financial interests of Arnelle and Jason to protect.

The agreement stipulated that O.J. and Nicole's property be kept separate. He gave Nicole sole ownership of the San Francisco condominium, specifying that he would complete mortgage payments on it and, if they divorced, give it to her free and clear. Its minimum value at the time of the agreement was estimated at $450,000. The condominium is all the property she would receive, if they divorced.

During the period that this agreement was being hammered out, Denise got married in January 1984 to a fashion photographer.* The wedding was held at Fred Levinson's house, which Nicole had decorated. As Lou Brown walked his third daughter down the aisle (the two from his previous marriage had also had weddings), Nicole thought of her own impending wedding. But sometimes she thought about it worriedly.

"Am I doing the right thing, marrying O.J.?," she asked her mother soon after Denise's wedding. "He's such a womanizer . . ."

---

*The marriage was short-lived; Denise considers it to have been such a mistake "that it's not even worth mentioning his name."

Judi's attitude was typically European. It seemed to her that O.J. didn't have to be faithful *before* they were married—"and I didn't know then how many girlfriends he had," Judi says. "I just knew about one woman in San Francisco." Nicole jettisoned her own doubts by talking hopefully of O.J.'s vowed intention to change his ways. He was even thinking about joining a prayer group to get him spiritually on track.

Nicole's ambivalence, however, was just under the surface when she and O.J. ran into Eve Chen and her TV writer-director husband Leslie Stevens, as both couples were getting off the plane for a Hawaiian vacation a few weeks after Denise's wedding. (Judi Brown booked Eve's travel tickets as well as her daughter's and often created rendezvous when their plans were close enough to mesh.) Eve and Leslie were in Hawaii for a vacation, O.J. and Nicole for the Pro Bowl. Both couples were booked into the Kahala Hilton.

Frank Gifford was also at the hotel for the Pro Bowl with his family, and as the two high-school girlfriends sat on the beach in front of the hotel's bungalows watching the Giffords at surfside, Nicole turned and said to Eve, "Isn't Frank Gifford the nicest man? He's such a nice husband and father." (In 1986, he would get a divorce from the woman Nicole felt he was such a nice husband to and eventually he would marry Kathie Lee Epstein.) "She said it in a way that made my heart twinge," Eve recalls. "There was a wistfulness in Nicky's admiration of this other man, a touching quality, as if seeing Frank Gifford and his family made her realize that the marvelous man she *thought* she had wasn't so wonderful."

That night Eve and Leslie and O.J. and Nicole went out to dinner. Eve noticed that Nicole's dress was "a little bit more constructed than the natural, sporty things she had always worn before. When I said, 'I don't know if I like that dress,' she said, 'You don't *like* it?' She was hurt. I was shocked. The Nicole *I* knew would have said, 'You don't like it? Eh, so what.' She had lost some of her natural confidence. I could feel a tension in her now."

The evening was "so completely overwhelmed by O.J. talking, it was lucky we got to order food. He was so dominating. He was so pushy. He just talked and talked."

"O.J. seemed to be controlling Nicole," Eve says now of the impression she was left with. "He seemed to need all of her and more."

Yet however controlling O.J. was becoming with her, Nicole's native toughness, even her pugnacity, were not qualities the relationship with O.J. had muted. One day Nicole called Ron Shipp and asked him to accompany her to the apartment of her housekeeper, whom we'll call Carmen. Carmen was a good housekeeper and an outstanding cook. Unfortunately, however, one of Nicole's prized diamond drop earrings, a Christmas present from O.J., was missing, and Nicole strongly suspected Carmen had taken it.

Ron Shipp, who found it hard to say no to people who needed him, nevertheless had misgivings about such a house call. He was a police officer; he couldn't spend off-duty hours facilitating a civilian's search mission on her employee's home. He voiced these reservations. Nicole begged him to help her. He said he would, but only if Nicole promised she would be calm and quiet and let him do the talking. "I promise! I promise!" she said.

But when they got to Carmen's apartment in the Miracle Mile area, no sooner did they ring the bell and Carmen answer than Nicole stormed right in and said, "*You* stole my diamond earring!"

Carmen denied the charge and demanded, "I want you out of my house!"

Ron gestured for Nicole to come out, but she was too angry to notice or leave. "I'm not getting out of this house until I get my earring back!" she shouted.

"And I want *you,* Officer Ron"—Carmen knew his name from his visits to Rockingham—"out of my house, too!"

"Nicole, let's get out of here!" Ron said. He finally managed to get Nicole out, and all the way back to the house he worried that Carmen would file a complaint and get him suspended from the force for a month.

The mystery of the lost earring was never resolved.* What may be most apparent from the incident is how Nicole could push things with people to the edge. And not heed warnings.

And by now there were warnings aplenty about O.J.'s radical mood swings and his propensity for fits of violence. One of the most dramatic came one evening at Rockingham. Denise cannot recall the exact date but believes it took place in this period before Nicole and O.J. were married. Although Denise described this incident sketchily on television in November 1994, she did not give the full story. Here it is:

Denise had a date with Ed McCabe, a major New York advertising man, then co-owner of a Madison Avenue agency, Scallion/McCabe/Sloves, which handled a good share of the Hertz account. (Currently he has his own award-winning agency, McCabe and Company.) Denise and Ed joined Nicole and O.J. for a restaurant dinner, then they all went dancing. They ended up back at Rockingham.

O.J. and the girls did a little coke, and then the foursome sat in the den, listening to music.

Denise had long felt that O.J. took advantage of her sister. "Any time he had anything to drink, he'd start picking on her. He'd say, 'You don't look good.' Or, 'Look at your fingernails. They're all bitten down.'" Tonight, Denise decided to say something about it. "You take Nicole for granted, O.J.," Denise remembers saying. "She deserves better. You treat her like shit, and she's the best person you'll ever have."

The blunt and prickly but hardly over-the-top remark *did* something to O.J. "All of a sudden he became another

*Nicole would continue to bewail the lost earring for the rest of her life. In her will—made out, tellingly, one month before her murder—she left the remaining earring to her youngest sister, Tanya, remarking that she believed that the other had been stolen.

person!" Denise remembers. "He went ballistic!" A half-hour rampage ensued. First, O.J. did what he had done many times: He walked up the stairs and threw down Nicole's framed photographs of her family. But now he went further. He continued up to the bedroom and into Nicole's closet. He randomly, furiously, pulled garments off hangers, stomped over to the railing, and flung them downstairs, one after another—dresses, shirts, pants.

"Stop it! What's wrong with you?!" Denise and Nicole yelled. "Ed appeared scared," Denise says.

O.J. did not stop there. He stormed downstairs, stepping over the clothes. He was, Denise says, "screaming insanely—about what, I can't remember." He grabbed Nicole by the arm and picked her up bodily. By now, she was crying and so was Denise, crying and continuing to shout, "Stop it, O.J.! Stop it! *Please!*"

"Put her *down!*" Denise shouted as O.J. walked to the front door, Nicole over his arm. ("It was easy for him," Denise insists; "he is *strong!*") He opened the front door and roughly set Nicole down outside. Then he went back and pulled Denise by the arm, and then Ed, who is not a large man. He threw both of them out of the front door, as he had Nicole. They clung together—aghast and stunned and trying to console a furiously crying Nicole—as O.J. slammed the door shut and left them in the dark.

They got in Ed's rental car. He drove the sobbing sisters back to his bungalow at the Beverly Hills Hotel. "I hate him! I hate him!" Nicole insisted. Back in Ed's living room, Ed and Denise had a long talk with Nicole about how self-destructive staying in the relationship was for her. "You can't go back to him," Denise said repeatedly. "Not after this!"

"I'm *not* going back! I'm *never* going back! I hate him!" Nicole said. Just as she had said the night she spent with the Schulmans.

Nicole slept in Ed's living room. The next morning she said, "I'm just going back to get my stuff out of the house, that's all." In retrospect, the result was predictable. "He schmoozed her back in," Denise says.

On May 19, 1984, O.J. took Nicole and her family to dinner at the Ritz Carlton Hotel in Laguna Niguel, for her twenty-fifth birthday. The hotel had become a kind of second home to the Brown family; with O.J.'s help, Lou had taken over the hotel's Hertz rental agency. All of a sudden, as they walked into the dining room, "Surprise! Surprise!" in many voices came bellowing out of the room's darkened corners. Although she may have had an inkling of what was in store (she *was* dressed for a party), Nicole was plainly thrilled as friends rushed up to her and kissed her and wished her happy birthday. Twenty-*five*—that sounded serious! Waiters popped out with silver trays of champagne in thin-stemmed glasses, and a disco-deejay pumped out top dance hits like Kool and the Gang's "Tonight," Deniece Williams' "Let's Hear It for the Boy," and the infectious song "Borderline," by a new singer named Madonna. Nicole danced till she dropped. A lavish dinner was served.

But one guest, David LeBon, was not in the party spirit. He knew his "little sister" was being treated badly by her famous fiancé. David had never quite forgiven himself for not having tried to talk more sense into Nicole after she had come home from her first date with O.J. with the torn jeans. Tonight David was going to confront O.J. on a different matter.

Just two weeks before, one of David's photographic assistants came back from a shoot and reported that who had waltzed onto the set and waxed intimate with one of the models but O.J. Hearing the story, David, perhaps feeling a combination of sympathy and humiliation for Nicole, instinctively snapped into denial. "No way that could have happened," he said. "'Cause O.J.'s engaged to marry my friend Nicole."

David's assistant pressed on. "Hey, I'm tellin' ya, I saw it with my own two eyes. And then I talked to the model. She says they do it all night, then he goes home to Nicole, then he comes back the next day and they do it some more."

David was disgusted.

Now, at the birthday party, David followed O.J. into the men's room. As the two men were standing together at the urinals, David said, "Hey, are you screwing around on Nicole with some model?"

"Yeah," O.J. said. "So what? Look, you don't know what it's like to be O.J. Simpson. I have women all over me. They put their phone numbers in my pocket. What am I supposed to do? Say no?"

"Yeah, you're supposed to say no!" David answered.

O.J. washed his hands and exited.

When David got back to his table, his face was red with anger. "The guy's an asshole," he hissed to his wife, D'Anne.

In a few minutes, all the guests were herded outside the hotel in an atmosphere of grand anticipation. The busy motor court had been completely cleared of other vehicles. In the center of the court, against a backdrop of bougainvillea and impatiens with the dramatic desert mountains in the distance, was a white Ferrari with a big red bow on it.*

Nicole ran to the car and jumped up and down gleefully. "I *knew* I was gonna get it! I *knew* I was gonna get it!" she trilled. It was the car of her dreams, and a companion car to O.J.'s red one.

Just as he had done on this very day six years before, O.J. had redeemed his bad behavior with a gift-wrapped dream car. Except now his panache and generosity were being revealed not merely to the Brown family but to *all* of Nicole's friends.

Now he would have them all in his pocket.

* * *

*This would be the last car Nicole would ever own. Nicole eventually had vehicles with four-wheel drive to ferry her children around in, but these were all registered to O.J. and some were on "loan" from Hertz.

As spring turned to summer, Nicole began making plans for her wedding. She wanted the actual ceremony to be very private. In fact, she wanted no friend except Linda Schulman present. Her reason? "She didn't want people to see her getting married to O.J. after what everyone knew she had gone through with him," Linda says. "She didn't want them pitying her or whispering about her."

It was hard to hold on to the dream of a traditional wedding, with all the hope and piety involved, while dealing with such an imperfect relationship—and one that she had been struggling with for seven years. "Nicole came over to the house one day," Kris Jenner (then Kardashian) recalls, "a few months before their wedding. We were talking about O.J.'s not being true blue. She said that he had really promised to turn his whole life around. He was going to be baptized at the wedding. He was promising her that he wouldn't cheat on her anymore—that after they married, he would be faithful. He and Marcus and my then-brother-in-law Tom Kardashian were taking their Bible study class with Donn Moomaw [who had not yet admitted his own personal lapses*] and he was getting a lot out of it. They all were. I remember thinking, 'This is great. Everything's changing for them.' "

During Thanksgiving weekend in 1984, O.J. and Nicole were in Laguna with her family. A group of people had gone out to dinner, including one of Lou Brown's daughters from his previous marriage. They had taken two cars to the restaurant. As the group was leaving the restaurant, O.J.'s and Nicole's fighting made the others want to avoid getting into their car. ("The two of them constantly had that

*In February 1993, Reverend Moomaw, of the Bel Air Presbyterian Church, asked his parishioners' forgiveness for having "stepped over the line of acceptable behavior with some members of the congregation." It is widely speculated that this may have meant that he, a married man with five children, had been involved with a parishioner.

bickering in their life," Tom McCollum observes. "Whether it was about having a child, going to a celebrity event, or who they were socializing with.") O.J. and Nicole were alone in the first car; everyone else crammed into the second.

Suddenly, O.J. ground his car to a halt. Then he started up slowly again and—according to an account that Lou's daughter gave to another person—all of a sudden the passenger door shot open and Nicole was *pushed out* of the car.

O.J. drove off.

There was dead silence in the second car. The driver inched forward to where Nicole was, and she got in. Nobody said anything. Lou's daughter reportedly described this incident as follows: "It was the weirdest thing I have ever seen: The next morning it was as if nothing had happened. No one said anything. It was as if it was a normal occurrence."

At least one other act of violence seems to have occurred during the months before the wedding.

Ron and Nina Shipp dropped by one night. O.J. was alone. He invited them to a movie, but they declined. "Where's Nicole?" Nina asked, thinking about their girl talk on the bar stools of this very room three years earlier. Nicole had so envied Nina's being married; now Nina wanted to congratulate *her* on her coming wedding.

"She went to her parents'; we had a fight; she got pissed," is how O.J. put it.

In Nicole's version of the story, however, O.J. shoved her, and she fell and her leg got scratched on a metal table.

Ron didn't know what to think. As was the case with so many of O.J.'s friends, to Ron he was a hero. Ron was a junior in high school and the star running back on his school's varsity team when O.J. had his banner year at SC. The next year, Ron (who also went on to SC and joined its football team as a walk-on) changed his number to "32." Although their adult friendship had certainly knocked hero worship out of the equation—Ron's being a cop gave him a certain authority in O.J.'s crowd even though he couldn't, as he put it, "hang with them, economically"—it would still take a lot to get Ron to think ill of O.J.

But Ron Shipp had an inviolable sense of right and wrong, and despite his very apparent jocularity and his decided love of partying ("I ain't no saint," he liked to say), he was endearingly old-fashioned. Not many others in O.J.'s crowd used the words "heck" and "darn" in mixed company so often. Or had dinner with their long-married mother and father every other week. Ron Shipp grew up in a home where people did not hit one another. In his world view, striking a woman was one of the most repugnant—and most cowardly—things a man could do.

Could O.J. really have struck Nicole? For now, Ron pushed the question away. It was the only way he could deal with it.

Despite this escalating violence, Nicole proceeded with her wedding plans. Perhaps she believed marriage would improve O.J.'s temper as well as his faithfulness. Apparently, she had become skilled at blocking out the incidents of violence after they were over. She could recover quickly and pretend they hadn't happened. She drew a veil of privacy over her life, and her friends respected it. They say: "You didn't pry with Nicole." "She didn't invite a lot of questions." "She told you what she wanted to tell you—no more."

She must have known that dwelling on the abuse would force her to take real stock of her dangerous relationship. Taking stock would mean leaving O.J., and that she simply would not do. She had a gorgeous, glamorous, idolized, rich boyfriend—a man who, however violent he could get, was madly in love with her and showed it in private as well as grandly public ways that were romantic in the conventional sense of the word. The fact that he was black probably made the relationship more romantic.

Who could turn down that drama, that larger-than-life quality? Not a lot of young women. One's early twenties is a time for such relationships, most of which eventually turn out to be too exhausting to stay with.

Nicole stayed with hers.

Nicole wanted every detail of her wedding to be perfect, and Linda Schulman, as usual, was her partner in planning. "We made the party favors—with Nicole, there always had to be party favors—and put them in little baskets," Linda says. "She had to have real lace tablecloths—Ricky had them made for her—and there was going to be chocolate everywhere! Flowers everywhere! All over the tables." Linda also started off Nicole's registry purchase of beautiful Bernardo china.

"Nicole was so excited about her dress," Linda remembers—and so superstitious and traditional "she wouldn't even let me see it." She dressed for her wedding alone, in the bedroom at Rockingham, while her sisters waited downstairs. "She *did* have her wedding," Linda says, with a sad hint of triumph.

On February 2, 1985, Nicole was a beautiful bride in a quadruple-tiered white embroidered lace dress with a straight skirt and mesh see-through portions around the breast and on the long sleeves. Her new short hair was adorned with a seed-pearl ornament. Around her neck she wore a "tennis" necklace of diamonds, O.J.'s wedding gift to his bride.

She carried a bouquet of white lilies and baby's breath, and O.J. had a sprig of white flowers in the lapel of his tuxedo.

O.J. was baptized just before the ceremony. Denise was maid of honor*; Jason and A.C. were both best men.

Lou walked his daughter around the side of the house to the strains of "Lohengrin." When asked about how he felt at that moment, he says evenly, "I've always been happy when

*Denise's marriage had been annulled in July 1984.

my kids are happy—and I commiserate with them when they're unhappy, but I remind them that it was their own doing that got them into this unhappiness."

When Judi Brown interrupts her husband's distant and generalized answer to say, "Lou, you were pretty proud, I think, when you walked Nicole down the aisle," Lou says, "Proud?" His face and manner have been disciplined into calm acceptance, but his words betray a different emotion. "It is hard for me to separate my feelings then about her marrying him from what I feel about him now."

Guests flooded the tented backyard right after the ceremony and danced all night to a band's rendition of Motown hits. When it came time for toasts and speeches, Judi made a speech about how important respect is in a marriage. She said that O.J. and Nicole respected each other. A.C. and Wayne Hughes also spoke. Then the bride's surprise present to the groom—a thirty-five-foot-tall heart emblazoned with the words NICOLE LOVES O.J., with fireworks shooting off around it—was wheeled out and the six-tiered wedding cake was cut.

There was more dancing. "Most people stay at a wedding five hours, tops," notes Rocco Cedrone. "People stayed at *this* wedding eleven, twelve hours." At one point, D'Anne LeBon and Nicole found themselves in Nicole's upstairs bathroom, repairing the makeup on their flushed faces. D'Anne saw a pile of packets of birth control pills stuffed in a drawer as if they weren't needed. "Are you and O.J. trying?" D'Anne asked. "We-ell," Nicole answered, eyes dancing. "A little more than 'trying.' We *are.*"

Afterward, as dark turned to dawn, Nicole and O.J. collapsed in their wedding clothes on the couch in the kitchen. They looked like two kittens sleeping in each other's arms, one observer thought.

The wedding over, Nicole now prepared excitedly for the birth of her baby. If it was a girl (as she hoped), she would name her "Sydney"; she had long loved that name, with its jaunty androgyny.

O.J. and Nicole spared no expense in furnishing the baby's room. An oval white wrought-iron bed frame was suspended from a big arch; its mattress was custom-made and covered by sheets of fine linen.

Two showers were given for Nicole*: one was thrown by Wayne Hughes' wife, the second was co-hosted by Linda Schulman, Kris Kardashian, and Robin Greer, at Robin and Mark Slotkin's large, modern home on north Elm Drive (which was eventually sold to Jose and Kitty Menendez). As all the women sat around eating gourmet omelettes showily prepared over flames before their eyes by the Omelette Man, no one could know that in almost four years to the day, two handsome, privileged young men would burst into this very room with loaded rifles and assassinate their mother and father.

For O.J. and Nicole's crowd it seemed that babies were in the air. Linda had just given birth to a healthy baby boy, Matthew. In fact, Robin, Mark, Nicole, and Kris had been *in* Linda's hospital room right before she delivered (Nicole asking pointedly, "How much does it hurt? What do the pains feel like?"), all silently praying that this baby would be all right, unlike the stillbirth that had preceded it. O.J. held tiny Matthew Schulman in his arms, "and he was *so* full of love," Linda recalls, "it was like this was the most *wonderful* baby in the world."

Pam and Allen Schwartz had a brand-new daughter, Danielle. And Nina and Ron Shipp had recently had a baby son, whom they named David.

One day when Nicole was halfway through her pregnancy and David was a few months old, Nicole called Nina, sounding anxious and worried. "I've got to see a picture of David!" she said. "What does his hair look like? Is it nappy? O.J.'s hair is so nappy."

---

*Actually, Nicole hadn't needed the showers at all. She later told Cici Shahian, "I had no *idea* O.J. had so many fans until I had Sydney. People we never met sent presents. Old ladies in Minnesota crocheted sweaters! I didn't have to buy her clothes for two years."

Nina put Nicole at ease. (Ron, to whom Nicole had first asked that question, had laughed. He wasn't offended; he thought it was cute.) "David has very loose curls," Nina replied. Nicole seemed much relieved. "Don't worry, the hair will be fine," Nina said, adding, "The hair is the least of your worries."

Indeed, although Nina Shipp did not know this, Nicole did have more than her share of worries. For one thing, despite his Bible study sessions with Reverend Moomaw, O.J.'s fidelity vow seemed to be extremely short-lived. D'Anne LeBon, then a stewardess on American Airlines—the airline that was O.J.'s favorite*—encountered another stewardess who dreamily mentioned her recent liaison with him. "Don't you know he's *married?*" D'Anne asked indignantly.

The other stewardess seemed surprised. "He didn't say anything about *that.*"

"Well, he *is.* To a good friend of mine." D'Anne was as annoyed with this woman as her husband, David, had been with O.J. in the Ritz Carlton men's room. Did O.J. have to humiliate Nicole, practically to her *face?* "And they're having a baby."

D'Anne spared Nicole the news of this conversation.

But what Nicole could not escape from was O.J.'s displeasure with her physical appearance when she was pregnant. Though she was not the first wife in history to learn that the phrase "There's nothing as beautiful as a pregnant woman" is more easily uttered than believed, the realization that she wasn't alone in feeling her husband hated the way she looked didn't assuage her pain.

"She was the most miserable woman during her pregnancy," Judi Brown says. "O.J. really was not nice to her. 'You're too fat,' 'You're gaining too much weight,' he would say. 'Look at your legs . . .' 'Look at your arms . . .' It's hard to be pregnant, period. You're very sensitive. And when

---

*It was an American flight he took to Chicago and back right after the murders.

your husband doesn't like it, it's worse. She was happy to be having the baby, but it wasn't a happy time for her."

On top of O.J.'s apparent cheating and his criticism of her body, there was at least one incident of violence during the pregnancy. According to separate accounts Nicole gave to two people (one a friend, the other a trusted babysitter), one day she drove home from a lunch date to find O.J. "going freakin' nuts—*freakin'* nuts—with a baseball bat." He banged on the front windshield, cracking it, while Nicole was in the car. She was terrified. She ran into the house and called the police. When they arrived, O.J. said, "This is *my* car! I can do anything I want with it!" The police, Nicole told a friend, pronounced the incident a "love spat" and left the premises.*

On October 17, 1985, Sydney Brooke Simpson was born at St. John's Hospital in Santa Monica. Shortly before the birth, as a family videotape reveals, O.J., suited up in green hospital gown and surgical mask (they had taken Lamaze classes and he assisted in the delivery), said, "I feel excited. Nicole and I, we're having our first little Zebra," an obvious reference to the baby's biracial parentage. (Sammy Davis, Jr., pioneered this distasteful approach by saying he didn't care if his and Mai Britt's children "come out polka-dotted.") After the Caesarean birth, Nicole cradled tiny Sydney and as captured on videotape purred, "My little pumpkin. . . . I don't believe I had this baby!" O.J.'s line, borrowing from *Porgy and Bess,* was, "She's smilin' 'cause her daddy's rich and her mama's good-lookin'."

The birth changed everything for Nicole. Judi says, "She

---

*One of the officers who came out on this call was Mark Fuhrman, who, nine years later, would be the first officer to arrive at the scene of the murders of Nicole and Ronald Goldman, as well as the officer who found, at Rockingham, the right-hand glove that matched the left-hand glove that had been found at Bundy. According to police reports, both O.J. and Nicole stated that the police made seven other such calls (by December 31, 1988) and, each time, left without doing anything.

would not give me Sydney to hold! Her attitude was, 'This child—nobody can do this but me!' She was the happiest mother. That baby was just her heaven."

O.J., on the other hand, was having trouble finding his center, his goals. Within a year of Sydney's birth a project he was excited about—his Orenthal Productions' *Heart and Soul* (billed as the first African-American soap opera)—would be derailed and he would be let go from *ABC's Monday Night Football,* left to cover less important sporting events for ESPN. His life as an endorser had a momentum of its own by now, oiled by his charismatic geniality. He was a marvel at stockholders' meetings; nobody could work a crowd of middle-aged white guys like the Juice. O.J.'s acting career was stalled: He hadn't made a film since his 1980 NBC-TV movie *Goldie and the Boxer,* which was very successful and had been mounted by his own production company. (The film horizon would brighten in time when, in 1988, he created the role of the bumbling Detective Nordberg in what would become the wildly successful Leslie Nielsen/Priscilla Presley *Naked Gun* series.)

What O.J. *wanted* to be was an executive—and a politician. His dream of becoming a state senator was at its peak now, and the group he aspired to was the establishment elite. "In this he was very naive," says Tom McCollum, who did mix a bit with that crowd. "He had this oozing confidence that anything he wanted he could attain; it was far beyond his capability or willingness to pay dues in the business and social and intellectual worlds. He could literally look at Maria Callas, with Aristotle Onassis, and think she should be with the Juice instead. [But he might also look at the prostitutes on Hollywood Boulevard and think the same thing.] Nicole wasn't socially driven, though *she* loved the ride. She was perfectly happy as a homebody rising no higher than Laguna society."

After O.J. told him that he wanted to be on the board of directors of Hertz, Tom flooded O.J. with books on how to be a capitalistic entrepreneur. O.J. was, after all, a voracious reader. So Tom, hoping to nurture O.J. and get a protégé in business, "gave Juice registration books on how to go public, what the security rules were all about, all the way back to the 1933 Securities and Exchange Act, all kinds of entrepreneurial books on what it takes to set up a corporation and how to be a director. But the guy would rather read Ken Follett every time. The necessary homework just wasn't done. Eventually Juice realized he wasn't going to be on a board of directors, he wasn't going to run for office. 'I'm too lazy,' 'I am what I am,' he would say. He accepted it without bitterness, but with a sadness. It had been a dream."

O.J.'s relationship with his son Jason had become troubled. In 1983, he had sued Marguerite for custody of Jason and his request had been denied by the court. But if the custody suit was an act of love, it may not have felt that way to Jason.

Though by most accounts a sweet, likable boy, Jason wasn't athletic or even terribly well-coordinated (though he did eventually play on the SC football team). Joe Kolkowitz tried to teach him tennis, but he didn't get the hang of it too well. A.C. took him to his Little League games, but he wasn't a star. In a commercial Fred Levinson used him in, he had a difficult time catching a football. One friend of O.J.'s says, "Jason seemed always to be floating around on the perimeter, trying to be a part of things. I think when you have a famous father you have to do one of two things: either be as good as he is or accept the fact that you're not." O.J.'s friends say he did not push Jason to be an athlete, nor did he evince disappointment in the boy. But then, perhaps they didn't know everything that went on between father and son.

One night in 1986, when Jason was fifteen, Rolf and Maria Baur were in the house with him and a group of his friends. O.J. and Nicole were vacationing with Sydney, and Arnelle was at her mother's house in the San Fernando Valley. The kids downstairs were hanging out, but the loud, banging noise, punctuated by angry screams, went frighteningly beyond the typical sounds of rowdy high-school boys.

Rolf threw on a bathrobe and raced downstairs and into the backyard. There he came upon an angry, seemingly inebriated Jason swinging a baseball bat at the life-sized black bronze statue of his father. O.J. *loved* that statue! One of Rolf's jobs was to spray it with WD-40, an oily liquid compound, to keep it nice and shiny. Now Jason was whacking at it so hard its bolts came out and it was starting to topple off its pedestal. (Which, to furious Jason, may have been the point.)

But the most shocking thing wasn't what Jason was doing but what he was *saying*. "I hate my father! I hate my father! I hate my father! I hate my father!" he screamed as he swung.

Rolf anchored the statue and tried to calm the fevered Jason, but it did no good. Rolf was terrified of what might happen next. He picked up the phone and woke up Ron Shipp and begged him to come over.

Shipp drove there at once and calmed Jason down. He sat for over an hour with the boy. According to someone who heard the conversation, Jason said, "My dad's never around. And when he is, all he does is criticize me."

"You've got to approach your dad," Shipp was heard to say. "Say, 'Let's talk. There are things that are bothering me.'"

"I can't tell him that," Jason protested. "And he can't find out what I did tonight, or he'll kick my butt."

"Look, dude," Shipp reassured him, "*I'll* talk to your dad for you. I'll explain it, and he *won't* kick your butt."

When Ron Shipp went to O.J. and told him that he had spoken to Jason, O.J. insisted on being told the substance of that conversation. Ron demurred, saying he had promised Jason he would not tell. O.J. then promised Ron he would *not* punish Jason—he just *had* to know what Jason said and did. Ron decided to take O.J. at his word. "Look," he said, "Jason's upset. He says he never gets to see and talk to you. That you don't understand him. . . ." He continued along this vein.

Later Nicole told Ron that O.J., breaking his word to Ron, had "beaten the shit out of Jason." Ron felt terrible that

Jason was punished and that he had unintentionally betrayed him.

But then, Ron Shipp knew that dealing with families in turmoil was full of betrayals and broken promises. One of the biggest of these promises was the one never again to be violent. Ron understood this all too well because he was now teaching the dynamics of domestic violence to his fellow officers at a special class set up at the Los Angeles Police Academy. Ron was one of six LAPD domestic violence experts. Teaching the course was grueling—and Ron and his partner understood why domestic violence was the *only* class the department would not allow the press to sit in on: Bored and derisive remarks abounded—"Hey, Ron, why are you teaching this crap?" It almost seemed as if half of the cops who took the class were batterers themselves! And the female cops (Ron thought this was particularly sick) tended to *side with* the batterers in their critiques of the role-playing sessions. *They* had come from families where a man's use of force on a woman was considered normal.

Ron's immersion into the dynamics of domestic violence opened his eyes about himself. Even though he would never lay a hand on Nina, he began to wonder about his verbal behavior, his assumptions and attitudes.

"Do I ever try to control you?" he asked his wife one day.

She immediately answered, "Yes!"

He and Nina then had a long talk. As a result, Ron was now going out of his way to change his behavior—assumption by assumption, response by response.

Ron Shipp and Rolf Baur went out and got drunk one night after their exhausting evening with Jason. As a result, word of Ron's new work in the field of domestic violence eventually got back to Nicole. It was something she would not forget.

As for Jason, the next year, when he was sixteen, he started experimenting with cocaine with some neighborhood friends. During one session, he had a seizure and was rushed to the hospital. The incident was kept out of the press. The parents of all the teens involved held a sober meeting at another house on Rockingham. O.J. said several times that evening, "I want to get to the bottom of this. *Who* gave my son cocaine?"

Someone present at that meeting, who knew about Simpson's own cocaine use, listened to O.J. and wondered, "Why all the surprise and indignation? A son picks up things from his father."

After another incident, when Jason took off with one of the Ferraris, he was sent to military school.*

Shortly after Sydney's birth, the Simpsons undertook a healthier lifestyle. Nicole started first. In an effort to lose weight, she would get up early in the morning and work out in her home gym in the garage: pop her Jane Fonda Workout tape into the VCR and jump on the treadmill (later the Stairmaster too) and pick up weights. Kris Kardashian often came by. Kris had had another baby—a boy—in March of 1987. "She and Nicole were always dieting," someone who saw them in the house a lot says. "Always taping what-to-eat signs on the refrigerator."

Kris' own needs were starting to shift a bit now that she had had her fourth child. She had come to Beverly Hills an impressionable young girl, on the arm of an older man for whom she had promptly made a home. But Kris would soon begin wondering if she loved Robert Kardashian in a romantic way, or merely as a brother. However glamorous and seemingly fast-track Kris' life was, she had never gone through the stage that most young people need to go through: rebellion.

(Nicole, too, snapped up right out of high school by an older man as Kris had been, hadn't gone through rebellion either—hadn't even had a devil-may-care dating binge. But

*Jason Simpson's problems followed him into young adulthood. He received a citation for drunk driving in 1990 and in 1992 received two years' probation for assaulting his employer, a restaurateur (Jason has worked intermittently as a chef).

Nicole's and O.J.'s highly tempestuous relationship obscured the fact of her very substantial innocence.)

If Kris and Nicole had led somewhat restricted lives, they were soon to meet someone whose experience had been far different. One day, at a parents' meeting at the Beverly Hills Presbyterian Church's preschool, Kris saw a young mother she hadn't noticed before at the endless round of school events that had been her life for six years. "She had this huge smile on her face, and she was happy and upbeat and bubbling around and she had this great style and great personality. And I looked around at all the other women, who looked somber and bored, and I thought, 'Who *is* this girl? I want to be friends with her!' "

The two women did become friends and so did their same-aged daughters, Khloe and Francesca. The woman was a firecracker with her high-fashion clothes and her foxy airs and her penchant for misbehavior and adventure. She was one of those women whom other slightly more naive women instinctively turn to for a certain brand of life lessons.

Her name was Faye Resnick.

One thing that kept the conflict level between Nicole and O.J. high was money—he was always telling her that her need to keep every vase in the house filled with fresh flowers was pushing them over the limit of the $5,000 monthly household budget Skip Taft had put them on. However, there were also many tender moments. "They were romantic," says Rolf Baur. "There was lots of romance. They'd go around hugging each other. He called her 'Nick' and 'Sweets.' " Their bedroom itself was certainly romantic—French country curtains and bedspread, a Louis XV canopied bed. (The room would be modernized in the 1989 renovation.) They often took walks through the neighborhood with Sydney in the carriage or stroller; or, when she was asleep under the nanny's watchful eye, alone with each other, each holding the leash of one of the two blue-tongued chows, Chubb and Shiba.

Soon after Nicole started her morning schedule, O.J.

switched to one, too. He had fallen in love with golf. Between the tennis and the golf, he would roll into the house in the early evening and say to Rolf Baur, "Rolf, talk to me, I'm tired," then would go upstairs and fall asleep with the TV on.

Eventually, when O.J. was diagnosed with arthritis (it is possible he has lupus as well), the Simpsons completely changed their eating habits. Nicole bought juicers, and both of them—she the German cook and he the barbecue fan—reduced their intake of red meat and fat. Parenthood had toned them down—sort of.

The golfing, for example. It was, of course, a staid, suburban sport, but O.J. played it his own way.

"With golf as with so much else, O.J. could never shut up," says Tom McCollum, who teed off with him for years, mostly in Laguna but also on "almost every golf course known to man." "He'd walk in front of you; you'd be putting and he'd start talking to someone at the four tee and you couldn't concentrate," says McCollum. "But if *you* ever did that to *him,* he'd go crazy." O.J. also had his own rules. "One of the wonderful things about golf is that it's a gentleman's game and one calls penalties on oneself. But *that* would be very un-Simpson-like," says McCollum. "He wouldn't dream of calling a penalty on himself. And there was always an argument when it was brought up that there was a penalty due."

O.J., McCollum, and Kolkowitz played each other for hundreds of dollars, and to this end, O.J. made an "off-the-premises" rule, whereby a bet was off if the losing player left the golf course before the winning player collected from him. "So, constantly, Simpson would go run and have one of the stewards or caddies very surreptitiously put his golf bag in the back of his car right after we finished," says McCollum. "And then we'd be sitting down and Juice would start off on one of his stories: 'When I was in the huddle . . .' and everybody was mesmerized—all these sycophants on the edges of their chairs. In the meantime, you're trying to get your two hundred dollars from him. You get up to go to the bathroom and you come out—and all of a sudden he's in his red Ferrari or his Rolls-Royce, taking off down the road, giving you a one-fingered salute and a grin so big you could stick a banana in his mouth sideways."

But O.J.'s favorite trick during a round was this: He carried an extra ball in his pants—"between his underwear and his slacks," McCollum explains. When his real ball would go off the green and everybody went to look for it, "he'd slide the spare ball down out of his pants leg. Everybody's out there looking for the ball—behind a tree, between houses—and suddenly he'd go, 'Hey!' Now, *we've* seen him walking around; he's out of the cart and nowhere *near* a ball! But he goes, 'Hey!'—and there's the ball, like an Easter egg, in the rough, with a very nice shot at the eighteenth green. And all our money is riding on it. Once he even had the ball sitting on a tee. I said, 'Juice, come on, let's play fair.' He said, 'I can't help it if the ball landed on the goddamn tee!' Finally, one day in Laguna Beach, Kolkowitz and I caught him at it—'cause he couldn't get the second ball out of his pants."

The fellows at Riviera Country Club on Sunset Boulevard, which O.J. joined in the late eighties and upon whose course he played almost every morning he was in town (up to and including June 12, 1994), wondered about these propitious ball-findings. And they wondered why O.J. would "sweat," as one put it, when his favorite caddy, a famous comedian's son, wasn't available. This caddy had an uncanny knack for finding Simpson's out-of-bounds ball in positions very convenient for his next putt.

One evening shortly after O.J. joined Riviera, he and a number of Riviera golfers—Alan Austin, now-deceased rock-group manager Tom Hewlett, Simpson, and McCollum—were having a dinner meeting at a restaurant on Canon Drive. When O.J. got up to go to the bathroom, the others started telling a story about how a ball O.J. had hit, which they all could have *sworn* went behind a tree, ended up in a position very advantageous to him. These guys had played gin with O.J., so they *knew* the explanation already. All faces turned to Tom as one of them asked, "Is it *possible,* McCollum, that . . . ?"

". . . that Mr. Simpson"—Tom spin-controlled their accusation with his ever-ready formality—"pre*var*icates slightly?"

"Cheats!" one of the men amended bluntly.

"Yeah, *cheats!"* said another.

"Now, now, gentlemen," Tom said, "I wouldn't use that word. Gentlemen, he's new, he's very competitive. Perhaps a gentleman-to-gentleman talk is in order."

Instead of that talk, the guys solved the problem by showing up on the green with an extra caddy. "What's that fifth caddy for?" O.J. asked.

"We hired him to watch *your* caddy!" came the answer.

The group played the entire eighteen holes with the extra caddy standing vigil.

O.J., McCollum, and often Kolkowitz played golf almost every summer morning at Monarch Bay in the last couple of years of the eighties. They played for $200 or $300 a game and referred to one another as "Bitch"—the vowel drawlingly elongated, the tone gutteral—during their hours on the fairway. Nicole and O.J. owned several condos in the development, using one and renting the others. Eventually, Skip Taft took a condo in the development. So did Marcus Allen. It was the old turf, transferred south.

One night, in order to get to Laguna from the *Naked Gun* set in the Valley, O.J. took the 405 at 120 miles per hour. When a cop finally flagged him over, he almost charmed his way out of a ticket by offering the officer his car keys and asking him if *he* could drive his Ferrari Testarossa under the limit.

Soon after, it appeared that O.J.'s penchant for speed had once again gotten him in trouble. "I was going a hundred and forty this time," he cried out to McCollum, waking him up at four in the morning. "I was arrested. Your boy is in jail. I only got a couple of hundred dollars on me and it's a fifteen-hundred-dollar fine. If you hurry up, we can still tee off at six."

McCollum scrambled out of bed, dressed, tore down the 405, almost getting a ticket himself, to get to the Crown Valley Parkway police station by six. "Where's O.J.? I've got the money! Here it is! Let him out!" he ran in, screaming. "The cops went, 'O.J. who?' and looked at me like I was ranting and drunk."

At that moment McCollum's cellular phone rang. "April Fools, you dumb bitch," came O.J.'s voice (Kolkowitz was with him). "We're on the first tee."

There was a Dagwood and Blondie aspect to the Simpsons' relationship, and the day that Tom McCollum moved into the Monarch Bay condo he rented from them afforded a prime example of it. The apartment's refrigerator hadn't yet arrived, so Nicole promised Tom she would go out and buy one herself and have it in the condo by the time he moved in and unpacked (he had been staying at the Ritz).

"Fine," Tom said. "I'm playing golf with Largehead and Kolkowitz this morning, so it will probably be there when we get back."

Nicole blew up at O.J. *"You're* out there, your buddy's going to rent my place, and I'm delivering the goddamn refrigerator while *you're* playing golf!" O.J.'s golf habit was really beginning to get under her skin.

"I'll hire someone to deliver the refrigerator," Tom offered, to ease her annoyance.

"No, no, no, I'll be there with the refrigerator," Nicole promised. ("Nicole was honorable as usual," says Tom.)

So the threesome played their golf game while Nicole, leaving Sydney with her parents, drove down to Sears, bought a refrigerator, and arranged for its delivery. O.J. lost the golf game and, invoking his off-the-premises rule, sped off in his own golf cart, chug-chug-chugging down the public road toward the country club exit. Kolkowitz and McCollum floored their own cart and were fast on his tail. A hot golf-cart chase ensued—it must have looked like an outtake from an old Walt Disney movie—with O.J. shouting, "You bitches . . . !" as Joe and Tom overtook him and beat him out the gate.

Right outside the gate, "there's Nicole," Tom recalls, "with her hands on her hips, leaning on her white Ferrari, madder than hell. 'Where have you been? The refrigerator's not here yet! Where's Largehead?' "

While O.J. was still catching up with them, Tom, Joe, and Nicole went back up to the Simpsons' condo and waited. And waited and waited. *Where* was O.J.? they wondered. He had been right on their tail. How long could it take him to cart up the goddamn hill?

Suddenly, sirens wailed outside the window. Tom became alarmed. "Joe," he asked, "is it possible he got hit?"

The prospect of their strong, macho friend being totaled by a Mack truck sent them racing outside. False alarm—the sirens were for someone else. But what they did see was typical O.J. "There's a big fat Mexican guy sitting on the wall, with the refrigerator in his hand cart. And there's O.J. standing there going, 'Yeah, and you know, I'm hitting this bitch three hundred yards, three hundred yards . . .' We're like, 'Juice, we're *waiting* for that refrigerator!' And he's, 'Oh, yeah, the refrigerator.' He takes out five bucks and hands it to the Mexican, 'Here, thanks a lot, man.'

"And the guy says, *'No hablo ingles.'* He doesn't understand a word of English, and Juice has been talking to him about an old football game for twenty minutes! And Nicole is shaking her head and rolling her eyes and going, 'What an asshole. . . .'

"And that's typical O.J. and Nicole: the big fight, then the big production. Then they'd stand there and argue and have a few beers. Finally, they'd be all lovey-dovey—kissing and hugging—and he'd tell everyone, 'My woman's got the greatest booty,' and that would be the end of that."

But the fights did not always end amicably. O.J. by now had a permanent mistress—Tawny Kitaen, the layered-haired actress (who now appears on television's *America's*

Funniest People). Nicole had discovered the depth of his attachment to Tawny when, one day in going through O.J.'s home office, she came upon a jewelry box. Opening it, she found a pair of diamond stud earrings set in white gold. Because her birthday was coming up, she put them back where she found them so as not to spoil O.J.'s surprise. But her birthday came and went, and this particular gift was not proffered. Eventually Nicole learned that the recipient of the earrings had been Tawny.

By now, Nicole was seriously worried about the risks of being married to so flagrant a philanderer—not just the risks to her fraying emotions, but the risks to her health. What if O.J. contracted AIDS from one of these liaisons?

She begged him, again and again, to wear a condom when they made love. He refused, claiming condoms were uncomfortable. "What do I *do?*" she asked a female friend. "If he won't wear one with me, you can bet he's not wearing one with anyone else!"

Nicole became desperate. Even though others saw her as brisk and private, Tom McCollum—who had been the first to notice her bitten-down fingernails years before—had always seen a deeply vulnerable woman. He says: "Nicky was so lonely, so insecure, so dying for companionship and to get her woes about O.J. out, sometimes she'd just talk to anybody. She was a sweet, darling girl and so visceral—she was close to the earth. She would get so pissed at O.J., she would pour her whole heart out. 'Nicky, you've got to learn who the hell you can trust,' I would say to her. 'I know you're going through living hell occasionally but don't tell everybody.'"

Eventually, Nicole began to call Tom, who had, after all, developed the forerunner to the HIV test kit, to ask questions about AIDS and beg him to get O.J. to get an AIDS test. Tom never told O.J. about her calls to him. He did not think O.J. would take too well to an exhortation to be AIDS-tested—"Juice was better at giving criticism than getting it," says Tom, but he knew how vulnerable O.J. was when he felt he had pushed things enough so that Nicole might actually leave him. At those moments, he was like Jell-O. Tom waited for the proper time, when O.J. would be more receptive to doing something to please Nicole.

That time would come in short order.

It began to seem to some people that, as one male friend puts it, "O.J. was driving Nicole crazy. When you're with someone who says green is pink and day is night, it makes you crazy. You can't respond normally anymore. O.J.'s other women—it was endless. And it hurt her and made her furious every time. She couldn't adjust to it like some wives do. She couldn't lie down and accept it." The friend sighs. "Guys like that, they need a passive woman. It's part of the deal. Nicole, she was too much of a fighter, bless her heart . . . for all the good it did her."

One male friend says he saw Nicole "slap O.J. and kick him in the balls at least three times during the eighties. (Not that he didn't deserve it!) Of course he acted like it didn't hurt—he was Mr. Macho. But when he said, in that note he wrote [on June 17, 1994], that he was a 'battered husband,' that's what I think he was referring to."

Then there was the Jennifer Young and Victoria Sellars incident.

The two young women, the daughters of Gig Young and realtor Elaine Young (who sold O.J. the Rockingham house) and Peter Sellars and Britt Eklund, respectively, were waiting for a table at LaScala Boutique one afternoon (Jennifer believes it was in 1988) when O.J. and Joe Stellini walked in.

Their recounting of the incident reveals how O.J.'s Teflon charm protected him from any blame for his years of emotional abuse of Nicole—abuse that finally made *her* act out publicly in a way that *he* knew not to. This is a chillingly classic scenario: A man (or mate of either gender, actually) who is *so* good at presenting an appealing facade to the world provokes his spouse to "prove" to others, in a humiliating and public way, that their problems are *her* fault. That *he* is lovable, easygoing, reasonable, and that *she* is crazy.

According to Jennifer Young, this is what happened:

"The maître d' came over and said, 'O.J. and his friend would like you to join them for lunch.' We said, 'Sure, why not?' He was at the height of his career; I remember my mom had sold him his house; we were flattered.

"So we sat down and had lunch. He was super nice, very genuine, very sweet. 'What can I get you?' 'Would you like dessert?' That kind of stuff. After lunch he was nice enough to say, 'Why don't I walk you two girls to your car?' So we said, 'Sure.' "

So far so good: O.J. is Prince Charming.

They all walked down Rodeo Drive, "and all of a sudden out of nowhere Nicole pulls up in her black convertible Mercedes with her hair pulled back in a bun. I remember *verbatim* what she said because it scared the hell out of me: 'You mother*fucker,* if you're going to fucking *cheat* on me why don't you pick someone *pretty?!'*

"She just pulled up and *screeched* it. We were shaking! Was she gonna beat us up? Gonna kill us? Oh, my God . . .

"We walked into a store, hoping that Nicole would calm down. We stayed in the store ten, fifteen minutes, hoping we could get back to our car safely. That was *not* happening. She kept circling around the block. She pulled up at the corner of Brighton and Rodeo, screaming at the top of her lungs. O.J. was as calm as could be. You would think if he had such a bad temper, it would really show, but instead he walked to her car and tried to calm her down, like, 'Listen, Nicole, this is nothing, these girls . . .' But she wouldn't take no for an answer. She was just screaming. He was embarrassed! She circled the block again, we walked into another store.

"She pulled up again. She pulled something out of her glove compartment, opening the door. I'm thinking, 'A gun?! A knife?!' We were shaking!

"As fate would have it a cop either heard her screaming,

or else he was just passing through . . . but he pulled up right behind her. She looked at him in the rearview mirror, saw that it was a cop, shut the glove compartment, closed the door, took off. Phew. . . ."

Jennifer Young is one of many people who believe, as she puts it, "O.J. could never have committed those murders because I *saw,* with my own eyes, how lovely and calm he is."

From time to time, fatigued and honest friends would tell the two of them, "You know, you're both wonderful people, but maybe you shouldn't be *together."* However, they both had an image of the perfect family, and that included another child. Mommy, daddy, sister, brother: that was how it was supposed to be. And that is what they would get for themselves.

At the end of 1987 Nicole became pregnant again. Now Sydney would have a baby sibling. But the pregnancy carried harrowing moments for Nicole—if not medically, then emotionally.

According to an account she wrote, which was found in her Bundy Drive house after her death and disclosed to someone close to the Brown family, one night early in her pregnancy, she came home with Sydney later than O.J. liked, after the two saw "Disney on Ice" with her family. A.C. was also in the house. O.J. had been drinking. He started yelling. A.C. grabbed Sydney and took her into another room so she would not hear the commotion.

O.J. angrily told Nicole that he didn't like Sydney being out so late at night, then he derided Nicole's weight gain, calling her a "fat ass," telling her to have an abortion and, after Sydney had gone to bed, screaming, "I want you out of my fucking house."

Nicole says in her written account that when she tried to reason with O.J., he shouted, "Let me tell you how serious I am. I have a gun in my hand right now. Get the fuck out of here."

Nicole wrote that she quickly packed a suitcase, grabbed Sydney, and left.

Justin Ryan Simpson was born on August 6, 1988.

Nicole was still in Laguna with Sydney when she went into labor early. O.J. was at Rockingham. "It started to be evening," Judi recalls, "and Nicole was having labor pains every two minutes. I said, 'Nicole, have the baby here.' She said, 'No. I have my doctor in L.A. and Sydney has to be in her own bed. She misses her own bed.' "

So Nicole, Judi, Sydney, and Ruth (the German nanny) got in the car for the drive to L.A.

"I said, 'Nicole, I'm driving.' She said, '*No* way! You're too nervous. *I'm* driving.' " Judi tells this with that Oh-my-stubborn-daughter-I-can-never-win-with-her look on her face, a look every mother knows about. "So there she was—labor pains every two minutes, and *she's* driving!

"She's racing in the left lane—eighty miles an hour—thank God she didn't get a ticket! Of course we have O.J. on the car phone—he's standing in the driveway, he has the bag waiting. He's going, 'I can't *believe* she's driving! I can't believe she's having labor pains *on the freeway!'* We drive in, he's *way out* of himself, he's so angry and nervous! 'How could you *wait* so long?! Wait!' He's holding the bag and jumping up and down—like *he* was in labor. She's ignoring him and calmly walking Sydney inside, with *her* labor pains every two minutes. He's, 'Nick, *where are you GOING?*' " ("O.J.," Nicole once told a friend, "is a little old Jewish woman.")

Only after she put Sydney into her pajamas, said her prayers with her, and put her to bed did Nicole consent to be driven to the hospital. Calm, steely Nicole knew exactly what she wanted. "You know, you can have this baby normally," the doctor told her. She said, "No thank you. I've had enough labor pains. I want another Caesarean." Then she wrote a note: "I do not want my husband in the delivery room."

Despite having been shut out on the moment of his son's

birth, "O.J.'s face was shining all over—he was really proud," says Rolf Baur, who arrived at the hospital right after the birth. "He had another boy. He wanted a boy. He was so excited."

Home videotapes show Nicole cradling the baby in the hospital room and saying, "I was waiting for you! I saw you out the window!" as O.J. and Sydney walk into the room, ready to fetch them home. O.J. calls Justin "Crubby." Sydney is beaming. O.J. kisses Nicole, then the baby. Sydney delights in her tiny brother. They seem like such a happy family.

The same month Justin was born—August 1988—a new, multi-level upscale shopping structure named Brentwood Gardens opened right next door to O.J.'s office on San Vicente and Barrington. The intimate three-story center had elevators and an open plan: fashionable boutiques catering to the young and wealthy giving off onto shaded patios. On each level there were balconies with Babylonian-style hanging ferns. O.J. became a highly visible presence here; he came by a lot and shot the breeze with the Gardens' security man, James. He also started frequenting the boutiques in a low-key way.

The Gardens—and a handsome red-brick two-story esplanade of stores and restaurants across the boulevard from it—heralded a change in commercial (as opposed to residential) Brentwood. Over the last ten years, Brentwood and adjacent Santa Monica had become flagships for the screenwriter/TV producer elite, who had the million-plus it now took to nail down a home in the neighborhood. Although this group was largely responsible for San Vicente's coral-tree-dotted grassy center median becoming the hippest running track (and pickup place) in town, the shopping areas of Brentwood had remained charmingly stodgy. The small cluster of eucalyptus-shaded alley-like streets—Old Brentwood Center—near the post office, just south of Sunset on Barrington, had a secure dowdiness far more typical of Bennington, Vermont, than of West Los

Angeles. Farther west, the Brentwood Country Mart, a collection of food stalls flanking a patio with umbrella-shaded tables, was similarly quaint and smalltown. It was here that Brentwood mothers shopped, buying their young children's patience with the promise of a few turns on the quarter-a-ride oscillating car and pony.

But now, Montana Avenue, a diagonal main shopping street to the south of San Vicente, was sprouting boutiques catering to the young affluent residents, and there was rumor (and hope) of it becoming like Venice Beach as a street of stores and galleries. Farther east, on San Vicente between Barrington and Gorham, the opening of the Brentwood Gardens marked the official yuppification of Brentwood.

Gyms and yogurt bars appeared, though in decorously low numbers. Eventually, Starbucks Coffee would open, a block east of the Gardens. An arrowhead-shaped adobe-like building with bottle-green canvas awnings, it jutted out into the busy intersection of San Vicente and Gorham. Its patio would become a town hitching-post and water well for what would emerge in 1994 as the new Brentwood people: guys in do-rags or turned-around baseball caps, unlaced basketball shoes, enormous T-shirts and baggy shorts; women who had had breast enlargements and bodies that were banded by a minimal amount of Spandex, bodies hard enough to bounce a Spalding off of.

A tall-windowed blond stucco building with patios—elegant amid the more ordinary architecture—sat on the southwest corner of San Vicente and Gorham, exactly catercorner from the spot that Starbucks would eventually occupy. It was as sharply triangle-shaped as Starbucks. There was an urgent geometric edge to that pulsing intersection. The building had sat there for several decades, as if watching the neighborhood change. In 1988 it was the Santa Pietro restaurant. In two years it would be sold and its name would change—to a more romantic one—faintly melancholic, a dim warning of duality. Mezzaluna. Half moon. Half-dark, half-light.

The premier boutique in the Gardens was Theodore, which had originated as a classic Rodeo Drive woman's clothing store. Theodore's owner, Herb Fink, and his wife, Norma, were local movers and shakers. Almost as much as Jack Hansen and Giorgio's Fred Heyman (and certainly as much as Marvin Chanin and Alan Austin), Herb Fink had helped make Rodeo Drive a trendy movable retail feast. The Finks were at the Daisy and the Candy Store several times a week in those clubs' heydays. Their daughter Leslie grew up understanding the connection between the nightlife, retail-fashion, and sports worlds of Los Angeles.

The new Theodore in Brentwood Gardens was operated by Leslie Fink LeTellier. She was a chic, pretty woman with a helmet of black hair, a size-three figure, and an engaging, friendly manner. She tended to hire sales help cut from her general mold: tiny, tan, vivacious Jewish girls who knew how to assemble one pair of jeans, one white tee, one belt, and two bracelets with the austere perfection of a Japanese flower arranger, and who knew how to listen to people with the perky empathy of a summer-camp bunkmate.

Leslie's store would soon become a popular daily stop for the new Brentwood guys—a more wholesome genre of males-on-the-town than the gold-chain-bedecked Billy Kehoes of Rodeo Drive. These were boys who had been toddlers in the seventies, who didn't have to be told girls were independent creatures; boys so young their *babysitters* had watched *Gilligan's Island.* These young men grew up in eastern and midwestern cities and suburbs, places that only seemed provincial once they got to L.A. They had energy and enthusiasm and, for all their immersion into rap music and Attitude, no woman ten or more years older than they were could meet them and not think them anything but safe and adorable. They lived three and four to an apartment and took jobs as caterers' helpers, waiters, and exercise trainers on their way to some hoped-for score in the film or the nightlife business.

Leslie—an L.A. sophisticate, a warm older sister—would eventually become their casual adviser and confidante. Her store would evolve into a kind of salon. The guys would bop into Theodore daily, between a basketball game or a casting call and their evening's work (which was often in the neighborhood). They would sit down on Leslie's big floor cushions and hang out with her and the salesgirls, many of whom went to the same special "nights" at the new local clubs as the boys did.

This new, young Brentwood that was signified by the opening of the Brentwood Gardens was a world within which Nicole would later find a new source of hope and energy. The boys in that world—her future buddies—would help her recapture the freedom she had surrendered when she took on the difficult task of loving O.J.

And one of those boys would be killed along with her.

In late December 1988, Tom McCollum won $6,900 from the California State Lottery, through a ticket he had purchased at a store "owned by a homosexual guy Juice used to tease all the time. This guy was so enthralled by O.J. that even though merchants are only supposed to give winners up to two thousand dollars in cash before the state comes in, *he* gave me the whole sixty-nine hundred!"

"C'mon, since I got you that, now you've got to come to Hawaii with us," O.J. said. He, Nicole, Denise and A.C., Lou and Judi, and all the kids were going for Christmas and New Year's. A.C. didn't play golf. "Come with us," O.J. exhorted.

Tom didn't want to go. Going meant taking along the tempestuous Lebanese girlfriend he was trying to break up with, but O.J. insisted. So Tom called his girlfriend and they packed.

The trip would turn out to be the beginning of the end. Not for McCollum and his lady friend—but for Nicole and O.J.

6

Separation

DURING THE HAWAII VACATION, DENISE, A.C., AND TOM'S GIRLfriend went out dancing at night; Tom and O.J. played golf from 6 A.M. to noon every day; and Nicole—relief from her parents notwithstanding—kept the exhausting hours of a breastfeeding mother. (Justin was four months old.) O.J. had thought that his golfing was a big concession to Nicole. As he once told Tom, "At least she knows I'm not out screwing around. At least now I come home to the family, and now she can't bitch about that."

"Well, she *did* bitch—even though we were only playing golf till noon," Tom says, taking up for his friend and expressing the male point of view on this issue. "Even before this trip, she couldn't stand it that he was out playing golf and she was with the kids. She was on his case all the time—and on my and Kolkowitz's case, too. 'Oh, it's such a stupid game,' Nicole would say. 'He's never with the kids. It used to be women—now it's golf.'"

On the evening of December 29, 1988, when they were all out at dinner, Nicole put her foot down. The next day was the second to last day of the year. "Tomorrow, I don't want any golf," she said. "I want to spend the whole day with all of us together, and I want to go to Charo's"—a scenic restaurant on the other side of the island.

"So," Tom remembers, "we take the kids, pile in all the rental cars, drive all the way around the island and we get there for lunch and we're having a hell of a nice time. But then, everyone's drinking a little too much and neither one of them could drink—once they would drink, they got mean. Nicole, especially.

"There were these two homosexual guys sitting at a table next to us. Now, Nicole liked to talk to certain types of people—sometimes she would just pick people out. It was like O.J.'s thing—except *he'd* talk to anybody, just to talk. Nicole was more selective—she did have a cool aloofness about her (and I can see from it how people would be buffaloed into thinking she was this tower of strength, when inside she wasn't).

"Now," Tom says in no uncertain terms, "O.J., for one thing, does not like homosexuals. And, number two, the two of them had been going through their horrible AIDS conversations, although Nicole, of course, was still sleeping with him." (This would change, in short order.) "So one guy's sitting there and he's got lesions on his hands and he's talking about how this is his lover and he's dying. Nicole, who's holding Justin, is talking to them sympathetically and I'm watching O.J. and he's *livid."*

(O.J.'s gay father, of course, had died of AIDS three years before this fateful lunch meeting.)

Denise vociferously disputes Tom's account. "Neither of those men had lesions! And they were not talking about AIDS. Nicole was *such* a protective mother. They were perfectly fine-looking men. They were admiring Justin, saying, 'What a cute baby. . . .' "

However Tom's and Denise's memories may diverge, on the next point they do agree. Nicole let one of the men either touch the baby or, as Denise recalls, "give him a tiny kiss on the forehead. And then O.J. got *pissed."*

Tom says, "All of a sudden he got up and walked over and grabbed Justin and said, 'I don't want any infected faggot touching my kid!' And he grabbed Justin and started walking out to the parking lot."

The two versions are instructive in terms of how differently men and women remember the same incident.

Tom continues, "They went out to the parking lot"—Nicole had handed the baby to Judi—"and Nicole really started raising shit—screaming and yelling. It was embarrassing. Lou and Judi went, 'Oh God, not again. . . .'" But in Denise's interpretation, Nicole doesn't embarrass O.J.; she leaves a bullying O.J. She says, "We sat in O.J.'s rental car—Nicole and O.J. in the front, me and A.C. in the back. They were fighting and O.J. was screaming at Nicole and then she said, 'I don't need to take this,' and she got out of the car and got into my parents' car."

Nicole's leaving angered O.J. all the more. He turned to Tom, who had come out to the parking lot to try to calm them down, and said, "Come on, McCollum, we're getting out of here!"

Tom thought this ironic. Two days before, Tom had been in O.J.'s position: angry at his difficult lady friend (whom O.J. couldn't stand because she was a better golfer than he was); he had decided to go back to Los Angeles. O.J. had caught up with him in the lobby, looked at his packed bags and airline ticket, and pleaded, "Don't leave me here! You go, I won't have anyone to play golf with! What am I gonna do, sit here and get drunk all day?" Tom had done what he almost always did when O.J. pleaded: He knuckled under and did what O.J. wanted.

This time, however, Tom got steely.

"Hey, man," Tom said, "I'm not going with you. You're all pissed off. Why don't you go by yourself and cool off."

So the group headed back to the hotel in two cars, the beautiful afternoon ruined.

According to Tom, O.J. was seething. He went into his room and slammed the door, refusing to talk to anyone.

Then Tom's phone rang. "Pack your shit, man," O.J. said. "We're outta here. We're going back to L.A. *Right* now."

Tom vividly recalls that O.J. changed *everyone's* plane

reservations. Denise recalls that the flight they ended up taking home that day was the flight they were scheduled to go back on.

In any event, Tom was not scheduled to go back that day. "Why should *I* leave?" he told O.J., angrily. "*I* just went through this two days ago! Let's finish the vacation!" But when Tom called the airline, he found that the change was irreversible: Because New Year's Eve was the next day, there was no other way to get back.

"So everybody left. In total silence. Juice and I played gin all the way back. We didn't talk to anyone. Nicole drank brandy the whole flight. Juice got plowed on whatever he was drinking."

The next night, New Year's Eve, Nicole and O.J. went out to dinner with Marcus Allen and his girlfriend, Kathryn Eickstaedt, a pretty, blond model. A photograph shows O.J. and Nicole as they were leaving for the dinner and, later, club-hopping (including, of course, Stellini's): she in a royal blue, sequined, long-sleeved silk dress with a high neck, a nipped waist and a short, puffed skirt; he in a tux. They looked like they were ready to ring in 1989 with love and happiness.

This is not how they would end the evening.

When they got back to Rockingham—both having consumed a good deal of alcohol—they started arguing. Nicole told a close friend that she was angry at having discovered that O.J. had purchased yet another piece of jewelry for Tawny Kitaen (a bracelet this time) and that she had refused to make love, a reluctance that had been growing ever since she had become worried about contracting AIDS from him.

O.J. made no mention of the bracelet in his version of how the fight started. He told a male friend that, after engaging in part of the sex act with his wife, "when it came time for her to give me some head, she said 'No.' *Can you believe* that shit?" O.J. had then looked at the friend as if asking, man to man, "You understand *now* why it happened, don't you?" The secretly astonished and disapproving friend thought, "*This* was his reason for the violence?"

O.J. told a Los Angeles Police Department officer who interviewed him two days after the incident that his anger is what turned their dispute physical. Nicole told this same investigator (Officer Farrell) that O.J. punched her on the forehead and slapped her repeatedly. O.J. saw the details differently—it was "a mutual wrestling-type altercation" (this is Officer Farrell's paraphrasing). He claimed to be surprised when he saw the bump and bruise on Nicole's forehead.

The passage of time, however, altered O.J.'s recollection of the evening. When he described the incident on June 13, 1994—under questioning by Detective Philip Vannatter—he said *Nicole* was the assailant. "We had a fight and she hit me," he said. "And they never took my statement, they never wanted to hear my side, and they never wanted to hear the housekeeper's side." The housekeeper was an Israeli woman named Michelle, who did not get along with Nicole* and who was extremely loyal to O.J. "Nicole was drunk. She did her thing, she started tearing up my house, you know? And I didn't punch her or anything, but I . . . I wrestled her, is what I did. I didn't slap her at all. I mean, Nicole's a strong girl, she's one of the most conditioned women."

Others tell it differently. After he started striking her, Nicole—"strong girl" though she may have been—was sufficiently frightened to run out of the bedroom and try to hide from O.J. And he was apparently so determined to hunt her down that he landed in the nanny, Ruth's, bed-

---

*Michelle is described by several of Nicole's friends as having been almost "militaristic" in attitude. Nicole thought Michelle was cruelly strict with the children—"the woman from Hell," is how she once described her. When Nicole and O.J. reconciled in 1993, after their 1992 divorce, she wanted O.J. to fire Michelle. (He didn't.) In the winter of 1993–94 Nicole and Michelle had a verbal fight that escalated. Nicole struck Michelle in the face. She finally resigned.

room, thinking Nicole might be hiding there. Like Nicole, Ruth had blond hair. In the darkness, O.J. looked at the sleeping Ruth, reached into the bed, picked her up, and carried her out of the room and halfway around the house, stopping only when Ruth screamed, "O.J.! It's *me*! It's Ruth! It's *not* Nicole! Put me down, please!" (This incident, which is described here as Ruth told it to a family friend a few days later, *did* make for subsequent laughter—even from Nicole—in the retelling. But while it was happening it was, for *both* women, decidedly more serious than comic.)

Nicole got to a phone and called 911.

In the exact words* of the two police officers—female Officer Milewski and male Officer Edwards—who came to the door at 3:30 A.M., here is what happened next.

"Officers Milewski and Edwards received a 911 radio call, 'Female being beaten at 360 North Rockingham' could be heard over the phone." This from Officer Milewski. "Upon arrival, my partner and I could not enter the above location due to the locked electronic gates. My partner phoned the residence, and was told by a housekeeper that everyone was fine and that the police were not needed. My partner told the housekeeper that we needed to speak with the victim [Nicole Simpson] to determine if she needed our assistance."

Officer Edwards: "A female [housekeeper] . . . said that everyone was fine and that we were not needed. I told her that I must see and speak to the woman who had dialed 911 and I would not leave until I did. About that time Nicole Simpson came running out of some bushes near her house. She was wearing only a bra and sweat-type pants. She had mud down the right leg of her pants. She ran across the driveway to a post containing the gate release button. She collapsed [on it] and pushed the button hard several times.

"She was yelling during this time, 'He's going to kill me. He's going to kill me.' As she said this the gate opened and

*Taken from their police reports.

she ran out to me. She grabbed me and hung on to me as she cried nervously and she repeated, 'He is going to kill me.'

"I asked her who was going to kill her. She replied, 'O.J.' I did not know this was O.J. Simpson's home, but at this point I felt she might have meant O.J. Simpson. I ask[ed] her, 'Do you mean O.J. Simpson the football player?' She said yes."

Officer Milewski: "Nicole Simpson . . . told us that [the suspect] her husband (O.J. Simpson) had beaten her up. She stated that he had slapped her with both open and closed fists, kicked her with his feet, and pulled her hair. Nicole Simpson also stated that suspect (O.J. Simpson) yelled, 'I'll kill you.'"

Officer Edwards: "I asked her if he had a gun, she said he's got lots of guns. (The question had been for my protection, since she had maintained he was going to kill her.)

"I could see clearly that her face was badly beaten, with a cut lip, swollen and blackened left eye and cheek. I also noted a hand imprint on her left [side of her] neck."

Officer Milewski also noticed "many scratch marks on her neck" as well as "multiple trauma bruises [including] swollen bruises on her rt [sic] forehead, scratches on her upper lip [and] a cut on her inner lip."

Officer Edwards: "I saw that she was shaking, so I had my partner put her uniform jacket on Nicole, then had her sit in the back of the police vehicle. As she was giving the crime info to my partner, she kept saying, 'You never do anything about him. You talk to him and then leave. I want him arrested, I want him out so I can get my kids.' She also made the statement that police have come eight times before for the same thing.

". . . . At about this time O.J. Simpson arrived at the closed gate inside his yard."

Officer Milewski: "He remained in the front yard of his house behind a brick wall. O.J. Simpson stated that he didn't want this woman (Nicole Simpson) sleeping in his bed anymore, and that he did not beat her up."

Officer Edwards: "At first he did not speak directly to me but yelled for about 30 seconds towards Nicole seated in the police car. He yelled, 'I don't want that woman sleeping in my bed anymore, I got two women and I don't want that woman in my bed anymore.'

"When he slowed down, I told him Nicole wanted him arrested for beating her. He blew up again* and yelled that he did not beat her up, he just pushed her out of the bedroom and nothing more. I again told him that Nicole wanted him arrested for beating her and that I could clearly see physical evidence on Nicole that confirmed she had been beaten.

"I then told O.J. I was going to have to place him under arrest for beating Nicole.† He yelled back, 'The police has [sic] been out here eight times before and now your [sic] gonna arrest me for this. This is a family matter. Why do you want to make a big deal out of it? We can handle it.'

"O.J. was wearing a bathrobe only. I told him to put on some clothes and then come outside. I told him, 'When my supervisor gets here, I'm going to have to arrest you.' O.J. then went inside."

Interestingly—despite O.J.'s demonstrated use of physical force against Nicole, despite Nicole's obvious fear of him, despite his anger at her and at the police officers,

---

*Two days later, according to police investigator Officer Farrell, O.J. stated that he, to quote Farrell's paraphrase, "became angry with uniform [sic] officers as they conducted their investigation."

†The California state legislature had recently upgraded domestic violence from misdemeanor to felony status. (Such charges, however, can be reduced to misdemeanor status after arrest.) Under this then-new policy, if officers responding to 911 calls saw a "traumatic condition"—any evidence of abuse on a possible victim, even a small bruise—arrest was made, whether the victim wanted it to be made or not. If, in a disputed incident, there were no witnesses to say who assaulted whom first, and if the man displayed any bruises at all, often both the woman *and* the man were arrested. There is no indication in the police report, however, that in O.J. and Nicole's case on this day, the officers considered arresting the woman.

despite all of this effectively flaunted machismo—what O.J. did next was send a woman out to do battle for him. According to Officer Edwards: "In approximately two minutes, the housekeeper"—Michelle—"came out the other gate and walked directly to the police vehicle. She opened the rear door and started pulling on Nicole's arm and saying, 'Nicole, don't do this. Come inside now.' "

Officer Edwards promptly became assertive on behalf of Nicole. "I pulled the housekeeper back and closed the door [of the police car]," he reports. "I told her to leave, she was interfering with a police investigation and could be arrested. She left."

His proxy-defender thus warned and dismissed, O.J. now turned sheepish. Officer Edwards continues: "About three minutes passed and O.J. peeked over the wall, now dressed. He again complained that I was the only officer to come to his house that made a big deal out of this. I told him again that I was going to have to arrest him, based on Nicole's injuries, and that the law required me to arrest him."

The arrival of Edwards' and Milewski's superior sent O.J. back into hiding. ("Sergeant Vinger drove up and O.J. disappeared from the wall.") Finally, while Edwards was conferring with Vinger, he "saw O.J. drive out of another driveway" (Milewski, in her report, accurately described this as a "side electronic gate")—"in a blue Bentley."

O.J. had gotten away!

Officer Edwards' written report continues: "He sped off s/b [southbound] Rockingham, 35 to 45 mph. We were out of our cars at the time and faced in the wrong direction. We drove s/b after O.J. but never saw him again. We fanned out through the nearby streets with five units but could not locate him. Red lights and sirens were not used during chase due to distance. Nicole was still in our police car and wanted to go back to her kids. She had already signed a crime report but refused medical treatment." (Denise believes that Nicole's initial refusal of medical treatment was made to spare O.J. publicity.)

Nicole then consented to having her bruised body and

face photographed at the West Los Angeles police station. Officer Edwards took three pictures and Officer Milewski checked her for additional injuries. Then she was brought back to Rockingham.

Fifteen minutes after an exhausted Nicole was delivered home, she called Officer Edwards to tell him that O.J. had returned. Edwards drove out and parked three houses away. He waited for O.J. to drive out of the driveway again to arrest him. After a futile forty-five minutes of waiting, Edwards had the station call Nicole. Nicole said that O.J. had left before Edwards got there.

Later, at the station house, Officer Edwards seemed very embarrassed at having had O.J. escape on him. Officer Milewski told a colleague that she was "mind-blown" by the whole incident.

O.J. may have gone to sleep at Allen and Pam Schwartz's house that morning. He was definitely at the Schwartzes' later that day, according to Joe Kolkowitz, who came by. "O.J. was absolutely remorseful that day," Kolkowitz says emphatically. "He felt horrible about what had happened." Joe adds, almost indignantly, "O.J. is *not* a batterer. The portrayal of him as a wife-beater is totally false."

Meanwhile, Nicole called A.C., who, according to Denise, became furious at O.J. on her behalf. After driving Nicole to St. John's Hospital (where she received treatment for bruising and soreness to the head), he confronted O.J. According to Denise, A.C.'s exact words to O.J. were, "You sick motherfucker, if you ever lay a hand on her again I'll kill you."

Despite the remorse Kolkowitz saw in him and the angry warning A.C. gave him, O.J. did what he always did on New Year's Day: He went to the Rose Bowl game that afternoon. Ordinarily, he took part in the pre-game fanfare. This year his presence in the ceremonies was especially important to him because it was Jason's first year at the university. But when the ceremonies started, O.J. was conspicuously absent.

O.J.'s friend Ron Shipp was present, however, in a group of former SC players in special seats on the sidelines. O.J.'s friend Mike Ornstein, L.A. Raiders senior administrator (and team owner Al Davis's right-hand man), was looking for Ron at O.J.'s request. When Mike found Ron, he hurriedly handed him a note. In O.J.'s handwriting it read, "Emergency. Call me tonight at Orny's [O.J.'s nickname for Ornstein]." Ornstein then told Ron what had happened at Rockingham during the predawn hours. "Don't turn around," he whispered to Ron. O.J. was in the stands, watching the game in some kind of disguise.

Twenty-six years ago to the day, O.J. had listened to this event on radio and his determination to have a brilliant career had sprung from that moment. The white Trojan horse and the bugles had inspired him. Today, he was a wife-beater hiding from the police in the stands of the very stadium in which he had shone, in which the whole football-watching world had roared its praises.

Before he was an SC football player, a cop, a domestic violence teacher, and even O.J.'s friend, Ron Shipp used to sit in this stadium, in awe of the Juice's magic. Now he was shaken. *O.J.—a batterer?* Granted, Ron had heard things over the years from his fellow cops, but he had loyally ignored their comments. When he and his partner gave their domestic violence classes at the Academy, they fleshed out their lectures with diverse examples of wife-beaters. Lyle Alzado, one of the most violent men in football, who was booked twice in Venice Beach for spousal battery, was an obvious example; corporate achiever John Fedders, the chief of enforcement for the Securities and Exchange Commission during the Reagan Administration, a 6′10″ man who had battered his wife (and the mother of his five children) for years, was a more surprising specimen. Once in a while during Ron's mention of these "celebrity" alleged batterers,* a voice from the audience would pipe up, "Hey,

*To this list of well-known men who were said, by their wives or girlfriends, to have been physically abusive, the following can be

Shipp, how come your friend O.J. isn't on that list?" The eight visits the LAPD made to Rockingham, responding to Nicole's 911 calls, may not have resulted in arrest but they had resulted in squad-room gossip. Ron had ignored that gossip.

When Ron called O.J. at Ornstein's later, O.J. told him, "Me and Nicole had a little argument last night, and now I'm a fugitive." O.J. wanted Ron to help him smooth things over with the police department and he wanted Ron to help him get back in Nicole's good graces. "Ron, it was an isolated incident; it just got out of hand," he told his friend, the domestic violence teacher. Nicole was refusing to let him come back home. He was camped out at Ornstein's for the duration.

Nicole called Denise to come over and take pictures of her injuries. Denise did so. She was stunned by her sister's appearance. Later, however, when Nicole showed her father the photographs Denise had taken, he reacted (Nicole later told a friend) by telling her she should *still* try to make a go of the marriage. "My parents," Nicole later told two people, "did not take up for me. They blew it off. They wanted me to stay with O.J."

One person Nicole did feel she could count on in this hour of need was Ron Shipp. On January 3, she called him. "O.J. really did it to me this time," she said. "I don't want to be married to him anymore. Please come over."

As soon as Ron got off work the next day, he went to see Nicole.

Even though Nicole's bruises had faded a bit, she appeared shockingly vulnerable, sitting in the TV room smok-

---

added: actors David Soul, William Hurt, Sean Penn (his alleging victim was his then-wife, Madonna), and Mickey Rourke; baseball player Darryl Strawberry; and singer-songwriter Jackson Browne (his alleging victim was actress Daryl Hannah). None of these men was ever convicted—and some were never even charged—in connection with the alleged abuse.

ing Marlboros, her whole body stiff. She seemed like a frightened child.

"O.J. wants to come home," she said. "I won't let him."

Remembering what O.J. had told him, Ron pled on his friend's behalf. "Well, it was just an isolated incident."

"Isolated incident?! Is that what O.J. told you?!" Nicole leapt to her feet. " 'Isolated incident,' *bull*shit!" She headed for the stairs, calling out over her shoulder, "Let me show you something, but you have to swear you'll never tell anybody about them."

Ron promised that whatever she showed him would remain a secret.

A few minutes later, Nicole came back down, carrying a manila envelope. "I've never shown these to anybody," she said, handing about a half-dozen photographs to Ron one at a time: close-ups of various parts of her body, deeply bruised and black and blue.* "I took these myself," she said, not specifying the date or circumstances. "I said to myself, when this happened, if he ever did it again, I would give these to the *National Enquirer.* I want him to hurt like he's hurt me."

Nicole started crying. Ron hugged her. The photographs stunned him—both for what they revealed about the true nature of the Simpsons' relationship and for what they revealed about O.J.'s psyche. Batterers almost always have low self-esteem, which is why Ron had for so long resisted the notion of O.J. as a batterer. Low self-esteem? *O.J.?!* But now, finally, Ron was convinced: O.J. was a batterer just as clearly and obviously as he had been a world-class athlete.

Holding Nicole as she sobbed, Ron felt every ounce of

---

*No one else had ever seen these pictures—which were *not* the pictures that Denise had just taken—and their elusiveness was a source of frustration for the prosecution for months after Nicole's murder. Finally, in early December of 1994, these photos, as well as the ones Denise had taken, were found in a safe deposit box Nicole had kept in a Brentwood bank. The box had to be drilled open.

respect he had ever had for O.J. vanish. As far as he was concerned, O.J. Simpson was now and forever an asshole.

Ron sat with Nicole for four hours. She talked about how she felt O.J.'s father's homosexuality (a revelation she made Ron promise not to repeat) was why he was violent. She told Ron about the black eye she had received from O.J. right before her nineteenth birthday—and the black Porsche that he gave her to make up for it. She told Ron that O.J. had once pulled a gun on her. (She would later tell this to other friends as well.)

"Ron, I'm so scared," she said. "One day O.J.'s going to kill me."

"No, he won't," Ron reassured her, just as everyone else to whom she made that same fearful prediction had said. A man with so much to lose committing murder? It was inconceivable, even to a teacher of domestic violence.

But *as* a teacher of domestic violence, Ron knew that, as he put it to his classes, "Domestic violence happens when two particular people—a woman with the characteristics of a classic victim and a man with the characteristics of a classic batterer—gravitate to one another. It can't be any old two people—it's not like a woman comes into a bar and says, 'Hey, Bad Boy, why don't you come over and kick my ass.' Only *certain* men and women mesh like that. And when they do, their personalities come together magnetically."

What kind of people? Nicole wanted to know. Ron said the next time he came over he would bring his lesson plan and show her. They agreed to show it to O.J., too.

In the meantime, Ron told Nicole, she was *not* to let O.J. back in the house unless he got counseling. She must promise him this. She did.

Before Ron left, the conversation drifted once again to fear of death, this time more hypothetically.

"What's the way of dying you're most afraid of?" Nicole asked Ron.

"Drowning," he replied.

As she would say to many other people over the years—very likely including her husband—Nicole now said to Ron,

"Mine's stabbing. To be killed with a knife—to me, that would be the most awful."

Over the next two weeks, O.J., who hardly ever called Ron, now started calling him daily ("Did you talk to Nicole?" "What did Nicole say?" "Tell Nicole I'll never do it again . . ." "Another thing to tell Nicole . . .") first from his outpost at Ornstein's and then from his closer-in exile at the Rockingham guest house. (Nicole had let him move back in after about a week as long as he stayed out of the main house.) He could barely eat and he was losing weight rapidly. He was now calling all his male friends at all hours, obsessed with the real possibility that Nicole would leave him. He seemed a broken man: desperate and focused only on getting his woman back.

Part of getting Nicole back was getting her to "sign off" on the complaint: to agree to drop her charges.* Because Ron Shipp, an LAPD officer and domestic violence expert, was seeing and essentially counseling the Simpsons, the detective in charge of the case asked Ron, "What do they want to do?"

O.J. knew what he wanted Nicole to do. "Hey, Ron, get her to sign it [the request-to-drop-charges form]," he said.

But O.J. wasn't controlling Ron. On his next visit to Rockingham, Ron said, "Nicole, here are the papers. O.J. wants you to sign off on the charges, but I don't think you should."

Nicole was confused. "I don't want to embarrass the

---

*Despite the new upgrading of domestic violence to felony level (making it a 273.5, in California police jargon) and the attendant de facto mandatory-arrest policy, the victim's discretion could be taken into consideration. Had Nicole signed the papers stating that she wished charges against her husband dropped (which she did not do), it is not clear what would have happened to the charge. Nicole did not sign the papers but she did tell the investigating officer that she did not want to prosecute but did want the case sent to the city attorney's office.

children," she said, taking the papers but putting them aside. "But I want the world to know what he did."

Meanwhile, after receiving O.J.'s charm-soaked and sincere-sounding apology and his promise to seek counseling,* the police passed the case on to the city attorney's office.

Ron now spent almost every day at Rockingham, talking to Nicole and O.J. separately; she would call Ron and arrange to be out of the house so that O.J. could go from the guest house to the main house and meet Ron there.

Ron spoke to each of them about religion. O.J. had been baptized before his wedding to Nicole—maybe it was time to go back to church more actively. Finding God—having "spiritual food," as Ron put it—could bring them together in a positive way *after* he started counseling. Both reacted affirmatively to the suggestion. "I'm a Christian; we haven't been going to church, but I want my kids to know right from wrong—maybe we should start again," Nicole said. O.J., too, seemed open-minded to Ron—"Yeah; church; yeah, it's something to consider . . ."—but in the way, Ron would later tell his wife, that manipulators have of pretending to be in agreement with someone they need to keep in their pocket.

O.J. needed Ron now because Nicole was listening to him.

And she was especially listening to Ron's descriptions of the link between classic victims and classic batterers. Although Nicole never thought of herself as a "classic victim" —she was much too tough and forthright—many of the

---

*Officer Farrell's follow-up report states that O.J. called Farrell on January 5 and "stated that he regretted the entire incident and that I, as the police, had to get involved with his personal problems. Mr. Simpson then went on and stated that he knew that what he did was wrong, and that he didn't mean any harm to his wife, Nicole. Mr. Simpson went on and stated that he planned to schedule himself and Nicole for counseling, and would appreciate it if the city attorney would take that into consideration when making a final determination."

descriptions in the lesson plan Ron showed her did have a striking familiarity. For example, *VICTIM: Often receives disbelief and denial from friends, relatives, and service agencies* was one description. (Her mother's blithe reaction to O.J.'s throwing down her framed family pictures and tossing out the antique desk . . .) *May give up hope when no one believes them or will not help* was another. (The fruitless 911 calls, O.J.'s constant charming of the police when they did come . . .) *May be immobilized by fear.* (The way she had felt being beaten up and locked in the wine cellar; the way she felt crouched in the bushes on New Year's Day . . .) *May turn to alcohol or drugs to cope.* (She did drink, and that drinking often escalated the animosity between them, leading to beating episodes.) *Societal pressures to keep the family together.* (Most of her family—with the exception of Denise—*wanted* her to stay with O.J., as did many in their circle of friends.)

Nicole was relatively quiet as she sat with Ron and turned the pages of the manual. In retrospect, however, it seems that she must have seen herself in these descriptions of frustration and desperation.

More certain is the fact that when she turned the page to *DYNAMICS OF THE BATTERER,* the man she encountered on those pages was O.J.

For "the Batterer," Nicole read: *a. Violence is a tool used to feel powerful and to have control over others.*

The Batterer: *b. Witnessed or experienced domestic violence as a child.*

c. Often blames others (spouse, boss, society, etc.) "They made me do it."

d. Often is afraid, jealous, or obsessed with controlling mate's activities.

After each description, Nicole slapped the table and exclaimed to Ron, "That's him!"

e. May become desperate with fear of living without mate.
"That's him!"

f. Uses violence/aggression in reaction to conflict or anger.
"That's him!"

g. May not be violent or aggressive outside the home.

"That's him!"

h. May have low self-esteem.

Yes, even this: "That's him!"

The next day, Ron opened the same page of the lesson plan* and went down the list with O.J. O.J.'s reactions were the mirror opposite of Nicole's: *"That's* not me!" *"That's* not me!" "That's *not* me!", all the way down the line.

O.J. had lingered on only one criterion—jealousy. "Well, maybe *that* one's me," O.J. had conceded. Ron's hopes briefly rose as O.J. considered facing the truth about himself. But then he took it back. "Nah, that's not me."

But Ron did not give up on him. O.J. desperately wanted to be back with Nicole—and, just as desperately, he did not want to lose his image. Nicole was still undecided about going public with the events of New Year's Day—women's groups had gotten wind of them and were calling her; the *Los Angeles Times,* though it had not yet run a story (this would not happen until February 2, ironically, the Simpsons' fourth wedding anniversary when Nicole was in Mexico with the children), had contacted her. She was agonizing over her options: Break her silence and let the world know what her hero husband was really like (to punish him—and perhaps prevent further violence by making the public vigilant)? Or: Keep quiet and protect her children from the humiliation and shock of having their father labeled a wife-beater? It was a hard choice and she was confused by it.

O.J., meanwhile, saw his whole future hanging in the

---

*In September 1994, it was reported that Cathy Randa might appear in Judge Ito's courtroom to answer questions regarding whether she had shredded certain domestic violence materials in O.J.'s office, which officers say they had seen there during the initial investigation. Whether or not these were the materials given to him by Ron Shipp or were materials given to him by some other person or agency in connection with the 1989 beating, it is interesting that O.J. kept the domestic violence pamphlets for so many years.

balance. "I'm afraid I'm going to lose my Hertz thing!" and "I don't know how she can *do* this to me!" he said repeatedly.

Over the course of these frequent talks, Ron saw O.J. try out all his manipulations. He took Ron to lunch at the California Pizza Kitchen in the Brentwood Gardens. He was "on"—the charming O.J.—refusing to let Ron's exhortations penetrate below the surface ("Juice, face it: *You* are a *batterer"*). Instead, he presumptuously regarded Ron as his PR man, his mouthpiece. "Tell Nicole . . ." this and that, he kept saying.

Ron wasn't having it. If O.J. was pushing his I-want-Nicole-back line with Ron, Ron was pushing a different line with O.J. "You've got all the traits of a batterer," Ron said.

"I love her; I would never hurt her," O.J. replied.

"What do you mean, you '*would* never'—you *have* hurt her!" Ron said, his voice rising. "You *already* hurt her." Batterers were like alcoholics, Ron explained. You're never really healed, though you can go into remission. The tendency is always in you. You're okay if you know this and stay on top of your own worst tendencies.

O.J. continued to deny that he was a batterer. In his relationship with Marguerite, for example, "She battered me!" O.J. said. Ron shook his head, thinking of the quiet, conservative Marguerite and the O.J. he knew. O.J. was in deep denial.

Ron used himself as an example. He told O.J. how he had once asked his wife, Nina, "Do I ever try to control you?" and how she had shocked him by retorting with an emphatic "Yes!" and how he had worked consciously to change. Hell, he was *still* working on himself.

But it was clear that O.J. cared more about results (getting back in the house, saving his image) than in process. All right, Ron thought, I'll think results. Once night he decided to propose something radical, something that would appeal to O.J.'s preoccupation with his image while at the same time making him change. He prayed O.J. would go for it. He knew everything would be different, from there on in, if he did.

"Juice," he said, as the two men sat in the Rockingham kitchen, "the media's gonna find out about this. Why don't you beat them to it—be a man and admit it. Get out there in public and say, 'I have a problem. I am a batterer. I need help. I'm coming clean and telling you. I want to change and I'm *going* to change. *Watch* me.' Man, the women's groups will *love* you for it!"

To Ron's surprise, O.J. did not say no. He said, "Hmm, you really think so?"

"Absolutely!" Ron said. "Alcoholics do it. People who've attempted suicide do it." Betty Ford had gained America's respect by admitting her drinking problem. Robert McFarlane, former President Reagan's National Security Adviser, had attempted suicide after the Iran-Contra affair and had talked about it on ABC's *Nightline.* It was the era of public repentance; America seemed to love public figures who confessed their fallibilities. Half the Watergate conspirators were either on the lecture circuit or finding God. In a month, Kitty Dukakis would announce her problems with diet pills and alcohol. A likable public personality need only ask America's mercy to watch his stock go up. Even if O.J. pursued this path for self-serving purposes, Ron believed that change would be enforced.

O.J. looked at the floor, thinking it over. "Yeah . . . ," he said. He looked up. "Yeah. Hey, I like that idea."

This was the O.J. Ron always thought he knew. *Stay* with that decision, man, Ron whispered to himself, prayerfully.

Ron stood up to leave. He and O.J. hugged.

The next day, O.J. called Ron and told him that, after talking it over with one of his advisers, he had changed his mind. The idea would lose him his endorsement contracts, the adviser (lawyer? agent? publicist? Ron never found out) had decided.*

---

*Indeed, O.J.'s career improved after the New Year's Day incident was made public; among other things, he signed a lucrative contract

"He came *this* close . . . ," Ron told Nina, shaking his head in an anguish that would increase a hundredfold six years later.

Nicole also had a meeting at the deputy city attorney Robert Pingel's office with a female victim's advocate, her supervisor, and a city attorney. According to one of those present, Nicole seemed typical in her desire to have the violence against her cease while hoping not to get her battering husband in trouble "for the sake of her children," this participant in the meeting recalls, "who were clearly her first priority. She wasn't hysterical sobbing and she wasn't vindictive, but she did seem confused. I didn't get the feeling that she knew what she was going to do."

Meanwhile, O.J. remained in the guest house. He was arraigned on January 30, 1989, and as the case bumped along from hearing to hearing over the next five months, with Howard Weitzman (or an associate from his office) representing O.J. at these hearings and O.J. almost never present, he changed his plea from not guilty to no contest.

O.J.'s entire financial assessment for battering Nicole turned out to be less than two moving violations: a mere $470 (a $200 fine, a $270 penalty; the disposition of his case was "convicted") and 120 hours of community service. He initially attempted to use, for the latter, services he had provided to a charity (Camp Good Times, for children with cancer) with which he had an existing relationship. To this end, the camp's director, Pepper Edmiston, wrote an effusive letter praising O.J.'s "unselfishly donated" time as well as the donation of his "personal funds to our charity" for which "we will be forever grateful."

But some of what Simpson did for Camp Good Times was to seek corporate sponsorship of it, and Judge Ronald R. Schoenberg assessed that these efforts were not true commu-

---

with NBC Sports. O.J. happily noted that Hertz had been *"so supportive"* of him following disclosure of the incident.

nity service but, rather, "part of what he does as a celebrity." Judge Schoenberg ordered thirty-two additional hours of community service; Simpson eventually fulfilled these.

O.J. Simpson was never jailed for the incident,* but perhaps the most telling turn of events in the proceedings occurred in May 1989 when prosecutors asked the judge to make Simpson attend a special treatment program for batterers (just like the one Ron Shipp had urged him to enter voluntarily). Howard Weitzman balked at the idea, strongly assuring the judge that his client was already receiving counseling to get at the "cause behind the problem." Schoenberg did not order Simpson into the batterers' program; he ordered individual counseling with a court-approved clinician (Dr. Burt Kittay), allowing such counseling to be by telephone when Simpson had to go to New York to fulfill his sports commentating commitments. Judge Schoenberg was criticized in the press during the summer of 1994 for allowing such telephone counseling.

At one point Nicole, voluntarily—in hopes of improving the marriage—went to see Burt Kittay for individual sessions. Then she and O.J. had couples sessions. At a certain point, Nicole began to wonder about the efficacy of the couples therapy. She told a friend that she felt that, even in the serious sanctum of the psychologist's office, O.J. was worshipped. Was there *no* man he couldn't snow?, Nicole wondered, in frustration. The couples therapy broke down.

However many victories O.J. accrued after he beat Nicole on New Year's Day—the successful escape from the cops, the nonarrest, the luck-out on jail time, the paltry fine, the support from Hertz, the obliging judge, the temporarily finessed "community service"—he still didn't have what he wanted most: Nicole.

---

*In June 1994, Judge Schoenberg claimed that Pingel did not ask for jail time for Simpson and Pingel claimed that he did ask for it, though not in open court. The *Los Angeles Times* concluded that the judge and prosecutors were "pointing fingers at each other."

For three months (January through March) he stayed in the guest house. In April Nicole let him back in the main house but for several weeks she refused to sleep with him, according to a friend she confided in.

O.J.'s litany during these months was that of a lovesick penitent. "What a lucky guy I am to have her." "She's such a wonderful mother." "I'm going to do anything to change." "I know I'm an asshole." These exact quotes were recalled by one friend. He would make these comments in telephone calls to one male friend after another at four, five and six in the morning.

The physical abuse was just part of it for Nicole.

One of her biggest reconciliation issues was AIDS. She simply would not sleep with O.J. again unless he got a blood test. The issue was exacerbated when rumors reached Nicole that O.J. may have been having a fling with a beautiful black celebrity who had been married to a professional athlete. For Nicole, "married to a professional athlete" had come to be synonymous with "married to a man who does it like a rabbit."

"That sonuvabitch is getting HIV; can I come down to your lab and get a test?" Nicole asked Tom McCollum one day. "He's nothing but an asshole. You know that, Thomas."

"I don't want to be in the middle of that," Tom said, referring to the bad-mouthing. "But I'll do anything you want, medically."

Nicole never got her test at Tom's lab, but he does believe—as do her friends—that she was tested. Convincing O.J. to be tested was a harder project. But Tom threw himself into it. "I begged him, out of common respect, to have it done for the sake of his family and his children. Clearly Nicole was worried—and she had a right to be. They were both, in fact, obsessed with it. He was always worried about AIDS. But did it ever slow him down? No."

At one point during those months in early 1989, O.J. told Tom that he had gotten an AIDS test, but when Tom asked him a few questions about the procedure, it seemed clear from O.J.'s answers—he said he had a buddy get the results—that he had not gotten one. He seemed concerned that he might not be able to get an AIDS test without the public knowing. After all, *if* they found out, what would they think was the reason for the testing?*

Tom offered to do both of Nicole's and O.J.'s tests by mail—they could be identified by number; no one would ever know it was O.J. Simpson. "Your private life, Juice, is your private life, but get this thing done now," Tom counseled. He reminded O.J. that O.J. had very recently given him good, strong advice about his own difficult girlfriend, which resulted in Tom's breaking up with her, "the best thing that ever happened." Now he urged O.J. to take his advice.

Still, though AIDS was a big worry, O.J.'s real obsession during this period was that Nicole would do what was for him the unimaginable, the *unbearable:* have sex with other men. Through all his endless philandering, she had to be his alone. McCollum says, "It's a real male jealousy thing. Actual vaginal penetration by another male. Men are obsessed by it."

One day, while O.J. was still in the dog house at Rockingham, so to speak, he and McCollum had one of their 5 A.M., pre-golf, O.J.-instigated phone calls. O.J. was obsessing again.

"Look, Juice," Tom told him, "it's so simple. You're only worried about one thing, period. And that is that Nicole—I didn't talk to him like a scientist—is going to go out and get fucked."

At that point Tom heard O.J. break down and sob. "Thomas, I know it! I just couldn't take it! I just couldn't take it!" he cried.

Tom tried to comfort O.J. "I know what you're talking

---

*And this was before the announcement by Magic Johnson (on November 7, 1991) that he was HIV-positive—an announcement that set off a swirl of talk about his sexual promiscuity and rumors (denied by Johnson) that he may have been bisexual.

about," he said. "I've heard it from many guys before. And in my life I also went through a divorce with someone I deeply loved. And if you think old rational McCollum didn't think about that, and it didn't hurt my feelings, you're wrong. But it's something you've got to keep to yourself." As he did whenever the opportunity presented itself, Tom tried to make O.J. see how incendiary he and Nicole were as a couple. "Look, Juice. You two don't belong together. Why can't you just be friends? You've got lovely kids. Look, you told me about my relationship, and I took your advice. *I* broke it off." Tom knew that if the Simpsons were going to finally break up, O.J. had to really let go of Nicole. "Look, man, about Nicole and some other man—if you stay broken up, it's *gonna* happen. Maybe it already did."

Long conversations with one confidant were never enough for O.J. No sooner had he drained one friend of sympathy and advice, than O.J., as Tom puts it, "would immediately hang up and speed-dial Kolkowitz or Austin or somebody else, and start the whole conversation again, so he could hear something new. He wanted to hear what he wanted to hear. Did we tell him it was very female, that obsessive telephone style of his? Yes! But we used a cruder word than 'female.'"

By April 1989, Nicole officially took O.J. back. It just seemed unnatural for them not to be a family unit. She missed him, she loved him, she needed him. She could not fight the inevitable.

As he had on her nineteenth birthday and on her twenty-fifth, he made her birthday—this time, her thirtieth—a special occasion, an observation that implicitly included penitence for his wrongdoings. As Kris Kardashian Jenner observed their pattern: "He would do all these things wrong but she'd still leave the door open a crack, so he'd have to make good to get back in, and then he'd be *so* relieved. That happened a *lot.*"

O.J. invited Robert and Kris Kardashian and Alan Austin and Alan's then-girlfriend Donna Estes, down to Las Brisas

Hotel in Acapulco, "and we all just laughed for four days straight," says Kris. By day, there was waterskiing and crazy competitions (pole-hangings and one-armed push-ups) among the men, and driving around in the hotel's little pink Jeeps. At night, there was dancing and drinking margaritas till dawn. After one such night, Kris remembers, "I drank so much that when Robert and I came back to our hotel room—I don't usually drink so I really got sick—I just *lay* there with a wet washcloth on my pounding head until I fell asleep. The next morning I hear this guy singing, 'Y-M-C-A . . .'—and it's O.J. and he comes *blasting* into the room, singing at the top of his lungs, and there's everyone else behind him—Nicole, Alan, Donna—throwing confetti all over me!"

But despite the nonstop laughter of that vacation, Kris' and Robert's marriage was coming apart even faster than Nicole's and O.J.'s. In 1988, not long after she gave birth to Robert Junior, she fell in love with a young man named Todd. He was twenty-three, ten years younger than she. As decent as Robert Kardashian was, Kris now realized that their marriage lacked passion. "Robert was more like a brother to me."

The affair came out in the open. Kris did not sneak around or deny it. But the honesty cost her. Her luncheon ladies dropped her. "I was the straightest person," Kris says today with a rueful smile. "I've never done a drug in my life. When I ask for forgiveness in church, it's for gossiping or for not being nice to my kid on Thursday." Suddenly, through the affair, the world opened up to her. "I went dancing and I had fun all the time and I felt, 'I'm out of jail!' "

Nicole would experience that feeling herself, soon enough. But before she did, she found it hard to countenance Kris' affair. "Nicole at first was very disapproving of what I was doing, very angry. She believed in total fidelity. When O.J. would come home and tell her things that Robert told him, she'd get upset. O.J. would say, 'Nicole says, Kris has four kids and she's got Bobby' "—the Kardashians were still living together despite her affair—"'so why is she going out dancing all night? Nicole's pissed.'"

O.J. would soon become obsessed with the same questions in regard to Nicole.

In the meantime, however, he was determined to be a good big brother to Kris. He told her that the young lover she was so crazy about was on the verge of handing her an unhappy surprise—who knew better than O.J. about this? He invited Kris over to Rockingham for a little brother/sister talk one night when Nicole and the kids were in Laguna. Michelle (the housekeeper) made dinner for them and then left. Over dinner, O.J. looked at the thirty-three-year-old woman who had been a sweet, naive teenager when they had met back when all of them had hung out at Tom and Bob Kardashian's house, and he dispensed classic O.J. wisdom. "Look," he said, "this guy you're dating is going to cheat on you—believe me, *I* know. And he'd have to cheat on you double-time for the next ten years to keep up with me, with what I've been through. So I know what I'm talking about. I've been through a divorce, you haven't. I'm telling you. They're not fun."

Kris sat taking it all in. Years ago, she had helped O.J. when he asked her. Now O.J. was returning the favor and being a mensch. "He refused to take sides between me and Robert, the way so many people do when couples split up. He would have preferred to be able to 'fix' me and Robert, but since he couldn't—since he'd taken my temperature and found out I really loved Todd—he wasn't going to let this friendship that the two of us had all these years fall by the wayside just because I didn't love his friend Robert anymore. And *as* my friend he was thinking, 'What is Kris getting herself into? I don't want her to sink.'"

To make sure she didn't, O.J. then picked up the telephone and called Kris' young boyfriend and "he more or less told him, 'You know you're going out with someone I consider Snow White and she's got four kids and a husband. The stakes she's playing with are big, buster. So if you're not serious about her then back off because she's a good person.' I remember sitting there, thinking, 'This guy doesn't have to do this for me. He's got a good heart.' "

Kris pauses, then says, "Sometimes, when I think about those times—about that side of O.J.—I'm just so sad . . ."

Indeed, O.J. was complex—and beneath his facile charm could be a genuine decency. He was so heartsick when Wayne Hughes' baby son was diagnosed with leukemia, he couldn't bear to speak about it. And during the very same months in 1989 that he was trying to wangle his way out of a domestic violence conviction, he was not only playing big brother to Kris but uncle to the Kehoes' sons, whose father was now in prison. Whenever Sean or Christopher needed school sports uniforms, they called O.J., who replied, "Go get yourself outfitted. Cleats, shoulder pads, whatever you need. Just call Cathy [Randa] with the amount and we'll write you a check." When Susie needed a foot operation, O.J. paid for it.

Susie had finally divorced Billy, just before he was sent to Tehachapee. She finally realized that staying with Billy wasn't doing anyone any good. "Do what you gotta do; we're behind you; we love you," Susie remembers Nicole saying. In return for all her years of standing by Billy and turning a loyally blind eye to his schemes, Susie received no money—there was none *to* receive; it had been made illegally and it had been squandered. Susie didn't have time to be bitter. She got a job as a manicurist at a Beverly Hills beauty salon and she baked apple pies to sell at local farmers' markets. O.J. and Nicole bought apple pies galore and helped her with the arduous task of taking her three children to visit their father in prison. "This was a man who sent his food back if the vegetables were on the same plate as the steak—imagine him dealing with prison food?" Susie muses, recalling her fussy husband. O.J. would smile sadly when she said this, probably never imagining that in five years he would be in the same position as Billy.

With problems in the lives of their friends to divert their

attention—Billy's imprisonment, Susie's divorcing him, Kris' affair, and her young lover's cheating on her—the genuinely more serious problems that O.J. and Nicole had at the center of *their* relationship could remain obscured.

One day in May 1989, while Nicole was out in the car on errands with Sydney, O.J. was at his office, and a German-speaking babysitter (not Ruth of the New Year's Eve incident) was alone with Justin, the boy fell off a swing and cut his head open; blood gushed. It was clear he needed medical attention. Unable to reach Nicole, the babysitter phoned O.J. in a panic. O.J. became hysterical. Justin was twenty-one months old; his daughter Aaren had been twenty-three months old when she had her eventually fatal accident in the same backyard. He called for an ambulance to pick up Justin and the babysitter, then he dashed to meet them at Santa Monica Hospital.

Justin turned out to be fine but O.J. didn't get over it. After Nicole (who would certainly have raced to the hospital had she been reachable) got back home, O.J. supposedly flipped out; he and Nicole had a screaming match, while the babysitter fled into her room, afraid to come out. (The woman never babysat for the Simpsons again.)

And yet despite these incendiary altercations and despite Nicole's now-constant pain over O.J.'s unfaithfulness and his fits of physical violence, life at Rockingham continued to be, in many respects, a luxurious high-bourgeois dream. Sydney was enrolled in the Sunshine School, a highly regarded private preschool in Brentwood (Justin would also go there); the next year she would go to Marymount Junior, the elementary wing of the prestigious local Catholic high school and college. The Simpsons were generous with their house and their grounds, offering both regularly for school fundraisers and parties.

One day, as they were walking their dogs down Rockingham, Nicole and O.J. saw a big, newly built play area in the front yard of the house down the road. They went up and introduced themselves to the owners, a pleasant if plain-looking man, and his wife, a tiny Asian woman.

And that is how the Simpsons met Ron and Cora Fischman, whose daughter, Leslie, would become Sydney's best friend, and whose second daughter—coincidentally named Nicole and, in the context of the new friendship called "*Little* Nicole"—was close to Justin's age. (The Fischmans also had a son, Michael, then eight.)

Although the Fischmans might not have picked it up, all was not well with their new neighbors, who were engaged in a diversionary home improvement frenzy. It has been observed that couples trying to shore up a dying marriage often indulge in massive house renovation, using their energy to alter the structure they *can* fix in lieu of the structure they cannot. In the latter half of 1989, the Simpsons completely remodeled their house: filling the old pool and putting in a new one with a waterslide, a waterfall, and a Jacuzzi; relandscaping; sanding the floors and beams on the ground floor and adding glass doors (lightening the house many times over in the process); modernizing the master bedroom (gone was the canopy bed in favor of a sleeker arrangement); and adding more guest houses. As she had with the Schulmans', Fred Levinson's, and Marcus Allen's homes, Nicole did the decorating herself.

During the reconstruction, Nicole and O.J. and the children moved to New York for five months, living in their Fifth Avenue condominium. They usually spent part of each football season in New York because it was the base for O.J.'s television commentary; the Kardashians often joined them, staying at a Fifth Avenue hotel. Bob was then the president of MCA Radio Network. While the men did their media business, the women jogged in Central Park, right across from the hotel and the condo, and shopped. Sometimes all four adults went ice-skating at Wollman Rink and took the kids to the Central Park Zoo. And they always celebrated Kris' November birthday with a fabulous restaurant dinner and many glasses of champagne. "We always had a ball," Kris says.

Not this trip, however.

"Nicole and I spent a lot of time jogging together in Central Park, sharing our grief," recalls Kris. As they ran a half-loop—from the Metropolitan Museum's Temple of Dendur, past the 72nd Street boathouse, south by the Carousel, around the curve that took them parallel with 59th Street and over to Tavern on the Green—"she talked a lot about the problems in her marriage and about perhaps not wanting to carry on with it. She was very, very unhappy. And so was I. It was my last year of being married to Robert—he and I knew it was over. And I had dated somebody—had been in *love* with somebody—who wasn't faithful, and as I listened to Nicole talking about all the things she'd put up with from O.J. over the years, I could understand, from my own experience, what it was like to want a guy to tell you something, just tell you *any* excuse that you could sort of believe."

"You know," Nicole said, as she jogged, "years ago I used to try to find him at two in the morning on the road, and it was impossible. I used to call the apartment in New York—I'd call wherever he said he was going to be. And I could never find him until the next day. And yet with me, it's different. He *has* to know where I am, every minute of the day."

With Kris it had been different too—although in quite another way. If a man, long married and seemingly stable, a good father to his children, suddenly falls in love and wants to leave his marriage, and indeed does, society is often quick to note his steadfastness in having put his shoulder to the wheel of domestic life for as long as he did, and quick to overlook his actions. But a woman who does the same thing is viewed as selfish and immoral. Where Kris was concerned, even her friend Nicole reflected this attitude at first.

Nicole had come to terms with the permanence of O.J.'s mistresses—in addition to Tawny Kitaen, there were others whose names Kris didn't even know—but it was a sad and grinding accommodation. Nicole would never stop getting mad at O.J. over his women, fighting with him—it wasn't in her nature, or her upbringing, to accept such indignities. She had been raised by a mother spunky and temperamental enough to have a take-no-crap attitude with a man. *But* that mother had always found her center in marriage and motherhood—in having a house full of kids and friends and kids' friends. And that life had been so warm, so good—and that mother had remained so beautiful and glamorous—that a daughter, *this* daughter anyway, couldn't *not* be pulled into trying to duplicate it. Even now, Lou and Judi (and Mini and Denise and their sons) were coming to New York for Christmas, along with Jason. Few other couples today—especially not "celebrity" couples in a purportedly roots-free place like L.A.—had the woman's parents and grown siblings as deeply and consistently a part of their social life as did Nicole and O.J.

There was so much—*so* much—keeping Nicole in this marriage. Not the least of which was her own good-mother instinct. And parental guilt. Nicole told Kris how much she wanted to keep the family together. "She knew divorce would hurt her children and I think the children were probably very verbal about that fact."

Kris tried to help Nicole solve her ambivalence. Even though she and Bob were together on this trip, Kris had already decided to file for divorce. "I would say to her a lot, 'Look, I'm getting through this, and it's going to be hard. It was the hardest decision I've ever had to make in my life. And I didn't have an abusive situation—I didn't have somebody who was hitting me or cheating on me. I was very lucky in that respect. I married a very decent guy. I just wasn't in love with him. I loved him but I wasn't in love with him—there's a big difference, I discovered."

But Nicole's situation was different. She *loved* O.J. Lack of passion was not the problem; misery and unfaithfulness were. And fear, though that component was not mentioned.

"We never discussed her being hit or getting beaten—there were those things you just didn't discuss with Nicole. It was just the betrayal, the infidelity. She had just given up. She didn't care *where* he was at night anymore."

It was during one of their last runs around the park that Kris said, "I don't like it from Todd—the infidelity. I don't know how you can take it so permanently. I'm leaving. I'm leaving my marriage *and* my affair, both of them. If you don't like how O.J.'s treating you—if you don't like the constant cheating, then you should leave O.J., too."

But Nicole did not leave. Not yet, at least. The big family Christmas and New Year's in Gotham came and went, and the Simpsons flew back home to L.A. to delight in their beautifully reconstructed and refurnished home. Nicole had had the play yard built in front. Whenever Linda and Ricky Schulman's two children (they had had a daughter, Kristina, a year after they had their son) and Ron and Cora Fischman's three kids came over, they all hated to leave.

Many of the Simpsons' friends were now parents of young children: Pam and Allen Schwartz had a daughter; the Shipps were having a second baby; D'Anne and David LeBon had the first two of their four sons. The Simpsons got caught up in the happy world of obsessed parenting, a product of the baby boomers' prolonged postponement of what for every previous generation had been taken for granted as part of married life. Some of the Brentwood manifestations of this rapture at being a parent were ludicrous, to be sure; one birthday party on Rockingham for a four-year-old girl, which Sydney and her parents attended, featured a camel ride, a hot dog cart, a popcorn cart, and a fashion show (runway, commentator and all) during which the guests modeled different lavish individualized costumes (flapper, princess, cowgirl, etc.) provided by the hostess' parents. (Each "model" then got to take home the costumes as a party favor.)

Nicole and O.J., and their friends, disapproved of this

excess. O.J. remembered where he came from and so did Nicole. Just as Judi had, Nicole clipped coupons before going to the supermarket (actually, O.J. did not like this; he didn't want his wife behaving as if they had to scrimp), and she bought Sydney's and Justin's sandals in the bins at Target, a discount chain because, as she put it, "kids' feet grow so fast." The day the children set up a lemonade stand in front of the house, Nicole trilled into the videotape, "Here's your first customer! You guys have a customer!," while O.J. smiled proudly, possibly remembering his years of turning in seat cushions for a nickel apiece at the 49ers' stadium.

"They were both very good parents," says a person high in the administration of the Sunshine School, which Justin eventually also attended. "And he [O.J.] participated in the school activities more than most of the dads."

Nicole and O.J. seemed determined to keep the children's biracial identity as much of a nonissue as possible. Although Denise, when asked if Sydney had any black dolls, replied, "I think she might have had one or two," no other friend of Nicole's remembers any. D'Anne LeBon recalls being with Nicole and Sydney one day in the spring of 1990 when, out of the blue, Sydney asked, "Mommy, am I black?"

Nicole said rather defensively, "No! You are not black. You are black *and* white. You are white *and* black."

When D'Anne asked Nicole why she seemed so upset, Nicole replied, "I wouldn't want her thinking she was 'white,' either. She's both."

D'Anne couldn't tell if Nicole was annoyed that society's categories thoughtlessly excluded her children—or if she was avoiding the likelihood that the children would move toward more of a black identity as they got older.*

"Nicole," D'Anne said, "I know you want the children to

---

*Today, at six, Justin Simpson says proudly, "I'm black"—and when asked in a school exercise to name his family, he did not list any members of the Brown family (all of whom he now lives with) but, rather, said, "Daddy, Sydney, Jason, and Arnelle."

always feel they have two heritages to honor and to draw from, but Sydney is going to grow up and be a black woman one day. That is probably how the world is going to see her. Don't you think you ought to prepare her for that?"

Again, Nicole got defensive. "They're not into black versus white—they are who they are," she said, quite reasonably. "Besides," she added, "O.J. would be pissed off if he heard Sydney asking, 'Am I black?' He doesn't like that." O.J. liked to think they were "above color," Nicole explained—that their wealth and privilege would put them above the fray—beyond the need for categorization.

One day in 1990, Kris Kardashian was on the phone with Nicole from Faye Resnick's house—as planned, she had left Robert and Todd. "Oh, I *wish* I could be more like you," Nicole said, with a sadness deeper than envy. "I wish I could just walk away. But I could never leave. O.J. would kill me."

In September 1990, Kris met Bruce Jenner and they fell in love. Five months later they were married.

In 1991, Nicole began to make serious plans to leave O.J. She had developed a crush on her hairdresser, Alessandro Cassalino. Although Cora Fischman contends Nicole was having an affair with him, Robin Greer merely says, "She was having a flirtation with him—the extent, I don't know. She had a glint in her eye for him."

But she was, as ever, confused. One night Nicole went to see a gospel play in which Ron Shipp (who had quit the LAPD and was now trying his hand at an acting career) was performing. She brought Mini along and talked with Ron afterward about how she wanted to come again, this time with O.J., because of the play's strong spiritual message. But the minute she mentioned bringing O.J., she threw her hand over her mouth and said, "Oh, wait! I can't bring O.J.—I'm leaving him!" It was as if she had to remind herself that she was leaving him; she was that confused, and it was that much of a habit for her to stay.

As for O.J., when Ron (who was still hoping O.J. would

embrace religion, as a way to face the truth about himself) mentioned that Nicole wanted him to see the play, O.J. said, half-sarcastically, "Yeah, I'll come see the play—if she doesn't change her mind." He seemed to feel he was being jerked around by Nicole.

O.J.'s friends observed that he was losing weight. One night a friend was visiting Rockingham when Nicole was out. O.J. was putting the children to sleep—chasing them around distractedly, trying to get them into their pajamas. The befuddled single father role was one he was stepping into and he seemed grim about it. But he also seemed to think Nicole's leaving was just a "phase"—a phase that would pass. "She can get all that stuff out of her system," he told his friend, "but if she ever crosses that line, I won't take her back." Without need of interpretation, the friend knew what "crosses that line" meant. Later that evening O.J. restated it even more explicitly to his friend. "If she ever gives it up, she's not coming back." *Crosses that line. Gives it up.* O.J. was talking about his thirty-two-year-old wife as if she were a teenaged virgin.

Nicole and Linda Schulman began drifting apart. Nicole had always been so comfortable with the down-to-earth couple, the three of them had almost been a unit. It was *them*—Linda-Ricky-Nicole, the easygoing, normal, non-famous ones—and *Him,* the friendly but difficult icon. But as Nicole got ready for life as a single woman—as she prepared herself to mine certain freedoms for the first time in her life—the perfect marriage the Schulmans lived in their storybook cottage may have suddenly seemed irrelevant—or newly threatening. Just as Nicole had been (in Linda's analysis) "embarrassed" to show any friend but Linda how bad her relationship with O.J. really was, now perhaps she was embarrassed to go running with abandon into the dating world with the ever-sane and protective Linda and Ricky close enough to watch—and judge—her new behavior.

One day just after New Year's 1992, Nicole called Linda and asked for Robin Greer's number. She said she was leaving O.J. and she wanted to get to know single women. (Robin had been divorced from Mark Slotkin for a number of years.) Linda was hurt. Nicole wanted to confide in *Robin,* a more distant friend? Linda gave Nicole Robin's number and, in a turn of events that haunts Linda today, she stopped calling Nicole.

Nicole called Robin in mid-January 1992. "I'm breaking up with O.J.," she said. "I need to talk to you."

They made a lunch date at Toscana, a Brentwood restaurant. Nicole talked frankly to Robin, who was now a realtor and who hadn't been in the Rockingham group since she and Mark split. ("The guy stays in the group while the woman is ostracized," Robin says. "The guy and his new paramour stay in. Those are the unwritten rules.") She told Robin that she had wanted to leave O.J. ever since the New Year's Day beating in 1989 but that she was afraid if she did he would lose his endorsements. She couldn't take his violence or his womanizing—she wanted to lead "a normal life with normal men."

Nicole told Robin that her parents had not been supportive of her desire to move out—O.J. had "browbeat and manipulated them," as Nicole put it, into lobbying for Nicole to stay in the marriage. "I think it was hard on her family," Robin says now. "O.J. was relentless in persuading them to dissuade her from leaving."

Robin recalled to Nicole those nights at Rockingham when O.J. had—mysteriously but charmingly—told her that Nicole couldn't come downstairs and Robin should not go up.

"Yeah, I didn't have enough cover-up," Nicole said.

"Oh fuck, Nicole!" Robin responded. "Let's get you out of that house!"

Within a week she found Nicole a rental—a sweet little three-bedroom house with a pool on Gretna Green, a minute away from Rockingham, though in the considerably less grand neighborhood south of Sunset. Nicole felt exhilarated. "I found a great little house!" she told Rolf and Maria. "I love it! I'm gonna be free!"

But her leave-taking had an in-your-face quality. In anticipation of the help she would need as a single mother, she made a sign—"PART-TIME BABYSITTER WANTED," with the Rockingham phone number on it—and tacked it on a tree on the next street over.

7

Divorce, Reconciliation, Separation

A MARRIED COLLEGE STUDENT WHOM WE WILL CALL RIZA GOMEZ saw the sign for the babysitter posted on the tree and called the number listed. "Hello, I'm answering the ad for the babysitter," she said to the deep-voiced man who answered the phone.

Riza recalls that the man sounded upset when he told her his wife wasn't home, although he proceeded to take Riza's phone number. (She would not know until after she was hired by Nicole that he was O.J. Simpson.)

Within a couple of hours Nicole called Riza and, after a brief conversation, told her that the family was moving. She asked Riza to come to 325 North Gretna Green Way in several days, to meet her and the children.

On the day of the meeting, Riza was running very late, and, after calling the Gretna Green number and finding it busy, she called the Rockingham number. "O.J. answered," Riza remembers, "and this time he was *very* upset. He said, 'She doesn't live here anymore. You'll have to call the other number. I'm not going to see her today.'" That was the first time Riza realized that the "we" the woman had used in "We're moving" did not include her husband.

When Riza got to Gretna Green, movers were unpacking a dining room set, three sofas and two chairs. In her eagerness to leave, and given her spontaneous nature, Nicole had taken a bare minimum of furniture and supplies from Rockingham. ("O.J. hung on to everything," her mother, Judi, recalls. "She even left her wedding china in the house. He said, 'Don't separate any of the sets! I guarantee you, Nicole, we'll be back together. On February 2 [their wedding anniversary], 1994, we'll get remarried—in Aspen.' He said that for three years. This year he changed the '1994' to '1995.'")

Although it was late January, the weather was so warm it felt like summer. Nicole, in T-shirt, jeans and ankle-high boots, walked Riza through the empty rooms, into which the movers were setting down large cardboard boxes. Justin was napping on the one sofa that had been cleared of its movers' quilting.

Nicole and Riza walked outside, where Sydney, who seemed almost sullenly quiet, was in the Jacuzzi. The two women sat on chairs by the brick-edged swimming pool, and Nicole told Riza that she and her husband had just separated.

Sydney spun her head around. "But it's only temporary," she piped up.

Nicole winked at Riza. "Yes," she said, going along with Sydney's fantasy. "It's only for a couple of months."

Nicole and Riza spoke for a while and then Nicole asked for her references and driver's license. It is likely that Nicole was struck by Riza's very apparent sensitivity and maturity, rare for a young woman in her early twenties. Nicole turned to Sydney and asked, "Do you like her?"

Sydney shrugged and said, "She's okay."

The little girl was clearly not thrilled with the separation, but Riza says, "I sensed Nicole was happy; she was starting a new life. That's how she would always refer to that period: her 'new life.'" O.J.'s new life, however, was not happy. He was devastated by Nicole's leaving, friends report. As he had after the 1989 beating, he lost a great deal of weight.

Riza, whose young husband was away in the Gulf War, was hired to care for the children on the weekends. (Maria remained part-time during the week.)

"And from day one," Riza recalls, "O.J. would call and would talk to me as if we were friends forever. Oh, *long* conversations! And *all* about her. 'I can't believe this is happening, but we're gonna work things out . . .' 'This is a phase she's going through.' He would talk and talk and talk and talk, and it made me uncomfortable because he was my boss—I didn't see us as equals—yet he was confiding in me like that. It was so weird."

These particular conversations took place when O.J. called the house during the day and Riza answered the phone. More often, however, he called in the middle of the night—at two and three in the morning.

"He would call ten, fifteen, twenty times a night," Riza remembers. "She would yell at him, 'Leave me alone! Give me my space! *Please* leave me alone!' But he would call and call and call and call."

He also began calling Judi. "He was crushed by her leaving," Judi says in a whisper. "He would call and talk—I think he wanted the sympathy of everyone—until I would have to say, 'You know, O.J., you're on the phone exactly fifty-five minutes and you're still on the same subject—you're still lamenting.' And he would say, 'I miss her. It's just so hard.' I sensed his obsession, but I never took it as danger." Judi sighs and shrugs self-deprecatingly at her own naïveté. "I thought it was love."

Despite the breakup—or, perhaps, to counteract its painful effects on the children—O.J. and Nicole initiated a weekly tradition: They took the children to church together—sometimes to Reverend Moomaw's Bel Air Presbyterian, which was O.J.'s selection; at other times to St. Martin of Tours Catholic Church, Nicole's choice. Sometimes Riza would get a call from Nicole: "Don't bother staying the night; we'll be back late." And she wondered if the long day together—and, quite possibly, a night to be spent together—meant that her new employer and her husband were thinking twice about continuing their separation.

Certainly O.J. was. As Judi remembers, "He was trying very, very hard to change—to get her back. He would say, 'It's my ego [that's behind my having] all those women. I'm going to change.' "

But now it was too late. If his years of "all those women" had finally driven her to leave him, *she* was now discovering the world of men. It was as if she had turned back the clock to the age—eighteen years, one month—she was when she first met him. "She was single for the first time after all those years with a very manipulative, controlling man—of *course* she wanted to be free and have fun and go to parties," says Robin Greer, who was herself dating "everybody" and who often spent the weekends at Nicole's new house, which she had furnished like her Laguna condo—white couches and pine furniture and lots of white candles, lit at night to give the living room a romantic glow.

As Riza puts it, "I have been told that when you get divorced after a long marriage, it's like somebody opens a cage. That was what it was for Nicole. Some people said, 'Why does she party so much?'* But who are we to judge?"

One of the people who most encouraged Nicole's partying and who helped her unlock the "cage" was Faye Resnick. Nicole had met Faye through Kris, whose own mad-divorcée days were solidly behind her now that she was married to Bruce Jenner. Although Faye was still married to businessman Paul Resnick, this did not seem to keep her from kicking up her heels when her husband was not around. "Once, when Paul was out of town," says someone who knew the Resnicks well, "I saw Faye and Nicole—in their expensive sports cars, wearing hot outfits, at a club—charm all these young guys. It was okay for Nicole—she was legally separated. But Faye was not yet separated from Paul. Once I

*"You know what?" Judi says today, in an adamant whisper. "I'm *glad* she had that experience! I'm glad she got a chance to do it!"

saw the two of them, each with a young boy, sitting outside by Faye's and Paul's swimming pool at ten in the morning, drinking margaritas." (Nonetheless, when Faye turned from play to work she did so with commendable dedication. Volunteers working on a Beverly Hills parcel-tax election referendum remember her coming in to get out the vote even though she had a 102-degree fever.)

According to Riza Gomez, Nicole's first official post–O.J. boyfriend was "a blondish boy with a short, cute name. He was very young—*so* young I don't want to speculate: maybe under twenty. He was like a playmate to the children. I don't remember his name; all I remember is that he stayed over at the house, and then he moved to Hawaii and sent the children funny straw hats and leis."

When her employer went off with this young man, Riza "sometimes used to think that Nicole did not know what to do with her freedom." But as Nicole began to confide in her, Riza realized that Nicole's abandon was at least in part an attempt to assuage years of pain.

"She would ask me to give her a massage on her back," Riza says. "She gave me a medicinal cream. She would lie down and as I put the ointment on her back she would say, 'Ooh, it hurts. Look what O.J. did to me. Look what he did . . .' I did not see any scars, but she would flinch, like she was in pain. 'He beat me,' she said. 'He beat me *a lot.*' "

"Oh, my God," Riza remembers saying, "he could have *killed* you."

To which, she says, Nicole replied softly, "I know. I know. But I got out in time."

One night in the early spring of 1992, while Nicole and Cora Fischman were having dinner at Giorgio's, a restaurant in Santa Monica Canyon, they ran into Kris Jenner and her ex-husband Bob's cousin, Cici Shahian. The two women had been close ever since Cici had come to Kris' defense during the bruising divorce from Bob—they now referred to each other as "my cousin."

These four women, who would form a close group, were

very different, both in personality and in circumstances. With the separation scandal behind her and her recent marriage to Bruce Jenner, Kris now had an air of womanly composure and authority. Cora, forthright, preoccupied, yet disarmingly perceptive, was a harried mother managing three kids under eleven. Cici, the only single one, was warm, sensible, always ready to listen, analyze, make things better. And Nicole, new at this girlfriend routine, was cool, fun, no-bullshit, ready for anything. On the surface, her life seemed easy to sum up: newly sprung from her difficult superstar husband, she was testing her freedom as a Brentwood beauty. But under her insouciant veneer was a thread of constant danger, although it was not visible, even to Kris, who had known her and O.J. for so long.

Absent from this foursome at Giorgio's that night was Kris' and now Nicole's friend Faye Resnick, the most adventurous one. They would soon become a tight group, all five of them.

At dinner that night, Nicole asked Kris about a male friend of hers whom she had seen but not yet met. "How's your friend Joseph?"

"Fine," Kris said.

"I'd love to meet him," Nicole told her. The next day, Kris set up a dinner for herself, Nicole and her friend, dark-haired actor and Neiman-Marcus shoe buyer Joseph Perulli. Shortly thereafter, a romance bloomed.

Even in a town full of handsome men, Joseph Perulli was, by all accounts, extraordinarily good-looking. He was closer to Nicole's age than the first boyfriend (who moved to Hawaii) and more serious in style. "The first boyfriend wore baggy shorts and sandals," Riza notes, "but with Joseph, you could see the creases in his T-shirt, you could smell his cologne; he was very well mannered and very cleancut. When he and Nicole started seeing each other, he was at the house all day and then they would go out at night. The kids liked him a lot."

O.J. did his level best to wish Nicole well in her new romance. "He told me"—Riza imitates a maudlin, self-sacrificing voice—" 'Now that she's seeing this guy, I hope that she's happy.' " And Alan Austin, who played golf with O.J. several times a week, says, "He accepted the breakup. He was resolved that she had the right to do what she wanted to do. He stepped out of her life when she got a boyfriend."

But O.J. may not have been as sanguine as he wanted people to think. Later, one of Nicole's friends would say, "Of all Nicole's boyfriends, after Marcus, Joseph was the one who really got O.J.'s goat. My impression is that he was jealous of him."

"Something curious started happening when Nicole was dating Joseph," Riza recalls. "Every time O.J. was in town, if I took the kids somewhere, ten minutes later O.J. would be there too. Let's say we were at the park on Barrington; there would come O.J. He'd walk over to us and very pleasantly say, 'I was driving by and I saw the van.' This happened three or four times. Another time I was eating with the children at the Soup Plantation on San Vicente. He walked in and said, 'I saw the van when you were parking.' Another time I was driving the kids down Sunset—they always liked to be way in the back of the van, looking out the back window—and Justin goes, 'Oh, there's Daddy! There's my daddy, right behind us!' We were at Cliffwood and Sunset, right by Rockingham, waiting for the light to change. There, in my rearview mirror, was O.J.: smiling, waving.

"I was so naive, I didn't put two and two together until I mentioned these 'coincidences' to Nicole and she said, 'Oh, no! He's following *you, too!* Oh, gimme a break!' She was really upset.

"One night, Nicole heard noises in the bushes outside by the alley where she had the trash cans," Riza continues. "When she told me about it the next day, she was still very, very scared. She told me that somebody had been following her and she was pretty sure it was O.J. but she didn't know for sure. So she went out and bought these *huge* locks and put them on the gate to the alley, so that whenever we wanted to dump some trash we had to bring a key. The next night, when I was going to pick Sydney up from a playdate across the street, she gave me a can of Mace. She said, '*Please* do *not* go out without this! I'm pretty sure that it's O.J., but I want to play it safe.' "

Actually, the night she heard the noise she called Ron Shipp immediately. "I saw a face in the window," she told him; then, when Ron arrived: "I'm not sure, but it looked like it was O.J. or Jason. I don't know—maybe O.J.'s even bugging my house!"

Ron checked around the house and stayed two hours, but the stalker, whoever he was, did not reappear. Once Nicole relaxed, she got Ron and herself a beer and as they sank into her big white couches, she talked of how happy she was to be on her own, even though some of the friends she and O.J. had had as a couple had made their loyalties known: to O.J., and certainly to the life that he, and not she, could provide —the tennis court, the swimming pool, the vacations, the Super and Pro Bowls.

She didn't care about a lot of those people, but some of the defections had hurt her. She said: "Marcus Allen called the other day, to say hi. I said, 'Stop by sometime.' And he said, 'This is a difficult situation for me; I don't know what side to take.' I said, 'Don't worry about it, Marcus. I understand.' And after I hung up the phone, I thought about it for a minute and I said to myself, 'Fuck Marcus Allen! I don't need Marcus Allen!' "

When Nina Shipp heard that story from Ron later that night, they both thought it was an amusing example of Nicole's spunkiness. Today, however, given what we know of the affair Nicole would (according to what she told friends) eventually start with Allen, O.J.'s protégé's apparent conflict might be interpreted as having weightier implications.

In any event, the spunkiness that seemed so evident in Nicole that night took great effort. Riza, who was becoming very fond of her generous and secretly vulnerable employer, saw much that was life-affirming in Nicole—the list she had on her refrigerator, for example. (*1. Lose 15 pounds. 2. Treat people the way I want them to treat me.* And on and on until *10. Get a life.*) She was a wonderful mother—sensible with the children, who were overwhelmingly her first priority, "always involved with their lives, always telling me to give them fruit and cheese instead of cookies if they wanted a snack." She found a stray dog on the street, fed it and gave it a bath and briefly took it in before taking it to the pound. She checked in on her elderly neighbor and bought groceries for her whenever she went to the market.

But underneath this effort at joyfulness, Nicole had been terribly afraid, almost all of the time. "She walked into my office in a major depression; she looked like a waif," says Dr. Susan Forward, the therapist and authority on the psychological dynamics of battering relationships, whom Nicole sought out for two sessions in March of 1992. Nicole had been reading Dr. Forward's book *Men Who Hate Women and the Women Who Love Them* (she would also be reading Forward's next book, *Obsessive Love,* at the time of her murder) and she had said of it to at least one friend, "This is the story of my life."

Dr. Forward, who, days after the murders, disclosed the fact of Nicole's sessions with her,* described her as a terrified, exhausted young woman who soon revealed that she felt she would never be able to get away from her husband, no matter what she did or who she was with or where she went.

Nicole told Dr. Forward that she had been beaten "regularly" by O.J.—"pounded" and "kicked" and "punched" were her words—and that now he was stalking her.

Dr. Forward told Nicole what she told all women in this situation: She must cut off *all* contact with O.J. Giving him a little contact was simply feeding the fires of an insanely jealous, possessive man.

---

*An act that some thought was inappropriate publicity-seeking but others believed to be an important service to battered women and to the cause of justice in this case.

Nicole could not do this. She told Dr. Forward that she believed if she placated O.J., if she spent a little time with him and meanwhile tried to get on with her life, sooner or later he would calm down and go away. Besides, Nicole said, she couldn't completely cut off from him because "that would hurt his feelings" (revealing herself, by this sad turn of phrase, to be, in Dr. Forward's view, a "classic" battered woman).

Dr. Forward had heard this misplaced sympathy for the batterer countless times before, and she told Nicole, gently but firmly, that things did *not* work that way. She *must* cut off all contact with O.J. It was the only way to get him to stop hounding her: to force a defusing of his obsession.

But *how,* Nicole wondered, between her two sessions with Dr. Forward, *could* she *do* that? O.J. was the father of her children. She wanted Sydney and Justin to get as much parenting as they could from the daddy they adored. And she was financially dependent on him—and dependent in other ways as well. The kids' playground was Rockingham. It still felt like their "real home." Even the van that she and Riza used for the kids was O.J.'s, not hers.

Riza could see the tension in Nicole. And she could clearly see Nicole's guilt over the separation—guilt that was not without justification, for Sydney was taking the divorce very badly. "She felt she had lost so much—her father, that house," Riza says of the little girl she became so close to. "There was so much less that we had, after what Sydney was used to—we had ten glasses and six plates. Sydney was very angry. She would get furious at the tiniest things." Nicole started taking her to a child psychologist.

Almost every friend of Nicole's and O.J.'s, at one time or another, supported their reconciliation—and for the same reason: "for the sake of the children."

So, when Nicole talked to Dr. Susan Forward, the therapist's prescriptive—Cut all contact with O.J.—seemed an impossibility. "Nicole's terror—her fear of this big man—was so pervasive," Dr. Forward recalls. "She said, 'I am so alone. Where do I go? The police won't help me. My family's not supportive. They wanted me to 'work it out' with him*—and they're my only support system!" O.J., Nicole made clear, had charmed her family.

It was precisely that charm, alternating with rage, precisely that Jekyll-and-Hyde quality, Dr. Forward explained to Nicole, that made O.J. so dangerously hard to deal with. As she observed: "The switching from charm to rage leaves you totally off balance. Everything that's right on Monday is wrong on Tuesday. So you're always watching—you're on emotional alert all the time." (In Nicole's particular case, of course, O.J.'s immense charm was most disarming to *others* —people adored him and felt him simply incapable of violence. Nicole's own style toward O.J. was considerably less timid than what Dr. Forward describes as the most classic battered woman's wariness: She dove right *into* the fray; she went hand-to-hand with O.J.)

Nicole told Dr. Forward of other threats O.J. was now making: "I'll take the kids"; "I'll cut you off without a dime." She told the doctor, in her usual broad strokes, about evenings like the one Denise and Ed McCabe had witnessed: when O.J. had tantrums and screamed and threw things—and people.

Both sessions were filled with Nicole's fear and anxieties and Dr. Forward's exhortations that she could not placate O.J. and at the same time get free of him. She could not do both.

Nicole said she did not think she could do anything but continue to see him and talk to him.

Dr. Forward says she spoke clearly and emphatically to Nicole: "Nicole, how can I help you? I cannot figure out a way for you to make nice with him—and to empower yourself and have a life. *The two things cannot coexist.*

---

*Again, the Browns sincerely state that Nicole—to use Denise's word—"minimized" and sloughed off and made light of the abuses, mentioning them so matter-of-factly that she did not invite a serious reaction. This description of Nicole's presentation of her problems with O.J. is corroborated by Linda Schulman.

You've got to take the only steps I know of that will get him to start to take you seriously, which means to make clear to him: 'I am no longer available for you. You cannot have a relationship with me.' And if you're not willing to do that, I don't know how I can help you."

Toward the end of their second session, Dr. Forward told Nicole, "I really fear for your life."

Nicole looked at Dr. Forward, and the expression on her face left no doubt that she understood that the therapist was not exaggerating.

Tears streamed down Nicole's cheeks.

As spring turned to summer, Riza recalls that O.J. seemed to accept the fact that Nicole was going to file for divorce. By now the conversations had changed from his obsessive hopes for winning her back to plaintive—and often indignant—lamentations about her metamorphosis. "She's changed so much," he would say to Riza, calling at night and finding Nicole not home. "I don't know what's wrong with her! What is she trying to prove?" This line was one of his leitmotifs. *"What is she trying to prove?"* O.J. told Riza that when he and Nicole had been together, her clothes had been "modest"; now, as Riza remembers his complaint, "he said her clothes 'embarrassed' him. She *did* wear tight tank dresses in summer—that was true. And he did not like that at all."

In his conversations with Cora Fischman, O.J. analyzed his error as having been a simple one: "It was my mistake to show Nicole Hollywood." Cora herself has come to sum it up this way: "Nicole wanted stability and O.J. gave her glamour because that was all he had to give. He gave her financial security, though that didn't make her happy. I've come to see it as the classic case of a woman getting married young and not really knowing what she wanted.

"O.J.," Cora says, "said to me many times, after she left him, 'She was my life.'"

And it was at those moments when he most felt his life with Nicole, as he had known it, was slipping away that

O.J.'s phone calls had greatest resonance. Over Easter, he called the house only to discover that Nicole had taken the children to Aspen. Riza, who was at the house feeding the cats, recalls that that is when the "What is she trying to prove? Why is she living this way?" questions were so painfully heartfelt.

Another night around this time, "Nicole left on a date and it was understood that she was spending the night out," Riza remembers. "She left me money for the kids, and I took Justin and Sydney and Leslie Fischman out to Shaky's Pizza and then dropped Sydney at the Fischmans' for a while. O.J. called from New York and he got *so* mad. He said, 'Why is she [Sydney] eating so much pizza?' And I said, 'Well, I was never told she was not allowed to eat pizza.' And he said, 'Yes, but it's not good for her, that much pizza. And where is Nicole?'

"I said, 'I don't know where she is.'

"'And when is she coming back?'

"'I don't know when she's coming back.'

"'So you're telling me you're alone with Justin?'

"And I said, 'Yes.'

"He explodes. 'I *can't believe* she's doing this! I can't believe she's leaving the kids like this!'" When O.J. was Justin's and Sydney's age, he was left alone with his siblings almost every night while his mother worked; the suppressed fear and loneliness of all those evenings may well have been partially the reason for his anger on his own children's behalf.

"O.J. called five or six times more that night. And the excuse was that he was worried about Sydney—'Where is she? Why isn't she back yet?'—when he knew she was just with Cora and the kids. Sydney and Justin didn't know their mother wasn't coming back that night—they would have gone to sleep fine with me there—but he made it worse by calling and, after giving Sydney his hotel room and phone number, saying real loud, 'Well, if she's not back yet, I'm sure she's not coming back!' Sydney started crying."

The shoe had been on the other foot hundreds of times

before, but O.J. could not bear the reversal: *his* calling Nicole and finding *her* gone for the night, with somebody else, destination and details unknown. Still, there was something undeniably sad about his realizing he no longer controlled his family's life.

The 1982 Albert Finney–Diane Keaton movie *Shoot the Moon* showed a controlling but genial screenwriter turning into a jealous, destructive yet somehow poignant madman after his divorce. At the end of the movie, he drives his car into his ex-wife's brand-new tennis court, completely destroying it. Many mild-mannered men who had survived divorces watched that movie and understood the emotional truth of that tennis-court scene, just as many mild-mannered women understood *Thelma and Louise.* For O.J. Simpson, that truth may have been quite literal.

Nicole, on the other hand, could bear O.J.'s taking on a new girlfriend—or so it appeared. While she was dating Joseph, O.J. was dating a woman whom Riza and Nicole called "the Victoria's Secret Girl" because all they knew is that she modeled for that famous lingerie catalogue (this was someone other than Paula Barbieri). Riza had seen her at Rockingham one day ("Since I took the kids there and back, I brought all the gossip home to Nicole") and when she told her, Nicole seemed calmly philosophical. "Yes, people have told me about her," she said. "I just hope the two of them are happy so he'll leave me alone."

But when the new Victoria's Secret catalogue arrived in her mailbox, Nicole's calm aloofness vanished. She ran upstairs with the brochure, thrust it at Riza and, bursting with curiosity, demanded, *"Which one is she?"* When Riza identified her, Nicole took a hard, appraising look, then, in a tone of voice that in Riza's re-creation combines suppressed jealousy with relief, said, "Hmmh, okay. Fine. Whatever."

But given O.J.'s apparent logic, there was no reason that his involvement with another woman should interfere with his obsession with Nicole—it never had before. In fact, in early April, just as his new romance was under way, his stalking of Nicole intensified.

She had just started a three-week-long affair with Keith Zlomsowitch, the director of operations for the Mezzaluna restaurants in Aspen, Brentwood and Beverly Hills. Like Joseph Perulli, Keith was dark-haired. He was not, however, as "pretty" as Perulli—his good looks were more rugged.

Keith's and Nicole's relationship was plagued by O.J.'s stalking.

One night, Nicole and a group of friends joined Keith at the Beverly Hills Mezzaluna, which was in the old Jax-and-Daisy grid of streets. As Keith would testify, in June 1994, to the grand jury, O.J. suddenly "walked into the restaurant and approached our table. . . . leaned over . . . , rested his hands on the table and sort of stared at myself and the other male individual at the table and . . . [said], 'I'm O.J. Simpson and she's still my wife.'" O.J.'s tone of voice, Keith testified, was "serious . . . , deep, threatening to the point [that] we were very intimidated. I was for sure intimidated. I was shocked a little bit. I simply leaned back. I was scared. I was afraid of a possible confrontation."

Nicole made a remark to O.J., Keith stood up, "a little shaken," and Nicole and O.J. walked outside where they talked about O.J.'s intrusion: "he was gesturing with his hands and she was . . . acting like she was trying to appease him."

O.J. left and Nicole came back into the restaurant, "visibly shaken," Keith recalled to the grand jury. Later, when she got home, she told Riza the incident had scared her and ruined her evening.

The next time (or *one* of the next times, at any rate) that O.J. followed Nicole and Keith to a restaurant, he upped the menace level. Nicole, Keith and a few other people, including Robin Greer, had just been seated for dinner at a new West Hollywood restaurant named Tryst. O.J., Keith told the grand jury, "walked into the restaurant, walked directly by our table, looked at everybody . . . as he walked by, made it very clear that his presence was there [sic], walked over to a table approximately ten feet away from ours, pulled the chair sideways, as if to face our table directly, sat down and just stared. . . . This actually was so uncomfortable that one of the guests at our party felt so shaken she got up and left the restaurant. She said, 'I just can't handle this.' "

Keith, too, was nervous. O.J. "made a point when he sat down of looking directly into my eyes." Nicole was "very, very nervous, very uncomfortable."

However, Robin Greer, whose cool wit had always enabled her to see through O.J. and his circle of friends, kept her composure and her humor. When O.J. asked her, "Don't you think Nick and I should be together?" she remembers that she replied, without missing a beat, "Not unless it's *without* a prenuptial agreement."

Nicole wanted to leave, but Keith did not want to be bullied, so they finished their dinner with O.J. staring at them from "ten feet or so" away.

But this was not the end of it. A week later, Keith and Nicole went to a show at the Comedy Store. A male friend of O.J.'s who had always been very sympathetic to Nicole remembers running into her there that night and feeling surprised at how "funny it seemed seeing her with another man after all those years of her being O.J.'s woman." Despite this man's intellectual, if not emotional approval of the Simpsons' separation, "it was hard to get used to. Seeing her on that date with that other guy gave me a pang. It's hard to watch your woman, or even your friend's woman, with another man."

But the sight that this man accidentally happened upon, O.J. apparently actively *sought*—and never more concertedly than on that evening. And though this friend of O.J.'s says, "I never said a word to O.J. about seeing Nicole that night," he didn't have to. O.J. apparently was already tailing the couple.

After the show at the Comedy Store, Nicole and Keith went dancing at a club called the Roxbury. There, according to Keith's testimony, "Nicole came up to me and made a comment: 'O.J. is here,' " whereupon Keith and Nicole beat a hasty exit.

But apparently not hasty enough.

When they got to Nicole's house, they thought they were alone. "We lit a few candles, put on a little music, poured a glass of wine and we sat on the couch in the downstairs living room . . . and we began to become intimate," Keith testified. A few hours later, "Nicole thought it was best that I should go home and she should go to bed. So she did and I did."

The next day when Keith returned to the house, Nicole mentioned her neck was stiff. They went into a bedroom off the swimming pool (so that they could see the children swimming) and Nicole lay on her stomach while Keith sat on her back and began massaging her neck. Both he and Nicole were fully clothed.

"Very soon after . . . I began giving Nicole [the] massage," Keith said, on the grand jury witness stand, "I looked up and Mr. Simpson came . . . directly in through the back door right up on top of us, physically within two feet. . . . I looked up. I was startled. Nicole looked up and was startled as well." O.J. said—in what Keith recalled as an "angry" tone of voice: "I can't believe it. I can't believe it. Look what you are doing. The kids are right out there by the pool. Look what you guys are doing."

Then O.J. sat down on the bed and said, "I watched you last night. I can't believe you would do that in the house. I watched you. I saw everything you did." (The minute O.J. left, Keith examined the three layers of curtains on the living room windows—and they were, indeed, partially open.)

O.J. talked on; by this time Keith was feeling "extremely uncomfortable" sitting on Nicole and slowly moved off her back. "I didn't want to jump, run. . . ." When O.J. said he wanted to talk to Nicole, Keith bravely said, "I'm not leaving the room."

"Is this what it's come to?" O.J. said to Nicole. "I can't even talk to you alone? Is this what it's come to?"

Keith stood his ground, but Nicole finally said, "It's okay, Keith. Just wait in the kitchen. It's okay."

Keith waited anxiously for fifteen minutes, until a subdued O.J. walked into the kitchen and extended his hand. He said, "No hard feelings. You know, I'm a very proud man and"—here Keith is approximating O.J.'s words—" I'm very visible in this community." Then O.J. left.

Nicole's friends give Keith a great deal of credit. "He was the only one of her boyfriends who stood up to O.J.," one of them says.

This is not quite the end of the Keith story. According to his grand jury testimony, another day he was at the house in Laguna watching a game on TV while Nicole, her children and sisters were outside on the beach. The phone rang, and when it wasn't answered after a number of rings, Keith picked it up. It was O.J., abruptly demanding, "Who is this?" (He sounded "very, very angry," Keith recalls.) When Keith identified himself, O.J. angrily said, "Put someone else on the phone."

Keith ran down the beach to get one of the Brown sisters, who came inside, picked up the phone, and proceeded to try to calm her brother-in-law down, repeatedly saying, "O.J., relax. Relax, O.J. It's no big deal."

Shortly after that incident, Keith and Nicole ended their romance.

In the midst of the enormously taxing task of fending off O.J., Nicole now had to deal with the details of their divorce. Two things in particular hurt her, Riza remembers. One is that O.J., hewing to their prenuptial agreement, didn't want to give her any real estate except the San Francisco condominium, whose value would exactly translate into nothing more than a three-bedroom Brentwood town house without a pool. "I don't care for myself," Nicole said to Riza, "but I care for the children. They're used to a big house with a yard and a pool; why does he want to deny them what they've always had?" Worse, Riza says, "She knew O.J. wanted Justin but he didn't want Sydney—that hurt her a lot. But she knew he wouldn't dare fight [for the custody of Justin] in court because he knew that if he took

Justin he would have to take Sydney, too; no judge would separate the children."

Despite these considerable pressures, Nicole threw herself a big thirty-third birthday on May 19, 1992. "It was a huge, wonderful party," Riza recalls. "She had somebody come and barbecue fish and chicken, and inside we made tacos. Fifty or sixty people came, and there was music and dancing." When Eve Chen arrived, Nicole was delighted—she walked her high school soulmate around and introduced her to all her new friends. Riza recalls, "It really hit me that everyone at the party was saying the same kinds of things to Nicole: 'We're so glad you're talking to us again!' 'We haven't seen you in so many years!' 'Welcome back to life.' "

One fact that marred the party, however, was Nicole's tremendous concern over a big dent and scratch she had recently gotten on her white Ferrari. The bodywork would cost thousands; she seemed as terrified of revealing this fact to O.J. as a teenage daughter would to her father. "Her fear did not make sense," Riza says. "After all, it was *her* car." The incident drove home to Riza once again how dependent Nicole was on O.J., how complicated their ties were.

"It seems so strange dating, with children," Nicole said a few weeks later, sitting on the beach with D'Anne LeBon. Nicole was now unburdening herself of many long-pent-up worries that she had never wanted her adored Pinky (David LeBon) and his wife to know. Magic Johnson's wife, Cookie, had just had their baby—a healthy one, thank God—and Nicole was talking about how agonizing it had been living with the fear that, sleeping around, O.J. could have gotten AIDS (he didn't) and infected her. And when she told D'Anne of some of the violence she had suffered at O.J.'s hands, D'Anne said, "Nicole! Why didn't you tell us?"

Nicole replied calmly, "I didn't think anyone would believe me."

After all, Nicole's father had seen the pictures Denise had taken of her after the New Year's Day 1989 beating and yet he still suggested that Nicole stay in the marriage. Lou Brown loved his daughter, but something about the dangerousness of it all just did not sink in. Similarly, Nicole told several friends that O.J. said he would kill her if he found her with another man (Denise had heard him make that threat), and yet the very patness and gross exaggeration of that threat lulled the hearers into disbelief. Nicole alone believed it—alone knew how serious it was.

Women who are loved by dangerously obsessed men suffer a terrible loneliness. The laws that govern other marriages and divorces simply do not apply to theirs, and they are the only ones who know it. Dr. Penelope Grace, a psychologist and domestic violence expert who was affiliated with Harvard University Medical School's Children's Hospital, has said, "The woman who knows her husband is serious when he says 'If you leave me, I'll kill you' is like a woman locked up alone in a cubicle, screaming. The people outside the cubicle's walls can hear her screams in a dim, muffled, general way—and they respond to what they hear with advice based on good intentions. But they can't hear the clarity and the bottomlessness of her terror. And they don't know what she knows in her bones: That he's going to make good on his promise."

Nicole, fearful that O.J. might be serious in his threats, felt like that woman in the cubicle. And although she and D'Anne sat side by side on the beach that day, separated by nothing, there was perhaps a wall dividing them—dividing Nicole from all her loving friends—a wall only Nicole could see. It is not that people did not *want* to "believe" her fear or pain. They didn't have the language. They did not live in the foreign country that was her marriage.

On July 7, 1993, O.J. turned forty-five and, as usual, he celebrated with a big party, this one a catered outdoor affair at Rockingham. He had by now settled into a relationship with Paula Barbieri, a lushly pretty southern model and sometime actress who, despite a propensity to tout her resemblance to Julia Roberts, had a kind of dignity and rectitude. Paula was religious—she and O.J. shared a "spiritual" connection, she has said—and she was decent. The children liked Paula, and Nicole liked her, as did those friends of hers who met her. "She seemed warm and down to earth," recalls one woman friend of the Simpsons', who met Paula at O.J.'s birthday party.

At that party, the toll the divorce was taking on the children seemed evident. According to one concerned guest (herself a mother), Justin was wild and Sydney was petulant. "I found myself thinking," this woman recalls, " 'I would love O.J. and Nicole to get back together, for the sake of the kids.' "

As O.J. raised his glass in a thank-you toast, it was clear that he was very drunk. "It was not a pleasant scene," a guest recalls. He left the party early to go upstairs; Paula went with him. There was no temper tantrum or falling down, just the sense that all his adoring friends—and even his lovely new girlfriend—couldn't save him from the deep loss that he was experiencing.

Over the course of the time she spent in the Beverly Hills offices of Jaffe and Clements, the law firm that was handling her divorce, Nicole got to know a very attractive young paralegal. His name was Brett Shaves; he was in his early twenties—twelve years younger than Nicole—and he had the same dark good looks as Joseph Perulli.

Of all the men she dated after leaving O.J., Brett had the background most like hers. He grew up in an upper-middle-class gated-estate section of Fresno—as she had grown up in gated-estate Garden Grove and Laguna. Brett had a wild side; he and his best friend had once spun out in the middle of the 405 just as Nicole and Pinky had spun out in Pinky's car in the parking lot. Brett had laughed at his close call, just as Nicole had.

Still, despite his Harley Davidson and his weekend Club Tatou and Viper Room mufti (jeans, vest over bare chest, large cross, two earrings in one ear, hair slicked back by a bandana), Brett was essentially a small-town preppy. He drove a BMW, wore Armani suits by day, and kept his well-appointed one-bedroom Beverly Hills apartment impeccably neat.

Brett was used to being the most handsome guy in his crowd—at Clovis West High in Fresno and at his UCLA fraternity—and having his pick of girls, but after he started dating Nicole Brown (she was now using her maiden name) in July 1992, he was hooked. He was, he told a friend, deeply in love. And he was crazy about Nicole's two adorable young children.

Brett's friend said, "Whoa, this lady comes with lots of baggage. Be careful."

Brett was Nicole's longest-term boyfriend—they dated for six months. And those dates—Brett told this friend—were often dogged by O.J. Simpson.

Brett and Nicole would go out to restaurants—Nicky Blair's or Brentwood Mezzaluna—and, suddenly, there was O.J. Nicole and Brett would drive down the street (Brett often drove Nicole's Ferrari) and, again, there would be O.J., right behind them. Once even as they were driving down Brett's street—Reeves Drive in Beverly Hills, miles away from Brentwood—they saw O.J.'s face in the rearview mirror. Brett made a quick getaway, losing O.J.

Still, Brett did not seem to be personally afraid. Whenever O.J. came up to him and Nicole at the restaurants they all just "happened" to be frequenting, Simpson was always civil. "O.J. was nice to Brett," says a friend of Nicole's. "He was not threatened by him as he was by Joseph"—and he wasn't angry and intrusive, as he had consistently been toward Keith, whose romance with Nicole had been, in comparison, very short-lived. Perhaps O.J.'s growing happiness and preoccupation with Paula Barbieri accounted for the difference.

Despite Brett's friend's warning, Shaves told him that he wanted to marry Nicole and be a stepfather to Sydney and Justin. Nicole's friends do not think that she took Brett nearly as seriously as he took her; still, his earnest intentions and his work in her lawyers' office led to frequent talks about the progress of her divorce negotiations.

Nicole was seeking $4,000 a month for medical expenses for herself and the children; O.J. claimed most of this would go to a nutritionist and fought that figure. Nicole wanted $6,200 a month for clothing, travel and entertainment and $2,500 for incidentals. O.J. thought those figures were much too high. In papers he filed, O.J. described bad turns of fortune—he claimed that his NBC contract was $100,000 a year less than the last one, that he had lost two fast food restaurants he owned in the L.A. riots (Rolf Baur had been employed at one of them), and that three of the six Honey Baked Ham gourmet stores he half-owned had been shut because of the recession. He cited the need to support his ailing mother, as well as Jason and Arnelle.

Nicole wanted O.J. to buy her the Gretna Green house or one of equal value—one-million-two. He refused. She wanted $7,000 in alimony and $13,000 in child support, adding up to $20,000 a month. He wanted to halve that amount, and succeeded in doing so. Nicole ended up receiving $10,000 a month child support (from which she had to make the children's private school payments), no alimony—and a lump sum settlement of $433,750.

During one of Nicole's discussions with Brett about how unfair she felt O.J.'s position was, O.J. walked in. The friend to whom Brett told this story does not know if the incident took place at a restaurant or at Nicole's house. Wherever it was, "O.J. walked in and, seeing Brett there, got angry. He said to Nicole, 'Why should I give you more money when you're fucking around! I should take the kids anyway!' " O.J. finally left, but Brett was nervous.

"Yeah, it was getting a little spooky," Brett finally admitted to a friend, just after he broke up with Nicole. Then he predicted, "I'm scared for those kids. I have a feeling something bad is gonna happen."

* * *

Nicole's and O.J.'s divorce was final on October 15, 1992. Still, despite months of O.J.'s stalking her and causing her pain, she was, up to the very last minute, ambivalent about signing the papers—about breaking the bond with him.

Nicole was to drop Sydney off at Cici Shahian's Beverly Hills apartment before going to sign the divorce papers. Cici was taking both Sydney and Leslie Fischman for the evening, to give their mothers a night off. When Nicole dropped Sydney off, she lingered at Cici's doorstep. She looked so wistful and hesitant that Cici had to ask, "Nicole, are you *sure* you want to go through with this?"

Nicole replied softly, "I don't know."

But everyone was already waiting at the lawyers' office.

Later Nicole told Cici that even as she and O.J. signed the document ending their marriage, they felt a connection to each other. As they walked to their separate cars, they both, in Cici's remembrance of Nicole's words, "looked back at each other and had expressions that said, 'Wait a minute, what just happened?' "

By now, according to Nicole's friends, she was involved with Marcus Allen.* She had also acquired a nonpaying lodger, Brian "Kato" Kaelin, whom she had met in Aspen. Kato, Robin Greer says, was a funny guy and "like a Pied Piper to the children." Nicole let him stay in her guest house for free, and Nicole, Kato and Robin often club-hopped together.

Riza had stopped working for Nicole, but they stayed in touch. In late November 1992 she called and Nicole told her she hoped they would soon be moving; she had received the San Francisco condominium in her divorce agreement and was going to sell it and buy a house in the neighborhood. "She told me, because I'd been with them when things were rough: 'We're very happy now.' "

*Again, through his agent, Ed Hookstratten, Marcus Allen denies that he was ever romantically involved with Nicole.

Still, spending Thanksgiving and especially Christmas away from Rockingham was painful. All the warmth of those years. Being in the kitchen of that big house with O.J. and Jason and Arnelle and A.C. and Lou and Judi and Denise, Mini, Tanya. Their friends popping over: the Schulmans, the Kehoes, the Schwartzes, Tom McCollum, the Kardashians, Ahmad, Marcus, Stellini and Kolkowitz. The Nat King Cole carols. The champagne and mistletoe. Nicole missed it. And the children missed it terribly.

Years before, after a fight with O.J., Nicole had driven from San Francisco to Laguna, only to turn right around and drive back that same night. Now, less than three months after her divorce, she began to long to make another—bigger—hairpin turn and go back into his arms, into his life.

Still, Nicole was confused. Did she want O.J. back—or did she want a younger O.J.?

Marcus Allen's career had certain strong echoes of O.J.'s He had just wound up the unhappiest of several frustrating seasons with the Raiders—just as O.J. had simmered for three years with the Bills. O.J.'s beef with the Bills' John Rauch was that he wasn't being played enough (or in the right position). Marcus' beef with the Raiders' Al Davis was similar: Despite the fact that Marcus had been the team's best running back in eleven years, Davis had virtually refused to play him on much more than third downs ever since he held out for more money in 1989; Marcus was so upset, he actually said, in a television interview, "What do you think of a guy who has attempted to ruin your career?" (By spring, via the players' new free-agency clause, Allen would be able to leave the club and sign with the Kansas City Chiefs.)

On January 13, Nicole gave a party. Marcus, despite his earlier reservations about seeing her, attended. Nicole's friends were impressed by him. "He's *so* charming; he has such a nice spirit about him," one friend said.

"I know," Nicole replied, looking at him admiringly.

Between mid-January and early April, her friends say,

Nicole and Marcus saw each other, discreetly.* They were seen by Robin Greer's sister Lysa, allegedly acting very affectionate at the Gotham Hall bar and pool hall (where Lysa worked as a barmaid) in Santa Monica.

One of Nicole's friends says, "Nicole fell in love with Marcus. She said, 'If it isn't O.J., it will be Marcus.' O.J. was the love of her life, and Marcus came second."

Still, that first man on her list was really the one she wanted back. And yet, all of a sudden, how mututal was the feeling?

"I'm getting tired of younger guys—they're more possessive, less stable," Nicole told Susie Kehoe one day early in 1993. Susie had come in to town to visit; she was now remarried, living in the desert community of Temecula and selling water filtration devices for an environmentally minded company with an evangelistic marketing regimen. "I don't like the dating scene. I miss O.J.," Nicole said. "I think about him."

Susie could relate to what Nicole was saying. "I feel that way about Billy sometimes," Susie said sadly. Billy was very ill with cirrhosis of the liver and Susie's long, complex life with the charismatic but ultimately impossible man was still fresh, particularly when she and the children visited him. "It's hard to let go of the past, even if it's only in your thoughts."

Nicole thought Susie was misunderstanding her. "I don't mean I'm having trouble letting go of O.J. I mean I want to go back to him."

Actually, Susie hadn't misunderstood; she was just tactfully moving the conversation in the direction she thought it should go. For she had just visited O.J. and she had come away feeling that he was finally getting used to the divorce. "I don't know, Susie," she remembers him saying, "I love

---

*As stated before, Marcus Allen, through his agent Ed Hookstratten, denies having had any romantic involvement with Nicole.

her, I love the kids, but I'm getting older, I'm getting tired." Susie had empathized. When she had finally divorced Billy, after all they had gone through, "I felt, 'Phew, it's over—the door is finally closed.' You've stopped asking yourself if the person will ever change. It's finally quiet. The thought of putting it back together again after all the legal and money issues have been worked out—it's the last thing you want. Besides, who can get the feeling back? O.J. seemed to agree with all of that."

He was finally beginning to let Nicole go. He was settling in with Paula. And yet he was keeping the door open, too. " 'If you wanted me back, I would drop Paula in a minute,'" Cora Fischman says O.J. told Nicole at one point. Cora claims that O.J. tried very hard to understand Nicole's need for freedom. "I was thirty-three myself once—I know what that feels like," he said. Cora says that Nicole appreciated O.J.'s tolerance of her. "He understands that I don't know what I want," she quotes Nicole as having said.

On their daily nine-mile runs, around UCLA and down and up San Vicente, Cora kept Nicole abreast of O.J.'s shifting plans. He was now starting to talk about selling Rockingham—he said he was tired of L.A.—and moving to Florida.

Rockingham—gone?! O.J., gone?! Although she spent so much of her time, since the separation, ducking him as he stalked her, the thought of him *not* being near was shocking.

"He's going to change his life," Cathy Randa told one of O.J.'s male friends one day in March. "*This* week it's Florida," she said, laughing good-naturedly, as if he now had a different plan every week.

On the runs with Cora and Cici, Nicole would say, "If only he could stop womanizing. If only things could be different. . . ."

She had begun to believe that, with enough inner determination, a person could change. On a recent trip to Aspen—Aspen and Cabo San Lucas in Mexico were her new crowd's chief holiday destinations—she had met a young actor named Grant Cramer, who was the actress Terry Moore's son. He had introduced her to a New Age-style group therapy program: Releasing the past and attaining self-empowerment were its two main themes. Nicole was now beginning to believe that she could, as she told her friends, "release on" the past with O.J. Forget the bad—the cheating and beatings. Start the future with today, not yesterday.

One day in the early spring, as Cici and Cora were running up San Vicente with Nicole, she stopped—and they stopped too, and turned, and looked at her.

"I wanna go home," Nicole said, very simply.

By that she did not mean: Jog back to Gretna Green. She meant: Go back to Rockingham. To O.J.

"It was so Nicole," Cici remembers. "A simple, direct statement." Home was the place she had created with the love of her life. Even though they had just divorced, even though their life together had often proved impossible, her heart was telling her that she had to go back and try again.

A few days later, during another run, Cora mentioned to Nicole that O.J. had called her and said he *was* putting the house on the market. (Indeed, he had called realtor Elaine Young and had started talking to her about this possibility.) "So we thought," Cici recalls, "that maybe there was a time limit."

A few mornings later Nicole called Cici and said, "I've made a decision. I'm going to go back to O.J., *if* he'll take me."

Cici remembered what Cora had said about the house going up for sale, the move to Florida "Well, then," Cici says, "you better call him—*soon!*" Today, Cici pauses and turns very sad when she thinks about that conversation. "This is the part that breaks my heart," she says. "We thought that, for *all* the good reasons—the kids, the family, the relatives, the beach, the birthdays, the holidays: for all the things she loved . . . we encouraged her." Cici sighs. "We encouraged her to go back. Nobody wants to be lonely."

Nicole called O.J.'s office and left a message with Cathy Randa to have O.J. please call her back, but, according to

Cici, Nicole did not believe that Cathy gave O.J. the message. At any rate, O.J. did not call. Nicole then called the house and left a message with Michelle. O.J. didn't call her after *that* call, either.

"When he didn't call back," Cici says, "we coaxed her to call again. She called the next day, and the message must have been relayed because he called back—maybe he thought there was something wrong with one of the children." But when he realized that the reason for the call had nothing to do with the children—when he divined its true purpose, "he avoided her," Cici recalls.

Cora elaborates. She says that O.J. told Nicole: "Don't call! I *like* my life now! Stop calling me!"

But theirs was a bond as sick as it was loving, and Nicole's fervor was only stimulated by O.J.'s rejection—by the astonishing thought that he could actually get over her. She kept calling; he did not take her calls.

She grew desperate. All she could think of was how wonderful their life had been at certain moments. To this end—and to get him to remember these moments as well—she duplicated the videotapes of their marriage and of the children's births and she either mailed or delivered these to Rockingham, along with a note, on an index card: *O.J., I understand that it's probably too late but I have to do it for myself and the kids or I would never forgive myself. I'll call Cathy from now on and I'll only call you in an absolute emergency. Please believe me and return these calls immediately.**

O.J. asked Cora, "What's going on? I'm used to life without Nicole. I come home and nobody's screaming and yelling. I've gotten over her. I've put my life back together."

---

*These tapes and this note were found by police searching for evidence in O.J.'s master bedroom shortly after the murders, leading reporters to erroneously report that they were sent by Nicole in the weeks before her death, not as a reconciliation plea but as a Dear John letter.

To a male friend he said, "Man, she wants to get back together. I don't want to."

Nicole panicked and became aggressive. "Cathy [Randa] said she started calling and showing up at the house a bunch of times," says a male friend. "Cathy said he didn't want to see her, but he was also getting a kick out of it. He was kind of excited by it."

One day in April, this friend was at O.J.'s house, about to play tennis. When he and O.J. stepped out front for a moment, the friend, walking ahead, was startled to see Nicole parked outside the gate. "I'm telling you, man, it was a Nicole I'd never seen before. She looked like she was *chasing* him. I walked up and said, 'Hi, Nicole!' When O.J. heard me say that he looked at me like, 'I'm not here! I don't want to talk to her!' He ran back in the house.

Nicole had told Cici what she was wearing that day—a $40 shift and a pair of rubber Zories. ("Who but Nicole," Cici asks, "would show up dressed like that to try to get her husband back?")

Nicole was super friendly. "Hey, you gonna play some tennis?" she asked O.J.'s friend.

"Yeah," the friend replied. "What are you up to?"

"Oh, I just want to talk to O.J. . . ." The pleasantries continued, but the friend got the distinct sense of Nicole being different than he had ever seen her. Gone was the breezy cool. *This* Nicole was a bit of a predator. And she was anxious. Nicole never *used* to be anxious.

As Nicole talked and waited, she pushed and re-pushed the button at the gate, but O.J. would not let her drive her car in. Finally, after she waited and pushed the bell for no less than twenty minutes, O.J. came out.

Nicole got out of the car and they took a walk down the street on which they used to stroll, with Chow and Shiba on each leash, with Sydney and then Justin in the stroller.

Cora conveys the essence of the walk, as described to her by Nicole: "Nicole *begged* O.J. to take her back. O.J. told her that he liked his life the way it was." According to what

Nicole told Cici, O.J. said, "I'm happy with Paula." Nicole cried as she said, "I wanna come home." She proposed that they somehow forget about their pasts and start anew. Cora and Cici both remember Nicole telling them that O.J. was *shocked.* Even though he had certainly told others, like Cathy, that Nicole wanted him back, perhaps to hear it from her this explicitly and emotionally was stunning. In any case, he girded himself: He said he would have to think about it—he couldn't respond to her proposal to try a reconciliation right away. It was just too much to swallow.

Nicole drove back to Gretna Green. That night O.J. called her—he said he couldn't sleep; he couldn't think about anything except what she had told him. He was talking a mile a minute. From that moment on, Nicole's friends say, he changed from someone who didn't want to go back, who liked his life, who had to think about it—to someone elated and driven and obsessed by the idea of coming back.

In May, they took a trip to Cabo San Lucas with a number of Nicole's friends to officially begin their attempt at reconciliation.

Nicole had walked to the brink of zero hour and won him back.

Nicole had some conditions for the new life she and O.J. would have together. The first was: "This time, my girlfriends come with me." She loved the new friends she had made, her evenings with her girlfriends at the restaurants; as much as O.J.'s morning golf games were part of his life, her girlfriends had to be part of it, too. O.J. conceded.

In an effort at greater togetherness, Nicole also took up golf—and was very good at it. ("Look at her; she's better than *you,*" one of the Riviera regulars kidded O.J.) O.J. walked her around Riviera, proudly—if no longer accurately—calling her "my wife"; he seemed delighted to be using that word again. One of Nicole's best friends observed his pride, and the vulnerability that went along with it. ("I'm a very proud man and I'm visible in this community," he had said to Keith Zlomsowitch.) Later, in sad hindsight, Nicole's friend says, "You don't leave a man like O.J. Simpson twice—it's too humiliating for him." Did Nicole not understand that the stakes in her reconciliation were higher than the stakes in her marriage?

But the most important ground rule O.J. and Nicole made for their attempted reconciliation was the promise to each come clean about their recent pasts—to tell each other, with immunity, about everyone they had slept with. "Nicole said that *he* insisted upon this 'cleansing,'" says Kris Jenner. Indeed, he had seemed proud of initiating these truth sessions when he talked to Judi. "I told her about all my girlfriends—the girls I had, how long I had them," O.J. told her. "O.J.! Why'd you do that?" Judi asked. O.J.'s reply (Judi paraphrases it with her own charming twist on the American vernacular) was, "I want to get the table cleared! Clean air!"

But, given what one might imagine O.J.'s history of indiscretions to be, those "cleansing sessions" were "fatiguing" for Nicole, recalls Kris Jenner. "When Nicole told me about them, she said, 'It was so draining, it was three hours of just talking.'" Still, Nicole was heartened by O.J.'s promise to "release" the past. "They were starting over fresh," Cici says. "Nicole said they both decided that they *could* forget the past."

Yet this proved untrue. Cora says, "O.J. could not take the fact that Nicole had had other men. She said, 'I don't bring up *your* past, your women . . . ,'" as if she could appeal to his sense of fairness. But try as he might to change, O.J. had an ironclad double standard. And the alleged betrayal that hurt had to do with Marcus Allen.

According to what Nicole told one friend, she told O.J. about her involvement with Marcus. O.J. then talked to Marcus—O.J. was, according to this friend's sense of Nicole's reading of the situation at the time, "angry but he had no choice but to live with it." When Marcus decided to marry his long-time girlfriend, Kathryn Eickstaedt, O.J. had apparently forgiven him enough to offer to host the couple's summer 1993 wedding at Rockingham. Marcus accepted O.J.'s offer. According to this same friend, before the wedding Nicole and Marcus had some heart-to-heart talks during which Nicole said, "Don't cheat on her," and Marcus said he intended to be a faithful husband. Nicole's friend says, "Nicole and Marcus had known each other so long, they could talk like that. They *were* friends. But their own passion and sexual attraction eventually outweighed their values and morals."

A day or so before the nuptials, however, Nicole picked up the phone at Rockingham (she was now dividing her time between the two residences; she did not want to uproot the children again until she was sure the reconciliation was working) and encountered the voice of Paula Barbieri. O.J. had promised fidelity; *why* was Paula calling? They had a fight; Nicole was angry. She chose not to attend the wedding. Right after the wedding, however, Nicole told a friend, O.J. rushed over to Gretna Green and spent the night with her.

It was during one of these rocky patches in the reconcilliation attempt that O.J. and Nicole found themselves with a not unexpected tragedy to attend to: Billy Kehoe's funeral.

He and Nicole had arrived at the funeral separately. (O.J. came with Joe Stellini.) With the same generosity that had informed his whole relationship with Billy and Susie during all of their previous dark hours, O.J. paid a good deal of the bill for the burial. As the old crowd stood at the graveside and mourned the man who thought he could out-hustle everyone, the mourners' thoughts turned to their own vulnerability. Some golden period in life was over. People in the group now struggled with medical problems, difficulties with their kids, second marriages that had proved to have problems just like their first ones. Stellini's restaurant had fallen on hard times and in a couple of months Joe would close it. These men might still throw footballs and bat softballs in parks on weekends, and they could expertly coach every big game they watched on their state-of-the-art TVs from the sofas in their expensively furnished living rooms, but time was passing. Middle age was here.

One of the bumpiest moments of the summer occurred one night when Nicole, O.J., Faye Resnick and her boyfriend, chiropractor Christian Reichardt, were waiting at the bar at a spirited little Hermosa Beach sushi place called California Beach, where the sushi chefs whack and mold the fish and rice while they cheer, groove, laugh, boogie and high-five each other.

The restaurant's manager Tonē, a cool, ponytailed sometime-UCLA student, remembers saying to himself, "Wow, it's O.J. . . ." as he seated the foursome at the sushi bar. At one point, O.J. went downstairs, apparently to make a phone call. Tonē says a regular customer later told him, "While O.J. was down there on the phone, he tried to hit on my date." At some point after O.J. returned upstairs, according to Tonē, "All of a sudden one or both of the girls said something and O.J. flipped like a switch." This "something" was, according to Faye Resnick, the name of Nicole's old boyfriend, Joseph Perulli. Tonē continues: "He just got up off his seat and started yelling, really loud, 'That was the wrong thing to say!' As he was walking out of the lounge into the bar area, the girls were chasing him, trying to catch him and get him to calm down and he's just going, 'Fuck you, bitch! Fuck you, bitch!' "

The other patrons stared as O.J. "stormed" out of the second-floor restaurant and down the wooden stairs to the parking lot. Nicole and Faye ran after him. "He had his Ferrari parked right out front and we were watching him and we could hear him yelling at the girls, 'Fuck you!' and 'I'm leaving!' The screaming went on for about five minutes." Then he got into his Ferrari and sped off in the night. Nicole, Faye and Christian left shortly thereafter.

These blow-ups were things Nicole either did not mention

to her family or, if she alluded to them, they did not mar her parents' affection for O.J. In August a big party was given for Lou Brown's seventieth birthday. O.J. stood up and gave a toast to his ex-father-in-law. According to one guest, it went: "I want everybody to know, at the beginning, when I started dating his daughter, Lou Brown was not supposed to know that I was around. And then he accepted me and we became good friends and I'm very happy about it." O.J. and Lou slapped each other on the back and hugged and hugged and everybody smiled.

"What does Nicole want? One day she wants me, one day she doesn't," O.J. would rail to Cora. She was attempting a reconciliation but she was also hanging out a lot with Faye Resnick. She wanted to move back to Rockingham and she wanted to buy a house of her own. She was tired of paying the $5,000 a month rent on Gretna Green; she wanted to be amassing equity. With the proceeds of the sale of the San Francisco condominium, she could do so.

In October she called the Brentwood office of Jon Douglas, a huge realty enterprise. (Douglas happened to be a good friend of Nicole's first and only employer, Jack Hansen.) Nicole had seen a FOR SALE sign on a very dramatic Mediterranean-style townhouse. The realtor handling the property was Jeane McKenna, with whom, serendipitously, Nicole had a lot in common: Jeane, though older than Nicole, was also a strikingly pretty blonde with a spirited personality who was divorced from a professional athlete—Dodger Jim Lefebvre. She and Nicole got along right away. And to Jeane, Nicole made mention of O.J.'s cocaine use—"in the present tense," Jeane remembers.

The townhouse did have one drawback: It was south of Montana Avenue and located right on Bundy Drive, which, being a busy north-south thoroughfare, was noisy. Its neighborhood (of apartments rather than houses) was one big step down from Gretna Green (a street of houses, not apartments) just as Gretna Green was a big step down from

Rockingham (a street of estates, not houses). But Nicole didn't care that she would be downscaling twice within a year—she wasn't a snob. Besides, the main drag of Brentwood—San Vicente from Gorham to Darlington—would now be within walking distance. The area she would be moving into was the young, urban Brentwood. Nicole now wanted to be a part of that neighborhood.

She went into escrow on the house.

But, as happy as Nicole was made by the prospect of purchasing it, at least one person was temporarily angered: O.J.

On the night of October 25, O.J. drove over to Nicole's house on Gretna Green and, according to what she told a 911 operator in a trembling voice, broke her back door down. "Can you send someone to my house? My ex-husband, or my husband, just broke into my house, and he's ranting and raving," she is heard begging the operator on the 911 tape. In the background O.J. can be heard sarcastically saying, "Oh . . . *now* it's different. . . ." and referring to the act of fellatio which he claims to have witnessed between Nicole and Keith in the living room in April.

When asked by the operator if he had been drinking, Nicole says, "No. But he's crazy."

A squad car is dispatched to the house, but O.J. leaves before it gets there.

Nicole calls a second time a few minutes later. "He's back," she says, crying. When asked who "he" is, she says, "He's O.J. Simpson, I think you know his record. . . . He's freaking going nuts." When the operator asks her to stay on the line, Nicole protests, "I don't want to stay on the line! He's gonna beat the shit out of me! The kids are up there sleeping and I don't want anything to happen. . . . He's in the backyard, screaming at my roommate"—Kato—"and at me."

The operator asks Nicole what O.J. is saying. She sighs deeply and replies, "Oh. . . . something about some guy I know [this is later assumed to be Joseph Perulli] and hookers and Keith, and I started this shit before and it's all my fault. . . ." Nicole abandons the weary paraphrase of O.J.'s litany to say, "He broke my door, he broke the whole back door in."

"Is he upset with something you did?" the operator asks.

Again, Nicole sighs and replies, "A long time ago." Here she means the April night with Keith. "It always comes back." She cries as the operator asks if she is talking back to O.J. "No! *Who* could talk? Listen to him . . ."

Now O.J.'s voice is heard on the tape.

"I don't give a fuck anymore. . . . ," he rants angrily.

"O.J., O.J., could you please just leave?" she pleads.

"I'm leaving with my two fucking kids, is when I'm leaving," he replies. He mentions Keith yet again and—after Nicole says, "O.J., please! The kids!"—he says, "I had to read this *bullshit* all week in the *National Enquirer* . . ." It is not known here what he is referring to. The last audible statement O.J. makes on the tape is typically self-pitying, "I try my goddam best." Then he says, "I ain't puttin' up with no goddam . . ."

The tape fades into a series of radio calls.

Three days after this incident, O.J. and Nicole were reunited.

When Tom McCollum heard of the incident and the reconciliation that postdated it, he exhorted O.J., "Dear God! *Both* of you! For God's sake: Move five thousand miles from each other!"

In October Riza Gomez had a baby. The minute she called Nicole and told her, Nicole said, "Oh, bring the baby over! I want to see him!" Riza drove to Gretna Green right after Thanksgiving. Nicole held Riza's infant in her arms and rocked him and said, "If somebody gave me a baby right now, I'd take it in a heartbeat." Nicole told her she had spent Thanksgiving with O.J.; despite her terror during his "break in" at the house (something Riza did not know about), she had been able to have a warm holiday meal with him—and she was buying a house. She seemed happy, if conflicted. "We owe you so much," she said. "Any night you need a babysitter, bring the baby over—I'll take care of him." Nicole took another peek at the tiny infant before Riza drove home. "They're babies for so short a time. It all goes so fast," she said wistfully.

Just before Christmas, O.J. popped into Theodore boutique in the Brentwood Gardens to buy a present for his loyal housekeeper Michelle. He started talking to owner Leslie Letellier, the way the male customers of Theodore so often did. "I don't remember how the subject came up," Leslie says, "but he seemed to want to put his marriage back together. He was *very* excited about it. He pretty much blamed the breakup on his infidelity; he said, 'You know, there's so much temptation out there.' But when I said, 'Sure there's temptation, but you can look the other way. Do you *always* have to get what you want?' he got a bit agitated and defensive, like it wasn't any of my business anymore. I backed off."

Leslie, by now, had a trio of cute young guys coming into her store daily, plopping on the floor cushions, talking to her and her cute salesgirls, Jodi Kahn and Arina Hanciulescu. "They were all wholesome boys—even when they talked about sex it was like they had just discovered ice cream," says Leslie. "They weren't jaded—just nice boys from nice families: always polite, always remembering their manners. It was very refreshing."

One of the boys was Jeff Keller. He had just moved to town from Boston. Another was his roommate, Mike Davis, who had just moved from Connecticut. Hanging out at the Wall—the stucco balustrade of Starbucks—Jeff and Mike met a guy Jeff remembers as "a warm kid who, like us, obviously wasn't from California—he was originally from Chicago. Basically we were all young guys transplanted from somewhere else: networking at Starbucks, wanting to get into television, acting, theater, commercials, club promotion or the restaurant business." The guys would sit on the Wall in their big shorts and cut-off-sleeveless tee shirts—do-rags swathing their brows, pagers clipped to their waistbands: talking about which clubs to hit that night and watching the local women sit down on the patio with their *grande lattes* and their oat bran muffins. "I'd never seen so many boob jobs in my life till I moved to Brentwood!" Jeff says. "We'd go, 'Peep this.' And, 'Hey, *no way* those are real, man.' "

The fellows all had starter jobs—waiter, gourmet food courier, gym trainer—located right in the neighborhood. Of the three of them, the Theodore's ladies clearly thought the boy who was originally from Chicago was the most vulnerable and the most appealing. "He was the one who was not afraid to show his feelings," Jodi noticed. "He was like my little brother," says Leslie. "He would say, 'Oh, I go out with these guys and they're all better than me, and everybody's interested in them and I feel like a big oaf.' But it was clear to *me* that *he* was the most desirable." He had gone through a difficult breakup—he told the other salesgirl, Arina—with a girlfriend who, he claimed, had taken most of his furniture out of their apartment when they separated and who then "started holding hands with guys at clubs, right in front of him." He was too good to be treated like that, the three Theodore ladies agreed. He had a poignant, yearning quality. He dreamed of opening a restaurant. He had the details all figured out, right down to the doors and the menus. He even had the blueprints drawn up. And he had already chosen a name for it: The Ankh—a similar Egyptian sign to the one the pop music star Prince had just adopted in lieu of his written, pronounceable name. These three guys all loved Prince's music, especially his brand-new hit, "The Most Beautiful Girl in the World" (who—the three were getting the distinct sense—probably resided in Brentwood). "He explained to me, 'The ankh is the symbol of eternal life and I want my restaurant to last forever,' " says Jeff Keller.

The young man's restaurant was not to be; but, sadly, the young man himself would shortly attain an unbidden piece of eternity.

His name was Ronald Goldman.

On Christmas Eve, O.J., Nicole and the children tried to be a family again, but tensions flared. They were at Rockingham, dressing for a lavish party at Kris and Bruce Jenner's when Nicole, according to Kris, walked into the kitchen and found a holiday gift basket. She glanced at the card—it was to O.J., from Paula: She got mad.

"By the time she got to our house," Kris remembers, "she and O.J. were in a very tense mood." Kato was with them—and a recent decision about his future accommodations was adding to their tensions. Nicole's new Bundy house, which she was about to close on and move into, had no detached guest quarters; in order for Kato to remain as Nicole's rent-free boarder, he would have to live in a room in the house proper, and, according to Kris, "the thought of that made O.J. crazy." So he had co-opted Kato: offered him one of the guest house rooms at Rockingham. And Kato had accepted. Nicole was mad at Kato for what she considered a betrayal: After her months of generosity, he was moving over to O.J.'s orbit (and eventually, friends say, spying on her for O.J. by turning up at the restaurants she went to with her friends). "O.J.," Nicole said ruefully to Kris, "always gets what he wants."

So here were the Simpsons on Christmas Eve: several battles simmering, as so often was the case. Walking into the Jenners' elegant party—fifty people; caviar; champagne; dinner; Christmas music and a dazzling tree—calmed their tempers slightly.

"Then in walks Joseph Perulli to deliver a Christmas basket to us," says Kris. "He's always invited to our Christmas parties, but this year I didn't invite him because O.J. and Nicole were coming."

But there he was—with his holiday gift. And, "because he knew everybody at the party, he stayed to shake hands, to give Christmas kisses and hugs. And," Kris continues, recalling how nervous it made her, "I'm sitting here thinking, 'This is never going to end. He is never going to leave.' O.J. started to stew. He just got angrier and angrier—you could tell by the look on his face. He was tense. Quiet. Bruce talked to him a couple of times and he was just blank—sort of getting crazed." Finally, O.J. stormed out of the Jenners' house with Nicole—and Christmas Day, for the Simpsons, came on the heels of a day's worth of mutual anger.

Nicole was very excited the day she moved into her house on 875 South Bundy Drive in January 1994. "She had on an old sweatshirt and sweatpants and I'm thinking, 'If her butt looks this good in those sweatpants then *I* want those sweatpants!'" says Kris. "Faye and I were helping her unpack, and we were all laughing—we were giving her a hard time because she had saved all these old tee shirts. We were throwing out old stuff and helping her organize.

"She was *so* happy that she was able to buy the place herself, that she hadn't had to ask for help from anyone. She had the most beautiful kitchen—all granite with cabinets you could see through, and she had all the dishes perfectly, and everything was so well organized—I hugged her and said, 'I'm so proud of you!'"

O.J. was there a lot, from the start. In fact, Nicole got a special four-poster bed, just because he liked them. They traveled to Atlanta for the Super Bowl, then chartered a boat in Florida.

By spring, however, Nicole was still conflicted. Keep trying to make a go of it with O.J. or be a free woman? Stay with the old crowd, the O.J.-centered social life, or strike out on her own, with new friends?: These were her questions.

She solved the dilemma by doing both. In March, looking glamorous in a slinky Jean Muir slip-dress that someone else picked out for her ("Who's Jean Muir?" Nicole had asked, when Cici got excited about the designer), she accompanied

O.J. to the premiere of *Naked Gun 33 1/3: The Final Insult.* Justin—his eyes scrunched up in a goofy smile—and a sweetly smiling Sydney posed for photos in front of their parents. (Leslie Fischman also came along, and got into some shots.) It was the last time they would be photographed as a family. Later that same month, she, O.J., A.C. and Joe Kolkowitz went to Marcus Allen's thirty-fourth birthday party at a restaurant on Melrose Boulevard. "Happy birthday—you finally caught up with me," Nicole said to Marcus, according to a friend, making fun of the ten months she had on him. But perhaps those words had a double meaning. For, according to Nicole's friends, she had cooled things with Marcus when she went back with O.J. Would seeing him again make things different?

Over Easter vacation, Nicole went to Cabo with friends. O.J. had been filming his new TV pilot, *Frogman,* on location in Puerto Rico; after filming was done, he flew over and joined them. The new *Naked Gun* had vitalized his acting career—in this pilot he was a Navy SEAL–type hero. One of the things he had to learn to do for the role was to perform a swift, complicated attack with a large, sharp knife. Soon, in fact, during a break from local filming he would wander into a downtown Los Angeles knife store, Ross Cutlery, and purchase an addition to his knife collection—a folding stiletto.

After the Cabo trip, Nicole was as confused as ever. "She said she had the best time," Cora Fischman says, "but that she was tired of being 'so into him.'" But Nicole told Rolf Baur that O.J.'s presence in Cabo had made her "very uncomfortable."

"Toward the end," says Kris Jenner, "you never knew in the morning *where* you'd find Nicole." Did Kris believe that Nicole was reeling out of control? Kris says, "Yes."

Shortly after that trip, O.J., during a golf game with Alan Austin, said, "Man, it's too much trouble, the relationship." Still, Austin says, "He was in love with her, until the very end."

* * *

By now Jeff Keller and Mike Davis—and probably their friend Ron Goldman, too—knew who Brentwood's contender for the "the most beautiful girl in the world" was. She was Nicole Brown, O.J. Simpson's ex-wife, the incredibly neat lady with the figure and the spirit of a girl their own age, whom they had met one day in March when she had jogged by Starbucks with her friend Cora and her big white Akita, Kato.

Jeff, who was white, and Mike, who was black, had became her buddies. (She knew Ron much less well.) To them, she was the *best:* She took them out to dinner (and paid) and let them take turns driving her Ferrari both ways. "This is the *baddest* car going!" Jeff would say, gunning the engine down Wilshire. She would call them and say, "What are you guys doing?" And Jeff or Mike would say, "Well, *Melrose* is on in a half hour"—*Melrose Place* was their favorite TV show—and she would say, "Can I watch it with you guys?" And she would come right over.

"She kind of lived vicariously through us," Jeff says. "We were in our twenties; she wanted to see what we were all about. Her life had been so different: She was married to this big celebrity, she was tied down with her kids. It was a total friendship thing, and one time, to show you the kind of person she was, when I said, 'Hey, I really like your DKNY sweatshirt,' she said, 'Here, try it on. If it fits you, it's yours.' She gave it to me!"

Jeff goes on: "She said, 'I feel comfortable with you guys. You guys have a good sense of morals and you give me good advice.' She didn't want synthetic B.S. people. She wanted real people—who didn't have anything, who just had what we were given by our families, what we got by our trials in life."

Mike and Jeff were her new Pinkys, and perhaps with them she could pretend she was again seventeen—that she hadn't met the man who she couldn't seem to leave even when she thought she desperately wanted to. The man who seemed to dog and provoke her—every day that she wasn't dogging and provoking him. The man she was in love with—in that compelling, tempestuous, no-win way that she had somehow come to define and experience as love.

Jeff and Mike were Nicole's lost innocence.

Jeff Keller recalls: "She said she wanted to resolve her relationship with O.J., to bring her kids up properly and show them the life they deserved and be a great mother. By May, it was extremely clear to Michael and myself that she didn't want to go on with O.J. She wanted to have her freedom and her life."

Faye Resnick was now spending a lot of time with Nicole—in her book, Faye contended that she and Nicole had a brief lesbian liaison, a contention which resulted in tremendous pain and anger on the part of Nicole's family and some of her oldest friends.

At least one of Nicole's other best friends learned from Nicole that she had started seeing Marcus again. "Oh, Nicole, just be careful!" that friend said worriedly.

On Saturday, May 7, Nicole went to Laguna for Denise's son Sean's First Communion. O.J. attended as well. The next day, Sunday, May 8, Nicole made out her will.

The very next week, on Saturday, May 14, Sydney's First Communion was held at St. Martin of Tours Church on Sunset. O.J. did not show up. Rolf Baur says that the reason Nicole did not invite O.J. to have dinner with the family at Mezzaluna on June 12 was because of his inexplicable slight, which hurt Nicole a lot.

That week, "O.J. and Nicole had a big fight over money," Cora remembers. On the heels of that fight, Cora had picked up Sydney and Justin to take them to school and O.J. called her and said, inexplicably, "I don't want my kids in your car!" After that, Cora says, Nicole talked to O.J. about what she called his "violent temper" and he agreed to see a therapist about it.

Referred by a mutual friend who was in treatment with this man, O.J. began seeing a licensed clinical social worker for private sessions. He continued the sessions until—in the therapist's words—"very close" to the time of the murders. This therapist makes it clear that the "Terasoff" warning (whereby any mental health professional whose patient or client voices a threat to the life of another is legally obligated to report that threat to the police) was not warranted by O.J. Simpson's sessions with him. The therapist declined to be interviewed for this book.

Nicole caught pneumonia the week of her thirty-fifth birthday. She was in bed, very weakened and sick. O.J. extended himself to her, almost as never before. He took the kids to and from school. He went shopping for her (or sent Michelle to do so). He came over with chicken soup that Michelle had made and with Nicole's favorite comfort food—candy from L.A.'s premier chocolatier, See's.

On May 19, O.J. gave Nicole a stunning piece of jewelry—an estate bracelet of rows of diamonds and a row of sapphires all set in platinum. It was the most ravishing jewelry he had ever given her.

That same day, Ron Shipp called Nicole to wish her a happy birthday. She did not sound good. Aside from her being sick, there was something in her tone of voice that worried him. It seemed to Ron as if she was now leading a confused and fast-track life. He wanted to stop by and visit her but, for some reason—some vestige of loyalty, some sense of propriety—he felt the need to clear the visit with O.J. first. When he called O.J. and said he was thinking of stopping by Nicole's house, O.J. said, "Nah, don't bother going over there." Ron, reluctantly, scrapped the visit.

A week later, Nicole met Cici and Cora for their morning jog. She looked elated—free. Cici noticed that the antique bracelet O.J. had just given her was not on her wrist. "I broke up with him!" she told her girlfriends, about what she had done a few days before on May 22. "I finally feel free! I gave him back the bracelet*—I did it nicely—and I told him, 'I can't be bought.'"

To Cici and Cora, Nicole seemed so different—so certain,

*Nicole added later to Rolf Baur, "O.J. said, 'Well, then you might as well give me back those diamond earrings I gave you, too!' I did!"

so *free.* Cici and Cora could feel it. They knew she had finally made the decision that had eluded her for all these years. They could not believe that O.J. could not see the difference, too. "It was obvious," Cici remembers. "She was over him."

O.J. now tried to woo Paula Barbieri back in earnest. A male friend of his ran into him and Paula at the House of Blues, the Sunset club owned by Dan Ackroyd. "O.J. was drunk. He was still in the process of trying to get Paula back, but she had her guard up. Instead of their usual cuddling, she sat there stiffly while he made jokes. She was standoffish—she had that 'After what *you* did, I haven't decided to let you back' attitude. I felt bad for the guy. He had totally cut it off with Paula to get Nicole back and now Nicole had dumped him. I saw a really hurt person."

As reported on television, on May 27, a local prop outlet called Cinema Secrets, which specializes in makeup for actors, received a call from someone ordering a short mustache, a short beard and surgical glue. The store's manager took the order. O.J. Simpson's credit card was used for the purchase. A woman named "Cathy"—later identified as Cathy Randa—picked up the order. O.J. Simpson had been a regular customer of the store, often buying custom-blended makeup. When the purchase was revealed, in August, O.J. Simpson contended that he often wore disguises when he was in public with his children, so he would not be bothered by his fans. But several people who know him well say that this is not true—he loves attention.

During the end of the first week in June, Nicole told Rolf Baur that she was very upset—a key to the house had disappeared from her key chain. She had her housekeeper looking all over the house for the key—under papers, in cupboards, in drawers. The key was not found.

On Sunday, June 5, Nicole, in a panic, called her friend and realtor Jeane McKenna and told her that O.J. had just informed her that he was going to report her to the IRS for something she had been doing for six months: When she sold the San Francisco condominium and bought the Bundy house, she was supposed to rent out Bundy in order to receive a tax break, just as she had rented out the San Francisco condo. But she hadn't done that—she had lived in Bundy pretending to rent it, reporting her permanent residence as 360 North Rockingham. If caught—or turned in, as now seemed likely—she would owe the government money. "Ninety thousand dollars," she told Jeane McKenna, "is all I have left!"

"Oh, Nicole, O.J.'s not going to report you!" Jeane had said. She couldn't imagine a father displacing his children —for the third time in a year and a half.

"Yes, he will. Believe me, he's crazy. He'll do it," Nicole replied. "So we gotta go find another place and we gotta list Bundy to lease." They made a date to look for a new place for Nicole to rent and move the kids into so she could properly rent out Bundy.

On Tuesday, June 7, Nicole called the Sojourn Shelter for battered women, seeking help. She said she was being stalked and she said O.J. was the person stalking her.

On Friday, June 10, Nicole and Jeane drove around looking at houses: a place in Mandeville Canyon, Allen Schwartz's street; a place on the corner of Sunset and Carmelina. These houses would put her back in the Rockingham neighborhood—but at what emotional cost? "I've been reading Susan Forward's book *Obsessive Love,*" Nicole told Jeane. "I finally get it. O.J. is a classic obsessive. He fits the pattern in every way."

Yet, in her own way, she had been his perfect mate. Hadn't she been as hooked on his obsession toward her as he was obsessed? What had Ron Shipp said about the dynamics of those relationships—it can't be just one person, brutalizing another—*both* have to mesh. "And when they do," Ron had said, "they come together magnetically."

Nicole looked at the houses Jean was showing her, virtually right next door to Rockingham. "Take me to Malibu," she said, referring to another listing Jeane had mentioned.

Malibu was far away from Brentwood.

The house Jeane took her to see was a sprawling four-bedroom contemporary with a pool and a spa and lots of grounds for the dog. It was on the peak of a hill, overlooking the Pacific Ocean. It was the beach girl's homecoming, a coming home to herself. And it was affordable: Its rental price—$4800 a month—was what she was asking for Bundy.

"She seemed excited," Jeane says. "And very hopeful. She turned to me and said, 'You know what, Jeane? I can *do* this!"

All the way back to Brentwood, Nicole seemed happy.

The next day—Saturday, June 11—Nicole called Jeane and asked her if a "For Lease" could be quickly gotten for Bundy—she was really looking forward to making the deal on the Malibu house and moving in with the children. Jeane said she would get the sign from her office and put it up the next day, Sunday.

Shortly after calling Jeane, Nicole took Sydney to the dress rehearsal for Eileen Blake's Dance for Kids annual show, which was to be held the following night. Sydney Simpson was in the group that was to perform to the soundtrack of the movie *Footloose.* Footloose: free of cares; free of her difficult relationship; moving to the beach—the music was apt for mother as well as for daughter. Nicole stood watching the rehearsal—smiling at Sydney as she kicked and leapt, talking to Pam Schwartz. (Pam's and Allen's daughter Danielle was also in the program.)

Another woman whose daughter was in the group noticed Nicole, so beautiful with that long blond hair, the jeans and boots, the sunglasses stuck in the V-neck crevice of her sleeveless shirt. The woman remembered the performance the previous year—it had been held on Father's Day and, though they were divorced, O.J. and Nicole had come and gone together. How nice, this mother had thought. What a civilized divorce. What a good relationship.

The rehearsal was finished and Sydney ran up to Nicole; jumping, excited. Nicole kissed her daughter on the top of her head, then pulled her daughter's arms straight out. Sydney, smiling broadly, playfully lifted her chin way up and pressed herself to her mother's body. Nicole started play-ballroom-dancing with her daughter. Both laughed. Their lives seemed full of sweetness and abandon and promise.

8

June 12, 1994

ON THE MORNING OF JUNE 12, 1994, O.J. SIMPSON PLAYED HIS usual golf game at the Riviera with one of his regular partners, producer Craig Baumgarten, whose wife, Melissa Proffit, was Tawny Kitaen's manager. A young golfer who played the eighteen holes behind them noticed that Simpson was having, as this young man later put it to a third party, "extreme mood swings" all through the course of the game. During the game, O.J. lamented to his caddy, Mitch Mesko, "I'm a pathetic person." "No, you're not," Mesko responded. "You're just a pathetic golfer." O.J. laughed.

Later that afternoon, Simpson called a young model and the then-current *Playboy* centerfold—Traci Adell—whose number he had been given although they had never met. According to what she later told reporters, he kidded that she "was not his typical type. He said he'd dated blondes and said 'I guess that hasn't worked out for me.'" He also said, "I've had enough, I've lived my life. I've done things most people couldn't do in a hundred lifetimes."

Nicole spent the morning shopping for toys for Justin and Sydney. She spoke to Judi and Denise by phone later, making plans for the whole family to drive up for Sydney's dance recital. Nicole, Denise says, was "up." Rolf Baur believes that Denise being at Sydney's recital meant a lot because Nicole and Denise had danced and performed together when they were Sydney's age.

The parents and relatives filed into Paul Revere Junior High starting at 4:30 P.M. Nicole, holding two bouquets of flowers for Sydney, sat with Lou, Judi, Denise, Mini, and, animatedly shifting in their seats, the three little boy cousins: Sean, Justin and Aaron. O.J. came late and sat a few seats away. Denise says Nicole did not talk to him. The father of a child in Sydney's dance group observed O.J.'s attitude as "friendly and smiling."

Sydney, however, may have felt a tension her parents refused to outwardly acknowledge. When her group of dancers—in their black sleeveless unitard bellbottoms, beaded belts and silver-fringed vests—lined up in the positions they had rehearsed, she decided to stand in a different spot than the one she was supposed to take. According to the mother of another girl in the group, "The girls all pounced on Sydney and said, 'No! *This* is where you stand!' Sydney started to cry." The other mother does not recall if Nicole heard Sydney cry and ran over or if she had been standing in the wings. But, wherever she had been, Nicole was now instantly at her daughter's side. She listened to another little girl explain the problem, then bent to comfort Sydney and negotiate her return to her assigned position. "She held her and coddled her and it was all straightened out," the other mother observed. "Sydney got back in line."

Nicole and O.J. sat apart, without speaking. After the dance, everyone filed out into the bright, setting sun—this time of day in summer and this close to the ocean, you had to wear sunglasses when you faced west. The happy parents hugged their costumed kids and the kids let off steam by running around the parking lot. Cameras were raised as dancers and families posed against cars. O.J. tried to get the

Browns to pose with him for such a picture but it did not come off. Families made plans to go out for dinner straight from the event. The Browns were going to Mezzaluna; O.J. asked to come along; Nicole said no, he could not come.

Was this rebuff of Nicole's any different than so many others she had made, increasingly, over all these seventeen years when O.J. stepped over the line, after he had done something that often justifiably infuriated her? Several of Nicole's friends believe that her disgust at O.J. for threatening to report her to the IRS meant that a line had finally been crossed in her mind. His act—so purely spiteful, so punishing to his own children—was repugnant to her in a way that may well have filled in the gaps of doubt in her mind about this last breakup. He had threatened to report her to the IRS in order to intimidate her *back*—yet the act may have had the opposite effect, constituting the final wedge between them. The disgust it produced in her released her from his grip and it showed him that, after all this time—all this exhausting possession and repossession of her—he didn't know her enough to predict her reactions, after all.

To an obsessed and controlling man, the idea that you don't know the person you thought you controlled is perhaps the most threatening truth of all. Kris Jenner had long thought that O.J. played a game with Nicole—a game called: How Far Can I Go? How badly can I misbehave, the premise of that game goes, and still charm you back?

Tonight, seeing her unmistakable contempt, he may well have gotten the answer.

At some point before he left Paul Revere Junior High, O.J. told Ron Fischman (according to what Ron Fischman reported to a friend), "I'm not done with her. I'm going to get her, *but good.*"

Nicole and her family went to Mezzaluna, taking along Sydney's friend Rachel. Ron Goldman was working that night, but he was not the waiter for their table. Nicole and

Ron did say hello, however—she knew him chiefly as one of Jeff's and Mike's buddies. A week and a half before, Nicole had taken Ron and Jeff to dinner at Locanda Veneta, a restaurant on Third Street, and she had let Ron drive her Ferrari to the restaurant and Jeff drive it back.

Ron had spent the morning playing softball with Mike, Jeff and some other guys on the Barrington field, right by Sunset; the day before, he and Mike had beaten their friends Doug Coupe and Dave Chokes at volleyball four games in a row on Will Rogers Beach. In between the two days of sports, Ron and some of his friends had gone to the club Tripps. Tonight, after work, he and Mezzaluna bartender Stewart Tanner planned to go to a Mexican restaurant (that turned into a singles' bar club after ten) in the Marina. Since the Mezzaluna staff wore uniforms—black tuxedo-like jackets and white shirts over their own dark pants—Ron was going to walk to his nearby apartment to change first.

Ronald Goldman's was a life of hard work and simple pleasures. He was a sweet, amusing, good-looking, fun-loving young man who was finally getting it together to make "the restaurant thing," as people called his dream, work. He deserved a good life.

At dinner that night, the talk among Nicole and her parents and sisters was joyous and full of future plans: a trip to Yosemite was discussed, the summer in Laguna mapped out. Nicole had been thinking about renting a place in Redondo Beach for a month, near the LeBons and their four sons, but new hope of renting the Malibu house would obviate the need for that temporary beach house. Now instead of taking the kids south to Redondo and Laguna, everyone could come up to Malibu!

Jeane McKenna was moving swiftly on the Malibu house for Nicole. In fact, while Nicole and her family dined at Mezzaluna, just across the street, in the Brentwood Gardens office of John Aaroe and Associates (Jeane had just switched over from Jon Douglas), she was getting a FOR LEASE sign out of a closet. Jeane was on her way to a dinner party up the canyon, and she was considering driving by the Bundy house afterward and putting the sign up to be good and ready for any people driving around on a sunny Sunday, looking at houses.

When the Browns were sitting down at Mezzaluna, O.J. was back at Rockingham talking to Kato in the kitchen. According to Kato's testimony to the grand jury on June 20, 1994, O.J. had talked briefly of his daughter's dance performance: "He said, 'She was wonderful, beautiful' and he was proud of her." He had mentioned Nicole "in a good-natured sort of way. He had mentioned who—she was with girlfriends, I believe* . . . —that he was wondering if they were going to age gracefully and what kind of outfits they were going to be wearing." (When pressed by the prosecutor to recall Simpson's words, Kato said, in less than fluent syntax: "It was about wearing tight-fitting clothes in reference—good natured, can't you wear that . . . when she's going to be older, joking, like wearing tight-fitting clothes, good-naturedly, like a grandma." Kato told prosecutor Marcia Clark that O.J. Simpson was "nonchalant" and not angry during the part of the evening they spent together.

(Although Kato Kaelin has, in the intervening months, resumed his trademark charm and has, by way of hosting of a cable TV show, reaped some benefit from his moment in the spotlight, this halting testimony—given eighteen days after the murders—seems to reflect his original nervousness.[†])

---

*The "friends" Simpson was referring to may, more likely, have been a reference to Nicole's girlfriends in general, none of whom accompanied her to the recital.

[†]That halting quality makes more sense when one understands what preceded it. On the previous Friday, Kato had stonewalled the grand jury, reciting the statement: "On the advice of my attorney, I must respectfully decline to answer and assert my constitutional right to remain silent" six times in a row—to virtually every

Kato then got into Simpson's Jacuzzi. At 8:30 P.M.—just as Nicole was leaving Mezzaluna with Justin and Sydney, and just as Judi, without realizing it, dropped her glasses on the curb—Kato went to his guest house bedroom and made a phone call to a friend named Tom O'Brien. O.J. came in and asked Kato if he was finished with the Jacuzzi, "because I had left the jets on and . . . I felt bad because I felt like I had screwed up" (by failing to properly turn off the jets).

O.J. then left—"but I didn't see where he went to"—and Kato got back on the phone with his friend Tom. O.J. returned to Kato's room. "He went 'Kato, Kato' and I told my friend, 'Hold on, O.J. calling.' And he said that he was embarrassed but he needed to borrow some money. And I said, 'Sure.' He told me he needed five dollars for a skycap"—for his flight to Chicago, scheduled for 11:45 that night—"and he was going to get a burger." Kato says he then "went to my drawer and I had forty-five dollars and I invited myself to go along because I was hungry."

Nicole kissed her family goodbye and said, as the Browns always said to each other at leavetakings, "I love you," and walked the children to Ben & Jerry's for ice cream.

Just as she was settling the children at home, Kato and O.J.—with O.J. at the wheel of his Bentley (Kato thought it

---

sentence put to him. Then, after the grand jury foreperson warned him that he would be held in contempt of court, and thus subject to imprisonment if he continued to refuse to answer the questions, Kato requested to see his attorney; after a private session with his attorney, he got back on the stand and issued the same sentence. Kato was then declared in contempt of court and was transported, by order of the sheriff, to a department of Superior Court for a hearing on his ability or inability to invoke the right of exemption from self-incrimination. On Monday, June 20, presumably after that hearing, Kato was back on the stand, this time answering the questions put to him.

was a Rolls), wearing a long-sleeved sweat-style outfit—were driving to a nearby McDonald's. O.J. seemed "very tired," Kato noticed. Kato had a grilled McChicken sandwich, O.J. a Big Mac and fries. Kato paid for it, then gave him $20 for the skycap. "Sorry to do this to you," O.J. joked, as he started to eat while he was driving. Kato nibbled some fries but saved his sandwich for when he got back to Rockingham.

"He just drove home," Kato said on the witness stand on June 20. "Nothing unusual. I got out of the car, had my food and started walking toward his door and said, 'I'm going to eat in my room' and he was out of the car."

It was 9:40 or 9:45, Kato estimated. If 9:40, it was just the time that Judi Brown called Nicole, having arrived home in Laguna. Judi had already called the restaurant to see if they could look for her glasses. Karen Crawford, the restaurant's Sunday manager, had found them on the curb outside. Nicole, too, had called and spoken to Ron Goldman, who offered to take the glasses to her. If it was 9:45, it was just about the moment Ron Goldman left Mezzaluna with Judi's glasses.

Ron walked through the pleasant, cool night, Judi Brown's glasses in a white business envelope. At home, Nicole waited. But for whom? Candles were lighted. O.J., she knew, would be safely on the way to the airport, then even more safely in Chicago overnight.

At a quarter to ten, Kato went to his room with his McChicken sandwich. "And that's the last I saw him," Kato testified, about O.J.

According to motorist Jill Shively's grand jury testimony,* an hour later, she ran into O.J. Simpson as he drove

---

*As previously noted, Marcia Clark instructed the grand jury to disregard Shively's testimony, that Shively had been untruthful to Clark in regard to her acceptance of $5,000 from a tabloid TV show.

through a red light out of Bundy Drive north through San Vicente, toward Sunset.

At midnight Sukru Boztepe, a neighbor of Nicole's, was walking with his wife, Bettina Rasmussen, and a dog that their neighbor had found inexplicably wandering down the street with blood on its paws. He was led, by that dog, to the courtyard of Bundy Drive. There he saw a sight he would never forget.

And there starts the story we have lived through together —and will live through again as the trial of O.J. Simpson for the murder of Nicole Brown Simpson and Ronald Goldman begins.

Acknowledgments

Sometimes a book comes along that is more than a fulfilling project and dream career break; it is also a story that allows the writer to revisit and tie together so many disparate themes of her career and her life that it takes on a personal resonance. This is what this project was for me.

My ability to take the time and emotional energy to find and enter this story was one hundred percent dependent on the support, generosity, and forbearance of my family: my husband, John Kelly, and our son, Jonathan Kelly—both of whom I thank first, last, foremost, and without equal. None of this could have happened without their blessings and their sacrifices. John encouraged me not to give up in the darkest early hours. He worked with me for days, until I got the tone right. They both did without me more than they wanted to and far, far more than was convenient; and they held in check all (justified) complaints about my absence and my absorption. You are my brilliant, handsome heroes, you guys—and I am one very lucky lady.

Bill Grose, Pocket Books executive vice-president and editorial director: When you picked me to do this story, I felt like Cinderella being tossed the glass slipper. The great trust and free rein you gave me, your elegant irony, and your willingness to take risks make you a stand-out class act, even in an industry that's full of them.

Ellen Levine, agent extraordinaire: You kept me going when all I had was the dream for this book and mountains of hotel message slips full of interview refusals. You did every deal with your masterful creativity and attention to detail, and you encouraged and advised with your commodious heart, as always. Diana Finch and Anne Dubuisson, your skills and enthusiasm were greatly appreciated.

Eileen Stukane: Who but another battle-weary freelancer would have cracked, over coffee on Eighth Avenue on June 20: "O.J. Simpson is the only person in America whose problems are bigger than mine are." You sent me home that day with an order—"Fax Bill! *Yes,* you *are* the one to do this story!"—that brought me to this moment. Eileen, Carol Ardman, and Mark Bregman have always been there, through any crisis—including a few that pocked this road—at any hour. Thanks, pals. Ditto, Elizabeth Weller Fiman. You can take the Weller girls out of L.A. but you can't take L.A. out of us.

Lydia Boyle: You helped me, as a research collaborator and much more, in uncountable ways, and in fact you never counted. There was not a request too small or too big or too frequent for you to accommodate with your classy aplomb and your sweeping connections. Endless *gracias*es

Molly Allen, magnifico Pocket Books editor and Village neighbor: Your tart wit and grand good nature, in the midst of the frenzy of flying manuscript pages, is one of the reasons Pocket feels so much like home to me. And so are:

Jennifer Weidman, Simon and Schuster associate counsel: Cool legal eagle, you make the impossible easy. You briskly came up with perfect substitute phrasings in seconds. Eric Rayman, vice-president, deputy general counsel: Thanks for your help, served up with great geniality.

Gina Centrello, Pocket Books publisher—the most down-to-earth high-powered woman I know and a decisive and gutsy risk-taker; Helen Atwan, superb director of marketing; Liz Hartman, ace director of publicity, and Cindy Ratzlaff, energetic associate director; Sheila Browne, who wrote the great jacket copy; Irene Yuss, director of production, who miraculously pushed this book onto and off the printing presses faster than anyone expected; Joe Gramm, droll, soothing troubleshooter; director of contracts Peter Anderson, who masterfully performed under pressure; copy editor/proofreader Jonathon Brodman and proofreader Steve Breslin: We were all a M*A*S*H unit (again), and wasn't it fun! How boring it would be to do a book with you guys on a normal production schedule.

Kelly Leisten: As freelance manuscript supervisor (and, Ed, as my sports-details czar), you were a marvel of precision, enthusiasm, and reassurance when the craziness got craziest. Dave Newman of Research Unlimited: I threw you guys weird questions to rush-answer; you came through unfailingly. Lisa Grossman of Gordian Knot: You were there for every computer glitch, plus one surveillance mission. Richie Haeg: Thanks for getting me to Buffalo.

The staff at a particular L.A. hotel was wonderful. Journalists wanting to know where to stay and never have to worry that your faxes are being read: Call me.

Jose at 380 Services made copies of thousands of pages on rush schedule. Dawn Guerin made scrapbooks of all the clippings and did my errands. Rennie Weller, one of my two beautiful nieces, took me right into one of this story's major side entrances. Radio stations 94.7 "The Wave" in L.A. and CD 101.9 in New York provided (along with my vintage Curtis Mayfield and new Boz Scaggs) a 24-hour-a-day soundtrack for my cogitating on and telling this tale—Andy Snitzer's, Bony James' and Peter Gallagher's plaintive saxophone riffs are embedded in every sad sentence. Randy Young, premiere local historian: Your work inspired me to link present with past. And your seriously important tip was enormously appreciated.

The Simpsons had wonderful friends—that's as sad and ironic a fact as any in this story. The people (named and unnamed) who became the kaleidoscope of voices herein are in a league of their own in terms of my immense debt to them. You gave me a piece of your life, each of you. You decided to take a chance and trust me when no one in L.A. trusted any reporters. I am enormously grateful.

The entire Brown family—and the Goldman family, who did not respond to my request to meet them—is a study of grace under almost unworldly stress. Let us all learn from them.

Judi: You are an elegant, gracious woman whose humor and conviviality survived this, the greatest nightmare a mother can possibly go through. No wonder everyone adores you.

Denise: Bravo for your spirit, your courage, your decency. I have so enjoyed getting to know you. As a close-in-age "big sister" myself, it would have pained me no end if I had had to write this book without your participation. You are your sister's keeper—I know how that feels, though hardly in the tragic way you do. Your childhood life with Nicole rings so many personal bells. I hope that I have captured it faithfully.

From this time I spent in their lives, I come away with so much affection for these special people:

Rolf and Maria: You opened every single important door. Thank you for your faith in me.

Cici: I'm *so* glad we're friends. You're the greatest!

Linda: I felt a connection the minute we got on the phone with each other. Nicole was lucky to have you.

D'Anne and David: You were instrumental with everything and you're both terrific. D'Anne, we were such good partners, sometimes I think we should go into business together!

Thomas: We instantly saw this story the same way. (Who says a Gingrich conservative and an open-minded feminist can't be soulmates?) And when you realized that, you sounded trumpets on my behalf. You are a kind, generous, eloquent man brimming with perceptiveness.

Finally: To Ron and Nina Shipp—and the handsome David and beautiful Danielle: How can I thank you enough?

Ron, you are one of the most moral and courageous people I have ever met in my life. And all of you are wonderful. As the months rolled on and this sad story became more full of exploitation and tawdriness—more rife with people who, at worst, sold out, and at least kept their heads down to stay comfortable—your characters were more and more apparent as exemplary. America needs more families like you guys. I'm so lucky you're my great buddies.

Afterword

September 15, 1995

A CORRECTION

When a book is written before a trial starts, conduits to the police are necessarily indirect. Police investigators might speak to authors afterward, but they will never consent to be interviewed before the trial has begun and the investigation ended. I relied on excellent sources who were talking to the principal detectives in the course of their own close involvement with this case. However, because this case was so riddled with news leaks (indeed, the defense would eventually try to make those leaks into part of a conspiracy argument), the principal detectives, it turns out, occasionally dispensed inaccurate information in conversations with close-in sources, perhaps to see where the leaks would wind up, perhaps because they did not have accurate information. One such inaccuracy ended up in this book.

It appears that Nicole Brown Simpson was NOT slashed in the neck-to-breast fashion described in Chapter 1. Instead, as was eventually brought out at the trial, her throat was probably slashed after she was unconscious; a foot was applied to her back and her head pulled up by her hair before the fatal slash was administered.

My apologies to my readers for this.

Raging Heart was shipped to the bookstores on Tuesday, January 24, a day after the opening statements in *California vs. Simpson.* The People's case started with domestic violence testimony, with Chris Darden, Marcia Clark's co-prosecutor, in charge of this portion of the prosecution's case. The 911 operator to whom Nicole had made her terrified phone call on January 1, 1989, testified, as did the police officers who responded to and evaluated that call.

On Tuesday, January 31, just as the fourth witness was about to be called, a bench conference was hurriedly convened, at the request of the defense. Cameras were banned—an unusual move that left both the Court TV and CNN commentators openly mystified. Chris Darden had just named a witness unfamiliar to the commentators, for the players known to the press and public—Kato Kaelin, Faye Resnick, Robert Kardashian—had represented only the most publicity-seeking of the Simpsons' friends.

So no one seemed to know what this emergency conference was all about.

Except I had a feeling that I did.

A few minutes later, Kristin Jeannette-Myers, Court TV's reporter covering the defense, stood in the hallway outside Judge Ito's courtroom, awkwardly balancing an opened book in one hand, holding her microphone with the other.

"What's going on in the courtroom, Kristin?" anchor Gregg Jarrett asked.

"Well, it's a strange story, Gregg," Jeannette-Myers said, in that overemphatic and breathless style of think-on-your-feet TV trial reporting. "It concerns a book and the testimony of Ron Shipp, which [sic] is the next witness scheduled to be called by the prosecution. This book is *Raging Heart* by Sheila Weller . . . and it came out this weekend. . . ." Jeannette-Myers went on to say that the book disclosed a conversation between Simpson and one "Leo" the night after the murders.

She continued: "Carl Douglas [one of Simpson's attorneys] just said in court that they are concerned about Ron Shipp's testimony because, if Ron Shipp is 'Leo,' . . . [then] what Leo has to say, according to this author, is that O.J. Simpson told him, 'I don't want to take a polygraph test because, although I didn't kill my wife I thought about it, and maybe that would make me fail a polygraph.' . . . Carl Douglas wants this aired outside the presence of the jury and frankly wants the jury *never* to hear [the conversation]."

"And, Gregg, that's not all," Jeannette-Myers said, after repartee between Jarrett and the broadcast's guest commentator, attorney Andrew Stein. "There's another story in this book that's a bit unusual . . . a passage about comments O.J. Simpson makes to this Leo [about] 'dreams haunting' him, and in some way the prosecution may feel that this goes to his consciousness of guilt. Again, this is something the defense is worried about. So when Carl Douglas went up to sidebar, he said, 'We've *got* to talk about this detective's testimony—detective Ron Shipp—because I read a book that talked about polygraphs and dreams and we've got to discuss this *before* the jury hears it. . . ."

Jarrett, Stein, and Jeannette-Myers agreed that Judge Ito would not let the polygraph half of Simpson's conversation with Ron Shipp—"They asked me if I would take a lie detector test. I don't want to take it"—be heard by the jury, since references to polygraph-taking are inadmissible in California courts. But what about the rest of the sentence?

"If this statement comes in," Stein opined, " 'I thought about killing my wife' [sic] . . . If *this* statement comes in, my prediction is O.J. Simpson's going to have to take the stand."*

It was clear that this testimony was being sprung on the defense. This self-congratulatorily smooth "Dream Team" was unprepared for someone to speak from a sense of morality, instead of from team loyalty. How could this have happened?

Here's how.

Five and a half months earlier, during one of our weekly meetings at the Hollywood Hills restaurant Yomishiro, Ron Shipp disclosed to me his June 13 bedroom conversation with O.J. Simpson. I knew it was an extraordinary admission the minute I heard it, but I pretended to take it in stride, grilling Ron carefully about which of them said exactly what when, while I scribbled furiously in my spiral notebook. He seemed relieved to have finally told a person other than his wife and his attorney. I believe that he meant for the disclosure's eventual pseudonymous appearance in my book to serve as the "Judgment Day" sign on the door of his conscience. Since the conversation would *one* day be revealed, he had an increment of time—the prepublication months—to meditate on the question: Do I testify about this? Do I owe loyalty to a living man I no longer respect and indeed believe is guilty, or to two dead victims, one of whom I loved as a friend, a woman who regarded me as the confidant who might have even been able to save her?

By that time, I had been talking to Ron for a month. I

---

*Instead, the statement's having "come in" eventually compelled the defense to open its case, in July, with the entire female side of Simpson's family—daughter Arnelle, sisters Shirley and Carmelita, mother Eunice—massed to try to discredit Ron and the damage done five months earlier by his testimony.

had gotten to know his wife, Nina, and their two delightful children. Ron's and Nina's personal decency was strikingly clear from the start. They did not want to advance themselves in any way through the tragedy. They would not take a dime from anyone. Belief in God plays a very real part in Ron's daily life, and the whole family holds hands and prays together before they go off to work and school every morning. He is that very rare individual these days: a person who isn't cynical.

The only reason Ron agreed to talk to me at all is that Rolf Baur told him that my publisher and I were donating a substantial sum of money for Justin and Sydney. "*Try* to get Ron Shipp to talk to you," Rolf had said. "He's who Nicole always called when O.J. got violent."

When we sat down at Yomishiro for our first meeting in mid-July, it was clear from Ron's tense, discomfited demeanor that he was burdened by information he wished he did not possess. Most of the close friends of Nicole's whom I had met during those first weeks were also raw and shell-shocked—Rolf had wept—and they, too, talked in that stop-start delivery of details that paradoxically combines intense wariness with the urge to recollect. And most of those people felt guilty about not having somehow prevented Nicole's murder. But Ron's feelings seemed to go farther than the others'. He was plainly tortured. At the end of our talk he told me why. "Because of something O.J. said to me that night, and the way he behaved, I *know* he did it."

"Are you ever going to tell anybody what that 'something' was?" I asked.

He paused, then said very firmly, "No."

Ron's conflict was fresh, and his dilemma was excruciating. He had just stopped visiting O.J. in jail—he could no longer stomach his own hypocrisy in doing so—and he was putting off Cathy Randa, whose puzzled, hurt imprecations—"Where've you been, Ron? Aren't you with us anymore?"—made him uncomfortable and guilty. Ron loved Cathy—he had been her confidant. Her son Gary was his buddy. O.J.'s sisters had relied on Ron. In fact, Ron was still in charge of security at the house (he had also handled security at Nicole's funeral), and during our meeting his pager went off with calls from one of the men he had hired, calling with emergency questions.

He was still assumed to be on the side of an Emperor who, as a result of this mysterious conversation, he suspected was wearing no clothes. But either nobody else could see that or—worse—they saw but did not want to acknowledge it.

Ron seemed to have a need to sort out his feelings about his participation in the lives of this couple, his principles as a former domestic violence teacher, and his own personal morality. During the several more conversations we had at Yomishiro, his answers to my questions about every aspect of life at Rockingham were often intercut with these other ruminations. After Ron and Nina read my previous book about a marriage that had veered into violence, and as the be-loyal-to-the-Juice machine cranked up and Ron felt increasingly repelled by friends' continued desire to blindly protect and serve a man who might be a double-murderer, he decided that he had to get the June 13 story off his chest, and that at some point down the road (book authors seem safer than newspaper reporters because the distance from notepad to publication is six months, not six hours) people should know what O.J. said in the bedroom. Later, he said: "Nina and I realized that my talking to you was like therapy."

While I was writing the book, last fall, I asked Ron several times if he wanted me to read him and Nina the "Leo" passage. He always said, "No. We trust you." Still, I worried. Did they know what they were getting themselves into? In December, I Fed-Ex'd them almost all of the book, so they would *have* to read it. They did so, and said that they loved it.

We were going on the willfully naive presumption that the passage, especially because of its reference to polygraphs, would not be admissible. Still, a reality check was in order, so when, in early January, a New York prosecutor friend of mine called me on a different matter, I took the opportunity to broadly outline the passage. "That *will* be admissible in some form," she said. "And it's dynamite. Your source should call Marcia Clark immediately."

I hung up and called Ron.

Since I increasingly assumed that Ron would eventually disclose the June 13 conversation to the prosecution, I was surprised when he answered, "Nah, I ain't doing it." As a police officer, he explained, he had always viewed himself as standing alone, not trusting either side in courtroom wars. So the plan we had made was still in place: I would never reveal him as Leo. If anyone claimed he *was* Leo, he would deny it. The defense would claim Leo was an invention. If the prosecution called me, I would call Ron. I doubted things would get to the point of my receiving a prosecution subpoena.

Meanwhile, I had had a call from Chris Darden, who asked to see the manuscript. I declined, but, to answer his stated area of concerns, and with the permission of the Brown family, offered to enumerate all anecdotes of domestic violence I had gotten from my interviews with the Brown family. At the end of the brief conversation* Darden said, "I hear you have something in there that might effect a conviction."

"Don't get excited; it isn't *that* good" was my answer.

On Friday, January 20, as the book was rolling off the

---

*During which Darden had said, "People will be surprised—our case will only take three weeks to present."

printing press at a secret location, *Prime Time Live* requested a copy of the first twenty pages of the manuscript in order to make its final decision about featuring the book as a segment. We had sent them a copy of everything *but* those pages, which obviously just whetted their curiosity. Now they said: Either send over the pages or we'll have to nix the segment. Their argument seemed to go something like this: "The book will be in the stores in a few days anyway, so why withhold the pages and lose the segment over it?"

Why, to me, was simple. The segment's producer, Shelley Ross, is one of the best producer/sleuths in the business—she had broken Tailhook and had uncovered major evidence in Menendez; I knew that if she got my book's first pages on a Friday night, she would find out who Leo was over the weekend. That meant going to those people—Bob Kardashian, Joe Stellini, Cathy Randa—who had been at Rockingham on June 13. I felt protective toward the Shipps and did not want the defense knowing about the passage before Ron had a chance to tell the prosecution, *if* he finally chose to do so.

I told the marketing and publicity people at Pocket that I would not release the pages to ABC without permission from my source, even if it meant doing without that coveted media. I called Ron in L.A. and told him the situation.

"What would you like me to do?" I asked.

He said, "Call Chris." Darden and he had met to go over Ron's upcoming testimony on his counseling of O.J. and Nicole after the New Year's Day 1989 beating.*

"Call Chris and tell him *what?*" I asked.

---

*As the trial went on, their bond would grow stronger as they shared the fate of two black men who had come out against O.J., a stand that earned them animus in segments of the African American community and made life very difficult for both of them.

"Tell him how the book begins."

"Including Leo's having law enforcement experience?"

Ron said, "Yes."

I called Darden. He was fresh from his stunning encounter with Johnnie Cochran over the admissibility of the "N word." In that confrontation, Darden had argued that Judge Ito disallow use of that word (which was expected to come up—and which did come up, and then some—in the defense's cross-examination of Mark Fuhrman) because it was too emotionally loaded and would force the mostly black jurors to reduce a carefully built case to a simple question: "Am I with the Man, the white police officer, or am I with the Brothers?" On the heels of Darden's extraordinary candor, Johnnie Cochran had waxed indignant at Darden's supposed implication that African American jurors could not be objective. Cochran got credit for taking the high road in that duel. Yet as soon as the trial began, Cochran—and F. Lee Bailey—did precisely what Darden accused him of setting out to do: seizing the race card and running with it. (Much later, of course, Mark Fuhrman fulfilled the defense's wildest dreams and became the prosecution's biggest—and most foolishly unanticipated—nightmare.)

It was 4:45 L.A. time Friday, and opening statements were Monday. I told Darden that, at my source's request, I was going to paraphrase an anecdote close to the beginning of my book.

When I finished, Darden asked, "It's Ron Shipp, isn't it?"

I said, "I'm not authorized to answer."

"I felt he was holding something back," Darden said. "*Is* it Ron Shipp?"

"I can't say yes or no."

"Thank you," he said, with great emphasis.

I called Ron in his car. No sooner did I say, "I did what you asked," than he said, referring to his pager, "That's the prosecution now. With a nine-one-one." He sighed —here it was: Judgment Day—and hung up to call Darden.

Ron was depositioned on Sunday and his deposition was made discoverable to the defense the following weekend.

On Tuesday, January 31—after the sidebar Jeannette-Myers described—Judge Ito, with the plucky weariness that would intensify in the months to come, said that Ron Shipp's proferred testimony had "broached to me an interesting legal issue that I had no idea was coming, *again.*" He invited both sides to fax him cases.

The prosecution filed papers arguing that Ron's testimony about O.J.'s statement was "about as relevant as any statement could be, save an outright confession." Hank Goldberg, of the prosecution, orally argued that it was "highly probative" testimony that went right to the issue of the defendant's "obsession" and that it "blows a hole in the defense theory of Simpson's 'circle of benevolence,'" which Johnnie Cochran had made a centerpiece of his opening argument. A smiling Marcia Clark added that "Jiminy Cricket said it well, Your Honor. 'A dream is a wish your heart makes.'" On the other side, Carl Douglas argued, self-contradictorially, that (a) the conversation absolutely *never* took place, but (b) if it *did* take place, Simpson was *joking.*

In a move that surprised almost all of the attendant "O.J. commentocracy"—as the assembled lawyers who have done a play-by-play of the case have come to be known—Judge Ito split the conversation in half, disallowing the "I don't want to take [the lie detector test]" portion but allowing the much more controversial "'cause I *have* had some dreams about killing her." Expressing the views of many, one CNN trial analyst, criminal defense attorney Maureen Kallins, wryly remarked that "Alan Dershowitz [who handles the appeals portion of the trial] is breaking out the champagne right now" about the ability of the illogically halved conversation to withstand an appeal court's review. Indeed, Ito's "dreams testimony" decision would turn into one of his most criticized.

Ron Shipp then took the stand, admitting under oath that he was the "Leo" in Chapter 1 of this book and that he had told me about the bedroom conversation with O.J. before he told the prosecution because it was "eating me up." Ron recounted his friendship with O.J., his counseling of O.J. and Nicole after the 1989 beatings, and his efforts to get O.J. to go public with, and seek help for, his battering problem (all recounted in Chapter 6). His testimony—not new to the early readers of this book but new to the rest of the country—caused the trial's major news of the day—indeed, of the week. (A few hours later, during a break in the proceedings, Court TV's reporter covering the prosecution, Dan Abrams, called *Raging Heart* "the gospel for this part of the trial," and told viewers what disclosures to expect on the basis of what appeared in the book.)

That afternoon, pages eight to twelve of the hardcover edition of *Raging Heart* were entered into evidence as defendants' exhibit 1000, while Carl Douglas, in biting, sarcastic tones, fired away at Ron, trying to make him look suspect and self-glorifying for telling an author the conversation with O.J. before he told the police or prosecution. "Did you *lie* to Marcia? Did you *lie* to the police?" he asked, about Ron's earlier conversations with them. If witholding information was "lying," then, "Okay," Ron answered calmly, "I 'lied' to Marcia."

In commentating about Ron's testimony, lawyers, reporters, and others frequently wondered why he had withheld the information from the prosecution for so long. This logical-*sounding* question misses the point of what was really going on in the summer of 1994. Far from being some highly regarded and omnipotent agency to which O.J.'s and Nicole's friends marched obediently to be depositioned, the D.A.'s office was being ducked by intimates of the couple right and left—boldly and proudly.

Even some of Nicole's best friends—people who loved her—were doing this. A woman who probably knew the most told me several times, in anguished whispers, how afraid she was of taking the stand—how she was trying, through a lawyer, not to have to. Another best friend of Nicole's remembers "going to sleep at night at an angle that would keep any bullet fired through my window from hitting me."

When a friend is murdered and the husband is a suspect, silence descends—and the richer, more charismatic and heroic the man and the more sophisticated the world the pair lives in, the easier it is to hoist that veil of arrogant silence. When, in September 1985, prominent artist Carl Andre was arrested for the murder of his wife, artist Ana Mendieta (she was found dead on the sidewalk outside their Manhattan high-rise apartment, having gone through an open window), so many of his friends in the New York art world refused to even speak to the authorities that the first prosecutor could not convince the grand jury to bring an indictment against Andre. (Andre was eventually indicted and, after a bench trial in which he waived his right to a jury in what was a virtual reversal of the Simpson situation—white, blond midwestern Andre was afraid a minority jury would be too quick to convict him of killing his Hispanic wife—he was acquitted.) In other recent cases in which rich, prominent men—stock analyst Joseph Pikul in New York, former Atlanta assistant district attorney Fred Tokars in Birmingham, and former Merrill

Lynch vice-president James Kelly in suburban Illinois—have stood accused of killing or arranging to kill their wives (all were convicted), a male-bonding phenomenon seems to occur: Wealthy friends of the wealthy defendant compete with one another to find him the best lawyers, financial advisors, and custody litigators. "It's quite a pissing match," a top female criminal defense attorney involved with one of these cases says wryly.

All through the summer of '94, friends of the Simpsons were afraid of having their privacy and anonymity ripped from them. They were afraid their children would be stalked and harmed. They were afraid their connection with the case would hurt them in business deals and with admissions boards of country clubs. They were afraid of the exposure of secrets. (One of O.J.'s best friends must have been especially glad he was spared a subpoena. Had he been called to the stand, this respected businessman might have had to admit that, within the course of one year, in two separate and unrelated incidents, he accidentally killed two people.) And, mostly, among the men: They were afraid of appearing to be traitors. They were even afraid of letting themselves stop believing in O.J.'s innocence. They were—these starstruck white men—so in love with their friendship with O.J. that, I believe, the loss of that faith and that bond itself was something they could not countenance.

The behavior of one of O.J.'s Inner Circle sums it up well: This man repeatedly said to another two of O.J.'s friends, right after the murders: "I know he did it; I'm sure he did it . . ."—then startled those same friends by popping up on TV shows, touting their famous friend's innocence.

"What happened?" the other two asked.

"O.J. called me and asked me to help him out," this man said. "So I said, 'Just tell me where and when; I'm ready!'" Still, the infinitely conflicted man was said to have spent much of his non-televised time telling near-strangers that O.J. had confessed to the killings.

One close friend of O.J., who had heard an extremely damaging statement from his lips, had run across his lawn to duck a process server. A young man who could have been a very good murder-day demeanor witness for the prosecution disappeared. One of the Inner Circle took up residence abroad, thus avoiding having to testify about one of O.J.'s beatings of Nicole.

A sports team junior executive who had covered for O.J. in the past, a famous world-championship athlete, and a garment industry executive and his wife were four people who were at a party, in the early 1990s, at which Simpson, according to another man present, wore Aris Light Leather gloves identical to the ones at the crime scene. However, none of the aforementioned party guests testified.

So eager were O.J.'s friends to believe that anyone but the Juice was the culprit that when O.J., early on, apparently started the outrageous rumor that Ron Shipp, of all people, had committed the murders, some friends were willing to believe him. One of Simpson's most intelligent friends was even willing to put credence in this "theory" months after the overwhelming DNA evidence was brought out in court. (Later, when the defense was preparing for the prosecution's rebuttal case, in which they believed Ron would be a witness, they dispensed one of their detectives to telephone gossip columnists with this "theory.")

This strange, almost religiously devotional loyalty seemed to have spawned a more official version in the courtroom. Eventually, as the months of the trial wore on, and his "Dream Team" burgeoned with one new *male* lawyer after another (so odd in a day and age in which female criminal attorneys are seen as distinctly advantageous for male murder defendants, especially when domestic violence is part of the evidence)—each a more self-important paper-ruffler than the next, each hysterically eager to balloon the most minor pathologist's error into a long cross-examination—the defense side of the room seemed to resemble nothing so much as a crowded bench of awed armchair jocks, elbowing in competitively, thrilled to be in this huddle of a lifetime. As I watched the trial, week after week, and heard this all-guy lineup proffer and elongate the most numbing minutiae, I thought of Robin Greer's remembrance of O.J.'s many-times-recounted football stories. And as we all witnessed F. Lee Bailey's fight with Robert Shapiro (who, increasingly, seemed the most dignified of the lot), I thought of Joe Stellini and Allen Schwartz both telling me (with no irony) that they had recently made up after a years-long fight over who was the better friend of O.J.'s

O.J. Simpson was re-creating his Rockingham sports den right there in Judge Ito's courtroom.

The more the ranks swelled, the more nervous these men seemed to be about thoroughly pleasing their captain. Peter Neufeld, one of Simpson's two DNA experts, was particularly exercised, almost pleading with Judge Ito during motions regarding his bloodstain witnesses—and Carl Douglas was rebuked by Simpson for temporarily leaving unclear the fact that the affable Juice had called the Hertz employee in Chicago back to apologize for rudeness. The sycophantism of these male lawyers seemed so bald—yet, in this otherwise wildly overanalyzed trial, so oddly unremarked upon.

More serious was the whole team's business-as-usual scribblings and chatting with Simpson during the playing of Nicole's frantic 911 call. Didn't they even have enough discomfort and self-consciousness to push the two mostly silent female associates—Shawn Chapman and Sara Kaplan—to the foreground for the interim (much as the Senate Judiciary Committee had stacked the Clarence Thomas hearings with females for the photo opportunities)? Not a single TV commentator noted how strange it was—in 1995—for so many public-reaction-savvy men to not even think they should throw a bone to the notion that scaring a woman out of her wits by breaking down her door and ranting is something that might be regrettable.

As if to pay Ron Shipp back for his defection from this retro-jock-pack mentality, Carl Douglas's cross-examination of him was vicious. No commentator failed to remark on its venom. Yet, through it, Ron made the angry, spontaneous remarks that were so eloquent and riveting: "Mr. Douglas, I could care less about an acting career! Do you think I would put my family through this for an acting career? I'm doing this for my conscience; I will not have the blood of Nicole on Ron Shipp; I can sleep at night, unlike a lot of others"; and, looking directly at O.J., the sorrowfully contemptuous: "This is sad, O.J. This is sad."

The ugliness of the cross-examination—Douglas made a big issue of Ron's past drinking problem and inaccurately turned his doubles-match tennis game with a family friend into a tawdry event with a "blonde in the hot tub"—became a benchmark for the kind of scathing personal attacks any witness brave enough to take the stand in this trial could look forward to. ("How many reputations have to be ruined," Chris Darden asked Judge Ito, "just because it suits Mr. Simpson?") The prospect of having every past mistake of one's life become the fodder of sound bites and headlines led valuable witnesses to panic—and one to disappear. Three told me, in almost identical words: "After what Ron Shipp went through, I don't want to get up there."

Ron Shipp's testimony was also a yardstick of the race

schism that started developing in this trial almost as soon as it began. As a number of other writers commentating on the case noted, white viewers and reporters found Ron highly credible and some found him moving and heroic, while black viewers and reporters were often condemnatory. Denise Brown, the witness who followed Ron on the stand, drew similarly race-based reactions.

Denise and I had spent time together and had had many conversations in the fall, but I didn't really know her until, in the middle of a lunch one day, she burst into tears when she was handed the photograph that appears on the cover of this book. She had always seemed so brisk and straight-shooting that the sudden vulnerability was stunning. That moment excavated for me the lost fact that she was a sister in the midst of a private grief that no amount of saturation media could ever let the American public come close to sharing.

So when Denise shed similar tears on the witness stand on February 6, it seemed very affecting. Yet the Los Angeles *Sentinel* (which serves the African American community) called her (and Ron) a "drunk"; a month later, dismissed-juror Jeanette Harris said disparagingly that she found Denise "acting—the way she pulled on her cross and everything." Tanya Brown was particularly upset at Harris's remark. Tanya told me, "That was *Nicole's* cross! That's what gets Denise through, wearing Nicole's cross and fingering it! How dare that juror say that!"

With Harris's dismissal, her remarks about the prosecution's case being "a whole lot of nothing" (and this, after much of the DNA evidence had been presented) and her positing of a profound racial rift within the jury, it became depressingly clear that this trial was now about little else *but* race. The Simpsons' life at Rockingham had been a melting pot, where class, ethnicity, race—all of it—was transcended. In that respect, it was the best of what California can be in terms of the offhand dropping of generations-old preconceived labels. Now all of that was bulldozed, and what was left was a dyspeptic, affectedly patrician old white lawyer shouting out the word "nigger" at every turn, and a slick, autograph-signing black lawyer invoking the address "Simi Valley" gratuitously and provocatively.

Race seemed to be lurking behind everything. The defense's great—and unsuccessful—effort to get Marcus Allen to testify, against his will, about his alleged affair with Nicole was so out of proportion with that testimony's minor declared value (to show that O.J. wasn't jealous); it struck me as meant for one—extremely cynical—purpose only: To impress upon the largely black and female jury that the white, blond female victim had taken *not* one but *two* handsome black heroes out of the pool of available men. Cochran's frequent references to Arnelle Simpson's attendance of Howard University (she had also attended SC, as had her brother) were conspicuous. The defense's coroner Michael Baden made special mention of the autopsies of *black* victims he had conducted, and he told the jury that his medical school was located in "the Harlem area of New York." Cochran's cries that Chris Darden was "racist" in attempting to introduce witness Robert Heidstra's opinion that he heard a "black" voice at the crime scene neglected the fact that the defense had cheerfully stressed that the two men whom Mary Ann Gerchas said she had seen at the crime scene were "Caucasian" and "Asian."*

---

*Still, the defense wasn't alone in trading on its members' minority status to hypocritically lob politically correct objections. Marcia Clark, at least once, did with gender what Cochran did with race: She made a big show of demanding that Cochran apologize to her for his "sexist"

And then of course, in August, came the Fuhrman Tapes—and, with them, the unmasking of Mark Fuhrman as exactly the kind of despicable racist F. Lee Bailey had been trying to make him out to be all those months earlier. As David LeBon put it, "Leave it to O.J. Simpson to keep on being that lucky."

The questions begged by this extraordinary turn of events—which brought the story back to its pretrial heights as an American Drama, after having been for so long a tedious and occasionally embarrassing courtroom slugfest—are many. Why did the LAPD and eventually the prosecution dismiss, or fail to act on, the clear signs that Fuhrman was a racist? As attorney Joseph DeGenova, one of the O.J. commentocracy, said, "The worst thing any prosecution can have is a bad cop because bad cops ruin good cases." Did the defense know about, or have hint of, the tapes early on, or did it build a sandcastle on the hunch that race anger and celebrity worship could be manipulated, only to have that construction, at zero hour, turn into a reality? And—a minor but fascinating question: What was behind Laura Hart McKinny's post–June 12 meeting with Fuhrman? Obviously, both of them knew how much was at stake when they sat down, this last time, to tape. They were no longer an anonymous "technical advisor" and a striving screenwriter engaged in an enterprise with import for no one but themselves.

The foreshortening of the domestic violence testimony surprised and frustrated many of Nicole's friends. They had been depositioned, and they wanted to get up

---

remark that she was "hysterical"—and she won points in the media and with the public for this action. Yet—as none of the commentators recalled—it was *she* who, very early in the trial, had *twice* loudly maligned the defense's "hysterical proclamations" about the discovery process regarding the DNA lab reports.

on that stand and tell their stories. Cici Shahian had briefly testified about Nicole's panic and dismay at O.J.'s threat to report her to the IRS, but she was also poised to be a rebuttal witness on another issue, which appears in Chapter 1: Ron Fischman's having told her that O.J. told him, at the dance recital, "I'm not done with her. I'm going to get her, but good." D'Anne LeBon had been promised, by the prosecution, that she would be able to repeat a threat Nicole had told her that O.J. had made—one D'Anne had not told me when I was writing this book, and one that is the most explicit threat I have heard reported in this case—"that," D'Anne says, "he would take Nicole in the middle of the night, cut her up and bury her body on Mullholland Drive so even her kids wouldn't know where she was. Nicole said he used to mentally 'torture' her with that threat all the time." Many of the incidents of beating and violence that appear in this book would have passed Judge Ito's admissibility requirement, and for those of us concerned with domestic violence, this trial at its outset promised the captive-audience American public a view of the dynamic of such relationships. This could have provided a valuable mass education.

But, of course, the prosecution pulled the plug on the domestic violence portion of the case and then never returned to it. Why? As someone in the prosecution explained to a confidant, "We found out from the dismissed jurors that they didn't like witnesses saying bad things about O.J." (This is what the commentocracy meant by saying that the prosecution was trying its case defensively.) Nonetheless, Chris Darden pressed to put on more domestic violence witnesses. He was outvoted.

Among the key testimony lost in this scrapping of the domestic violence part of the case was that of the woman who appears as "Riza Gomez" in Chapter 7 of this book. I found her to be an enormously impressive source—specific, precise, dignified, thoughtful. "Riza" was called by the prosecution in December. Her descriptions of O.J.'s stalking and harassing of Nicole, which appear in this book, were considered so strong that the prosecution had her set to go on immediately after the fiasco of O.J. trying on the bloody gloves. But after waiting in the wings for days, she was called and told that she was not needed.

"Riza" says today, "It is so wrong, what happened to Nicole. She was so good to me, so generous. And she loved those kids so much. She would say to me, 'Can you believe one day Sydney is going to have babies and I will be a *grand*mother?' This is what is lost in this trial, a sense of Nicole and Ron Goldman cut down in the middle of their lives, the sense of them as people."

Perhaps that is why one of the most poignant reminders in the trial was a letter the defense was trying to get admitted into evidence—a letter Nicole had written to O.J. in the spring of 1993 when she was trying so hard to effect a reconciliation. Yet it was the presumption that governed the intended use of that letter that was so disturbing.

The letter, which I wish I had had when I was writing this book last winter, reads:

Dear O.J.:

I'd like to see you, to talk to you in person. But I know you can't do that. I've been attending these meetings—to help me turn negatives into positives—to help me get rid of my anger. . . . I've learned to "let things go" (the most powerful, helpful thing I've ever learned). . . .

I always knew that what was going on with us, was about *me*—I just wasn't sure *why* it was about *me*—So I just blamed you. I'm the one who was controlling. *I* wanted you to be faithful and to be a perfect father. I was not accepting to [sic] who you are. Because I didn't like myself anymore.

I'm not sure exactly what went on with me these last few years. I know New Year's Eve started it. I sank into a depression that I couldn't control. I also agree with you now—that I went through some sort of mid-life crisis—"that 30s thing," you called it. My own self-esteem . . . etc. I know I gave up treating you like I loved you. . . . I never stopped loving you. I stopped liking myself and lost total confidence in my relationship with you.

. . . I want to put our family back together! I want our kids to grow up with their parents. . . . I want to be with you! I want to love you and cherish you and make you smile. I want to wake up with you in the mornings and hold you at night. I want to hug and kiss you every day. . . .

There was no couple like us.

We want to come home—we'd be there tomorrow if you'd let us.

. . . I'm sorry for the pain I've caused you.

In its desperation, self-abasement, and willingness to shoulder all blame, this letter is—to me—the most moving testimony of all to Nicole Brown Simpson's vulnerability and pathos, and her inability to live without the man she knows will never stop hurting her. But wait: Wouldn't such a sympathy-engendering letter be a *prosecution* goldmine? Did the "Dream Team" really think this letter would help *them?*

Was Nicole's most desperate reaching-out so completely unheard, not just before but *after* it may have killed her?

And if the defense was right in its hunch—if the letter had been admitted and had proved effective for them: How could a heinous act whose only up side was its consciousness-raising value on the subject of domestic violence have turned so neatly, over these months, into a sympathy-fest for the abuser/defendant?

As of this writing, members of the Inner Circle still talk to O.J. on the phone. Until it became obvious that he was not going to take the stand, many believed, as he continued to assure them long after there seemed any merit in this claim, that he wanted to take the stand—and that he would—to proclaim his innocence. One now rather disgruntled close friend believes many of the others are still "blindly believing bullshit. Their attitude is, as it always was, 'He's still the Juice; so I'll believe him, whatever he says.'" One friend had been asking others, "What do I do if he's convicted? Stay friends with him or not?" Now that friend is asking, "If he walks just on a technicality"—for example, Mark Fuhrman's racism—"do I stay friends with him or not?" So, one might say, there's been some maturing.

The prosecutors are exhausted. Marcia Clark, for all her toughness and cool, has had vulnerable and emotional moments: She burst into tears and cried loudly during Ron Goldman's unveiling, and she's supposedly made worried middle-of-the-night phone calls to her custody lawyer since her ex-husband, Gordon Clark, has initiated a suit for custody of their two sons, claiming that she is too busy to be a good mother. Chris Darden, whose mood of melancholy and beleaguerment, and whose flashes of anger, have been visible throughout the trial, has exploded in out-of-court moments. Referring to the defense, he told one Brown family friend: "Do you think I like these fucking assholes? They're all slime. They're in this for the money. Don't you think they damn well know that their client is guilty!?"

Meanwhile, the two youngest victims of the case, Sydney and Justin, "are healing as well as they can," says a family friend. They have each completed a year at their new school and they are happy living with the Brown family, relying partly on Judi and partly on Denise as a mother stand-in. Sydney, the graver and older one, has wisely told one adult, "I don't think about it [her mother's death] anymore. I don't want any more sadness. I've already been sad too much."

Their relationship with their father, over this past year, has—especially for Sydney—involved more strain than the public has known. For starters, one of the best-kept secrets has been that O.J., according to a family member, drafted a custody codicil to his will shortly after the murders. In the document, which implied that he was planning to commit suicide, he designated that custody of Sydney and Justin be shared by Denise and Arnelle. Arnelle would be given the Rockingham house to live in, and O.J., in the provision, promised to set aside money to buy what was described as a "mansion" for Denise. Both the custody plan and the promised house purchase were subjects of conversation at the wake and the funeral. Whether this custody plan is an indication that O.J. really intended to commit suicide, an indication that he hoped to buy the Browns' silence, or was done for some other reason is not known.

As for the children's relationship with their older half-siblings: Jason Simpson has been an admirable older brother to Justin and Sydney, visiting them frequently at the Browns' Laguna house, all through the year. "He has been a wonderful big brother—going out of his way to be a caretaker of those children," says a family friend. Arnelle, that same friend reports, has not been to visit her younger siblings quite as much as her brother has. "She just seems to be a real stronghold for her dad."

In fact, when the defense opened its case in July, Jason's and Arnelle's visits to Justin and Sydney increased radically. The two visited their younger siblings just about as much in that one month as they had the entire previous twelve. This markedly stepped-up interest by O.J.'s older children worried the Browns, since the defense was actively seeking to put Sydney on the witness stand to testify about the phone conversation she heard Nicole having shortly before she was murdered. The Browns adamantly opposed Sydney's taking the stand—they saw it as nothing short of child abuse.

Their concern is justified, especially since the children have been vulnerable to manipulation by their father, and Sydney in particular has been hurt by evasion and fabrication. In fact, despite O.J.'s camp putting out the word that he talked to his children from jail daily, the truth is that Sydney Simpson refused to take her father's telephone calls from jail for three months.

From the middle of August '94 to early November, Sydney told her aunts and a family friend that she didn't want to talk to her father until he told her the truth about where he was and why. A psychologist friend of a Brown family friend lent her services as intermediary. This woman first interviewed the children and said that they had neither seen nor heard anything on the night of the murders. Then she apparently went to jail and talked to O.J., telling him, according to the Brown family friend, something along the lines of: "You've got to be honest with your children and tell them the truth. You can tell them that you have 'information' and the police are keeping you in a safe place until they've finished the investigation." Shortly after she visited, the psychologist told the friend of the Browns (according to the latter) that "O.J. Simpson displayed none of the psychology of an innocent individual."

Sydney's phone boycott of her father ended after his conversation with the psychologist. When Sydney hung up the phone from that conversation, she said, "Daddy doesn't know how to be honest with me."

According to someone close to the family: One day this past spring when Sydney and Judi were out shopping Sydney asked her grandmother if her father was responsible for her mother's murder. Judi then replied that this was not the right place to talk about that. She then quickly took Sydney home and called a male psychologist whom the children had been seeing for a number of months. After that conversation, Judi apparently then told Sydney that her father was being accused of killing her mother.

The family friend says, "Sydney was then very calm and quiet and said, 'I knew.'"

Undaunted, O.J. has been wooing his children with grand plans for their life together after he is freed; he is more successful with his son than with his daughter. When he gets on the phone with the children—and, as of August, these phone calls had gotten down to about once a week—he tells them, says someone close to the family, "'After I get out, we'll travel all around the world and then we'll buy a big house on a ranch.'"

Justin takes these plans at face value, responding enthusiastically. He is, by all accounts, a daddy's boy—and the father-identified racial identity he began cheerfully forming in the fall seems now solidified. "I'm a black boy! I'm a black boy!" he was singing last July. Sydney, however, seems warier of her father's attempts to ingratiate at all costs. Though he says to her, "You're my Sydney Brooke Simpson," she remains slightly aloof.

"You know, I missed Justin's birthday," O.J. is said to

have said to her on the phone, shortly after Justin's seventh birthday this past August, "but I'll be there for yours and we'll take a big trip." If Sydney was happy about the prospect of a trip, she was at least more circumspect about her father's choice of birthday gift to her brother. "I'm getting your brother a drum set," O.J. told his daughter, on the phone.

"Don't," she replied, with the somber realism she has now settled into. "Drums are too noisy, and this house is small."

"But that's what he said he wanted, so I *have* to get it for him," O.J. said.

The electric drum practice set was sent to the Brown house—and, of course, O.J. employed a familiar stand-in at Justin's seventh birthday party on a Laguna beach: Al Cowlings. More recently, A.C.—and Arnelle—took the children to Wild River, a local water park.

One friend close to the family says that the Browns' continued friendliness toward the man who drove the accused killer of their daughter on a presumed getaway run on the freeways is simply their way of being "fair to O.J.'s side" and of preserving normalcy for Justin and Sydney. Other friends bemoan these accommodations, one saying, "I know they're operating from good motives when they do this, but how can they truly commit to Nicole, in death, if they continue to be so pleasant to O.J.'s sisters and mother in the courtroom?" Even after Shirley and Carmelita did their best to slam Ron Shipp's credibility, the two women seemed to feel they could take Judi Brown aside (as one Brown family member reports that they did) and ask her why she wasn't being nicer to their brother.

(Judi had responded, "*I* didn't get him in this trouble!")

The charm and celebrity and entitlement of O.J.

Simpson persists. So much so that the few raw, centering emotions one hears anymore are expressed by the Goldmans, who have come to epitomize integrity of grief and purpose, and who are unanimously admired among courtroom observers. "I just hate him so much!" Kim Goldman said of her brother's accused killer, to a guest at the unveiling of Ron's headstone.

This may be one of the few pure statements in an unpure year, when the dollar value of these murders has been so baldly celebrated. Nicole's family was not only approached with an offer to sell via internationally televised bidding on *Larry King Live* the Bundy Drive house where she and Goldman were killed (it was thought that wealthy Japanese American-pop-culture fanatics would buy it), but they also almost considered doing so.

As of this writing, the long-standing armchair consensus that there will be a hung jury has shifted to the belief that there may be an acquittal. If this happens, those of Simpson's friends who've hung in for him this year and a quarter will, no doubt, be considered by some to have bet on the winning side, if that is what is important. And, indeed, it is important in some quarters.

Meanwhile, it is worth reflecting on Nicole's prescience.

"She was smarter than all the rest of us," Cici Shahian says today. "She saw it all. Sheila, from the *day* she separated from him she lived her life to the fullest for *one* reason—she knew she was going to go down. She knew she would be killed for leaving him.

"Five days before she died, when I came over to her house for our morning run, she was so upset about his reporting her to the IRS. And she knew what would follow. 'He's going to kill me, Cici,' she said. 'And then he'll charm the world and get away with it, because he's O.J. Simpson.' "

But Nicole foresaw more than her murder those five days before the fact. She also seemed to understand the exploitation—and the fact that her friends would live in a fishbowl of bizarre notoriety, with money thrown at them right and left, for long after. " 'Cici,' she said—we were just finishing our run—'my friends are going to sell me out.' "

" 'Nicole,' I said, 'what do you *mean?'*

"She said, 'Just like after the divorce. He bought our friends.'

"I said, 'Nicole, I promise, I will *never* sell you out.'

"Nicole was a woman of few words. She said, 'Thanks, Ceece.'

"We looked at each other. It was understood that she knew she would be killed and I knew she would be killed. We just didn't know the day."

In mid-July, Sydney Simpson performed in her new dancing school's annual recital. As she took her bow, the memory of last year's dance recital was gently—and finally—supplanted.

The night of that previous dance recital—on June 12, 1994—Nicole had sat with her children, parents, sisters, and nephews at Mezzaluna. Everyone talked about a trip to Yosemite. The kids were very excited. This year, D'Anne LeBon tried to effect that promised trip. But when she called Yosemite National Park, it was booked solid. So, in late July, she and David, their four boys, and a family friend took Justin and Sydney with Denise and Sean to Sequoia National Park instead.

There, under the stars in the wilds of northern California, the children roasted marshmallows and climbed the mountains and rode horses. Sydney wanted to sleep in Denise's tent every night; sudden abandonment is still an issue with her.

Justin, however, has found a way to deal with it. One

day as he and D'Anne were riding down a path in the park, the little boy turned and asked, "Do you think Mommy can see me now?"

To which D'Anne replied, "Yes, I know she is watching you right now, Justin. And I know she'd give anything—*anything* in the world—to be down here, riding next to you, like I am."

On Tuesday, October 3—after a previous day's deliberation of an astonishingly brief four and a half hours—the jury found O.J. Simpson not guilty of the murders of Nicole Brown Simpson and Ronald Goldman. The brevity of the deliberations seems to indicate that the jurors virtually dismissed, wholesale, the prosecution case.